www.wadsworth.com

wadsworth.com is the World Wide Web site for
Wadsworth and is your direct source to dozens of
online resources.

At *wadsworth.com* you can find out about
supplements, demonstration software, and
student resources. You can also send email to many
of our authors and preview new publications and
exciting new technologies.

wadsworth.com
Changing the way the world learns®

INTEGRATING RELIGION AND SPIRITUALITY INTO COUNSELING

A Comprehensive Approach

MARSHA WIGGINS FRAME
University of Colorado at Denver

THOMSON

BROOKS/COLE

Australia • Canada • Mexico • Singapore • Spain • United Kingdom • United States

Executive Editor: *Lisa Gebo*
Sponsoring Editor: *Julie Martinez*
Marketing Manager: *Caroline Concilla*
Marketing Assistant: *Mary Ho*
Assistant Editor: *Shelley Gesicki*
Editorial Assistant: *Mike Taylor*
Technology Project Manager: *Barry Connolly*
Project Manager, Editorial Production:
Kim Svetich-Will

Production Service: *Forbes Mill Press*
Copy Editor: *Robin Gold*
Permissions Editor: *Sue Ewing*
Cover Design: *Roger Knox*
Cover Image: *Daryl Benson/Masterfile*
Print/Media Buyer: *Christopher Burnham*
Compositor: *Shepherd, Inc.*
Printing and Binding: *Transcontinental Printing, Inc.*

Printed in Canada
1 2 3 4 5 6 7 06 05 04 03 02

For more information about our products, contact us at:
Thomson Learning Academic Resource Center
1-800-423-0563

For permission to use material from this text,
contact us by: **Phone: 1-800-730-2214**
Fax: 1-800-730-2215
Web: http://www.thomsonrights.com

Library of Congress Control Number: 2002105836

ISBN 0-534-53093-1

Brooks/Cole—Thomson Learning
511 Forest Lodge Road
Pacific Grove, CA 93950
USA

Asia
Thomson Learning
5 Shenton Way #01-01
UIC Building
Singapore 068808

Australia
Nelson Thomson Learning
102 Dodds Street
South Melbourne, Victoria 3205
Australia

Canada
Nelson Thomson Learning
1120 Birchmount Road
Toronto, Ontario M1K 5G4
Canada

Europe/Middle East/Africa
Thomson Learning
High Holborn House
50/51 Bedford Row
London WC1R 4LR
United Kingdom

Latin America
Thomson Learning
Seneca, 53
Colonia Polanco
11560 Mexico D.F.
Mexico

Spain
Paraninfo Thomson Learning
Calle/Magallanes, 25
28015 Madrid, Spain

CONTENTS

CHAPTER   9
Religious and Spiritual Applications to Special Groups   239

CHAPTER   10
Ethical Considerations   281

PREFACE

INTRODUCTION

George is a 56-year-old white male who has been married to Dorothy for 30 years. Last month George was diagnosed with liver cancer and is not expected to live more than six months. George sought counseling to "come to terms with my eventual death" and to "develop some kind of spiritual peace about my life." George wants to work on his fear of death, but he does not want "some preacher trying to get me into Heaven."

Denise is a 32-year-old African American woman. She is single, the mother of 12-year-old Cedrick. She presented for counseling because she had been feeling "lost and lonely." Denise reported a series of unfulfilling relationships with men, but continues to hang onto her dream of someday being happily married. In addition, Denise indicated that she has not been able to "find a spiritual home." She said she had experimented with yoga and meditation from time to time and that she attends church with her family when she visits them in another city. She wonders how her "spiritual desert" might be connected to her sense of isolation and her failure with men.

Nathan is a 44-year-old white male who is currently single. He was married to Betty for 22 years. They have two sons: Andrew, 21, and Stephen, 18. Both Andrew and Stephen are attending colleges in the northeast. Nathan is seeking counseling because he is having difficulty with the breakup of his marriage eight months ago. He indicated that his wife had initiated the divorce because she had discovered Nathan was having a sexual relationship with Tim, a co-worker at the bank. Nathan indicated that he had had "this attraction to males ever since I could remember." However, he stated, "I couldn't begin to come out and say I was gay or anything. I still love Betty. Besides, I'm so afraid I am going to burn in hell for this." Nathan said he was seeking counseling so he could "figure out who I am" and "try to find some spiritual peace." Nathan said he was sure that the Bible says homosexuality is a sin, but he couldn't quote the chapter and verse. He reported that whenever he would have sex with other men he would feel guilt and shame and would be "tormented by the Devil."

In all these cases, ordinary people sought counseling for psychological, relationship, or emotional issues that had a religious or spiritual dimension. By sharing these vignettes, I am suggesting that in the context of their work counselors and psychotherapists have the opportunity to address clients' religious and spiritual concerns. Granted, there may be some limitations to raising religious and spiritual issues based on the particular counseling setting. For example, public schools would be more limiting than private practice. However, I argue that religious and spiritual values are legitimate issues for counselors to pursue in their therapeutic endeavors with clients. Most counselors would not claim to possess adequate training to function as spiritual directors or guides; nevertheless, it is appropriate for us to offer clients a safe place to explore their beliefs and values. In this context, we can use our well-honed counseling skills and our specialized training to assist clients in attaining personal growth and enhanced meaning in their lives. This book is intended to help counselors and other mental health practitioners make informed and effective interventions with clients for whom religion and spirituality are significant concerns.

Standing at the beginning of the twenty-first century, American culture appears to be ripe for a spiritual revolution. Countless magazine articles, books, television programs, films and college courses (Richards & Bergin, 1997) have been produced recently that attest to a resurgence of interest in issues of transcendence. Philosophically, we are living in a postmodern age in which the concept of absolutes, objective truth, and empirical knowledge continually are being scrutinized and questioned. The notion that people create their own realities based on their subjective experience of the world, the influence of their families of origin, their culture and values has given a new twist to how we think about what is real and true and meaningful. As a result, psychotherapists of all theoretical orientations are challenged to assist clients in grappling with their worldviews and wrestling with how their perspectives shape their thoughts, feelings, and behaviors. Thus, the intersection of religion, spirituality, values, and psychotherapy is fertile ground for the forward growth of our profession. Now more than ever, we are presented with the opportunities to focus on our clients as whole persons and to take into account their physical, mental, emotional, and spiritual dimensions when they present for treatment.

MY PERSONAL PERSPECTIVE

No less than any other author, I wrote this book out of my own particular context—that of being white, female, Western, and Christian. I have been especially conscious of the ways in which my socioeconomic status, religious tradition, geography, gender, and training influence my understanding of the psychotherapeutic process. I am deeply committed to issues of diversity in terms of race, ethnicity, culture, sexual orientation, religion, spirituality and the ways in which these intersect in counseling. In this book, I have made a deliberate effort to include chapters and cases that incorporate a variety of religious orientations and spiritual paths. In addition, I have taken into account strategies that draw from an assortment of theoretical orientations to counseling and psychotherapy. Despite these efforts at inclusiveness, much of this book is written based on theistic assumptions, that is, with the idea that clients' worldviews involve some God, Supreme Being, or Higher Power. Although I have been sensitive to definitions of spirituality that do not include a deity, I believe that many counselors feel more competent working with clients who do not possess a theist orientation than with those for whom a deity is central. Furthermore, most clients who present with religious or spiritual concerns do so from a theistic point of view. In fact, according to Barrett (1996) more than 88% of the world's population adheres to a belief system that is theistic in nature. Moreover, historically the theistic religions and spiritual orientations have provided moral and ethical frameworks that have shaped western culture. In addition, they have significant impact on personality and human behavior.

At this juncture, it is important to note that despite the empirical research linking the practice of religion with positive mental health (Bergin, 1983; Gartner, Larson, & Allen, 1991; Schumaker, 1992), I acknowledge that historically much harm has been done and continues to be perpetuated in the name of religion. The Crusades, the Inquisition, the Holocaust, and many religious cults across the centuries have wreaked havoc, destruction, and loss of human life. Also, religion and spirituality are often the media through which clients express psychological pathology and dysfunction. I describe and address the harmful side of religion and spirituality, even as I claim that religion and spirituality may be counselors' ancillary tools in assisting clients on their journey toward wholeness.

Finally, one of the major assumptions underlying this book is that counselors and other mental health clinicians must address their own personal issues regarding religion and spiritually before they can help their clients who venture into this arena. I believe strongly that we cannot facilitate our clients' personal growth unless we are willing to commit to that same kind of growth for ourselves. Thus, a prevailing theme in this book is how the counselors' own worldviews, beliefs, and values enter into the therapeutic process. In the cases and strategies presented throughout the book, readers are asked to contemplate their own struggles and convictions, and to consider how these issues affect their work with clients. Although the exercises and activities included in each chapter contain "person-of-the-therapist" concerns (Aponte & Winter, 1987) regarding religion and spirituality, the intention is not to convert readers to a theistic perspective. Instead, it is to enable them to gain clarity about their religious and spiritual beliefs and nonbeliefs, and to increase their awareness of potential countertransference with their clients. As a result of this objective, I have crafted a book whose purpose is twofold. First, my aim is to provide critical, well-researched information for working competently with clients' religious and spiritual perspectives, and second, I strive to offer a guide for counselors' who choose a spiritual odyssey as one of their pathways to personal growth.

ORGANIZATION OF THE BOOK

In Chapter 1, I differentiate the terms "spirituality" and "religion." Spirituality concerns a person's search for meaning, purpose, and value in life. It may or may not include a Supreme Being or a higher power. Religion, on the other hand, refers to a set of beliefs and practices of an organized religious institution (Shafranske & Malony, 1990). It tends to be expressed in ways that are "denominational, external, cognitive, behavioral, ritualistic, and public" (Richards & Bergin, 1977, p. 13). Also, in Chapter 1, I describe reasons why the mental health professions have neglected or opposed the inclusion of religion and spirituality in their disciplines, and I give a rationale for why they ought to be included in the realm of psychotherapy. In addition, I bring to the fore "person-of-the-therapist" issues (Aponte & Winter, 1987), and describe in detail situations that might act as "clinical triggers" (Guerin & Hubbard, 1987) for counselors working with clients' religious or spiritual concerns.

In Chapter 2, I present five models of religious or spiritual development. I highlight the work of Gordon Allport, James Fowler, Vicky Genia, Fritz Oser, and Michael Washburn. All of these theorists work from a developmental framework, though they take various theoretical approaches. Included in this chapter are case examples that will assist you in understanding how to use these developmental frameworks to organize your thinking about various clients and their issues.

In Chapter 3, I present the major theses of a variety of religious and spiritual belief systems. I begin by discussing the concept of worldview, or weltanschauung. From there, I set forth the basic tenets of the world's largest religions, both Western and Eastern. I introduce Christianity, Judaism, and Islam and discuss the concepts of liberalism, conservatism, and fundamentalism as they apply to these major Western religions. Then, I offer information regarding Eastern religions: Hinduism, Buddhism, Taoism, Confucianism, and Shinto. The last section of Chapter 3 focuses on the spiritual traditions of New Age and Wicca. Case studies and discussion questions are intended to assist you in conceptualizing clients' worldviews and applying counseling techniques and interventions that are sensitive to their belief systems.

In Chapter 4, I focus on the general principles of assessment and offer specific information regarding various forms of religious and spiritual appraisal. I include a sample intake form, suggested interview questions, and descriptions of formal paper and pencil assessment instruments. In addition, I offer criteria for helping counselors determine whether or not a religious or spiritual path is a "healthy" one. In the context of this discussion, I include a section dealing with cults. The remainder of Chapter 4 focuses on using assessment results in counseling. The chapter concludes with cases and discussion questions designed to assist you in applying assessment data to your clinical work.

In Chapter 5, I cover the intersection of religion, spirituality, and culture. I present facts regarding the five major ethnic groups in America: Caucasian/European, African Americans, Asian Americans, Latinos/Latinas, and Native Americans. These groups were selected for inclusion because they constitute the largest percentages of ethnic diversity in the United States. In this chapter, I provide information about the indigenous spiritual and religious practices of each ethnic group and indicate how these traditional rituals and beliefs are imbedded in the cultural context of each people. Also, I offer strategies for incorporating meaningful spiritual practices into psychotherapy, including consultation with indigenous healers.

Chapters 6 and 7 are dedicated to specific counseling strategies for working with clients' religious and spiritual concerns. I use a social constructionist framework for my theoretical approach. In Chapter 6, I focus primarily on work with individuals, and on the application of the micro-skills of counseling (Ivey & Authier, 1978) to religious and spiritual dilemmas. In addition, I discuss interventions based on classic individual counseling theory. In Chapter 7, I give attention to specific religious or spiritual interventions that focus on counseling individuals. I include a discussion of religious and spiritual authorities such as the Bible, the Koran, and the Pope, and how counselors may use these authoritative books, people, or practices.

In Chapter 8, I address working with couples and families by applying systemic intervention models to clients' religious and spiritual issues. For example, I discuss prayer and meditation, forgiveness, religious/spiritual cognitive restructuring, and engendering hope in clients. Also, in this chapter, I describe 12-step programs such as Alcoholics Anonymous as spiritual approaches to various types of treatment, especially in work with clients' addictions.

In Chapter 9, I focus on special groups including women, gay, lesbian, and bisexual clients, children, and adolescents as well as the dying and their families, describe the unique issues associated with each of these groups, and provide suggestions for effective counseling approaches. Case examples are designed to assist you in entering the subjective world of these particular clients, assessing their needs, and developing appropriate interventions to address their religious and spiritual concerns.

In Chapter 10, I present ethical issues that arise when working with clients' religious and spiritual dilemmas. The following topics are included: the welfare of the client, cultural sensitivity, personal and professional boundaries, imposing one's values on clients', and counselor competence. The cases associated with this chapter are fashioned for the purpose of having you wrestle with difficult ethical challenges that emerge as a result of taking on clients' religious and spiritual concerns.

SUMMARY

This book represents my best efforts at providing a comprehensive text for counseling students and mental health professionals who wish to integrate clients' religious and spiritual issues into psychotherapy. I am keenly aware of my own white, Western, liberal Protestant context, and, as a result, have been intentional about being open and respectful of traditions and world-views that differ from my own. I am deeply invested in celebrating diversity and in developing counseling approaches that emphasize multiple perspectives. My hope is that this book will be a resource for readers' personal and professional growth and that it will contribute to mental health professionals' knowledge and skills in addressing clients' religious and spiritual concerns.

ACKNOWLEDGMENTS

I would like to thank the following people who reviewed the manuscript and made helpful suggestions: John Barletta, Australian Catholic University; Mary Thomas Burke, University of North Carolina; Patrick Callanan; Mary Fukuyama, University of Florida; Joshua Gold, University of South Carolina; Pamela Highlen, Ohio State University; Virginia Kelly, SUNY Plattsburgh; Judy Miranti, Our Lady of the Holy Cross; and Kathleen Ritter, California State University, Bakersfield. In addition, I am especially grateful to my husband, Dr. Roger Frame, who read every chapter and contributed important ideas to this edition.

I have been blessed by the able support of Julie Martinez, my editor, and the rest of the Brooks/Cole team who have assisted in this project: Kim Svetich-Will, production editor; Shelley Gesicki, assistant editor; Mike Taylor, editorial assistant; Karyn Morrison, permissions editor; and last but not least, Robin Gold, production service.

Finally, I am deeply appreciative of my students in the Counseling Psychology and Counselor Education program at the University of Colorado at Denver for their interest in this material and their participation in my course that addressed spirituality and counseling. Their desire to learn these concepts and skills has been an inspiration to me.

Marsha Wiggins Frame

RELIGION AND SPIRITUALITY IN COUNSELING

INTRODUCTION

In this chapter, I introduce you to the concepts of religion, spirituality, and transpersonal psychology. I argue that these aspects of human experience may be significant in clients' lives and that counselors must be knowledgeable about them and open to helping clients explore these dimensions in therapy. I present reasons why the field of psychotherapy has neglected or, in some cases, intentionally excluded religion and spirituality in training and practice. I also provide a rationale for why these aspects of people's lives should be integrated into the therapeutic endeavor.

In this book, I will present models analyzing religious and spiritual development, information on various world religions and spiritual practices, cultural and ethical concerns, and strategies for working with clients' religious or spiritual beliefs. However, it is my judgment that confronting your own personal history with and current orientation toward religion and spirituality is critical. I believe that as counselors, one of the best tools we have to offer our clients is ourselves. In the therapeutic encounter, our humanness, authenticity, and empathy can be catalysts for change. If we are open to our own personal growth, are willing to move beyond our comfort zones, and are open to exploring what gives our lives meaning, then we are capable of being excellent role models for our clients. Likewise, if we are unaware of our own inner conflicts, have unresolved issues that are outside of our awareness, or are reluctant to confront our questions about meaning and values in our lives, we can severely limit or even harm our clients' growth process.

In this chapter, you will be asked to assess your religious or spiritual background, the role that these dimensions played (or did not play) in your family of origin, your current beliefs and practices, and your questions, doubts, and struggles. In the Suggested Activities section of this chapter, you will be asked to consider the types of clients whose beliefs would pose difficulty for you and those whose philosophical orientation would be engaging and energizing for you. The purpose of this self-study is to increase your awareness of your own issues with religion and spirituality so that you will be less likely to have countertransference negatively affect your work with clients. My hope is that through reading this book, completing the exercises, working with the cases, and doing some of the supplementary reading, you will make strides in your journey toward personal health and wholeness and that you will be able to provide assistance to clients who journey with you.

SPIRITUALITY, RELIGION, AND TRANSPERSONAL PSYCHOLOGY

Spirituality

Capturing a concept as ethereal as "spirituality" in words is challenging. Doing so is almost antithetical to the idea itself. However, in a book whose major focus is the integration of spirituality into counseling and psychotherapy, it is imperative to undertake the task. One place to begin is with root words for "spirit." The Latin word, *spiritus*, means breath, courage, vigor, or life. According to Sheldrake (1992), this word was an attempt to translate into English the Greek noun *pneuma* used in the Pauline letters of the Bible. *Pneuma*, like its Hebrew corollary, *ruach*, means "wind," "breath," "life," and "spirit" (Delbane & Montgomery, 1981; Roth, 1990). Indeed, the notion that "spirit" is equated with the life force is echoed in the first entry in *Webster's Ninth New Collegiate Dictionary* (1987): "an animating or vital principle held to give life to physical organisms" (p. 1137). Although "spirit" is associated with physical vitality—that is, breath—it is certainly more than mere respiration. A quality of "spirit" transcends physical, organic existence. This aspect of "spirit" is concerned with "otherness," and what Rudolph Otto (1958) called "the holy." Spirituality, then, is concerned with persons' search for meaning, purpose, and value in life. One's construction of spirituality may or may not include a Supreme Being or a higher power.

Several writers have offered definitions of spirituality that are helpful in understanding the rich texture and myriad meanings that this concept encompasses. Cervantes and Ramirez (1992) included in their definition of spirituality the notion that it includes the search for harmony and wholeness in the universe. Tillich (1959) referred to spirituality as that which is related to one's ultimate concern and is the meaning-giving dimension of culture. Booth (1992) described spirituality as an "inner attitude that emphasizes energy, creative choice, and a powerful force for living" (p. 25). Elkins, Hedstrom, Hughes, Leaf, and Saunders (1988) spoke of spiritual values that include an appreciation for the sacredness of life, a balanced appreciation of material values, altruism toward others, a desire for the betterment of the world, and an awareness of life's tragic side. Chandler, Holden, and Kolander (1992) defined a spiritual experience as "*any* experience of transcendence of one's former frame of reference that results in greater knowledge and love" (p. 170). Hinterkopf (1994) claimed that spiritual experience is currently felt in the body, that it involves an awareness of the transcendent dimension of life, it brings new meanings and leads to growth. Holifield (1983) described spirituality as "less a method than an *attitude*, a posture of one's very being that allows seeing not different things but everything differently" (p. 88). Winarsky's (1991) definition emphasized that spirituality may or may not involve a Supreme Being or God:

> It may be an inner-generated, thoughtful and sometimes skeptical search—a process rather than a product—for universal connections, with no *quid pro quo* from a higher power sought or intended. People who consider themselves to be spiritual may or may not participate in organized religion. Some may find solace in readings, discussion groups, and the like. (p. 186)

Participants in the 1995 Summit on Spirituality, comprising leaders in the American Counseling Association's division called the Association for Spiritual, Ethical, and Religious Values in Counseling (ASERVIC), were confounded by the task of defining spirituality. Instead, they chose to provide a *description* of spirituality rather than a definition:

> The animating force in life, represented by such images as breath, wind, vigor, and courage. Spirituality is the infusion and drawing out of spirit in one's life. It is experienced as an active and passive process. Spirituality also is described as a capacity and tendency that is innate and unique to all persons. This spiritual tendency moves the individual towards knowledge, love, meaning, hope, transcendence, connectedness, and compassion. Spirituality includes one's capacity for creativity, growth, and the development of a values system. Spirituality encompasses the religious, spiritual, and transpersonal. (p. 30)

From the previous discussion, we can see that *defining* spirituality is not an easy exercise. There are many components to our understanding of the construct. *Spirituality* includes one's values, beliefs, mission, awareness, subjectivity, experience, sense of purpose and direction, and a kind of striving toward something greater than oneself. It may or may not include a deity.

Religion

Religion, on the other hand, is easier to explain. Although the concept of religion may share the characteristics of spirituality, there are some important differences. A religion refers to a set of beliefs and practices of an organized religious institution (Shafranske & Malony, 1990). It implies a cosmic or metaphysical backdrop as well as some behavioral expectations (Marty, 1991). Religion tends to be expressed in ways that are "denominational, external, cognitive, behavioral, ritualistic, and public" (Richards & Bergin, 1977, p. 13). It is important to note that *religion* is one form of spirituality. The two concepts are not mutually exclusive. Many followers of religion find that its organization, doctrine, rituals, programs, and community are means through which their spirituality is supported and enhanced. Likewise, many persons who think of themselves as *spiritual*, rather than *religious*, find that the institutions of religion interfere with their private experiences of spirituality. It is possible, therefore, for these two constructs to be related in a variety of ways and played out differently in individual lives. For example, a person may care very deeply about the meaning of life, may be very committed to her purpose and direction, may even engage in spiritual practices such as meditation, and yet not be involved in a religious organization. Thus, one may be spiritual without being religious. Another person may be a member of a synagogue, keep a kosher kitchen, be faithful to Torah, and never really take these Jewish practices to heart. He may go through the motions of being religious without being spiritual. Yet another person may be an active member of a church, attend worship regularly, read the Bible, and pray, finding great inspiration in these activities and support through the institutional church. Therefore, one may be religious and spiritual simultaneously. Given that the terms *spirituality* and *religion* have different meanings and connotations, it is important that counselors clarify for themselves how these concepts are related to their own perspectives. It is also critical that they help their clients identify the ways in which spirituality or religion make sense for the clients.

Transpersonal Psychology

Transpersonal psychology is a relatively new yet increasingly popular approach to psychotherapy that "aims at the integration of physical, emotional, mental, and spiritual aspects of well-being" (Vaughan, Wittine, & Walsh, 1996, p. 483). Transpersonal experiences differ from other psychological experiences in that they involve "an expansion or extension of consciousness beyond the usual ego boundaries and beyond the limitations of time and/or space" (Grof, 1975, p. 155). Some examples of transpersonal experiences include out-of-body experiences, clairvoyance, past-incarnation experiences, time travels, telepathy, extra-sensory perception (ESP), experiences of other universes and encounters with their inhabitants, encounters with various deities (Grof, 1975), and near death experiences (Moody, 1975).

Transpersonal psychology has been influenced by the work of Abraham Maslow (1968). Maslow emphasized peak experiences as hallmarks of the transcended self-actualizers—those who had reached the top rungs of his schema of human development. Assagioli (1965), through his work in psychosynthesis, posited a "higher conscious" or "superconscious" that he believed was present in all humans. The inspiration for art, music, science, philosophy, altruism, contemplation, and ecstasy came from this "supercon-scious." Assagioli (1989) believed that *all* states of awareness that include values higher than average are to be considered spiritual. Perhaps the best-known spokesperson for transpersonal psychology is Ken Wilber (1977, 1980a, 1980b, 1983, 1993, 1995). Wilber's work involves integrating East-ern religions and psychological perspectives. Transpersonal psychology, then, is a way of working with clients that combines a variety of psychological con-cepts with spiritual interventions.

Vaughan, Wittine, & Walsh (1996) offered four postulates to describe the basic assumptions of transpersonal psychology. First, it is "an approach to healing and growth that addresses multiple levels of the spectrum of iden-tity—prepersonal, personal, and transpersonal" (p. 487). According to these authors, the levels of identity are both developmental and interpenetrating such that it is possible for persons to experience themselves in all levels simul-taneously. The first level of identity, the *prepersonal,* begins in the womb and extends through the first three to four years of life. In this level, conscious-ness is basic, driven by survival, safety, and attachment. The second level, that of *personal identity,* involves developing a sense of self, the world, and oneself in the world. This level, not unlike other approaches to psychother-apy, involves the development of a stable, cohesive personal identity or ego. The third level, that of the *transpersonal identity,* develops as persons become aware of a longing for a deeper sense of self, a kind of self-transcendence.

The second postulate of transpersonal psychology is that it "recognizes the therapist's unfolding awareness of the Self and his or her spiritual world-view as central in shaping the nature, process, and outcome of therapy" (Vaughan, Wittine, & Walsh, 1996, p. 491). This postulate asserts that a unique aspect of transpersonal psychology is the therapist's commitment to a spiritual orientation toward life that informs his or her work with clients.

The third postulate of transpersonal psychology is that it is a process of "awakening from a lesser to a greater identity" (Vaughan, Wittine, & Walsh, 1996, p. 492). This idea involves the notion that therapists assist their clients in gaining enhanced self-awareness that may involve relinquishing previously held ideas, attitudes, or beliefs. Such an experience may be likened to what St. John of the Cross (2000) called the "dark night of the Soul" or what Grof and Grof (1989) described as a "spiritual emergency." What may begin as a crisis often results in greater growth and higher functioning.

The fourth postulate of transpersonal psychology is that it "facilitates the process of awakening by making use of techniques that enhance intuition and deepen awareness of personal and transpersonal realms of the psyche" (Vaughan, Wittine, & Walsh, 1996, p. 493). Transpersonal psychology re-quires that clients look within and beyond themselves to gain a deeper sense of self and a greater consciousness of one's identity. The belief that such a journey into self-awareness is therapeutic in itself is similar to ideas espoused by Fritz Perls (1969), developer of Gestalt therapy. Increased wisdom and in-tuition are developed through techniques such as bodywork, meditation, im-agery and dreamwork, and altered states of consciousness.

Though many counselors who work from a transpersonal perspective would not consider themselves religious, some are able to integrate transpersonal ideas and experiences into traditional religious frameworks. For example, Christine, a counselor who identifies as a Christian and is involved actively in an Episcopal church, has had transpersonal experiences. She is open to exploring her "higher consciousness," and believes that her moments of self-transcendence are evidence of the work of the Holy Spirit in her life. Although Christine's perspective may not represent the majority of transpersonal counselors, it is important not to make assumptions about anyone's spiritual, religious, or transpersonal worldviews. Transpersonal psychology has a place in the efforts of counselors to integrate religion and spirituality in their work with clients.

UNDERSTANDING THE RELATIONSHIP BETWEEN SPIRITUALITY AND RELIGION

There is an unquestionable relationship between spirituality and religion and how the two concepts may be manifest in our lives and in the lives of our clients. Jaroslav Pelikan (1968) used the paradigm of "spirit versus structure" to describe Martin Luther's role in the Protestant Reformation. Essentially, Pelikan claimed that part of Luther's motivation to reform the Roman Catholic Church was based in his belief that the institutional church's structures (e.g., dogma, doctrine, monasticism, and papacy) had become so rigid that they were squelching the spirit of God. Luther also discovered, however, that the subjectivity of his free-floating personal spirituality needed the concrete structures of the Church to mediate and contain its power. Luther's experience suggests that individuals may oscillate between a need for their spiritual experiences to be freed from the trappings of religion and a need for some kind of structure to manage and make sense of them.

CASE | **PHYLLIS**

Phyllis, a 53-year-old Caucasian woman sought counseling because of a lack of direction and purpose in her life. Phyllis reported that her only child, Mark, had left for college, and that she had no place to direct her energies now that she was not focused on his needs. Phyllis reported she was sad, depressed, and "couldn't shake the blues." The counselor, Ricardo, asked Phyllis about the sources for support she had in her life. He also inquired about any religious or spiritual connections that might be tapped at this time of transition. Phyllis reported that she had been raised in a Baptist church but felt that she could not endorse some of the beliefs of her religious tradition. Consequently, she said she had spent the past 20 years of life "going it on my own." Phyllis told Ricardo that she would like to explore her spiritual side and was open to any suggestions he might have about how to embark on a spiritual journey. Phyllis said she wasn't ready to go back to church but that she wanted to do something by herself to re-kindle her spiritual fire. Ricardo provided Phyllis with information about learning to meditate and keeping a journal. Phyllis indicated that she was open to trying these two spiritual practices. She bought a book on journaling and attended a lecture and demonstration on meditation.

After several weeks, Phyllis reported to Ricardo that she was not feeling as depressed and that she was excited about giving herself permission to explore spirituality in a new way. After three months of intense journal keeping and meditation, Phyllis sought out Ricardo again. This time she reported that although she was growing in her spiritual self-exploration, that she found it to be lonely, and that she was longing for company on the journey. Ricardo was able to help Phyllis get connected with a meditation group for women. Phyllis attended the group for a month and indicated that it was just what she needed to feel balanced.

Phyllis continued to participate in the meditation group, added a yoga class to her schedule, and attended several spiritual growth retreats with her companions from the meditation group. Soon Phyllis was feeling overwhelmed and pressured by her new friends to attend every workshop and meeting offered on spiritual growth and meditation. Again, she sought Ricardo's help.

In the next session, Ricardo asked Phyllis how her spiritual activities were related to her sense of feeling pressured and out of control. Phyllis indicated that she no longer felt the exhilaration and energy from her spiritual meetings and retreats. Somehow, they had become a drudgery and a demand rather than a source of strength and support.

Ricardo helped Phyllis see her pattern of moving from a very structured form of religion in her young adulthood as a Baptist to a free-form spirituality in her early days of private journaling and meditation. He pointed out that her highly structured Baptist church had kept her from exploring her own faith and spirituality. He also helped Phyllis to see that in response to that structure, she had sought out very personal and solitary spiritual practices that freed her from the oppressive feelings she had about her Baptist upbringing. In addition, Ricardo was able to help Phyllis realize that she needed *some* structure, in this case, comrades, to help her make sense of her new-found spirituality and to give her support in her quest for a deeper knowledge of herself. However, when Phyllis' friends began making inordinate demands and prescribing for her how she should meditate, she felt confined by *too much* structure. In this case, the spirit versus structure paradigm was helpful to Phyllis in grasping that at times in her life certain structures such as organizations, friends, churches, or retreats might be the means needed for her to actualize her spiritual potential. At other times, however, Phyllis came to understand that too much structure made her want to escape. In the past, she had simply escaped from her religion altogether. After working with Ricardo, though, she realized that she simply needed space from structures that put too many limits on her spirituality.

CASE | PETER

Peter is a 20-year-old Native American factory worker. He left the Zuni reservation in New Mexico at 16 and has been in and out of work for the last four years. Recently, he returned to New Mexico because his grandmother was ill. When Peter reported back to work in Chicago after taking personal leave, his supervisor noted that he was not productive, seemed preoccupied, and did not socialize with his co-workers after hours. Within two weeks, Peter's absenteeism at work became an issue, and his supervisor referred him to the Employee Assistance Program. His counselor, Sharon, asked Peter about what had happened during the past month that had contributed to the change in his work habits and attitudes. Peter revealed that he had made an emergency trip to New Mexico to the Zuni reservation to visit his grandmother who was terminally ill. The visit was upsetting to him because it reminded him of how much he had strayed from his tribal connections and their spiritual practices. Peter reported that he felt guilty for abandoning his family and clan and for forsaking his heritage. Sharon helped Peter explore his ambivalent feelings about being part of the tribe. He valued and appreciated his Zuni background, but he felt that he would never "make it" if he stayed on the reservation. Because Sharon was not well informed about the Zuni tribe or their religion, she sought consultation from a Native American resource center. There, she learned that the identity of the Zuni male is almost totally wrapped up in the collective rituals and religious societies of the tribe. She discovered that individuality is a negative concept among the Zuni and that those who act too much on their own may be accused of witchcraft (Hultkrantz, 1993). As she spoke with the consultant, she began to grasp Peter's dilemma: his visit to his home and tribe had elicited serious questions about who he was and how he could forge a life in a culture that prized individual achievement.

In his next session with Sharon, Peter was able to acknowledge how torn he was between his current life and work and what he perceived to be his "true" life among his people. Peter revealed that he had left the reservation at 16 after a fight with his father. He said he felt trapped by the expectations for males in his culture, he was questioning the beliefs of his tribe about Sun Father and the kachinas, and he wanted a chance to see the rest of the world. If he left and explored other ways, thought Peter, he could decide for himself. Sharon helped Peter to see that in his attempt to be a "free spirit" he had lost his sense of self—a self that could be known only in the community of the Zuni.

Using the spirit versus structure paradigm, over time Sharon was able to help Peter understand in a fresh way that, for the Zuni, spirit is made known in structure—that by participating in the ritual dances and tribal practices he comes to understand himself and the spirits. In his adolescence, Peter had found the structures of his tribe to be too limiting and inflexible. He wanted to reject his cultural background, hoping that by shedding it he could be free from its claims on him. For Peter, however, the significant discovery was that he could be himself only in the context of his place within his tribe.

In each of these cases, the counselor assisted the client in understanding how either too much structure or too much spirit can threaten the welfare of one's religious and spiritual lives. Despite the attempts to categorize religion by its structures and spirituality by its freedom from structures, it is evident that pure spirit is amorphous without some structure and that overly rigid structures often deaden the spirit they were designed to proclaim.

NEGLECT OF RELIGION AND SPIRITUALITY IN CLINICAL PRACTICE

Psychologists, counselors, marriage and family therapists, and other mental health service providers trained in the last half of the 20th century probably had little or no introduction to the role of religion or spirituality in clinical practice (Bergin, 1983). There are several reasons for this lack of attention to religion and spirituality in the therapeutic arena: (1) the tenuous relationship between psychology and religion; (2) the conflict between the assumptions of the scientific world and those of religion and spirituality; (3) the association of religion and spirituality with pathology; (4) the belief that religion and spirituality are the prerogative of the clergy and other spiritual leaders; (5) a lack of training regarding how to integrate religion and spirituality into clinical practice; and (6) mental health practitioners' own unresolved religious or spiritual issues.

The Tenuous Relationship of Psychology and Religion: Connection and Estrangement

When studied in depth, we can see that the relationship between psychology and religion has been many-faceted. During the Middle Ages (and certainly before and extending beyond that period), many kinds of healers existed in every culture. These were of various religious persuasions and engaged in what was known as *cura animarum*—the care of souls (Kurtz, 1999). This enterprise involved the mental, emotional, and spiritual aspects of persons as a unified whole. When conceived in the 16th century, western psychology was closely linked with a religious worldview. It began formally with pneumatology, the study of spiritual beings. At the time, pneumatology was divided into three parts: (1) the study of God, (2) the study of intermediary spirits such as angels and demons, and (3) the study of the human spirit (Vande Kemp, 1996). In fact, the Latin term, *psychologia*, first used in 1524 by Marulic, referred to that division of pneumatology concerned with the human spirit. Later in that century, further classifications were made. Cassmann contributed the term, *anthropologia*, meaning the science of persons (Vande Kemp, 1996). That designation "was divided further into 'psychologia,' the doctrine of the human mind, and 'somatologia,' the doctrine of the human body" (Vande Kemp, 1982, p. 108). Initially, then, the two disciplines of psychology and religion were bound together because psychology emerged as the study of the human mind, soul, or spirit. At the time, distinctions were not made between *pneuma*, the spiritual aspect of persons, and *psyche*, the soul or mind of the person.

Everything began to change when the Renaissance gave way to the Enlightenment period during the 18th century. Enlightenment thinkers expected the Age of Reason to displace the Age of Faith (Kurtz, 1999). In many ways, these expectations came to fruition in the emergence of modern science that began in the 1600s and continues (Richards & Bergin, 1997).

Modern-day psychology, followed by counseling and other forms of psychotherapy, emerged in the late 19th and early 20th centuries as this division between science and religion was becoming an ever-widening chasm. The pioneers in psychology, Sigmund Freud, John B. Watson, Edward L. Thorndike, B. F. Skinner, and others aligned themselves with the scientific worldview and, as a result, gained credibility and respectability for their theories.

The Conflict Between the Philosophical Assumptions of Science and Religion

The development of modern science resulted in its separating itself from religion on the grounds that the two disciplines had fundamentally different orientations and philosophical assumptions. Proponents of the scientific mindset rejected the belief in God and claimed that human behavior was determined by outside forces. Subscribers to religion held to a belief in a Supreme Being and in the freedom of individuals to make choices regarding their behavior. Scientists thought of persons as machines with separate parts that worked together. Religious enthusiasts claimed that humans were more than the sum of their parts and that their transcendent spirits made them unique. When scientists suggested that there were no universal moral principles by which persons were to live, religious advocates held tightly to a set of values that were all encompassing and absolute. When epistemology (or the question of how we know what we know) was raised, scientists pointed to the physical world, to the senses, and to empirical evidence. Champions of religion ceded that these approaches to knowledge were partially correct but that other dimensions, those of transcendence and inspiration, were also valid ways of knowing the truth. Thus, science was, in the words of Mahoney (1976), "grounded in empirical facts that are uninterpreted, indubitable, and fixed in meaning; that theories are derived from these facts by induction or deduction and are retained or rejected solely on the basis of their ability to survive experimental tests; and that science progresses by the gradual accumulation of facts" (p. 130). Religion, on the other hand, was focused on "the realms of significance, meaning, values, ultimacy, and ethics; these are regarded as making no factual claims on human reality" (Jones, 1996, p. 117). Thus, science and religion were assumed to be incompatible because science was based on fact and religion on faith and because scientific assertions could be proven whereas religious ones were mere subjective speculation.

Since the late 1950s, however, the immutable differences between science and religion in general and psychology and religion in particular have been challenged. Postmodern thinkers such as Kuhn (1970), Gergen (1985), O'-Donohue (1989), and others have challenged this positivistic worldview. They have pointed out that scientific data are theory-laden (Jones, 1996) and that the expectations and perceptions scientists bring with them to the experimental process shape the outcomes. Rather than theory-building being an exclusively objective appraisal of data deduced from methodological tasks, there is a subjective aspect to the presuppositions scientists bring to the process. Contextual variables such as gender, ethnicity, and power also affect the way scientific experiments are conducted, analyzed, reported, and published. Postmodern thinkers have promoted the notion that *all* reality is socially constructed (Gergen, 1991), an idea that applies even to what had been viewed as *scientific* (and thus objectively true) reality. This postmodern, constructionist perspective opens the way for science and religion to be related to each other again in new and challenging ways.

The Association of Religion and Spirituality with Pathology

Many psychologists and other mental health practitioners have been supportive of addressing religion and spirituality in their practices and have identified themselves as religious or spiritual (Bergin & Jensen, 1990). Historically, however, most have disparaged religion, or condemned it as an example of pathology.

Freudian Psychoanalysis   Freud was perhaps the most well-known opponent of religion. He believed that religion is rooted in early childhood experiences, especially the experience of the father as omnipotent and omniscient as well as caring and protective. Thus, when individuals suffer crises later in life, they come to depend on the fantasy of a loving and benevolent father-god. Freud (1913/1953) understood this notion of a longing for a father-god to be what "constitutes every form of religion" (p. 148). Based on his concept of the Oedipus complex, Freud believed that the human father was also associated with guilt, fear, and resentment, and thus, persons have ambivalence associated with religion (Wulff, 1996). Freud held that "obedient submission to God as the projected infantile father finally restores the long-lost relationship" (Wulff, 1996, p. 51).

Besides the idea that religion is the result of wish fulfillment and fantasy, Freud also declared religion to be an illusion (1927/1961). He believed that when people were introduced to religious doctrine in their early years, such an exposure made them less likely to objectively evaluate religious beliefs, institutions, and other accouterments of society. Freud was convinced that religious indoctrination created fear-induced repression that resulted in a reluctance to exercise critical thinking.

The rituals and liturgies associated with religion caused Freud to refer to them as neurotic obsessions (Wulff, 1996). In his view, the blindly accepted patterns of religious practice, coupled with fear of divine punishment for sin, were related to obsessive neuroses. Freud explained these neuroses as defense mechanisms that protected religious persons from the anxiety created by unacceptable or evil impulses within them. In sum, Freud aligned himself with the scientific, rational positivism of the day. He was persuaded that human beings would act more maturely if they abandoned religion altogether.

Despite Freud's rejection of religion and his denouncement of it as pathological, Freud's critique made some positive contributions for counselors.

Kung (1979) wrote that Freud pointed out some of the excesses of religion and helped us see ways in which it can become pathological within some clients. For example, Kung (1979) pointed to escapism, self-deception, rigid thinking, and behaving that characterize some religious people. Kung (1979) also hailed Freud's ideas as a welcomed critique of institutionalized forms of religion that had rendered various abuses to vulnerable populations across history.

Freud's perspective continues to be influential in mental health training and practice despite a trend toward interest in and openness to religion and spirituality. Regardless of how one views Freud's position on religion, it is important to recognize that much of his theory was developed in response to his work with persons who embodied unhealthy religiousness. For both theoretical and personal reasons (e.g., unresolved religious and oedipal struggles), Freud was unable to acknowledge that there are varying forms of religion and spirituality, some which are healthier than others are.

Cognitive and Behavioral Objections   Cognitive-behavioral therapists believe that psychological distress is the result of distorted thinking. People come to hold various beliefs about themselves, others, and the world through socialization in the family and culture. One's religious beliefs are typically acquired in the family of origin and may be the root of his or her crooked thinking.

Albert Ellis, founder of Rational-Emotive Behavior Therapy (REBT), declared that atheism was the only way to optimal human functioning (1980). He wrote, "Religiosity is in many respects equivalent to irrational thinking and emotional disturbance" (p. 637). Thus, many of his followers in the cognitive-behavioral tradition assume that all religious and spiritual beliefs are irrational distortions that clients ought to give up.

Skinner (1953), most known for his contributions to behavior therapy, asserted that religious behavior occurs because it follows reinforced stimuli. Skinner believed that the clergy, liturgy, and behavior codes served as contingencies of reinforcement, serving not only the individuals involved but the institutional and social order as well (Wulff, 1996). It is interesting to note that Skinner did not object to the control religion exercised over people's lives. In fact, in his mechanistic theory of behaviorism he claimed that people were not as free and autonomous as they believed they were. Rather, Skinner held, they behave in the ways they do precisely because they are responding to reinforcement. For Skinner, religion was just another reinforcement. However, one of Skinner's major objections to religion was that much of the reinforcement that was used was negative reinforcement or in some cases punishment (Wulff, 1996). The threat of hellfire and damnation as well as the possibility of being excommunicated from the church are examples of the negative and punishing aspects of religion cited by Skinner. According to Wulff (1996), Skinner saw one positive aspect of religion in that its positive reinforcement may be a means of encouraging ordinary people "to forgo individual gratification in the present to ensure a better future for all" (p. 49).

The Humanist-Existential Critique   The humanist and existential theorists criticized psychoanalytic and behavioral models as too deterministic and mechanistic, but they had objections to religion on different grounds. The modern humanist psychology movement has its roots in Renaissance humanism. The major ideas that have been carried forth include the principles of free inquiry, individual expression, and the basic dignity of all humanity (Goud, 1990). Humanists' major thrust was a belief in the potential of humanity. They underscored the natural tendency of people to become self-actualized if surrounded by a positive, supportive environment. The idealism reflected in the humanistic perspective is similar to some religious and spiritual beliefs, yet those humanists with a scientific and rational bent generally rejected the notion of a Supreme Being (Goud, 1990). Their emphasis was on the human being as the apex of creation.

This unilateral position of humanists has undergone transformation over the decades since its inception. In his 1990 study of 388 members of the Association for Humanistic Education and Development, a Division of the American Counseling Association, Goud (1990) found that most participants exhibit ethical and spiritual pluralism. The overriding theme, however, was the freedom of persons "to choose or create their own spiritual orientation" (Goud, 1990, p. 573).

Secular existentialists, too, valued humanity and human agency. They emphasized ideas such as freedom, responsibility, anxiety in the face of death, and the crises of meaning that occur in life—themes that are also addressed in a variety of ways in religious and spiritual approaches. Some proponents of existentialism such as Yalom (1980), however, purported that beliefs in a personal God and in immortality were merely defenses against the anxiety surrounding death. He also held that following religious codes and their behavioral prescriptions were a way of avoiding personal choice and responsibility.

Although humanists and existentialists differ in significant ways, both sets of theorists support the notion that people have the inborn capacity for self-direction and the responsibility for making choices about their lives. Despite their departure from psychoanalysis and behaviorism and their common praise for humanity, many humanists and existentialists alike minimized or rejected religion. Humanists tended to regard transcendent experiences as nothing more than higher consciousness (Genia, 1995). Reliance on God or some other Supreme Being was simply a crutch for persons who had not altogether claimed the possibilities of being fully human. Existentialists (other than avowed Christian existentialists such as Kierkegaard, Tillich, Bonhoeffer and others) tended to support the notion that the search for meaning is a human endeavor, undertaken without the help of any Higher Power. Instead, the search for meaning involves embracing life and its vicissitudes, and is thus a "by-product of *engagement,* which is a commitment to creating, loving, working, and building" (Corey, 2001, p. 151).

It is important to note here that although psychologists from various theoretical perspectives pointed to the pathology in religious and spiritual expression, they have not been completely mistaken. Certainly mental health providers in most settings have had ample opportunity to observe clients in whom pathology is expressed in religious or spiritual forms. For example, some clients with schizophrenia or other thought disorders present themselves as divine figures such as Jesus Christ, or they maintain that they have heard the voices of angels or of God. As a result of interacting with religiously disordered clients, some counselors have erroneously assumed that religion itself is the source of mental illness. However, as Genia (1995) rightly observed, "It is the nature of the psychic organization that determines the spiritual health of the individual. Disturbed religious functioning is the external manifestation of pathological tendencies in individual believers" (p. 11).

Meissner (1996), in writing about the pathology of religion, commented on the truth-value of religious beliefs: "On what grounds is the content of religious faith judged unintelligible or delusional? Is there only one standard of truth, or is there a truth of scientific method and a truth of religious belief?" (p. 245). He claimed that religious beliefs were not necessarily pathological in themselves, but that pathology was determined by how the belief affects adaptive functioning (Meissner, 1996). (A more detailed discussion of the characteristics of harmful religion follows in Chapter 4.)

Religion and Spirituality as Domains of the Clergy

In writing about the parallel histories of the development of psychology and religion in America, Kurtz (1999) described the 1920s as a time characterized by the emergence of faith in professionals. Although for centuries the clergy of various religions had been viewed as authority figures, the elevation of other experts, including psychologists, shifted expert authority from the extended family to institutions and their leaders. The notion of expertness residing in the hands of "professionals" also resulted in each discipline carving out boundaries that separated it from other competing disciplines. A classic example of such boundary setting is evident in the current divisions among mental health providers. Psychiatrists, psychologists, counselors, social workers, and marriage and family therapists emphasize historical, theoretical, practical, and political differences to maintain a demarcation around their "unique" identities. A similar type of limit setting has occurred among religious and spiritual leaders and mental health providers. Thus, persons' needs are compartmentalized based on the expertise of the healers. For example, clients seek doctors for physical ailments, counselors for emotional problems, and religious leaders for spiritual distress. This context of professionalism and its accompanying "turf wars" partly explains counselor's reluctance to address clients' religious or spiritual concerns. As a result, the wholeness of the client continues to be divided, and its various parts taken to appropriate healers.

By advocating that counselors and other mental health service providers consider clients' spiritual beliefs and values and be willing to work with them, I am not suggesting that counselors themselves become religious or spiritual leaders. The appropriate boundaries around theological training and ecclesiastical authority must remain in place. However, to relegate counseling religious or spiritual clients solely to religious leaders is to abdicate our responsibility to provide psychological services, even if they must be offered within the clients' religious or spiritual worldviews. It is essential that counselors realize that even though clergy and other spiritual leaders may be well prepared to deal with religious and spiritual issues, many are not equipped to address psychological ones (Domino, 1990). Thus, while respecting the boundaries around the professions, simply dismissing clients' religious and spiritual concerns as belonging to the domain of the clergy is too simplistic. Gaining skills in counseling religious clients effectively is, in my opinion, a more suitable enterprise.

Counselors' Lack of Training Regarding Religious and Spiritual Issues

Another reason that counselors and other mental health service providers have given over religious or spiritually oriented clients to the clergy, or have neglected or opposed integrating religion and spirituality in their practice, has to do with competence. Virtually all the ethical codes governing the practice of psychotherapy proscribe practicing in areas in which one is not trained or competent (ACA, 1995; APA, 1995; NASW, 1996; AAMFT, 1991; NOHSE, 1995).

Until recently, very few psychologists or counselors had been trained in working with clients' religious or spiritual issues (Collins, Hurst, & Jacobson, 1987; Genia, 1994; Jensen & Bergin, 1988; Shafranske & Malony, 1990). Indeed, Kelly (1994) found that of 341 accredited and nonaccredited counselor education programs, only 25% reported that religion and spirituality were addressed in the curriculum. Pate and High (1995) surveyed 60 CACREP-accredited programs, and 60% reported that some attention was given to these issues in the social and cultural foundations courses. In a subsequent study, Kelly (1997) studied 48 programs that were accredited solely by Council for the Accreditation of Counseling and Related Educational Programs (CACREP) and found that just over half reported that religion and spirituality were presented in some aspect of their counselor education curriculum.

Studies of psychologists (Shafranske, 1996; Shafranske & Malony, 1990) revealed that formal education and training in religious issues rarely or never occurred. However, in their study, Shafranske and Malony (1990) found that of 228 psychologists surveyed, 10% had some degree of theological training, and 10% were members of the American Psychological Association's Division 36 pertaining to Psychology and Religion. Thirty-eight percent of the sample had read at least one of the books considered by the Executive Division of Division 36 of APA to be critical in the area of psychology and religion. From this data, it seems that although formal education pertaining to the interface between religious and spiritual issues and psychotherapy has been modest, practitioners often have sought additional training outside academic arenas.

Counselors' Unresolved Religious and Spiritual Issues

One reason that many counselors and other mental health practitioners have neglected or opposed the inclusion of religion and spirituality in psychotherapy has to do with their personal experiences. When we have unresolved issues in our lives, then we are more likely to avoid dealing with them in a clinical setting. And, if we do venture into an area such as incorporating clients' religious and spiritual concerns in our work, our countertransference may be so strong that it interferes with our effectiveness, or worse, harms the client (Genia, 2000; Kochems, 1993).

That a large number of counselors have negative feelings about religion may contribute to their difficulty in dealing with religious clients. In a national study of mental health providers, only 29% believed that clients' religious and spiritual issues were appropriate areas to be addressed in therapy (Bergin & Jensen, 1990). In addition, researchers found that in a national sample of clinical psychologists' religious and spiritual orientations, 25% expressed negative feelings about past religious involvement (Shafranske & Malony, 1990). Thus, it is likely that counselors whose background includes negative religious incidents might have a disapproving or cynical reaction to religious clients. These ideas are developed more fully later in this chapter under the heading, "Person-of-the-Therapist Issues."

Thus, there are a number of reasons that, until recently, psychotherapy and religion have been bifurcated. Now we turn to a justification for integrating religion and spirituality into counseling and psychotherapy.

RELIGION AND SPIRITUALITY
IN COUNSELING AND PSYCHOTHERAPY

Religion and spirituality deserve a place in the practice of counseling and other forms of psychotherapy for many reasons. First, the majority of Americans indicate some belief in a Higher Power, and many are actively involved in churches, synagogues, mosques, and other religious institutions (Hoge, 1996). These data imply that most clients will have some kind of religious or spiritual background that shapes their attitudes, feelings, beliefs, and behavior. Also, there is some overlapping in the values and goals between counseling and religion or spirituality. For example, both psychotherapy and religion offer ways of managing life's difficulties. In a related way, the counseling profession has matured in such a way that client and counselor values are acknowledged rather than ignored (Richards & Bergin, 1997). Moreover, empirical evidence suggests that religion and spiritual faith contribute positively to mental health, and thus, the religious and spiritual dimensions of clients' lives may be ancillary tools in the therapeutic endeavor.

In addition, evidence indicates that across the decades since psychology's inception, there have been those who have been open to making use of the positive aspects of religion in psychotherapy. The legacy of others such as Frank

Parsons, Jesse B. Davis, Carl Jung, Erik Erikson, William James, Gordon Allport, Abraham Maslow, and Victor Frankl are worthy models for current clinicians who seek to master ways of integrating spirituality and psychotherapy.

Another reason that religion and spirituality are appropriate for the counseling enterprise has to do with the shift in thinking that occurred in the latter part of the 20th century. The postmodern movement has been a bridge over the chasm between science and religion and has opened up new possibilities for integrating a wholistic approach to psychotherapy. That philosophical trend, coupled with a renewed interest in religion evident in the popular culture (Richards & Bergin, 1997), makes the time ripe for committing ourselves to using religion and spirituality in mental health practice.

Finally, the need to seriously consider clients' cultural background and context implies that counselors must look carefully at the role spirituality and religion play in culture (Pate & Bondi, 1992). For many clients, religious beliefs and practice are fundamental aspects of their culture. For example, the Black Church (Frame & Williams, 1996) has influenced many African American clients significantly. As a result, counseling interventions that incorporate clients' spiritual or religious beliefs and practices, or that rely on indigenous healers may augment counselors' effectiveness.

Demographic Data Regarding Religion and Spirituality in American Culture

According to a Gallup poll, 94% of adult Americans believe in God or in a universal spirit. In addition, 68% of adult Americans are members of church, synagogue, or place of worship, and 58% rate religion as being very important in their lives (Gallup, 1993). When asked about religious or mystical experiences, 40% of participants in a national survey responded "yes" when asked, "Have you ever felt as though you were very close to a powerful spiritual force that seemed to lift you out of yourself?" (Greeley, 1989, p. 59).

Another interesting factor related to religion in America has to do with the impact of immigration on the religious composition of the United States. Since 1965, immigrants from Mexico and South and Central America— mostly Spanish-speaking Catholics—have tipped the scales by increasing the Roman Catholic presence in the United States. Likewise, immigrants from the Middle East, Eastern Europe, and North Africa have brought Islam with them. In fact, the number of Muslims in America increased by 1.7 million between 1980 and 1993 (Hoge, 1996). These demographic changes in religious composition certainly will affect the world of psychotherapy by suggesting more diversity in culture and belief than previously experienced.

Besides numerical data on belief and affiliation, Hoge (1996) noted a definite trend in all religious groups toward increased individualism and autonomy in their decision-making. Over the past several decades, the authority of church officials such as the Pope and the clergy has declined. It has been impossible for church leaders to enforce their moral or doctrinal teachings (Hoge, 1996). Thus, according to Marty (1993), a dramatic shift has occurred in religious leaders: They have moved from being coercive to being more persuasive. Nevertheless, laity are thinking and acting for themselves, especially when it comes to social issues such as the role of women, premarital sex, birth control, homosexuality, and abortion. With the increased burden of having to sort out moral and religious beliefs on their own, and with the openness and tolerance of religious differences, counselors may find opportunities to help clients make sense of their own worldviews and their morality in ways that were not possible before.

Overlapping Values and Goals in Religion, Spirituality, and Psychotherapy

There are some etymological connections between the Latin root words for salvation and health. *Salvare* in Latin means "to save." *Salvus* means "safe" and is related to the Latin word *salus* meaning healthy or whole. Thus, the religious word, *salvation* is etymologically related to the psychologically oriented words *health, wholeness, and well-being*. A linguistic history binds the spiritual notion of what it means to be whole with the psychological assumption about wellness. The unity of the disciplines, then, is visible from the perspective of language.

Another way in which religious faith and counseling intersect has to do with a common focus. Both disciplines have as their goal the transformation of the mind and the emotions (Bianchi, 1989). Moreover, therapy and religion have overlapping roles. They "foster a sense of identity, give meaning to life, provide rituals that transform and connect, provide social support networks, support families, facilitate positive change for individuals, and look out for the physical and emotional welfare of members" (Stander, Piercy, MacKinnon, & Helmeke, 1994, p. 29). From this vantage point, we can see that both religion and psychotherapy are often about the same tasks, with a different language and set of activities and responses.

Going beyond the idea of parallel processes, Jones (1996) argued that psychotherapy overlaps with moral and religious aims because of the void it fills in American culture. He indicated that because of the decline in religious practice in America during the past several decades, counselors and other mental health practitioners are serving as the culture's *shamans* when it comes to answering questions about the meaning and purpose of life and providing more direction for clients. It is possible, then, for counselors to think of themselves as partners with religion and spirituality in striving toward common ends.

Beyond the notion that psychotherapy and religion have a common purpose and overlapping roles, London (1986) made the case for psychology as a moral enterprise. He claimed that counselors constituted a "secular priesthood" (London, 1986, p. 148) in which they perform moralistic functions. Jones (1996) explained the moral nature of psychotherapy and counseling by suggesting that clients do not separate psychological and moral or religious issues. Someone contemplating an extra-marital affair, for instance, does not dwell solely on the emotional aspects of such a choice but, rather, on the moral and religious dimensions as well.

Empirical Evidence Linking Religion, Spirituality, and Mental Health

In numerous studies during the past several decades, researchers have investigated the relationship between religion and mental health. The outcomes have been mixed: Some results indicate that religion and spirituality are positively connected to mental health. Other findings suggest an ambiguous relationship, and still other research results indicate that religion and spirituality are associated with psychopathology (Gartner, 1996). Moreover, several meta-analyses have been conducted for the purpose of summarizing and teasing out the variables in these contradictory findings (Bergin, 1983; Gartner, Larson, & Allen, 1991; Schumaker, 1992).

A constant challenge to such research is addressing methodological issues. This task involves managing the varying definitions of religion, sorting out the different measures of religiosity (e.g., commitment, beliefs, affiliation, church attendance), and dealing with the confounding variables and alternative explanations that plague many experimental designs. Having acknowledged these methodological hazards, several positive links remain between religion and mental health.

Bergin (1983) reviewed research studies through the 1980s and found that when religion was correlated with measures of mental health, 23% of the studies revealed a negative relationship, 30% found no relationship, and 47% found a positive relationship. "Thus, 77% of the obtained results are contrary to the negative effect of religion theory" (p. 176). Gartner, Larson, and Allen (1991) found a favorable association between religiousness and suicide risk, drug use, alcohol abuse, delinquent behavior, divorce and marital satisfaction, psychological well-being, depression, and physical health and longevity. Specifically, they found fewer suicidal impulses and more negative attitudes toward suicide in religious subjects. Eleven of the 12 studies reviewed revealed a negative relationship between religious commitment and drug use. In addition, those who reported a high level of religious involvement were less likely to abuse alcohol. Religious attitudes were moderately associated with lower criminal and juvenile behavior, but high religious participation *consistently* was associated with lower criminal and juvenile behavior.

Gartner and colleagues (1991) also found that the greater their church attendance is, the less likely couples are to divorce. Although this finding could mean that regular church-goers remain in unhappy marriages, further research reviews resulted in the discovery that religious folk were more satisfied in their marriages than were the less religious. Results of one such study (Glen & Weaver, 1978) revealed that church attendance predicted marital satisfaction better than any of eight other variables in a regression model. Religious commitment also appears to be positively related to psychological well-being. Several studies (Argyle & Beit-Hallahmi, 1975; Lindenthal,

Myers, Pepper, & Stern, 1970; Stark, 1971) reviewed by Gartner et al. (1991) showed a negative relationship between psychological distress and religious participation. Most evidence gleaned from studies of religion and depression indicated that religious persons reported lower levels of depression than did those who were not so religious.

The outcomes of researchers' investigations of religion and mental health suggest that religious attendance is significantly related to physical health in a positive way. There are many confounding variables in some of these studies, however, rendering it impossible to claim a unanimous association. Good physical health might allow people to attend church more often. Or, perhaps church attendance leads people to practice more healthy behaviors. Despite these challenges to data interpretation, frequent attendance at religious services seems to be a protective factor against a host of negative health outcomes (Levin & Vanderpool, 1987). Related to physical health, research results show that religious people tend to live longer than do those with less religious commitment. This same outcome appears to be true for religious participation as well as commitment (Gartner, 1996).

It is possible, then, to conclude that religious belief and practice have a positive relationship to measures of well-being, social adjustment, and emotional stability (Batson, Schoenrode, & Ventis, 1993; Batson & Ventis, 1982; Payne, Bergin, Bielema, & Jenkins, 1991). Given that so many studies support the salutary relationship between religion and mental health, these findings support the proposition that religion and spirituality are integral components to the psychotherapeutic enterprise.

The Legacy of Psychotherapy's Pioneers

Despite the negative view of religion presented by several psychologists mentioned in the previous section, others recognized the contributions that religion and spirituality could make to psychotherapy. Some of these pioneers, such as Parsons and Davis, came from the tradition of vocational counseling. Others such as Jung and Erikson came from the psychoanalytic orientation. Still others such as James and Allport worked from the perspective of the psychology of religion. Other contributors such as Maslow and Frankl represented the humanistic and existential viewpoints.

Frank Parsons   Known as the "father of guidance," Parsons' work focused on vocational counseling. Parsons (1909) was convinced that religion influenced persons' daily lives and that it contributed to their industriousness in the world of work. Although Parsons' attention was not directed toward the study of religion, spirituality, or its role in the unconscious (Kelly, 1995), nonetheless he was aware of the capacity of religion to foster tolerance, open-mindedness, social justice, and ethical decision-making.

Jesse Davis   A leader in the early days of vocational guidance in schools, Davis was equally concerned with students' development of moral character as with their vocational choices. He believed that people were successful in their work arenas because of the quality of their moral lives—something that was influenced by their religious commitment. Davis was careful not to assume that any practice of religion was to be construed as necessarily resulting in moral character. He was aware of the potential for religion to result in persons' becoming self-serving, authoritarian, oppressive, and rigid. Instead, he held that religion ought to motivate persons to serve neighbors, to assist in eliminating social misery, and to cater to the majority of citizens rather than to the elite (Davis, 1914). Although he did not see himself as a champion of the interface of counseling and spirituality, he was able to blend the two disciplines into a philosophy with a humanistic bent.

Carl Jung   Trained in the psychoanalytic tradition, Jung departed from Freud in significant ways. One of those deviations involved his view of spirituality and religion. Jung (1932/1969) did not emphasize the institutional aspect of religion, but he did suggest that a religious perspective could have a positive role in psychological adjustment. Jung's focus was not on the objective reality of a deity. He was not interested in arguing about the existence of God. Rather, he concentrated on the ways in which one's awareness of the holy assisted in the process of individuation.

Jung postulated the existence of a *collective unconscious,* "the deep universal layer of the psyche" (Wulff, 1996, p. 54), or the "powerful and controlling repository of ancestral experiences" (Schultz & Schultz, 1998, p. 92). The collective unconscious is made up of archetypes, or universal mythic symbols. The major archetypes posited by Jung include the *persona, the animus and anima,* and the *shadow.* The *persona* refers to the self-protective public presentation we make of ourselves toward others. The *animus* and *anima* denote the masculine and feminine aspects of the self. The *shadow* has to do with the dark side of human experience, including the dangerous, powerful, and socially nefarious thoughts, feelings, and behaviors that people project outward. The goal of human life is to achieve individuation—the integration of the conscious and unconscious aspects of the personality (Corey, 2001). To become individuated, or whole, people must be able to acknowledge the divergent dimensions in themselves and must be able to accept their shadow sides. According to Jung, the religious traditions with their myths, stories, rituals, and images in which the archetypes have been embedded have done much to promote individuation. Ultimately, for Jung, the open relationship between the unconscious and conscious forces in the personality is critical for personality integration—the sign of true spirituality (Mack, 1994).

Eric Erikson   Best known for his life-span theory of human development, Erikson's ego psychology also included a positive slant toward religion. Unlike Freud, Erickson did not view religion as illusory or immature but, rather, linked it to humanity's needs, fears, hopes, and yearnings. According to Erickson, religion is a means of sealing trust, the core issue of the infantile stage of development. In addition, religion "universalizes mistrust through a shared conception of evil" (Wulff, 1996, p. 58). Moreover, in the final stage of life, religion offers wisdom, a hallmark of the integrity that emerges as persons age. In addition, Erikson (1966) emphasized the importance of rituals, those that circumscribe daily routine as well as religious rituals that punctuate life stages. Although he acknowledged the potential for religion to go awry and to degenerate into pathological distortion, Erikson primarily believed in the place of religion on the path to human generativity.

William James   Author of one of the most significant volumes on the psychology of religion, *Varieties of Religious Experience,* James' notions of religion were similar to Jung's. His definition of religion was much more akin to my definitions of spirituality in that he did not focus on organized, institutional forms of religion. Rather, he emphasized a sense of transcendence in relation to the divine. James acknowledged the potential difficulties with religion in its extremes—such as dogmatism, oppression, violence, and rigid proscriptions about what constituted appropriate behavior for the religious person. However, he held to the belief that faith and reason in concert would lead people to attain human excellence.

Gordon Allport   In his landmark publication, *The Individual and His Religion* (1950), Allport, following in the tradition of James, underscored the positive aspects of religion in human development and functioning. Like James, Allport was cognizant of the psychopathology that can occur with the excesses of religion and spirituality; however, he denied that these negative qualities were the prevailing ones among well-adjusted religious people.

Allport's (1950) greatest contribution to the psychology of religion was his description of the six benchmarks of mature religion. These criteria included the following:

(1) Religion is *well differentiated*. It involves a cognitive process in which one evaluates knowledge and experience resulting in an organized perspective. (2) It is *autonomous and dynamic*. Instinctual drives, childhood wishes, dreams, or needs, or other negative qualities do not motivate it. Mature religion augments individual and social development. (3) It results in *ethical consistency* such that one's moral code is borne out in his or her actions. It fosters integrity. (4) Religious maturity is *comprehensive* in that it grapples with questions regarding life's ultimate meaning. It comes to some resolution that is connected and congruent. (5) Religious maturity is *integral* in that it pulls diverse elements of human existence, including human atrocities, into meaningful wholes. (6) It is *heuristic*. That is, it retains the quality of a hypothesis, embracing both faith and doubt. Religious maturity allows for ongoing growth, development, and transformation of beliefs, while constantly fueling persons with spiritual drive and grounding them in a value-based orientation toward life.

Abraham Maslow   A major spokesperson from the humanistic movement, Maslow (1968), is best known for his concept of "peak experiences" that take on mystical dimensions. For Maslow, these peak experiences culminated in persons' experiencing self-transcendence, unity with the cosmos, personal wholeness, and a deep sense of reverence for and marvel at the beauty of existence. Maslow believed that those who had peak experiences became more creative, were bursting with life and newfound energy, and reported having gained new insights about themselves, others, and the world. "Plateau experiences" were, for Maslow, an enduring state of less intense, but pervasively enlightening experiences that resulted in personal transformation. Ironically, Maslow, an atheist, wrote about peak experiences as spiritual or religious phenomena, but denied that they were in any way supernatural. Instead, he considered them the hallmarks of truly self-actualized individuals (1970). Maslow accused religious institutions of squeezing the vitality out of spirituality such that it became dry and petrified, ceasing to sustain life. He hoped that ultimately spirituality as embodied in peak and plateau experiences might be rescued from the religious forms of the day.

Viktor Frankl   From the humanistic-existential perspective, Frankl's perspective, shaped by the horror of the holocaust, focused on the human search for meaning (1963). For Frankl, self-transcendence occurred when persons made deep commitments to taking responsibility for relationships, personal dignity, or anything else that would humanize the social order and bring significant meaning. Frankl held to the notion of a spiritual unconscious that housed human freedom. He posited a religious unconscious, a concept that referred to transcendence that has not yet come forth but may emerge and develop. He also believed in the unconscious God, a term that referred to a latent relationship to a God whose self-revelation is not obvious. In the existential tradition, Frankl claimed that in their freedom, persons were responsible for making choices toward ultimate meaning. Thus, Frankl's view provided an opportunity for spirituality to emerge in the context of humanistic values.

Paradigm Shifts and Cultural Movements

Postmodernism and Social Constructionist Theory   If logical positivism and the scientific worldview were some reasons why psychology and spirituality parted ways, then postmodern constructionism partially explains why they are being reunited today. The postmodern perspective involves a paradigm shift regarding how we think about the world. In this worldview, "there are no metaphysical absolutes; no fundamental and abstract truths, laws, or principles that will determine what the world is like and what happens in it" (Slife & Williams, 1995, p. 54). Instead, there are multiple perspectives and varieties of ways of perceiving. Thus, individuals do not discover reality but rather invent it (Watzlawick, Weakland, & Fisch, 1974). Postmodern thinkers emphasize the context in which human beings find themselves. They claim that meaning and truth are not objective "givens" but that they emerge in light of human relationships, language, culture, and personal meanings.

Anderson (1990) related a joke about three umpires that illustrates the difference between an objective, scientific worldview and a postmodern subjective one:

> The three umpires are sitting around over a beer, and the one says, "There's balls and there's strikes, and I call 'em the way they are." Another says, "There's balls and there's strikes, and I call 'em the way I see 'em." The third says, "There's balls and there's strikes, and they ain't *nothin'* until I call 'em." (p. 75)

According to Anderson, the first umpire is an objectivist, the second a moderate constructionist and the third a postmodern radical.

What this shift in perspective means for counselors is that clients' religious or spiritual beliefs are considered human constructions of reality. It does not matter if those constructions include God or not (Zinnbauer & Pargament, 2000), or if they are congruent with the counselor's constructions (Neimeyer, 1995). Thus, counselors enter the subjective reality of their clients and work within those perspectives, using a common language involving shared metaphors and symbols (Bilu, Witztum, & Van der Hart, 1990). Such an approach enables counselors to avoid theological arguments with clients, and could reduce the likelihood that counselors will impose their values on their clients.

Cultural Changes   According to Benningfield (1998), besides the shift to a postmodern inclination, other events in late 20th century culture have contributed to a resurgence of interest in and support for integrating spirituality and religion into psychotherapy. First, the advent of alternative medicine and natural healing has set the stage for fresh ways of looking at wellness. The emphasis on holistic approaches that address body, mind, and spirit are becoming popular. Bernie Siegel's (1990) book, *Love, Medicine, and Miracles* is an example of the integration of holistic practices into modern medicine. Such a move has inspired a similar attempt in the mental health arena.

Second, Benningfield (1998) pointed to epoch-making publications by well-renowned counselors urging colleagues to consider religious and spiritual material in their therapeutic work. Examples are Scott Peck's book, *The Road Less Traveled* (1978), Lovinger's book (1984), *Working with Religious Issues in Therapy,* and Spero's (1985) edited work, *Psychotherapy of the Religious Patient.* The authors of these volumes have made unique contributions to the growing body of literature devoted to addressing clients' religious and spiritual concerns in therapy.

Third, Benningfield (1998) noted the impact of self-help groups, especially 12-step programs. The popularity of these programs resulted in a new wave of "converts" who placed their trust in a Higher Power. In addition, the number of volumes by writers claiming to help people manage their emotional distress and promising them spiritual growth has skyrocketed. Moreover, pop psychology has infiltrated American culture to such a degree that mental health clinicians are, by necessity, being forced to be conversant with their clientele regarding the major themes inherent in these publications (Butler, 1990).

Thus, clients are bringing their newfound or newly transformed spirituality with them and expecting their counselors to be able to deal with it.

Fourth, Benningfield (1998) acknowledged the surge of interest in Eastern religions and philosophies that has been expanding since the 1960s. These traditions focus on personal enlightenment and spiritual practices such as meditation and yoga. Eastern thought, too, has challenged the prevailing assumptions of the western, scientific, objective model of knowing. A sense of unity, wholeness, and acceptance characterizes Eastern spirituality. Clients who have found personal harmony and meaning through engagement with these Eastern spiritual practices will bring their worldviews into the counseling process. Counselors must then be prepared to enter into these clients' experiences and to use them in therapy.

Religion, Spirituality, and the Multicultural Context

Another compelling reason for counselors to integrate religion and spirituality into their therapeutic endeavors is to be able to work effectively within clients' ethnic and cultural backgrounds. Religion and spirituality are, for many clients, an integral part of their cultural experience. Indeed, the entire notion of "culture" in the broadest sense implicitly involves religion and spirituality. According to Pedersen (1990), "culture" includes "ethnographic variables such as ethnicity, nationality, religion, and language, as well as demographic variables such as age, gender, and place of residence [and] status variables such as social, economic, and educational factors, and affiliations" (p. 93). When thinking about culture, it is important to stress that although each ethnic group has some common characteristics, individual differences preclude stereotyping. These ideas are explored in greater detail in Chapter 5 in which characteristics of religion and spirituality are elucidated and therapeutic interventions provided.

The Summit on Spirituality

During the fall of 1995, leaders of the American Counseling Association's ASERVIC (Association for Spiritual, Ethical, Religious, and Value Issues in Counseling) division convened the first Summit on Spirituality. As a result of this meeting and subsequent ones in the following two years, ASERVIC leaders developed a set of nine key counselor competencies regarding the challenge of integrating religion and spirituality into counseling. These competencies are as follows:

> In order to be competent to help clients address the spiritual dimension of their lives, a counselor needs to be able to: (1) explain the relationship between religion and spirituality, include similarities and differences, (2) describe religious and spiritual beliefs and practices in a cultural context, (3) engage in self-exploration of his/her religious and spiritual beliefs in order to increase sensitivity, understanding and acceptance of his/her belief system, (4) describe one's religious and/or spiritual belief system and explain various models of religious/spiritual

development across the life span, (5) demonstrate sensitivity to and acceptance of a variety of religious and/or spiritual expressions in the client's communication, (6) identify the limits of one's understanding of a client's spiritual expression, and demonstrate appropriate referral skills and general possible referral sources, (7) assess the relevance of the spiritual domains in the client's therapeutic issues, (8) be sensitive to and respectful of the spiritual themes in the counseling process as befits each client's expressed preference, and (9) use a client's spiritual beliefs in the pursuit of the client's therapeutic goals as befits the client's expressed preference. (Burke, 1998, p. 2)

These competencies and their endorsement by ASERVIC are another reason why counselors should endeavor to work with clients' religious and spiritual concerns.

I have described some of the reasons that I believe that religion and spirituality are aspects of the human experience worthy of exploration in counseling. They are as follows: (1) demographic data suggest that a majority of Americans believe in God or a universal spirit; (2) overlapping values and goals in religion, spirituality, and psychotherapy; (3) empirical evidence linking religion, spirituality, and mental health; (4) the legacy of psychotherapy's pioneers; (5) paradigm shifts and cultural movements; (6) religion and spirituality in a multicultural context; and (7) the spiritual competencies developed by the Summit on Spirituality suggest a need for counselors to become able helpers in this area.

PERSON-OF-THE-THERAPIST ISSUES

The process of becoming a competent counselor involves learning not only technical skills, but it also involves a commitment toward becoming a professional and a person (Whitaker & Keith, 1981). Many counselor educators, psychologists, and family therapists (Aponte & Winter, 1987; Bowen, 1972; Liddle, 1982) have advocated family of origin work as part of their preparation to enter the mental health field. The theory is that because all counselors grow up in families, they tend to reproduce in subsequent relationships the interactional patterns they learned at home. Moreover, all students of counseling and other mental health disciplines bring with them their life experiences, worldviews, values, and personal relationships into the counseling process (Aponte & Winter, 1987). It is imperative to address "person-of-the-therapist" issues (Aponte & Winter, 1987) when working with clients' religious and spiritual concerns because they are often what Guerin and Hubbard (1987) referred to as "clinical triggers." This phrase means that clients enter counseling with issues that are similar to the counselor's issues. When these sets of issues collide in the therapeutic process, counselors are more vulnerable to being pulled into their clients' system (Kramer, 1985).

A myriad of experiences can color counselors' responses to clients' religious and spiritual issues, including countertransference reactions. For example, counselors who were raised in families where religion was eschewed and perhaps considered unscientific or irrational could find themselves feeling disloyal to their families of origin if they entertain their clients' spiritual or religious issues. These counselors could be vulnerable to being drawn into arguments or other conflicts with dogmatic clients that could result in cementing clients' rigid beliefs rather than opening for them new possibilities. Or, counselors with or without a religious or spiritual upbringing might be unaware of how significantly religion could influence their clients and thus not attend to it in ways that would be helpful to their clients (Benningfield, 1998).

Some counselors could have been raised in orthodox religious homes and disassociated themselves with their family's religion during adolescence or young adulthood. It is developmentally typical for people to question their religious or spiritual beliefs (Fowler & Keen, 1978). However, some people continue to struggle with unresolved theological questions that lead them to feel anxious when religious or spiritual topics emerge in conversation. When such anxiety strikes counselors in the context of their therapeutic work, they might consciously or unconsciously redirect the session to avoid addressing the religious or spiritual concerns that make them uncomfortable.

Some counselors might have the opportunity to work with clients who are examining their religious or spiritual beliefs and who are considering moving away from long-held fundamentalism to less stringent perspectives. A possible countertransference reaction occurs when counselors who are disturbed by such dogmatic religion are too eager to move clients beyond their inflexible views (Genia, 2000). As a result of counselors' critical reactions to clients' unmalleable religious worldviews, clients could feel lost and ungrounded in their faith.

Other counselors who have experienced significant losses and trauma such as the Oklahoma City bombing, school shootings, or the tragic and untimely death of loved ones, might feel disappointed in or angry with a God who is seemingly powerless to prevent such atrocities. These personal crises could also create crises of faith for persons who previously thought they had made peace with their Higher Power and reconciled with their religion. When clients raise spiritual or religious questions about evil, death, and "why bad things happen to good people" (Kushner, 1981), counselors might feel unprepared to deal with the powerful emotions these topics unleash for them. They might also feel incapable of responding effectively to their clients' distress, and thus could attempt to minimize or avoid it. Such difficulty for the counselor signals the need for supervision, personal counseling, and perhaps referral of the client.

Other counselors might have had deeply moving transpersonal experiences of higher consciousness, unity with others and the universe, and a palpable sense of self-transcendence. Despite the positive impact these encounters might have had, some counselors might not have a suitable religious, spiritual, or philosophical frame for integrating transpersonal experiences into their daily living. They might feel at once energized and apprehensive about what has occurred for them personally. When counselors find themselves in this situation, their countertransference reaction could cause them to over-identify with clients who present similar circumstances.

Or counselors' transpersonal revelations might be too intense and unexamined such that they cause counselors to refrain from entering that domain with their clients. Another possible scenario could involve counselors seeking help from clients to assimilate their transpersonal experiences. In such a case, counselors who rely on their clients would be placing their personal needs above the needs of their clients, an act that is clearly unethical (ACA, 1995; APA, 1992; NASW, 1996; AAMFT, 1991).

Another type of unresolved issue for counselors could be the conflict they undergo when faced with clients whose social and political positions, undergirded by a particular religious perspective, are diametrically opposed to the counselors' own. For example, clients could present with hostile and denigrating attitudes toward gay and lesbian persons and be seemingly justified in their views based on some religious authority such as the Bible. Or, perhaps clients are unwilling to consider abortion because of the doctrine of their church or because of their spiritual persuasions regarding the right to life. Counselors who hold opposing views could find themselves in an adversarial position with their clients. These practitioners might assume that their strong aversive responses are elicited by the religious or spiritual dogma that buttresses their clients' beliefs. Thus, counselors might be tempted to minimize clients' issues, to address only the social or political issue without its accompanying religious context, or to focus on freeing clients from what the counselors perceive as unsound religious or spiritual beliefs. All these detrimental possibilities are derived from counselors' internal conflicts that have not been adequately reconciled.

Another difficult reality that some counselors face is that of their having been sexually abused by a member of the clergy. This devastating event could result in counselors' severe depression, self-blame, and symptoms of posttraumatic stress disorder such as nightmares, hypervigilance, and flashbacks (Fortune, 1989). Moreover, it could seriously damage the counselors' trust in spiritual leadership, could result in a fracture in counselors' connection to a religious or spiritual community, and could be extremely confusing because of the intertwining of spiritual and sexual betrayal. Counselors who have survived this kind of victimization most certainly should obtain personal therapy. Despite engaging in successful psychotherapy, however, the psychic and emotional toll that is taken on persons who are abused by clergy or other spiritual leaders is tremendous. Thus, the potential for avoiding clients with religious or spiritual issues is compounded. Counselors who have survived clergy abuse could be exceptionally vulnerable to projecting their experiences on clients' religious leaders or reexperiencing personal trauma when clients present religious or spiritual issues.

The previous scenarios are illustrations of how "person-of-the-therapist" issues (Aponte & Winter, 1987) can emerge in the context of working with clients' religious and spiritual concerns. Countless other vignettes could reveal counselors' unresolved personal issues that could interfere with their counseling effectiveness. Following you will find some case examples that involve many of the issues discussed in this section.

CASE EXAMPLES
Isabel

Isabel is counseling Nadine, who requested assistance handling her boyfriend Mike's pressure for her to start attending church with him. Nadine, a Jew, was not interested in getting involved in Christianity, though she had virtually given up attending her synagogue and had not participated in any religious holidays in the past ten years. Nadine also reported to Isabel that she was afraid she would lose Mike if she didn't show some appreciation for his religion. Isabel, who was raised Catholic, had discontinued her relationship with her church when she decided she could not support its negative position on birth control, women's ordination, and abortion. Isabel was able to empathize with Nadine's reluctance to get involved in a religion she didn't believe in. In counseling, Isabel focused on gender issues and advised Nadine to be assertive regarding her opinion about religion, regardless of what her boyfriend thought. Although Nadine appreciated the support from Isabel, she remained torn between her religious heritage and her boyfriend, whom she hoped to marry.

Discussion Questions
1. How well do you think Isabel handled Nadine's issues around religion? Why?
2. What do you think are some of Isabel's personal issues?
3. Do you think that Isabel's own history with religion influenced the way she worked with Nadine? Why or why not?
4. What would you recommend that Isabel do in subsequent sessions with Nadine?
5. If you were Nadine, how might you be feeling about Isabel's work with you?
6. What facts, ideas, or other information presented in this chapter is related to this case?

Anthony

Anthony, a counselor in a community mental health center, is counseling Gloria, a recently divorced Caucasian mother of three young children. As a means of coping with the stress of her divorce, Gloria began attending a meditation group and reading numerous self-help books about overcoming depression through surrender to a Higher Power. Anthony, a champion of meditation and yoga, encouraged Gloria in her newly discovered spiritual path. After four weeks of counseling with Anthony, Gloria found herself spending all her free time attending lectures, meditating, and practicing yoga. She reported that sometimes she "forgot" to fix dinner for her children and that once she had left Tiffany, her youngest, at day care until the babysitter called her an hour after pickup time. Gloria indicated that she was afraid that Social Services might hear about her "oversights" and try to take her children. In response to Gloria's story, Anthony suggested they spend some of the counseling session meditating. He thought Gloria's anxiety might be reduced if she went into a meditative state. Although she was relaxed after meditation, as Anthony predicted, Gloria remained frustrated about how to manage her children and the other demands in her life without becoming overwhelmed and depressed.

Discussion Questions

1. In what ways do you think Anthony's work with Gloria was helpful or not helpful?
2. What "person-of-the-therapist" issues do you think Anthony needs to consider?
3. How would you respond to Gloria if she were your client?
4. How do you think Gloria's new found spiritual path is functioning for her?
5. What information from this chapter do you find especially relevant to this case?

SUGGESTED ACTIVITIES

Write a Spiritual Autobiography

Start with the earliest memories you have of religion or spirituality in your home or family life. Describe your experiences with religion and spirituality through childhood, adolescence, young adulthood, and beyond. Indicate incidents when your religious or spiritual beliefs and values were challenged or changed. Reflect on where you are with religion and spirituality at this time in your life. What directions would you like to take in this dimension of your life in the future? Following are some excerpts from counseling students' spiritual autobiographies. Perhaps these comments will spark your own thoughts and memories as you construct your spiritual or religious story.

Student #1: "Before I was conceived my parents had both accepted the Lord [Jesus Christ] as personal savior in their lives . . . for several years they attempted to conceive a child without success. At the climax of distress, my parents found themselves on their knees before the Lord begging Him, if it were His will, to bless them with a child. Lo and behold, one was sent to them—me! . . . There was never a time when I felt that the Lord was not in my life. I have always felt his comforting presence. Before college, I was close-minded about my beliefs . . . [but] I am thankful for the Lord leading me to a university that was able to give me the tools to think about His Word critically. I believe He [God] does not want blind followers but people who are able to think for themselves . . ."

Student #2: "Growing up, we attended a Reformed Protestant Church . . . although my mother had an open mind regarding religion and spirituality, I

definitely experienced the more dogmatic side of religion through my peers
. . . My early experience of [church] was that of a judgmental and critical
place where values and beliefs that were being taught were not engendered
in the lives of the congregation. Religion failed to make sense to me—it
seemed cruel and punishing while talking about kindness and forgiveness
. . . The moment I truly began to believe in the divine was one evening
when I was home alone. I was petrified, highly agitated, and unable to
sleep. I had a protection candle that had come with a prayer. I followed the
directions and said the prayer over and over. When I blew out the candle
and closed my eyes, there was a bright yellow light that completely en-
veloped me, and I felt instantly at peace. I could try to intellectualize it or
try to give a scientific explanation for it, but I chose to believe instead that
there is something greater than I that listens to me and answers me. This
something—spirit, god—may not always answer so directly, but I feel for
myself that I have proof that the divine works in my life. I believe that the
divine flows through all things and all people. I also know that I can only
find answers for myself and try to be open to the answers that others have
found for themselves."

Student #3: "From elementary school through most of high school, I
claimed and sincerely felt myself to be an atheist. All religious settings, literature, and ideas were tainted and conjured up the image of that which I re-
viled: blind followers of nonsense and ignorers of obvious reality. Therefore
. . . I adopted the natural/scientific model and asserted that there simply was
no evidence whatsoever for anything beyond that which we can sense. If it
could not be proven, I simply dismissed it . . . [Then] I encountered poetry
and literature and Eastern thought . . . and somehow I had come to believe
that personal, subjective experience could differ from objective experience yet
not be any less real . . . Initially, I focused my intention on my physical health
and well-being. My spirit (soul, mind, chi, tao—the terminology is not important) exists for now inside my body. Consequently, I find it beneficial to
make my body do good, healthy, life-affirming things . . . like running,
breathing fresh air and feeling sunlight, not smoking or taking drugs. These
behaviors provide a window into the second phase of my spiritual development, "learning to be . . . in the best way that I can . . . so that I and others
can promote harmony and balance throughout the world."

Student #4: "My spiritual journey began long before I was born. My
mother, her mother, and her mother before that were all strong Presbyterian
women with strong ties to the church. From the beginning of childhood, my
parents took my brother and me to Sunday school, then church. I was in the
choir and youth group. [During high school] I experienced a growth in my
spirituality by way of conferences and leadership opportunities. With every
new conference came a renewed faith, a stronger sense of self, and a promise
of hope for the future. While my faith roots are deeply embedded in organized religion, they are also branching toward a more personal spirituality."

Confront the Difficult Questions

Consider keeping a journal in which you can reflect on the difficult questions to which religion and spirituality provide responses. Remember that your clients will be grappling with these same issues. It can be very helpful for you to gain clarity on where you stand on these matters. Use the following questions to structure your thinking and writing. You may also want to use these questions as the focus of small group discussions.

1. How do you view human nature? Are people good, evil, neutral?
2. What about free will? Do people have the human agency to make their own choices or are their thoughts, feelings, actions determined by some other force such as instincts, reinforcements, God?
3. How would you respond to the question, "Why do bad things happen to good people?" Is God responsible for evil? Is there an evil spirit that struggles against a good spirit? Is God powerless to contain evil? Do bad things happen because people make poor choices? Do bad things happen to good people because the "good people" aren't really as good as they think they are? Do bad things happen randomly?
4. What happens to people after they die? Is there some form of afterlife? If so, what does it look like? Who decides what happens to whom?
5. Do you believe in a Higher Power? What are the qualities of the Supreme Being if you believe in one? Why do you believe in a Higher Power or God? If you do not believe in a Higher Power or God, what are the reasons for your disbelief?
6. What is your understanding of spirituality? How have you experienced it in your life?
7. Which of the "person-of-the-therapist" issues seems to fit best for you? In which areas do you believe yourself to be most vulnerable to counter-transference when clients raise religious or spiritual issues? What experiences have you had that lead you to believe that you are particularly vulnerable to "clinical triggers?"
8. Which types of clients or client problems involving religion or spirituality would be the most challenging for you? Why? Which ones would be the most engaging? Why?

Interview Another Counselor

Select someone who is currently working in the mental health field providing direct service counseling or psychotherapy to clients. Interview that clinician regarding issues raised in this chapter. Consider using some of the following questions to guide your interview:

1. How do you understand the differences between religion and spirituality?
2. How would you describe your own spiritual path if you have one?
3. What is your opinion about working with clients' religious or spiritual issues in therapy? How comfortable do you feel doing so?

4. How does your theoretical orientation to counseling shape your ideas about how to work with clients' religious or spiritual issues?
5. If you do address religion or spirituality in your work with clients, what is your rationale for doing so?
6. Which types of clients or client problems involving religion or spirituality would be the most challenging for you? Why? Which ones would be the most engaging? Why?

SUPPLEMENTAL READINGS

Reality Isn't What It Used to Be (Anderson, 1990). This readable book is a helpful treatise on postmodern thought and its implications for contemporary life. It includes a very enlightening chapter regarding psychotherapy from a postmodern perspective.

Humanistic and Transpersonal Psychology (Moss, 1999). This edited book is a comprehensive treatise that includes both the fundamental theoretical assumptions of humanistic and transpersonal psychology and a review of the major figures associated with each. Included are chapters that address humanism in Christian movements, transpersonal psychology's integration of Eastern and other world religions, and the future of humanistic psychologies. Detailed information about the life and work of major psychologists associated with humanistic and transpersonal thought is offered.

When Bad Things Happen to Good People (Kushner, 1981). Written by a rabbi, this book reveals the author's personal struggles with the question of how a loving God can permit tragedy to occur. Kushner addresses, in a very straightforward way, the difficult questions that most people raise when grappling with the problem of evil.

MODELS
OF RELIGIOUS
AND SPIRITUAL
DEVELOPMENT

CHAPTER 2

INTRODUCTION

In this chapter, I focus on the work of five theorists who contributed developmental models as means of describing how people grow and change in relation to their religion or their faith. As with most developmental schema, most of the systems described in this chapter have a linear and hierarchical organization. The implication is that each stage builds on the previous stage, and individuals must complete each stage successfully before moving on to the next one. In addition, these developmental stage models are designed more or less to follow a chronological sequence based on age or life stage.

Theoretical models oriented around religious and spiritual development are useful to counselors because they provide frameworks for understanding how clients incorporate their faith. These models assist counselors in assessing where clients are in their religious or spiritual growth. They also externalize religious or spiritual perspectives to reduce counselor and client reactivity. That is, when counselors and clients are able to acknowledge that there are predictable ways in which people grow in their faith, then it is easier to respond to particular manifestations of religion or spirituality in an open and accepting manner. Furthermore, these models provide counselors with the tools to make sense of their own spiritual journeys. Because gaining increased self-awareness is central to the work of effective counseling, having the knowledge of various developmental theories

TABLE 2.1 | ALLPORT'S THEORY OF RELIGIOUS SENTIMENTS

Stage	Description
Stage 1: Raw credulity	Children (and some adolescents and adults) believe everything they hear about religion and spirituality that comes from parents or authority figures.
Stage 2: Satisfying rationalism	Adolescents begin questioning their childhood beliefs, and might even reject their parents' religious or spiritual values outright.
Stage 3: Religious maturity	Persons move between uncertainty and faith. They are able to stay connected to a religious or spiritual tradition, but can approach it critically. Religion and spirituality are liberating rather than oppressive.

enables counselors to see how their own development compares with that of their clients. The developmental theorists' work described in this chapter offers explanations for how people grow and develop spiritually. Access to such structures might make counselors more open to the variety of clients' religious or spiritual beliefs and expressions.

In addition, under some circumstances it may be appropriate to share one or more of the models with clients who are interested in learning how their religious or spiritual orientation is related to the developmental theories presented here. Clients, too, can benefit from being able to understand how their perspectives are related to a larger schema.

One limitation of such an approach to organizing religious and spiritual development is that there are no nonwestern models. Although Michael Washburn's model is transpersonal, it has still grown out of a western context. There is a tremendous challenge, then, for practitioners to be able to apply these frameworks to persons whose worldviews are less individual, less linear, and less hierarchical.

In the following sections, I present a summary of the work of Gordon Allport, James Fowler, Vicky Genia, Fritz Oser, and Michael Washburn.

GORDON ALLPORT

The first contemporary psychologist to present a theory of faith development was Allport. His model focused on "religious sentiments" (Allport, 1950, p. 3), which were defined as "religious beliefs (empowered by affective energies) that lead to consonant religious and secular behaviors" (Worthington, 1989, p. 565). (See Table 2.1). According to Allport (1950), the development of religious sentiments occurs in three stages. Allport held that one's experience of religion as an adult is very different from that which is experienced as a young child. Allport offered the following ration-ale for this belief: "Neither intelligence nor self-consciousness is suffi-ciently developed [in young children] to sustain anything that might be called a sentiment, least of all such a highly complex mental organization as the religious sentiment" (Allport, 1950, p. 31). Thus, Allport claimed that a certain level of cognitive development must precede the possession of true "religious sentiment." Allport acknowledged that children might be engaged in religious activities such as saying prayers or singing hymns, but he held that these actions were "wholly social in character" rather than truly religious (Allport, 1950, p. 32). He held that kneeling for prayer or lighting a menorah has no more meaning to children than does brushing their teeth or listening nightly to a bedtime story. Allport noted that religious rituals, like other daily routines, are learned. Until they are more developed cognitively, however, children do not have the capacity to com-prehend religious meanings.

Stage One: Raw Credulity

According to Allport (1950), the first stage of religious sentiments is referred to as "raw credulity." By this term, Allport means that prepubescent children believe everything they hear about religion and spirituality coming from par-ents and other authority figures. During middle childhood, children need to feel a sense of belonging and to identify with the "in-group" (Allport, 1950, p. 36). Because of this necessary bond, children cling to their religious beliefs with an unwavering superiority and do not question them. This first stage of developing religious sentiment may be characterized as "authority based" (Worthington, 1989, p. 565). Although it is typical of children, such blind ac-ceptance of the doctrine and dogma of religious or spiritual persuasion may persist beyond childhood. Thus, many adults move into adulthood with an unquestioning stance toward the faith they acquired as children. According to Allport, when child-like beliefs continue into adulthood, these beliefs are con-sidered juvenile, illogical, and suppressive.

Stage Two: Satisfying Rationalism

The second stage of religious sentiments generally begins in adolescence (All-port, 1950). In this stage, teenagers begin questioning the beliefs held from childhood (Worthington, 1989). As they begin to seek an identity separate from their parents, adolescents may rebel against or reject parental values outright, including religious and spiritual ones. In the place of ardent faith, these emerging adults might ascribe to a "satisfying rationalism" that pro-vides a safe haven amid the turbulent waters of adolescence. Allport was aware that there is great diversity among teens in how they negotiate the de-mands of adolescence in general, and specifically in how they manage their religious or spiritual faith. He acknowledged that some youth remain excep-tionally devoted to their childhood belief systems. Others feel tremendously alienated from anything religious or spiritual. Still others may experience "wavering faith, with peaks of exhilaration and troughs of despair" (Allport, 1950, p. 38).

Stage Three: Religious Maturity

Allport's final stage of religious sentiments typically is entered after adolescence. Movement between uncertainty and faith characterizes it. Allport described mature religious sentiment as

> a disposition, built up through experience, to respond favorably, and in certain habitual ways, to conceptual objects and principles that the individual regards as of ultimate importance in his own life, and as having to do with what he regards as permanent or central in the nature of things. (p. 64)

Mature religious sentiment is not unidimensional. It involves the ability of persons to remain connected to a religious or spiritual tradition, but to approach it critically. Moreover, persons in the stage reflecting mature religious sentiment are able to maintain beliefs that are useful and meaningful to them and to reject those that no longer meet their needs. In addition, in this stage, religion is a positive, motivating, dynamic force in persons' lives. It has more of a liberating quality than an oppressive one.

Allport (1950) was quick to note that not all adults reach religious maturity. He indicated that some adults retain the faith of childhood that is characterized by egocentrism and wish fulfillment. Other adults, having endured the struggle of adolescence emerge with more faith than doubt, while still others identify as agnostic, having approximately equal amounts of doubt and faith (Worthington, 1989). Allport (1950) went so far as to claim that some adults never attain religious maturity. He believed that many persons have developed a meaningful life philosophy that did not include religion at all.

CASE | MIGUEL

Miguel is a 16-year-old Latino American who immigrated to the United States from Mexico when he was five years old. Both Miguel's nuclear family and his extended family are devout Roman Catholics. They attend Mass every day, enrolled Miguel in a parochial elementary school, and have high expectations that he will enter the priesthood. Until six months ago, Miguel dutifully participated in the rituals and practices of Roman Catholicism. He observed the holy days, went to confession, and learned the catechism. He even attended a retreat for boys who were interested in the priesthood. When he turned 15, Miguel entered public high school and, in the course of interacting with youth of different backgrounds, began to question the beliefs of his church. He asked the priests difficult questions about the doctrine of transubstantiation (the belief that the bread and wine of the Mass are transformed into the actual body and blood of Christ). He developed an intense relationship with his girlfriend, Margarita, and wondered aloud why priests could not marry and must remain celibate.

A program on career choice, offered by the high school counselor, exacerbated Miguel's dilemma. He was struggling with his personal religious beliefs, his deepening relationship with his girlfriend, and the pressure he was feeling from his family to become a priest. Miguel scheduled an appointment with his school counselor to discuss his career options. When she heard his story, the counselor, Marjorie, recognized that Miguel was in stage two of Allport's scheme, "satisfying rationalism." She was able to help Miguel understand that his religious queries were part of the normal process of growing toward religious maturity. Although she was sensitive to the cultural aspects of Miguel's dilemma regarding his future as a priest, Marjorie helped Miguel let go of some of his guilt about questioning religious authority. Informed by Allport's (1950) perspective, she supported Miguel's search for himself and for clarity about his calling.

Because Marjorie knew about Allport's theory, she was able to incorporate it into her thinking about Miguel's situation and to normalize his adolescent experience by sharing the theoretical concepts with him.

JAMES FOWLER

Fowler (1981) created the most comprehensive theory or faith development (Helminiak, 1987). Fowler was influenced by other developmental theorists such as Erik Erikson, J. Mark Baldwin, John Dewey, Jean Piaget, and Lawrence Kohlberg (Fowler, 1991). Indeed, Fowler's stages of faith are parallel to Piaget's cognitive development stages and the stages of moral development posited by Kohlberg (Gathman & Nessan, 1997). Fowler's theory of the stages of faith was based on an empirical study of 359 individuals who were interviewed from 1972 to 1981 about religion, values, and life-altering experiences. Each interview lasted approximately two and a half hours, and participants ranged from 3½ years to 84 years old (Lownsdale, 1997). Fowler used seven criteria to determine the stages of faith:

> (a) form of logic, (b) role-taking and social relationships, (c) forms of moral judgment, (d) bounds of social awareness of primary reference groups, (e) locus of authority, (f) forms of world coherence, or ways of forming and holding a comprehensive sense of unified meanings, and (g) symbolic functioning. (Worthington, 1989, p. 567)

Fowler held that faith was a process of development that spanned one's entire life (Lovecky, 1997). As such, Fowler believed the term "faith" had more to do with a dynamic, trusting orientation toward life, others, and God, than with the more static notion of faith as merely believing beliefs. According to Fowler (1996a), faith can be understood as

> an integral, centering process, underlying the formation of beliefs, values, and meanings, that (1) gives coherence and direction to persons' lives, (2) links them in shared trusts and loyalties with others, (3) grounds their personal stances and communal loyalties in a sense of relatedness to a larger frame of reference, and (4) enables them to face and deal with the limit conditions of human life, relying upon that which has the quality of ultimacy in their lives. (p. 56)

Fowler's model includes either six or seven stages, depending on whether or not one considers the first stage, "primal faith" genuine faith. In his earlier writings, Fowler spoke of stages 0–6, but later he described seven stages (Kropf, 1990). Fowler's stages are characterized as "invariant, sequential, and hierarchical" (Fowler, 1996a, p. 57). Accordingly, the stages correspond to certain age ranges, and persons pass through them sequentially. It is not possible to skip stages, but it is not inevitable that individuals will make transitions from one stage to the next. Some people remain in one stage for long periods in their lives. Fowler's stage theory does allow overlap in the stages such that one may be grounded largely in a particular stage, but have thoughts and beliefs that are more characteristic of earlier or later stages (Kropf, 1990). Fowler held that his stages were present in every religious tradition (Gathman & Nessan, 1997) and that the stages of faith development were not content specific. Furthermore, Fowler (1987) did not construe his stage theory to mean that those in lower stages were inferior to those in higher stages. Following are Fowler's stages, followed by a case example that illustrates how persons can embody the characteristics of various stages.

Primal Faith (Infancy)

The first stage, known as primal faith, occurs during infancy and the prelanguage period when babies are learning to trust their caregivers. Such trust enables infants to manage the anxiety that is created when they are separated from the ones on whom they depend for survival. During this time, the way is prepared for infants to differentiate themselves from others, and to form attachment bonds with parents and others who nurture them. This stage is similar to Erikson's (1963) stage of trust versus mistrust (Lownsdale, 1997).

Intuitive-Projective Faith (Early Childhood)

During this stage when language is emerging, children make meaning of their worlds through the joining of imagination with story symbol, dream, and experience (Fowler, 1987). At this stage, roughly between the ages of 3 and 7, children do not have the cognitive capacity for logical thinking. Instead, their perceptions and feelings combine to create enduring images that represent both dangerous and protective aspects of life. At this stage, children's images of God largely are reflections of their relationships with parents or other adults to whom the children are attached (Fowler, 1991; Rizzuto, 1981). Although this stage is most associated with children, occasionally some adolescents and adults demonstrate features of the Intuitive-Projective stage. Fowler (1987) stated, "Typically when the liminality and emotional lability characteristic of this stage are encountered in adolescents we are dealing with episodes of repression or psychotic breakdown" (p. 84). Fowler also noted that members of some fundamentalist cults exhibit characteristics of the Intuitive-Projective stage. For example, cult members who ingest poison to test God's saving power are behaving in ways that are more commonly associated with unrestrained childhood urges and fantasies.

Mythic-Literal Faith (Middle Childhood and Beyond)

The hallmark of this stage is the emerging cognitive abilities of logical thinking and separating fantasy and reality. In addition, persons at this stage are able to take the perspective of others and to understand that other people have different perceptions and experiences in the world. In this stage, people appropriate for themselves the stories, beliefs, and symbols of their traditions; however, the beliefs are one dimensional and literal (Fowler, 1981). People in this stage often develop a concept of God as anthropomorphic. They tend to understand the Supreme Being as a cosmic ruler who acts with fairness and moral reciprocity (Fowler, 1987). Persons in the mythic-literal stage often assume that God rewards goodness and punishes evil. They might exhibit either a kind of perfectionism in their efforts to be rewarded for their goodness. On the other hand, they could be self-abasing, assuming that because they have been abused or neglected by significant others, they are inherently bad and will be punished. Many persons become disillusioned when they discover that "bad things happen to good people" (Kushner, 1981). Although the mythic-literal stage consists largely of elementary and middle school aged children, adults can also remain in this stage. For example, in some fundamentalist circles, entire congregations are in this stage and are not interested in moving beyond it (Fowler, 1987).

Synthetic-Conventional Faith (Puberty to Adulthood)

This stage begins as young persons develop a capacity for formal operational thinking (Fowler, 1991). At this point, they have the cognitive ability to think abstractly and to manipulate concepts. Furthermore, individuals at this age have "the ability to reflect on one's feelings and thoughts, and see one's self through the eyes of others, and accept and value the evaluation of others" (Lownsdale, 1997, p. 58). During adolescence and beyond, persons' worlds are expanded, and they must make coherent meaning in the midst of diverse and complex experiences of family, school, work, media, and other social contacts. Faith must provide a unifying means of synthesizing values and information and must serve as a basis of forming a stable identity and worldview (Fowler, 1981). During this stage, faith is constructed through conformity to a set of values and beliefs with deference to authority. At this point in development, people might understand themselves to have faith, but their beliefs and values are typically unexamined. The synthetic-conventional stage is also characterized by a hunger for a close, personal relationship with God; one yearns to be known and loved by God (Fowler, 1987). Fowler maintained that this stage was characteristic of adolescents and normative for adults. A clue that persons are beginning to move beyond this stage is when they begin to question authority and established beliefs and values.

Individuative-Reflective Faith (Young Adulthood)

Before this stage can emerge, individuals must engage in two significant changes. First, they must be willing to examine critically their system of beliefs, values, and commitments. Second, they must gradually begin to take responsibility for an authoritative worldview that they themselves have chosen. Before this stage, people are quite content to rely on others' goals and values. Another aspect of this stage involves critical reflection on the stories, symbols, rituals, and myths of one's tradition and translating them into conceptual meanings. For example, in previous stages, persons might have ascribed to one of the creation stories that described how the world came to be. Critical reflection or "demythologizing" involves asking oneself what the significance of the creation story is. Instead of dwelling on the details of the length of creation or how people came to exist, one moves to the notion that the creation story is a theological assertion about a God who is powerful enough to create the world and the people in it. Analyzing and examining one's faith heritage does not mean that individuals must reject their religions. Instead, they commit themselves to faith through conscious choice rather than through unexamined acceptance (Fowler, 1991). People begin to be ready for the next stage when they become aware of the complexities of life that do not necessarily fit the neatly constructed worldview developed in this stage. They find themselves yearning toward a more dialectical and multileveled approach to life (Fowler, 1981).

Conjunctive Faith

Conjunctive faith, originally called paradoxical-consolidative faith emerges in midlife and beyond (Kropf, 1990). Most adults do not reach this stage. According to Lownsdale (1997), only one of six adults, older than age 31, meets the criteria for this stage. In conjunctive faith, one comes to "embrace the integration of opposites or polarities in one's life" (Fowler, 1991, p. 40). For example, God is experienced at once as both personal and abstract (Lownsdale, 1997), and life is considered simultaneously rational and mysterious. During this stage, people acknowledge and celebrate the multiple perspectives to faith without being forced to choose one direction or another. They are open to immersing themselves in the myriad of meanings inherent in myths and symbols. In the previous stage, these myths and symbols had to be analyzed and mined for a given meaning, but in the conjunctive stage, they resonate with truths hidden deep inside the persons themselves. There emerges a new appreciation for the stories, rituals, practices, and symbols that Ricoeur (1967) called a "second naïveté. This term means that there is a "new reclaiming and reworking of one's past . . . and an opening to the voices of one's 'deeper self'" (Fowler, 1981, p. 197–198). At this stage, people are open to new depths of experience in spirituality and religion. They develop a passion for justice that is beyond the claims of race, class, culture, nation, or religious community. These convictions enable people in the conjunctive stage to lay down their defenses and to tolerate differences in belief while staying firmly grounded in their own personal faith systems (Gathman & Nessan, 1997). It is rare that one moves beyond this faith stage. However, if transition to the last stage does occur, it happens late in life and in response to "the tension between universal ideal and life in an imperfect world" (Gathman & Nessan, 1997, p. 410).

Universalizing Faith

The apex of Fowler's model, universalizing faith is limited to few people, perhaps two to three individuals per thousand (Lownsdale, 1997). In this stage, people are "grounded in a oneness with the power of being or God" (Fowler, 1991, p. 41). Persons' awareness of and commitment to universal values such as peace and justice characterize this stage. People in this stage are likely to be activists for justice. They live as though complete love, justice, and the Kingdom of God are already a reality on the earth (Fowler, 1987). Some examples of persons who achieved stage six include Mahatma Gandhi, Martin Luther King, Jr., and Mother Teresa (Gathman & Nessan, 1997). Although these individuals' lives are focused in God, they have not attained perfection. They continue to exist as finite beings with "blind spots, inconsistencies, and . . . some distorted capacities for relations with others" (Fowler, 1987, p. 175).

See Table 2.2 for a summary of Fowler's stages of faith development.

| CASE | BETTY |

Betty is a 42-year-old white female who presented for counseling because she was unhappy in her marriage to Clifford. Betty and Clifford had been married for 21 years and were the parents of three children: Andrea, 19, Robin, 17, and Curt, 14. Betty reported that she suspected Clifford was having an affair with a woman in his company. She indicated that she and her husband had frequent fights, and they "did not do anything together for fun anymore." Betty told her counselor, Sandra, she was not particularly interested in saving her marriage. She said, "It was over a long time ago." Instead, Betty wanted help deciding what to do. On one hand, she wanted to divorce Clifford. On the other hand, she feared that he would divorce her. Despite her desire to divorce Clifford, Betty could not bring herself to contact an attorney. When Sandra asked Betty what was getting in the way of her moving forward with the divorce, Betty said that she "did not believe in divorce." She indicated that she was not raised in any particular religion during her childhood. After ten years of marriage, however, she and Clifford "got saved" and joined a nondenominational Christian congregation. Betty revealed that this congregation considered divorce a sin and that if she were to divorce Clifford, she would surely be banished from the church membership. She was worried that "God would not forgive her."

Sandra probed Betty's concept of God, the teachings of her church, and the doctrine against divorce. After talking with Betty, Sandra discovered a person who had deeply held beliefs and values that were unexamined. Betty had simply accepted a set of rules and rituals that had provided some stability in her life and her marriage. She had never been forced to question how these beliefs helped or hindered

TABLE 2.2 | FOWLER'S STAGES OF FAITH DEVELOPMENT

Stages	Description
Stage 1: Primal faith	Trust in caregivers is developed in infancy.
Stage 2: Intuitive-projective faith	This stage characterizes early childhood. Images of God and faith are reflections of children's relationships with parents and other significant adults.
Stage 3: Mythic-literal faith	This stage begins in middle childhood and may extend beyond it. In this stage, people appropriate for themselves the stories, beliefs, and symbols of their tradition. God's characteristics are often seen as anthropomorphic. Persons in this stage might believe God rewards goodness and punishes evil.
Stage 4: Synthetic-conventional faith	This stage begins when people are able to think cognitively. During this stage, faith is constructed in terms of conformity to a set of values and beliefs with deference to authority. This stage is characteristic of adolescents and normative for adults.
Stage 5: Individuative-reflective faith	In this stage, persons critically examine their faith and take responsibility for an authoritative worldview they have chosen. People commit themselves to faith through conscious choice rather than through unexamined acceptance.
Stage 6: Conjunctive faith	This faith stage typically emerges in midlife and beyond. People acknowledge the multiple perspectives of faith and begin to integrate the polarities in their lives. Persons in this stage develop an openness toward differences in belief while staying grounded in their own.
Stage 7: Universalizing faith	This stage is limited to a few people. In this stage, persons are committed to universal values such as peace and justice and are "grounded in a oneness with the power of being or God" (Fowler, 1991, p. 41).

her in facing life's dilemmas. Being aware of Fowler's (1981) stages of faith, Sandra determined that Betty was in the synthetic-conventional stage. Through her continued work with Betty, Sandra was able to assist Betty in critical reflection about her faith and her marriage. The crisis involving the demise of Betty's marriage was the catalyst that thrust Betty into the transition toward individuative-reflective faith. Betty struggled to make sense of how her idea of a loving God who wanted her to be whole and happy could be reconciled with her belief that the same God would condemn her to hell if she were to divorce Clifford.

FRITZ OSER

Oser (1991) developed a five-stage scheme for describing the emergence of "religious judgment" (p. 5). Oser described religious judgment as "a form or quality of acts of balancing different value elements against each other, struggling for faith, rehearsing and rejecting solutions, and building up religious 'views' of the world's ontological and cultural unevenness" (Oser, 1991, p. 6). Like Allport and Fowler, Oser held that religion was not static but, rather, a continually evolving construct. He also believed that as people age they undergo transformations of faith and relate their life experiences to an Ultimate Being (God) in qualitatively different ways across the lifespan (Oser, 1991). Also, Oser's work is similar to Allport's and Fowler's in that the stages he devised follow an invariant order and cannot be skipped. Persons move from one stage to the next when (a) they feel the old structure of religious judgment does not properly explain current situations; (b) an individual experiences a need for autonomy "toward and within the connection to the supernatural" (Oser, 1991, p. 13); and (c) an individual has the ability to reject the old structure and integrate a new way of thinking into many diverse situations (Oser, 1991). Oser's five stages of religious judgment explain how persons conceive their relationship to the Ultimate Being.

Stage One

Children at this stage view the Ultimate Being, or God, as all-powerful. They understand God to be one who intervenes in world events and in individuals' lives. God is conceived of as responsible for and causing everything that happens, even disasters and untimely deaths. God's will must be executed in the world, and persons in this stage perceive themselves as having little influence over God's ultimate decisions.

Stage Two

Although God is still viewed as all-powerful and external, in stage two there is a shift in thinking. Persons in this stage often believe they can influence God by prayers, vows, rituals, and good deeds. If individuals are devoted, faithful, and practice piety and good works, God will bless them.

TABLE 2.3 | FRITZ OSER'S STAGES OF RELIGIOUS JUDGMENT

Stage	Description
Stage 1	God is seen as all-powerful and responsible for everything that happens.
Stage 2	God is still powerful and external, but persons believe they can influence God through prayer, vows, rituals, and good deeds.
Stage 3	God has a special transcendent realm that does not influence the autonomy of individuals. That is, God does not control individual and secular concerns.
Stage 4	Persons on this stage regain a sense of God present in the world and active in concert with human will.
Stage 5	Universal aspects of all religions are central. God informs every moment and commitment in life.

Stage Three

In the third stage of Oser's framework, God has a special transcendent realm that does not influence the separate autonomy of individuals. This idea means that if an Ultimate Being exists, that Being is not in control of individual and secular concerns. In those arenas, the human will is operative. According to Oser (1991), adolescents commonly find themselves in this stage because it is congruent with their developmental tasks of gaining independence from parents and religious institutions.

Stage Four

Persons in stage four regain a sense of the Ultimate Being (God) present in the world and active in concert with human autonomy. Thus, humans are free, but God sustains that freedom. Another characteristic of this stage is that individuals ascribe to a divine plan that gives meaning to life's situations (Oser, 1991).

Stage Five

Like Fowler's last stage, Oser's final stage is relatively rare. For individuals in this stage, the universal aspects of all religions, regardless of their diversity, are central. Persons who develop into the fifth stage are intensely aware of the all-pervasiveness of God who "inhabits each moment and commitment, however profane and insignificant" (Oser, 1991, p. 12).

See Table 2.3 for a summary of Oser's stages of religious judgment.

CASE	DENNIS

Dennis is a 20-year-old African American student who was referred to the campus counseling center by his advisor because of poor school performance and infrequent class attendance following the death of his 18-year-old brother in an automobile accident. Dennis reported that he was devastated at the tragic death of his brother who was his "buddy and confidant." Dennis told his counselor, Aaron, that he "felt as if his world had come to an end." In addition, Dennis revealed that even though he had not had any exposure to formal religion during his childhood, he "had always believed in God." However, Dennis said that he wasn't sure he could believe in a God who would "take my best friend from me."

Aaron employed reflective listening skills and demonstrated empathy for Dennis' loss. Aaron was also able to use Oser's model of religious judgment to organize his thinking about Dennis' statements concerning his view of God. Although Dennis is a young adult, his religious judgment is underdeveloped. His concept of God reflects that of persons in Oser's stage one: They believe God causes all events, including automobile accidents, and that they have little influence over God's will. Although Aaron was a religious person, Dennis' anger at God, or his need to question God's existence did not offend Aaron. He understood that Dennis was responding from a serious loss and was using religious language that reflected his rudimentary faith. During counseling, Aaron was able to help Dennis begin to come to terms with his brother's death and to embark on a spiritual journey that led him to deeper exploration of who God was for him.

VICKY GENIA

Genia's five-stage developmental typology of faith is grounded in psychoanalytic theory. It begins with egocentric faith and progresses toward spiritual commitment in adulthood (Genia, 1995). Although there are similarities between Genia's work and that of Allport, Fowler, and Oser, she acknowledged that development does not always progress in a linear fashion, nor does it always move along smoothly. Instead, when people undergo crises, or when they endure unmet needs over long periods, they could regress to less mature coping strategies (Genia, 1995). Furthermore, some people could have peaks of spiritual growth alternating with long plateaus of maintaining the characteristics of one stage. Genia (1995) claimed that emotional difficulties could cause some people to stray into unhealthy forms of faith. In addition, she noted that traumatic experiences might explain why some adults fail to move along the continuum of faith.

Stage One: Egocentric Faith

According to Genia (1995), in stage one "religion is rooted in fear and needs for comfort" (p. 19). Adults who find themselves in stage one are often survivors of abuse or neglect, and, as a result, are incapable of forming trusting relationships with others or with God. Although people in stage one find religion a source of comfort, their relationship with God "becomes a reenactment of their traumatic relationships with their parents" (Genia, 1995, p. 21). When life hands them disappointments or emotional injury, adults in stage one feel victimized and tormented by God. Individuals at this stage often attempt to be perfect so God will accept them. Moreover, they tend to use prayer as a means of manipulating God to protect them against adversity. The major issue for adults in stage one is their self-deprecating beliefs and behaviors that arise because of childhood mistreatment and deprivation. That they behave in egocentric ways in relation to their faith is not surprising, but it signals a need for intensive psychotherapy before they can progress to the next stage of faith.

Stage Two: Dogmatic Faith

The organizing principle for those in stage two is untiring devotion to earning God's love and approval. Because religiously dogmatic adults fear disappointing God, they exhibit strict adherence to religious codes. They might feel extremely guilty about transgressing behavioral proscriptions against sex or aggression. According to Genia (1995), persons in stage two spent their childhoods trying to please authoritarian parents. As a result, in their religious lives, they tend to gravitate toward religious groups that are centered on self-denial and allegiance to religious authority. They are commonly intolerant of diversity and ambiguity.

Whereas religious egocentrics attempt to *appease* a vengeful God, dogmatics seek to *please* God so they will be rewarded and eternally blessed (Genia, 1995). Persons in stage two typically believe that religious affiliation and participation are critical. They are likely to adhere to religious dogma as a means of being accepted by God.

Stage Three: Transitional Faith

Individuals who dare to examine critically their religious beliefs mark this stage in Genia's (1995) scheme. They are open to exploring new spiritual paths and to trusting their own consciences rather than depending on religious dogma. During this period of searching, persons can feel disconnected and unbalanced. They might undergo surges of doubt that enable them to forge a faith that takes them to deeper levels of psychospiritual integration (Genia, 1995). Individuals in the transitional stage of faith might experiment with different ideologies, might switch religious affiliations, or might investigate diverse spiritual experience in the journey toward adopting a meaningful spiritual orientation.

Stage Four: Reconstructed Faith

Persons in stage four have chosen a faith that provides meaning and purpose and fulfills their spiritual needs. They have a strong sense of self undergirded by internalized morals and ideals (Genia, 1995). Because they have mature superegos, persons in stage four conform to religious behavioral codes because the content of the codes is congruent with their inner convictions. Stage four often comprises people who have grown up in a secure, nurturing, accepting environment. They relate to God as a caring, reliable parent who is "an ally and source of sustenance" (Genia, 1995, p. 98). In their prayer lives, they are apt to offer thanksgiving, praise, and devotion as well as intercession and petition. Persons in stage four are aware and accepting of their human frailties. They acknowledge their wrongdoing, seek forgiveness for their transgressions, and make restitution when possible.

Though persons in stage four have made significant strides toward religious maturity, they still have difficulty tolerating ambiguity and appreciating the paradoxical and multifaceted dimensions of spirituality. The dangers facing this group of people is that if they do not continue to push the parameters of their faith, they will not continue to grow beyond their current stage.

Stage Five: Transcendent Faith

Like Fowler and Oser, Genia (1995) believed that attaining the final stage in her model was rare. People who are committed to universal ideals, who are selflessly devoted to truth and goodness, and who experience community with others of diverse faiths characterize the transcendent faith stage. According to Genia (1995), there are several benchmarks of the fifth stage. First, persons in this stage have a transcendent relationship to something greater than themselves. Their lifestyle, including their ethical and moral actions, is consistent with their spiritual values. They are committed without absolute certainty, such that their faith is forged in the fire of doubt. Persons in stage five appreciate spiritual diversity. They have eliminated magical thinking, egocentricity, and anthropomorphisms (attributing human qualities to God). They have integrated reason and emotion and have developed a healthy concern for others. Persons in stage five acknowledge the reality of evil and suffering while celebrating human life and growth and promoting tolerance. The mature faith of stage five provides meaning and purpose to life while allowing room for traditional beliefs and private meanings (Genia, 1995).

See Table 2.4 for a summary of Genia's stages of faith.

CASE | YUSUF

Yusuf is a 34-year-old Muslim who works for a manufacturing company. His supervisor referred him to the employee assistance counselor because of his ongoing conflict with his co-workers. Yusuf reported to his counselor, Karen, that neither his supervisor nor his co-workers understands that his attempt to convert them to Islam is truly in their best interest. According to Yusuf, he spends his breaks speaking to others on the line about his religion and becomes agitated and defensive when they do not respond to his overtures. Moreover, Yusuf admits that he is not interested in having an intellectual discussion about religions, nor does he believe that different religions are simply other paths to God. In fact, during the first

TABLE 2.4 | GENIA'S STAGES OF FAITH

Stage	Description
Stage 1: Egocentric faith	Religion is rooted in fear and needs for comfort. Persons in stage one tend to reenact their relationships with their parents in their relationship with God. They might be self-deprecating or attempt to be perfect so God will accept them.
Stage 2: Dogmatic faith	The organizing principle for those in this stage is devotion to earning God's love and approval. They might gravitate toward religious groups that focus on self-denial and allegiance to religious authority. They are commonly intolerant of diversity and ambiguity.
Stage 3: Transitional faith	Individuals in this stage examine the tenets of their faith. They are open to exploring new spiritual paths, might switch affiliations, and could experience doubt that takes them to deeper levels of psychospiritual integration.
Stage 4: Reconstructed faith	Persons in this stage have chosen a faith that provides meaning and purpose and fulfills their spiritual needs. They are aware of their human limitations, acknowledge their mistakes, and seek forgiveness for them.
Stage 5: Transcendent faith	People in this stage are committed to universal ideals and experience community with others of diverse faiths.

session with Karen, he spent ten minutes quizzing her about her religious beliefs and attempting to convince her of the superiority of his religion.

Karen was quick to recognize dogmatic faith in Yusuf, and, despite her discomfort with his evangelizing, she was able to respond empathically to his frustrations. Furthermore, Karen was astute enough to know that she must not allow herself to be drawn into a theological debate with Yusuf. Instead, she worked diligently at establishing rapport with him. She concentrated on helping Yusuf relax and enabling him to begin looking at how his religious beliefs and his crusading posture was affecting his relationships and his work performance.

MICHAEL WASHBURN

Washburn (1988) proposed a theory of psychospiritual development based in psychoanalytic theory and transpersonal psychology. One of Washburn's fundamental assumptions was that both psychological and spiritual expressions of dynamic life derive from a single source (Washburn, 1988). He believed that the psychological and the spiritual were not two different dynamic realities but were, "rather, two different modes of appearance of the same power, the power of the Dynamic Ground. Libido and spirit . . . are ultimately one" (Washburn, 1988, p. 4). Washburn conceived of three stages: the pre-egoic, egoic, and transegoic stages. These stages reflect the process of the ego's unfolding interaction with dynamic life. In Washburn's schema, the movement between stages is not linear as in the other models presented earlier. Instead, there is a pattern of negation, return, and higher integration. Washburn (1988) describes the developmental process as

> involving a *negation* . . . a repressive submergence of the Dynamic Ground perpetrated by the very young ego—which brings the pre-egoic stage to an end and commences the egoic stage. Second, . . . involving a *return,* a regressive reconnection of the (now mature) ego with the Dynamic Ground—which . . . leads the ego through such transitional experiences as conversion, descent into the underworld, and the dark night of the soul. Third . . . involving a *higher integration,* . . . a transcending synthesis of the ego with the Dynamic Ground . . . through a period of spiritual regeneration and culminates in full transegoic realization. (p. 6)

The Pre-Egoic Stage

The first stage in Washburn's system is the pre-egoic or body ego stage. It corresponds to the pre-oedipal period in childhood in which the "Dynamic Ground dominates the weak and undeveloped ego" (Washburn, 1988, p. 4). This stage is characterized by a focus on the body and sensuality. In addition, there is a concentration on maternal presence experienced both externally (parent) and internally (archetype). The person in stage one has a deep connectedness to the sources of life within and openness to the rest of the world. Stage one is typically a dynamically charged experience in which the sense of the numinous is prevalent. Persons in stage one are creative, but have not advanced very far in their cognitive development. Their thinking is organized in concrete images of the world around them.

The Egoic Stage

This stage, also called the stage of the mental ego, is of the longest duration. It begins during the period Freud called latency, is consolidated toward the end of adolescence, and remains largely stable throughout the rest of one's life. This stage is characterized by a repressive infrastructure "which insulates the mental ego from the dynamic unconscious, and therefore also from the Dynamic Ground" (Washburn, 1988, p. 5). In addition, individuals in this stage experience a predominantly mental character that is anti-physical and anti-instinctual. Further, in the egoic stage, there is an emphasis on "ego independence, self-control, and autonomous command of the will" (Washburn, 1988, p. 5). In this stage, social norms, roles, and values shape personalities, and cognitive processing proceeds to formal operations. Finally, emptiness and alienation mark the egoic stage with a stimulus toward transcendence.

TABLE 2.5 | WASHBURN'S STAGES OF PSYCHOSPIRITUAL DEVELOPMENT

Stage	Description
Stage 1: Pre-egoic or body ego	This stage corresponds to the pre-oedipal period in childhood. Focus is on the body and sensuality. Persons in stage one sense a deep connectedness to the sources of life within and openness to the rest of the world. They are creative, but have not advanced very far in cognitive development.
Stage 2: Egoic stage	This stage is characterized by a repressive infrastructure "which insulates the mental ego from the dynamic unconscious, and therefore also from the Dynamic Ground" (Washburn, 1988, p. 5). In this stage, roles and values shape personalities. Emptiness and alienation mark the egoic stage with a stimulus toward transcendence.
Stage 3: Transegoic stage	This stage is also called integration. It usually begins in midlife. It is the result of a spiritual awakening and involves a transcendence of dualism such as body and mind, feeling and thought, creativity and logic. Individuals in this stage experience openness, dynamism, and spontaneity.

The Transegoic Stage

The third stage in Washburn's developmental framework is also known as integration. This stage begins at the earliest in midlife, but can conceivably begin in the latter years. This stage is usually entered as the result of a spiritual awakening or conversion in which the Dynamic Ground is reopened. The ultimate aspect of this stage is psychic reorganization in which persons move to a higher synthesis of their psychic resources. Stage three is characterized by a transcendence of dualisms such as body and mind, feeling and thought, creativity and logic, civilization and instinct, and ego and Ground (Washburn, 1988). What occurs in this stage is a transformation of dualisms into "harmonious dualities" (Washburn, 1988, p. 5) involving a synthesis of opposites. There is the infusion of the ego by the Ground, a sense of spiritual presence, and the realization of intuitive, contemplative, and creative abilities. Moreover, individuals in this stage experience openness, dynamism, and spontaneity. They are grasped by a sense of kinship and community that give meaning to their lives. Like the final stages of other theorists, Washburn's transegoic stage is rarely attained. Washburn claimed that although some people are awakened to a spiritual consciousness, most do not have enough power to get beyond the mental ego stage.

See Table 2.5 for a summary of Washburn's stages of psychospiritual development.

| CASE | NORMA |

James and Allison, a Caucasian couple in their mid-forties contacted their counselor, Gary, because of their concern about Allison's mother, Norma. Seventy-year-old Norma had been living with James and Allison for two years following the death of Norma's husband, Allen. During the past two years, Norma had made significant progress in grieving the death of her husband. However, what prompted Allison to call Gary was what Allison called her "mother's bizarre ideas and odd behavior." According to Allison, her mother had always been a "spiritual person," but during the past several months, she had become "a fanatic" about her spiritual practices, especially meditation. In addition, Allison reported that despite Norma's failing health, she was totally accepting of her physical limitations, and had become deeply immersed in a new political and social activism that was uncharacteristic. Allison indicated that people from all walks of life were calling Norma and asking her for advice for their problems—a situation that Allison perceived as disruptive to the family.

Gary, a family counselor, invited James, Allison, and Norma to a session so he could help them understand the changes that were occurring in their relationships. Gary asked Norma what had been happening in her life in the past few months. She calmly described "a spiritual transformation" in which she was in touch with her body and spirit and was "constantly in a state of bliss" as she contemplated the presence of the "holy" in her life. Norma told Gary she believed that she was "entering a plane of higher consciousness" and that this experience had helped her make sense of Allen's death and prepare for her own.

In working with James, Allison, and Norma, Gary was able to help them think about Norma's spiritual experiences in terms of Washburn's third stage, the transegoic. Gary reframed Allison's notion of her mother's "craziness" as her journey on a spiritual path toward wholeness. He was able to help them see that Norma was experiencing a deeper level of spiritual development, and that the expression of her spirituality was new and frightening for James and Allison. Although there was work to do in renegotiating their expectations and familial interactions, eventually James and Allison were able to appreciate rather than denigrate Norma's spirituality. Ultimately, they were able to make a space in their lives for her newly emerging creativity, sensuality, and charisma.

See Table 2.6 for a comparison of the five models of religious and spiritual development we have discussed.

LIMITATIONS OF THE MODELS OF RELIGIOUS/SPIRITUAL DEVELOPMENT

There are no perfect theoretical models that are at once cogent, comprehensive, and able to address the religious and spiritual experiences of all persons in all historical and cultural contexts. One major criticism lobbed against all frameworks that involve developmental progressions is the implication that

TABLE 2.6 | COMPARISON OF FIVE MODELS OF RELIGIOUS AND SPIRITUAL DEVELOPMENT

	Allport	Fowler	Oser	Genia	Washburn
Stage 1	Raw credulity	Primal faith	Ultimate Being viewed as all-powerful	Egocentric faith	Pre-egoic (body-ego)
Stage 2	Satisfying rationalism	Intuitive-projective faith	God external but influenced by good deeds and prayer	Dogmatic faith	Egoic (mental ego)
Stage 3	Religious maturity	Mythic-literal faith	God has transcendent and separate from human autonomy	Transitional faith	Transegoic (integration)
Stage 4		Synthetic-conventional faith	God is involved and collaborative with human autonomy	Reconstructed faith	
Stage 5		Individuative-reflective faith	God informs every moment and commitment in life	Transcendent faith	
Stage 6		Conjunctive faith			
Stage 7		Universalizing faith			

those in the more advanced stages of the schema are somehow more highly prized. There is the intimation that lower stages of development consequently are of lower worth. Most theorists have attempted to counter this assumption by alluding to the various stages as ways of organizing common characteristics; however, in systems that are admittedly linear and hierarchical, it is difficult not to make the inference that higher stages are more desirable.

In addition to the general liabilities of the developmental models, some criticisms are specific to the particular models themselves. For example, Allport, known for his contribution to the notion of religious maturity and its association with intrinsic religious experience, has been accused of being biased by ethnocentric and Western-liberal orientation (Beit-Hallahmi, 1989). Allport reported, however, that he had consulted with experts of different cultural backgrounds and perspectives to check himself for such blind spots (Kelly, 1995).

Fowler has not been immune to criticism regarding ethnocentrism, either. For example, in his original research, African Americans constituted only three percent of the participants (Fowler, 1991). In addition, Muslims, Buddhists, and Hindus were not included in the original sample. As a result, his work has been criticized for not including a stage that involves personal transcendence (Hendlin, 1989). Hendlin queried, "Is there room for the concept of personal 'enlightenment' in our Western theories, or are 'religious maturity' and 'faith' all that we are willing to accommodate" (Hendlin, 1989, p. 619)?

The major concerns registered against Genia's work have to do with her reliance on psychodynamic interpretations of clients' religious expression. Even though her work is groundbreaking, some counselors who do not share her theoretical orientation could have difficulty applying her analyses to their own clientele.

Counselors might find Washburn's theory confusing and abstract if they are not familiar with the tenets of transpersonal psychology. The concepts employed are especially abstract. Some counselors could be seriously challenged in conceptualizing how they would recognize clients who were in the pre-egoic, egoic, and transegoic stages.

Regardless of the critiques leveled at the developmental theories described in this chapter, these theories have made a significant contribution to counselors' understanding of religious and spiritual growth. Each theorist has enabled counselors to see that clients are engaged in a process of transformation that is dynamic and intimately connected to both chronological and cognitive development. These schemas offer counselors ways of organizing their thinking about their clients' progress relative to their religion or spirituality. These theorists also suggest ways that counselors can assist clients in moving toward spiritual wholeness.

CASE EXAMPLES

Rebecca and Michael

Rebecca Rosen is a 25-year-old college graduate who is working in a computer programming company. She is Jewish and has been dating Michael O'Malley, a Roman Catholic of Irish descent. Michael is 28 years old, is an urban planner, and is, according to Rebecca, "a nominal Catholic."

Rebecca is seeking counseling because her relationship with Michael is becoming more serious, and she is worried about the possibility of marrying a Catholic. On the intake form, Rebecca revealed that she was raised in a Reformed Jewish home, attended synagogue on holy days, and observed Jewish customs and holidays in her home with a large extended family. Rebecca indicated that she has not participated in religious activities much since she left for college, but that she does attend when she is in Chicago with her family. Rebecca reported that she "believes all the stories in the Torah" but that she "would have trouble articulating how her faith makes a difference in her life."

Although her younger brother, Samuel (age 20), is dating a young woman of Presbyterian background, no one in her family has ever married someone who wasn't Jewish. When asked to write about her problem on the intake form, Rebecca wrote, "I'm not a religious fanatic or anything, but being Jewish has been a significant part of my family life and my sense of identity. My parents would be so disappointed in me if I married someone who wasn't Jewish. In fact, my mother has said some pretty nasty things to Michael when she has visited here. I think she (Mom) is trying to break us up. She keeps asking me, "Why can't you find some nice Jewish boy?"

Rebecca says she is "in love" with Michael and would want to accept his marriage proposal. She reports that she and Michael have discussed marriage, have similar values regarding family, children, work, and money. The only thing Rebecca considers a problem is the difference in religion. Rebecca indicated that she had discussed "the religion thing" with Michael, and that although he isn't actively involved in a Roman Catholic parish, he would not want to give up his faith. According to Rebecca, Michael said he "could never see himself converting to Judaism" and that his family would disown him if he did.

Discussion Questions

1. Using the various developmental models described in this chapter, how would you assess Rebecca's stage of development? Michael's stage of development?
2. What questions would you want to ask Rebecca and Michael so you could learn more about their religious development?
3. How would you use one or more of the developmental models to assist Rebecca and Michael in understanding their differences?
4. What is your personal reaction to Rebecca and Michael's dilemma? How do you think your own stage of faith development might affect your work with this couple?
5. What counseling interventions would you consider appropriate in helping Rebecca and Michael address their religious differences?

Sherry

Sherry is a 52-year-old white female who sought counseling after ending her 20-year marriage to Ed, who abused her both physically and emotionally. Sherry had left her marriage on several occasions after abusive incidents occurred, but she always returned when Ed apologized and brought her a gift. After a particularly violent argument, however, Sherry resolved to leave Ed permanently. She moved to another state, stayed in a shelter for a few weeks, got a job, and started to build a new life. At the shelter, she was assigned to see Lois, one of the staff counselors.

Lois began working with Sherry by helping her take an inventory of her personal strengths and resources. When it came to religion, Sherry reported that she had felt trapped by a set of beliefs that no longer fit for her. She said, "When I married Ed I was a Lutheran, but he was a Southern Baptist. He insisted that I join his church. At first, that was OK because it was what he wanted. However, I've never been able to accept the teachings of his church. Of course, I had to keep my mouth shut for the last ten years or so, but I know there is a growing sense of spirituality within me if I can just get in touch with it." Sherry indicated she was ready to explore her faith in more depth and to make decisions for herself about what she believed and how she wanted to practice her faith. Lois was able to work with Sherry on her issues regarding the abuse by her husband and her subsequent divorce from him. She was also able to support Sherry's search for a viable faith in the midst of her changing life circumstances.

Discussion Questions

1. Which model of religious/spiritual development seems to be the most adequate in helping you make sense of Sherry's current situation?
2. In which stage of development would you place Sherry? What details from her case support your decision?
3. If you were to ask Sherry questions about her faith journey, what would you ask?
4. In what ways, if any, do you think Sherry's religious or spiritual beliefs are connected to her relationship with Ed?
5. What aspects of Sherry's case are particularly salient for you personally? How are you able to connect with her pain? What issues do you have with religion or spirituality that could make it difficult for you to work with Sherry?
6. What counseling interventions would you select to help Sherry on her quest for wholeness?

SUGGESTED ACTIVITIES

Assess Yourself

Using any one or more of the models of religious or spiritual development described in this chapter, assess where you are based on the stages presented. Be sure to provide an adequate rationale for why you perceive yourself to be in the stage(s) in which you find yourself. Think about what aspects of the stage(s) are comfortable for you and what dimensions of it do not seem to fit you well. Look at the stage beyond the one you believe you are currently in. What characteristics of that stage seem particularly attractive to you? Which ones seem unreachable? Which ones are not currently of interest to you? What would it take for you to make a transition to the next stage?

Interview Others

Select at least two friends or colleagues to interview about their religious or spiritual experiences. Try to incorporate some diversity into your choices. For example, if you choose someone who is a "born-again Christian," then you might want to interview a second person who is less connected to an organized religion, but is more involved in some type of spirituality. When you have finished the interview, select a model of religious or spiritual development that you think best fits the person you interview. You might share that particular schema with the persons you interview. Consider using the following questions as a guide, and add follow-up questions as you see fit:

1. How would you describe yourself in terms of your religion, spiritual path, or faith?
2. How did you come to this place in your journey? What other religions or practices have been important to you throughout your life? How did any of the changes you made in your religious or spiritual arena coincide with changes in other parts of your life?
3. What would you say is the content of your most rudimentary religious or spiritual beliefs? Does your belief system include a Supreme Being? If so, what is that Being like? If not, how did you come to reject the notion of a Supreme Being?
4. What do you think is your "next step" in your religious or spiritual journey? What is getting in the way of your taking that "next step?"
5. How much have you allowed yourself to question your faith? How do others in your family or community react if you question their beliefs or your own? What do you think is the place of doubt in a religious or spiritual system?
6. What are your sources of authority for religion or spirituality? For example, how important to you is the Bible, Koran, Torah, or other religious or spiritual texts? How much do you rely on the teachings of religious or spiritual leaders? What is the place of reason in your religious or spiritual system? How much do you trust yourself to make decisions about your religious or spiritual beliefs and practices?
7. What has it been like for you to reflect on these questions?

Evaluate a Spiritual Leader

Read a collection of writings, sermons, or speeches authored by a contemporary religious or spiritual leader. You may select someone who is well-known, such as Martin Luther King, Jr., Billy Graham, Ken Wilber, or a lesser-known individual such as the leader of your religious or spiritual community. Evaluate these writings to determine which model of religious or spiritual development seems the most appropriate for understanding the writings of the leader you have selected. Decide which stage of development the person is in. Give a rationale for your decision based on quotations from his or her writings.

SUPPLEMENTAL READINGS

The Individual and His Religion (Allport, 1950). This classic book on the psychology of religion reveals Allport's developmental approach to religious maturity. Allport writes in a way that enables readers to see the connections between religion and psychology and underscores the belief that religion can be a positive resource in people's lives.

Stages of Faith (Fowler, 1981). In this book, Fowler describes the stages of faith in his model, but includes some interviews that help elucidate his concepts. This book is the cornerstone of Fowler's work and the springboard for his more recent writings.

"The development of religious judgment" (Oser, 1991). In this book chapter, Oser explains his theory of religious judgment. He offered empirical support for his theories and indicated their cross-cultural applicability.

Counseling and Psychotherapy of Religious Clients (Genia, 1995). In this book, Genia describes her theory of religious development, but more than that, she explains the psychological characteristics of persons in each of her stages. In addition, she provides chapters that suggest how to work with clients in therapy.

The Ego and Dynamic Ground (Washburn, 1988). In this book, Washburn explains transpersonal psychology and the three-stage theory of psychospiritual development. The book is an excellent treatise on transpersonalism. Washburn provides a detailed explication of his theory.

VARIETIES OF RELIGIOUS SYSTEMS AND SPIRITUAL BELIEFS

CHAPTER 3

INTRODUCTION

It is impossible to do justice to the richness and diversity of the world's religions in a short chapter. Moreover, it is difficult to write about various religious systems from the outside looking in. They are better understood from the inside perspective. However, my purpose in this chapter is to provide an overview of the central beliefs and practices of the world's major religions so that as counselors you may come to appreciate the ways that these worldviews could affect your clients' thoughts, feelings and behaviors. I argue that with a greater understanding of religious and spiritual diversity, you will better be able to meet your clients' needs and enhance their well-being.

Weltanschauung

The term *weltanschauung* is a German word whose English translation means something similar to "worldview." A worldview is a total outlook on life. It includes persons' concepts of the universe, their answers to questions about the origins and destiny of human existence, and their value orientation (Dilthey, 1978). Worldviews shape individuals, societies, and cultures and affect human relationships (Kluback & Weinbaum, 1957; Sarason, 1981).

In addition, worldviews affect people's lifestyles and behaviors as well as their physical and mental health (Richards & Bergin, 1997). For example, a Seventh Day Adventist may hold beliefs that smoking and drinking are not acceptable behaviors for Christians and thus abstain from them. The result could be improved overall health.

Scholars in multiculturalism have noted the many ways in which persons of various racial and cultural backgrounds differ in their worldviews (Ibrahim, 1985, 1991; D.W. Sue & Sue, 1990). Ibrahim (1996) described five value dimensions that contribute to diverse worldviews: (a) human nature, (b) person and nature, (c) time sense, (d) activity, and (e) social relations. The dimension regarding human nature has to do with the judgment of whether humans are good, bad, or a combination of both. This aspect also involves the question of whether human nature is changeable or not. Persons' relationships with nature involve whether or not they hold a belief in the power of nature, in living in harmony with nature, or in controlling nature (Ibrahim, 1996). The time construct is based on whether or not individuals focus on the past, the present, or the future. The activity domain involves either an emphasis on spontaneity or a process of becoming. It could involve evaluating the spiritual or moral aspects of success based on internal standards, or it might focus on doing in which success is evaluated only by external standards and is sought at all cost. The dimension of social relationships refers to whether or not such relationships are organized on lineal-hierarchical, collateral-mutual, or individualistic belief systems.

How persons from various racial, ethnic, and cultural groups perceive human nature and humans' interaction with the natural world will influence how they direct their lives and their relationships with others. In addition, the manner in which relationships are organized in a culture—whether hierarchical, communal, or individualistic—will determine how clients present their difficulties and what alternatives they see for solving them. Furthermore, individuals' sense of time and whether or not they orient their lives by their watches also contributes to cultural functioning and lifestyle. Multicultural counseling experts emphasize that these differences in worldview are critical factors when clients from various racial and cultural groups present for counseling. These dimensions of worldview are also central to the world's religions, and clients' religious perspectives often shape their worldviews. Thus, as counselors, we must be aware that our clients bring to us not only their problems and their pain but also their views of the world molded by culture, religion, and the intersection of the two.

In the remainder of this chapter, I describe in broad brushstrokes the tenets of the major religions of the world. I begin my treatment of world religions by separating the Western from the Eastern religions. Western religions (Judaism, Christianity, Islam) are *monotheistic*. Their followers believe there is one Supreme Being or Supreme God (Honer & Hunt, 1987) who created and sustains the universe. Eastern religions (Hinduism, Buddhism, Confucianism, Taoism, and Shintoism) are either polytheistic or pantheistic, and some are atheistic or agnostic (Richards & Bergin, 1997). *Polytheism* is the belief in or worship of more than one God, whereas *pantheism* is a doctrine that equates God with the forces and laws of the universe. Pantheists believe that "God is all and all is God" (Percesepe, 1991, p. 469). Within my discussion of both Western and Eastern religions, I begin historically and address the various religions as they developed and influenced one another. Within these larger groups are diverse offshoots, small sects, and individual practices that may deviate somewhat from the overview I provide. At the end of the chapter are suggested readings that will amplify your understanding of the various forms of these religions.

WESTERN RELIGIONS

Judaism

Judaism was born in Palestine approximately 2000 B.C.E. (Before the Common Era) (Fishbane, 1993). The word *Jew* is derived from the term *yehudah,* or Judah, the Southern Kingdom of Israel that existed from 922 to 586 B.C.E. (Morrison & Brown, 1991). The state's Latin name was *Judaeus,* meaning "a resident of Judea." The name was later shortened to *Jew.* Today, a Jew is someone who is a member of a religious or cultural group or practices the religion of Judaism. According to Jewish law, a Jew is someone whose mother is Jewish or who has converted to Judaism (Morrison & Brown, 1991).

Basic Jewish Beliefs   The first tenet of Judaism is radical monotheism: There is only one God who created the universe and continues to govern it (Sarason, 1993–1996). This God is Yahweh, who is eternal, omniscient, omnipotent, and holy. God is made visible to Jews through the natural order, creation, history, and revelation (Sarason, 1993–1996). The second tenet of Judaism is that Jews were chosen by God to receive the divine law and to be a model for the human race. Jews were seen as being blessed by Yahweh so that they might be a blessing to all the peoples of the world. A third major concept in Judaism is that of covenant (berith). This is a contractual agreement between God and the Jews that if they acknowledged God and kept his commandments, he would reward them. If they failed to be obedient, God would punish them. All Jewish history is viewed through this lens of divine blessing and retribution. Another theme in Jewish faith is that at the end of time, Yahweh would send a messiah from the lineage of King David to redeem the Jews and restore them to sovereignty in their land (Sarason, 1993–1996). Some Jews believe that rather than being head of a theocracy, the Messiah will bring peace and love among all nations (Morrison & Brown, 1991). In addition, there is the belief that individual Jews, through study of the Torah and faithfulness to the commandments, could hasten the arrival of the Messiah (Sarason, 1993–1996).

Sacred Texts   The Tanach (an acronym for the three sections of the Hebrew Bible) is considered scripture and includes the Torah (the first five books of the Hebrew Bible), Nebiim, the prophetic literature, and Ketubim, the wisdom writings (Sarason, 1993–1996). In addition, there are more contemporary rabbinical writings called the Mishnah, a classical collection of laws and rules of behavior in ancient Judaism (Fishbane, 1993). From the second century B.C.E. onward, rabbinic discussions of the Mishnah resulted in the Talmud of Israel and later the Talmud of Babylonia. Gradually, these texts came to be understood as authoritative and sacred (Fishbane, 1993).

Religious Practices and Festivals   One distinctive practice among some Jews has to do with dietary laws. Because one's home table is considered the table of the Lord, certain animals, considered unclean, are not to be eaten. Fish without fins or scales and pigs fall into this category. Acceptable animals are those that have split hooves and chew their cuds. However, they must be slaughtered correctly, have the blood drained from them, and must not be served together with dairy products (Sarason, 1993–1996). Observing these dietary laws is called keeping kosher. Those who keep kosher laws have separate plates and utensils to prepare and serve meat, dairy products, and Passover meals (Morrison & Brown, 1991).

Some Jews observe the seventh day of the week as the Sabbath and perform no work. Instead, they spend the day in prayer, study, rest, and family feasting (Sarason, 1993–1996).

The Jewish year includes five major festivals and two minor ones. The major festivals were agricultural in origin. Passover, the spring festival, marks the beginning of the barley harvest. It is significant because during this period Jews celebrate the exodus from Egypt. Fifty days after Passover, Shabuoth occurs. This festival commemorates Yahweh's gift of the Torah at Mt. Sinai. Rosh Hashanah, the Jewish New Year, begins with the call to repentance and culminates in Yom Kippur, the Day of Atonement. This day, the holiest of Jewish holidays is spent in fasting prayer and confession (Sarason, 1993–1996). Hanukkah, one of the minor holidays, is a remembrance of the victory of the Maccabees over the Syrian King Antiochus IV in 165 B.C.E. On Purim, celebrated a month before Passover, Jews remember the deliverance of their Persian ancestors by Esther and Mordecai.

Contemporary Judaism   Most American Jews are descendents from European Jews who immigrated in the mid-19th century and those who were survivors of the Holocaust. There are three major forms of Judaism in America today: Orthodox, Conservative, and Reform. Orthodox Jews are traditionalists who are committed to maintaining their practices amid the demands of modern life. They believe that the Torah is the ultimate religious authority and reject modern interpretations of it as mythical (Morrison & Brown, 1991). They adhere to the strict laws of their religion and dutifully observe the Sabbath through rest and worship. Conservative Jews respect traditional Jewish law and practice, yet they are more flexible, less mechanical, and attempt to update the Law in response to contemporary life. Reform Judaism emphasizes reason and tends to be liberal and nonauthoritarian (Sarason, 1993–1996). There have been innovative changes in Reform Judaism, such as allowing families to be seated together instead of segregating males and females. Sermons are preached in English rather than in Hebrew, and women are permitted to become rabbis (Morrison & Brown, 1991).

Christianity

Christianity emerged in the first century c.e. (Common Era) in the context of Judaism and currently claims more than 1.7 billion adherents (Pelikan, 1993–1996). The entire religion is focused on the centrality of Jesus Christ, a Jew who taught in Palestine and whom his followers claimed was God's promised Messiah. In Christian teaching, not only is Jesus a powerful teacher, healer, and exemplar of the moral life, he is also the means by which people obtain salvation and eternal life. Christians claim that after his crucifixion in approximately 29 c.e. (Frankiel, 1993), God resurrected Jesus (raised him from the dead) and that he continues to live and reign with God. Christians also believe that Jesus will return to earth at the end of time to consummate the Kingdom of God (or bring in his eternal reign) that he inaugurated during his earthly life.

Basic Christian Beliefs Although there is significant diversity among Christians regarding the major tenets of their religion, several are held as decisive. One major tenet is that Jesus was simultaneously both fully human and fully divine. This statement means that Jesus is God in human form. God became human in Jesus to conquer the sinfulness of humankind. Although he was human, Jesus was not sinful. Instead, he suffered the punishment (death) for the sin of the world. One interpretation of Jesus' crucifixion is that he was the sacrifice for human sin or alienation from God. Jesus' bodily resurrection from the dead gave human beings the opportunity to be freed from the punishment of sin if they repented and accepted Jesus Christ and his offer of salvation. In addition, God offered Christians the Holy Spirit, or divine presence in their lives as an ongoing comfort and guide (Frankiel, 1993). Instead of achieving salvation through obedience to the law (as in Judaism), Christians believe that they are saved from the power of sin, death, and evil by the grace of God. Such grace is not earned by doing good, serving others, or heeding religious moral codes. According to Christian theology, it is a free gift. In response to the gift of salvation, Christians strive to model their lives after the example of Jesus Christ. For some Christians, Jesus' mandate to spread his gospel results in strong evangelistic endeavors. These Christians typically believe that Jesus Christ is the exclusive means of salvation.

Another concept basic to Christianity is that of the triune God, or the Trinity. This doctrine, though not set out explicitly in scripture, holds that even though God is one, God is also expressed in three personas: Father, or creator; Son, or redeemer (Jesus); and Holy Spirit, sustainer.

Another important component of Christianity is the church, the community of believers, also called the body of Christ. The ritual practices, study, worship, and service take place within this community.

Sacred Text   For Christians, the Bible is considered the authoritative word of God. The Bible comprises 66 separate books. Included are the Hebrew scriptures (or Old Testament as it is called by some Christians), the four gospels (Matthew, Mark, Luke, and John), Acts, the letters attributed to the apostle Paul, and Revelation. Although there are various perspectives on the nature and purpose of the Bible, all Christians ascribe some level of authority to it.

Rituals and Practices   Most Christian churches participate in at least two sacraments (ritual signs of God's grace): Baptism and the Eucharist (or Holy Communion). Baptism involves the use of water (either by sprinkling pouring water over a person or immersing a person's body into water) to signify remission of sins, new life, and initiation into the Christian community. The Eucharist or Holy Communion is a ritual meal in which bread and wine (or in some cases grape juice) are taken in remembrance of Jesus' suffering and death. Christians believe that in the sacraments Jesus Christ is mysteriously present with them.

Denominations and Sects   Across its nearly 2000-year existence, the Christian church has undergone many splits based on theological differences. The three major divisions in Christianity are Roman Catholicism, Eastern Orthodoxy, and Protestantism. The Roman Catholic Church, the largest single Christian body, is composed of those Christians who acknowledge the supreme authority of the bishop of Rome, the Pope, in matters of faith. Adherents to Roman Catholicism claim that their church is the only legitimate one because of its unbroken succession of priests descending from St. Peter to the present time (O'Malley, 1993–1996). Priests, as representatives of Christ, are not permitted to marry and must take a vow of celibacy. The Roman Catholic Church is hierarchically structured and emphasizes the liturgy of the Mass (Eucharist). Catholics believe in the real presence of Christ in the Eucharist such that bread and wine are changed into Jesus' body and blood. The other sacraments are baptism, confirmation, penance, holy orders, matrimony, and the anointing of the sick (O'Malley, 1993–1996).

The Eastern Orthodox Church, whose members number 4.5 million Americans (Young, 2000), shares many beliefs and practices in common with other Christians. It tends to comprise persons from central and eastern Europe. The Orthodox Church is conservative, traditional, and liturgical. In Orthodoxy, humans are believed to be created good. The purpose of humankind is to achieve *theosis* or divinization (Young, 2000). The Orthodox do not see scripture as inerrant nor do they believe that it is the sole authority. They also give credence to the writings of the early church Fathers. One of the most distinctive beliefs held by the Orthodox is that the entire church (bishops, priests, and all the people) is infallible (Young, 2000).

Protestantism began as a movement within the Roman Catholic Church in the 16th century to reform it, resulting in the Protestant Reformation. Despite the considerable differences among them in doctrine and practice, Protestants reject the authority of the Pope and focus instead on the authority of the Bible and the importance of individual faith. In addition, Protestants hold to the "priesthood of believers," a doctrine that underscores individual Christians' direct access to God without mediation by a (Roman Catholic) priest.

Although mainline Protestant denominations have unique histories and some specific theological differences, they have several common characteristics: (a) initial development from Europe's Protestant Reformation, (b) the influence of 20th century liberal Protestantism, (c) an optimistic view of human nature, (d) latitude in questioning scripture and church tradition, (e) rejection of biblical literalism, (f) openness to scientific discovery, as well as incorporation of medical, and psychological therapy, and (g) minimization of the distinctiveness of the denominations (McCullough, Weaver, Larson, & Aay, 2000).

Evangelical Christians and Fundamentalist Protestants constitute a significant force in American Christianity. During the past 30 years, their numbers have grown from 51 million to 77 million members (Thurston, 2000). Whereas Evangelical Christians tend to be moderately conservative theologically and socially, Fundamentalists are very conservative or traditional in these areas. Both groups tend to focus on converting nonbelievers to Christianity. Fundamentalists and some evangelicals hold to literal interpretation of the Bible and believe that it is the inerrant Word of God. There is an emphasis on tithing 10% of one's income to support church ministries. One of the biggest differences between Evangelicals and Fundamentalists is the degree of absorption into secular culture (Thurston, 2000). Evangelicals tend to want to reform the world from within its institutions and structures, but Fundamentalists often withdraw from them. Fundamentalists emphasize personal holiness and expect their members to refrain from smoking, drinking, dancing, gambling, swearing, and premarital sex. Some strict Fundamentalist sects require modest apparel for both men and women. Both evangelicals and fundamentalists tend to share a conservative approach to social issues. They oppose homosexuality, extramarital sex, abortion, divorce, and substance abuse (Marsden, 1987; Thurston, 2000). They may also call for women to be submissive to their husbands, not to work outside the home, and to refrain from seeking leadership positions in their churches.

These descriptions are but thumbnail sketches of the major facets of Christianity. There are subtle differences within and between each of the groups that are beyond the scope of this chapter. More likely than not, counselors will find clients who hail from a particular Christian tradition or denomination, but whose beliefs will be scattered across the continuum from conservative to liberal. For example, some Roman Catholics are very liberal, oppose the unilateral authority of the Pope, reject the church's stance against abortion, and advocate for the ordination of women to the priesthood. Likewise, one may discover Christians who are members of mainline, typically liberal Protestant denominations who hold to Fundamentalist views and practices. It is important, then, for counselors to know the general perspective of these Christian traditions, but not to assume that their clients adhere to the beliefs and practices typically associated with them.

Islam

During the last two decades, Islam has been the fastest growing religion in America (Hedayat-Diba, 2000). By 2010, Islam will be the second largest religion in North America after Christianity (Haddad & Lummis, 1987). There are currently an estimated six million Muslims in the United States. According to Power (1998), 12.4% are Arab, 42% are African American, 24.4% are Asian, and 21% are "other." The word *Islam* literally means "to surrender" but as a religious term, it means "to surrender to the will or law of God" (Rahman, 1993, p. 1).

Islam began in Arabia with the life of Muhammad (circa 570–632 C.E.), its founding prophet. Islam is a monotheistic religion whose believers hold that there is one God, that Muhammad is his last Prophet, and that the Koran is the final holy book of humankind (Hedayat-Diba, 2000). Muslims* also believe that their religion is primordial and universal and that "even nature itself is Muslim because it automatically obeys the laws God has ingrained in it" (Rahman, 1993, p. 1).

Basic Muslim Beliefs   According to Islam, the one God has four fundamental functions: creation, sustenance, guidance, and judgment. Muslims believe that they are called by God (Allah) to be grateful for their blessings and to choose to serve God. For Muslims, both faith and good works are required, but faith is also considered a gift from God (Denny, 1993). Muslims believe that people are essentially created good. Although they may make poor choices, persons can be forgiven if they repent and follow their repentance with ethical living. For Muslims, the greatest danger and the unforgivable sin is idolatry or "shirk" (Denny, 1993). The ultimate goal of a faithful life is "success" (Denny, 1993, p. 637). This concept entails both physical and emotional well-being as well as an eternal blessing in the life to come (Denny, 1993).

There are five major doctrines in Islam. The first is the belief in the divine unity, *tawhid*. The second doctrine is the belief in angels as divinely appointed agents of God's revelation and helpers in life's tasks. The third doctrine is a belief in prophecy as revealed especially in the Qur'an (Koran). The fourth belief is in the Last Day when there will be a final judgment of the living and the dead. The righteous will be saved and granted eternal bliss. The unbelievers will be cast into hell. The last doctrine is the Divine Decree and Predestination. It implies that Allah has already decreed which people will receive eternal salvation. Although this concept is mysterious, Muslims believe humans are given freedom and responsibility to make moral and spiritual decisions (Denny, 1993).

Sacred Texts   The major source of authority for Muslims is the Qur'an (Koran), which is considered the speech of God to Muhammad, mediated by

---

*The term *Islam* is used to refer to the religion, whereas the term *Muslim* refers to Islam's adherents.

Gabriel, the angel of revelation (Rahman, 1993). Because Muslims believe the Koran came directly from God, it is considered infallible. The book itself is a collection of passages revealed to Muhammad over 22 years (601–623). It has 114 chapters, some containing only 3 verses, others containing as many as 306 verses (Rahman, 1993).

The second source of Islam is the Sunna, or example of the Prophet. This text includes traditions of what the Prophet Muhammad said or did regarding various issues. This body of literature is not considered infallible because of its human transmission through the oral tradition. Some scholars have suggested that much of the Sunna was derived from the opinions of early Muslims, rather than from Muhammad himself (Rahman, 1993).

Rituals and Practices   The five *Pillars of Islam* contain the religion's most sacred practices. The first is shahada, or profession of faith. The faithful Muslim makes the following confession of faith, "There is no God but Allah, and Muhammad is his Prophet." The second pillar is ritual prayer. Muslims are expected to pray five times a day at dawn, noon, mid-afternoon, sunset, and evening. Before praying, they must undergo a ritual cleansing that symbolizes purity (Hedayat-Diba, 2000). All the prayers must be offered facing the direction of Mecca. Friday is the holy day for Muslims, and prayer is often conducted in a Mosque. The third pillar of Islam is almsgiving. Muslims are expected to give 2.5% of their income to the poor (Hedayat-Diba, 2000). In some countries, it is a tax, but in most places, it is considered a voluntary response to God's goodness. The fourth pillar of Islam is fasting. During the month of Ramadan in which the receipt of the Koran is celebrated, Muslims may not eat, drink, smoke, or have sexual intercourse between sunup and sundown (Hedayat-Diba, 2000). Children as young as 7 participate in fasting. Those who are elderly, disabled, or physically ill are exempt from this practice. The end of the month is *Eid fitr,* one of the two Islamic holidays. The fifth pillar of Islam is pilgrimage. Muslims are expected to make at least one pilgrimage to Mecca in their lifetime after age 16. Some writers suggest that there is a sixth pillar of Islam known as *jihad,* or "holy war" against Islam's enemies. Although the media tends to focus on extremist movements when using this term, *jihad*—rightly understood—refers to "exertion in the way of God" (Denny, 1993, p. 648). The term can refer to fighting against enemies, but it can also include attempts to spread the religion or even personal spiritual growth.

Subtraditions of Islam   Most Muslims worldwide and in America are Sunni (Denny, 1993). This group of orthodox Muslims accepts the Caliph as Muhammad's successor. He was the one designated to carry on Muhammad's teachings after his death.

Shi'ism is the branch of Islam practiced by approximately 10% of the Muslim population, mostly those in Iran and Iraq (Hedayat-Diba, 2000). These Muslims hold that Ali, Muhammad's cousin and son-in-law (he married Muhammad's daughter, Fatima) was the rightful successor to Muhammad.

African American Muslims have existed since the beginnings of slavery in America in the 17th century (Wormser, 1994). Although forced to give up their African spiritual traditions, some slaves developed an interest in Islam. The most well-known branch of African American Muslims is known as the Nation of Islam and led by Louis Farrakhan. Malcolm X was the best-known member during the 12 years he belonged to the Nation of Islam (Wormser, 1994).

Although there are differences among Muslims, their unity is more obvious than their diversity. Perhaps the biggest barrier for Western counselors working with Muslims is the prejudice that might have been absorbed from the images promulgated by the media. According to Wormser (1994), many Americans view Muslims as fanatics, warriors, hostage takers, and terrorists. These attitudes themselves are detrimental to counselors' successful work with Muslim clients. Learning about religious, cultural, and ethnic diversity that characterizes Muslims and developing acceptance is the first step toward effective counseling.

EASTERN RELIGIONS

Hinduism

Hinduism is one of the world's oldest religions, dating from about 1500 B.C.E. (O'Flaherty, 1993). Unlike other major religions, it was not founded by a single person but, rather, is the result of a coming together of many religious beliefs and philosophical ideas (Wangu, 1991). Originating in India, Hinduism has grown to be the third largest religion in the world with approximately 700 million members (Wangu, 1991). The word *Hindu* is derived from the Sanskrit word *sindhu* referring to the Indus River. In the 5th century B.C.E., Persians used the term to designate people who lived in the land of the Indus (O'Flaherty, 1993). Because it encompasses all of India and much of south Asia, Hinduism also carries with it social and doctrinal systems that are central to the culture of its people.

Basic Hindu Beliefs   Hinduism is a polytheistic religion. That is, Hindus worship more than one god. The three major deities are Shiva, Vishnu, and the goddess Devi. In addition to these, Hindus also worship hundred of other minor deities related to villages or even families (O'Flaherty, 1993). Hindus are united by some common observances: reverence for Brahmans and cows; refraining from eating meat, especially beef, marriage within the caste (jati), and the hope for producing male heirs (O'Flaherty, 1993).

Hindus believe there are four yogas or paths toward God based on individual temperaments (Sharma, 2000). Jnana Yoga is the path of knowledge designed for persons who are intellectual and philosophical. Their duty is to meditate to shift their focus from self to the Divine within. Bhakti Yoga or the path of love or complete devotion to and adoration of God (Sharma, 2000). Mantras are associated with Bhakti yoga as a means of bringing about one's change in consciousness (Sharma, 2000). Karma yoga is the path of work. On this path, God may be found through daily activities rather than through a life of contemplation. Raja yoga is the path of psychological experimentation (Sharma, 2000). This path is oriented toward scientific mind, and the experiments lead the devotee through meditations that reveal one's true nature (Sharma, 2000).

In addition to the four paths, there are the four stages, or wants, in life. These are rungs on a ladder that lead to liberation, or moksha. The first stage is brahmachari, or the student stage. During this period, Hindu males between the ages of 8 and 12 study the scriptures and tradition of their religion with a teacher (Wangu, 1991). The second stage is that of grahasthin, or householder. During this stage, the young male is expected to marry, earn a living, produce sons, and give alms to those who have passed to a higher level (Wangu, 1991). The third stage, or vanaprahasthin, is the forest dweller. This stage belongs to the elder Hindu males. They perform rituals honoring their ancestors. The fourth stage, or sanyasin, is the ascetic. This stage occurs when the Hindu is prepared to give up the world, physically and mentally, to achieve liberation (Wangu, 1991).

The concepts of karma and reincarnation are central to Hinduism. One's human life contains developmental stages, and so does the soul. Karma involves the law of cause and effect. There is a consequence to every action. All thoughts, feelings, and actions that are emitted from persons come back to them (Wangu, 1991). People are born into circumstances that reveal conditions in past lives. For example, those who find themselves in difficult situations are reaping the results of their actions in previous lives. Conversely, those who are enjoying the benefits of a good life are being blessed by their good deeds in past incarnations. Hindus believe that people continue to be born in physical form until they transcend all pain and pleasure and release themselves from all fears and all attachments. This concept is called samsara or transmigration. The Hindu religion rejects the Western notion of sin (Sharma, 2000). Instead, Hindus believe humans are divine and have only to "uncover our perfection by removing the layers of illusion in which we are wrapped" (Sharma, 2000, p. 345).

Another central belief in Hinduism, that of the caste system, is linked to the social order in India. The notion was that people were divided into groups based on how they could best contribute to society. The four original casts included the brahmans or seers, the kshatriyas or administrators, the vaishyas or businesspersons, and the shudras or laborers (Knipe, 1993). A fifth class of untouchables emerged over time and became subject to discrimination. Mahatma Gandhi is credited with dismantling the caste system and working to integrate the outcasts into Indian society.

Sacred Texts   Hindus hold several texts sacred. The *Ramayana* is the epic tale of Lord Rama's victory over the ten-headed demon, Ravana. The celebration of this triumph occurs at Diwali, the Festival of Lights (Sharma, 2000). The Mahabharata, the longest poem in the world, is often referred to as a library rather than a book (Knipe, 1993). The Mahabharata contains the famous *Bhagavad Gita,* which is composed of advice to the warrior prince Arjuna by Lord Krishna, his charioteer at the beginning of the Great War between the two families (Sharma, 2000). In addition, the *Vedas* (knowledge) consist of four volumes. One hundred and eight books compose the *Upanishads,* the spiritual truths, and ways of living them. The *Puranas* were composed after the epics and contain subsidiary myths, praise hymns, philosophy, and rituals (O'Flaherty, 1993). They are predominantly sectarian in nature and are dedicated to the worship of one of the gods: Vishnu, Shiva, or Devi.

Rituals and Practices   The Hindu temple is a cultural center where songs are sung, text is read aloud, and rituals are performed. There are rituals for every rite of passage (samskaras).

A classic practice associated with Hinduism is the chanting of the Vedas. The mantras, timeless universal sounds are believed to have the cosmic power to transform people and to enable others to turn in to the universe (Knipe, 1993).

Hindu icons, or sacred images, are also important to Hindus. Some icons are seen as personal deities and are believed to embody the presence of the god. By worshipping an image, the Hindu gains access to the deity (Wangu, 1993).

Daily worship, or puja, is a significant aspect of Hindu religious life. This practice involves offering food, incense, flowers, ashes, and other articles to a deity. After the offering, the host prepares food for the worshippers. Fire plays a major role in many Hindu ceremonies, including weddings and funerals (Sharma, 2000).

Many holy places or shrines (tirthas) are the objects of pilgrimages for people all over India. In addition, local shrines are visited at festival time.

Hinduism is an ancient and complex religion whose details are beyond the scope of this chapter. However, it is critical to realize that Hinduism is not limited to the geography of India and south Asia. It has become a vital religion in the United States and is undergoing transformation as its followers address women's issues and the caste system.

Buddhism

Buddhism is one of the world's largest great religions, claiming 150 to 300 million followers (McDermott, 1993). Siddhartha Gautama, known as the Buddha or Enlightened One, founded it in northeastern India. Originating in the Brahman Hindu tradition, Buddhism developed in distinctive ways apart from Hinduism. Buddha rejected many Hindu beliefs, challenged the authority of the priesthood, claimed that the Vedic scriptures were invalid, and rejected the sacrificial cults based on them (McDermott, 1993). Buddha rejected the notion that one's spirituality is a matter of birth, and opened his way to people of all castes.

Buddha   Scholars generally agree that Buddha was born in 563 B.C.E., the son of a ruler of a small kingdom near the current-day India-Nepal border.

Legend claims that Buddha was destined to become either a ruler or a sage. He was raised in luxury until age 29 when he recognized the emptiness of his life, discovered the reality of suffering and death, and embarked on a quest for enlightenment and release from the cycles of rebirths (McDermott, 1993). After practicing radical asceticism for many years, Buddha advised that neither extreme of pleasure or denial of pleasure was the path to Nirvana (release from suffering). He advocated a middle way that involved attaining purity of thought and deed. He believed that awareness was the path to overcoming death (Finn & Rubin, 2000). Buddha was adamant that he not be worshipped as a god or savior. He held that his role was to point out the path to freedom, but that all people had to "work out their salvation with diligence" (Burtt, 1955, p. 49).

Basic Buddhist Beliefs   At the heart of Buddha's teaching were the Four Noble Truths and the Eightfold Path (Wangu, 1993). The Four Noble Truths are as follows: (a) There is suffering; (b) Suffering is caused by desire, attachment, and craving; (c) Suffering can be overcome (nirvana) by ceasing to desire; and (d) the way to end desire is to follow the Eightfold Path (Lester, 1993). The Eightfold Path includes "right opinion, right intentions, right speech, right conduct, right livelihood, right effort, right mindfulness and right concentration" (Wangu, 1993, p. 26). These eight paths are often divided into three categories that are significant aspects of Buddhist faith: morality, wisdom, and concentration (McDermott, 1993). Although at first followers of Buddha belonged to monasteries or Sangha, Buddha recognized that not everyone could give up everyday life to become a monk. To those, he offered the Five Precepts or rules for everyday behavior: "to refrain from killing, from taking what is not given, from sexual misconduct, from false speech, and from using intoxicating substances that cloud the mind" (Wangu, 1993, p. 29).

Karma is a major facet of Buddhist belief. As with Hinduism, Karma involves a person's acts and their ethical consequences. Good deeds are rewarded and evil ones punished. In this system, there is no undeserved mercy nor unwarranted suffering (McDermott, 1993). Instead of a divine judgment, Karma functions as a kind of universal natural moral law. Karma determines one's destiny and whether one is reborn as a human, animal, or some other creature such as a devil or a god (McDermott, 1993).

Buddhism focuses on the psychological and the ethical aspects of human life (Finn & Rubin, 2000). Although Buddha did not deny the existence of gods, he did not attribute to them any particular role such as creators of the universe or controllers of human destiny.

Sacred Texts   Buddhist teaching developed from a long oral tradition in which the teachings were recited at councils. Eventually during the first century B.C.E., these teaching were written down. The Buddhist scripture is known as the Tripitaka or Three Baskets because it contains three types of writings: the Sutra Pitaka or discourses, the Vinaya Pitaka or code of monastic discipline, and the Abhidharma Pitaka or philosophical psychological and doctrinal material (McDermott, 1993). The Tripitaka writings are claimed by Mahayana Buddhists to be the revealed words of Buddha to his most spiritually advanced followers (Wangu, 1993). The Way of Righteousness is another Buddhist scripture that is composed of brief sayings of the Buddha made during his 45 years of teaching.

Rituals and Practices   Buddhists engage in rituals in their homes and temples through chanting and placing flowers, candles, and incense before a Buddha-image. The flowers remind followers of the impermanence of life; the incense is reminiscent of moral virtue; flame symbolizes enlightenment (Lester, 1993). There may also be the offering of food.

Rites of passage involve special rituals to mark life transitions. These occasions are presided over by monks, or in some cases elders in the lay community (Lester, 1993). The yearly festivals include celebration of the New Year and the Buddha's birthday. The New Year is the occasion for reflecting on one's karma, well-wishing, and cleansing (Lester, 1993).

At the heart of Buddhism is the spiritual practice of meditation. This process involves acute attentiveness and heightened self-perception. Meditation involves focused awareness of one's breathing, for example. It may also involve attentiveness to aspects of consciousness issuing in insight (Finn & Rubin, 2000). It is a means by which persons are able to disengage from the grasping and desiring that are thought to be at the root of suffering.

Schools of Buddhism   The two original schools of Buddhism resulted from a schism that developed as result of varying interpretations of how to follow the Vinaya rules (Finn & Rubin, 2000). The Theravadins are stricter about observing the Buddha's teachings than the Mahayana school is. The Theravadins maintain a rather unified tradition and are concentrated in Southeast Asia, parts of India, and in some regions in the United States. Mahayana spread north and east and eventually took root in Korea, Japan, Nepal, China, Tibet, and the United States (Finn & Rubin, 2000). Tantric Buddhism developed by the 7th century C.E. and consisted of a blend of Mahayana Buddhism and popular folklore and magic of northern India (McDermott, 1993). Tantrism is an esoteric tradition that became the dominant form of Buddhism in Tibet (McDermott, 1993).

Two other forms of Buddhism also developed, that of Ch'an or Zen and Pure Land or Amidism (McDermott, 1993). Zen Buddhism was influenced by both Confucianism and Taoism (discussed later) and the belief that people are basically good and need only guidance and support to access their innate wisdom (Wangu, 1993). Through the practice of Zen Buddhist meditation, persons come to realize their Buddha nature. The emphasis in Zen is on personal practice and enlightenment rather than on doctrine or scripture (McDermott, 1993). Pure Land Buddhism, which emerged in China, stresses devotion to the Buddha Amitabha (Infinite Light) as a means of being reborn into eternal paradise, or Pure Land (Wangu, 1993). The distinctively Japanese sect of Mahayana is Nichiren Buddhism, named after its 13th century

Japanese founder, Nichiren. Its focus is on devotion and chanting to bring about world peace (Finn & Rubin, 2000).

There are at least three major types of Buddhism practiced in the United States in addition to the small group of Theravadins, including immigrants from Asia who practice within their cultural and linguistic traditions and middle-class Caucasians who practice in English (Finn & Rubin, 2000). These persons tend to practice some form of Mahayana Buddhism, including Zen. In addition, Soka Gakka is a unique form of Buddhism that has attracted many African Americans and Latino members (Wangu, 1993).

Buddhism is an important religious and spiritual force in the United States today and has influenced a number of American-born clients in significant ways. Counselors working with such clients will want to be especially sensitive to the complex relationship between psychotherapy and spirituality and be open to ways of integrating the two. In addition, counselors should be aware of the potential for some Buddhist clients to be suspicious of traditional Western psychotherapies and to hold that the spiritual path is a superior route to psychological healing (Finn & Rubin, 2000).

Confucianism

One of the major philosophical systems in China, Confucianism, developed from the teaching of Confucius who was born around 551 B.C.E. (Smith, 1958). These teachings focused on good conduct, practical wisdom, and proper social relationships. Confucianism was the official ideology of China, but was never a religion per se (Liu, 1993). Confucius was considered a great teacher, but not a personal god. Confucius himself never claimed to be divine, and the temples built to honor him were designated for public ceremonies, not as places of worship (Liu, 1993).

Basic Beliefs   There are five major concepts in Confucianism. The first is *jen*, translated as love, goodness, humanity, and human-heartedness (Liu, 1993). Jen involves simultaneously "a feeling of humanity toward others and respect for oneself, an indivisible sense of the dignity of human life . . ." (Smith, 1958, p. 159). Other Confucian virtues include righteousness, propriety, integrity, and filial piety (Liu, 1993). The second concept is *Chung-tzu*, which refers to the notion of True Manhood [sic]. An appropriate image for this ideal is the perfect host who is so comfortable that he is able to be fully attentive to guests and to put them at ease (Smith, 1958). Confucius believed that only people who were Chün-tzus could transform the world toward peace. The third concept, *Li*, refers to propriety or ordering life so it fits social convention and such that people conduct themselves with grace and urbanity regardless of the circumstances (Smith, 1958). The fourth pivotal concept is *Te*. Literally, this word means power and its appropriate use. Confucius believed that those who govern should be honorable and benevolent and that the people in turn were to be respectful and obedient. The fifth Confucian concept is *Wen*. This term refers to the "arts of peace" (Smith, 1958, p. 165) that contribute to the esthetic dimension of culture.

Sacred Texts   The major ideas of Confucianism are recorded in nine ancient Chinese books handed down by Confucius and his followers. The *Wu Ching* (Five Classics), which originated before Confucius' time, includes the *I Ching* (Book of Changes), *Su Ching* (Book of History), *Shih Ching* (Book of Poetry), *Li Chi* (Book of Rites), and *Ch'un Ch'iu* (Spring and Autumn Annals). The *Shih Shu* (Four Books) contains the sayings of Confucius and Mencius (the second sage of Confucianism, 372–289 B.C.E.) (Statler, 1971) and commentaries on their teachings.

Although we can debate whether Confucianism is a religion or not, certainly the values and philosophy of this ancient thinker have had a significant impact on Chinese thought and politics across the ages. Counselors are most likely to see the influence of Confucius' thought in the cultural values of Chinese Americans who continue to carry his philosophy with them.

Taoism

Taoism (pronounced DOW-ism) is a Chinese philosophy and religion dating from about the 4th century B.C.E. Along with Confucianism, Taoism has exerted considerable influence on native Chinese schools of thought. The word *tao* literally means "the way." It has at least three distinct meanings. First, *tao* is the way of ultimate reality. It is ineffable (unspeakable) and transcendent, the ground of all existence (Smith, 1958). Second, *tao* is the way of the universe or the way of nature (Hartz, 1993). The cycles of nature and constant change in the world are signs of the universal force of *tao*. This aspect of *tao* also includes the principle behind all life. Third, *tao* refers to the way that people should order their lives to be congruent with the operation of the universe (Smith, 1958). The notion of *tao* as ultimate reality could suggest that it is a god or Supreme Being; however, such is not the case. Taoism is not monotheistic; its followers do not worship a god but, rather, focus on coming into harmony with *tao* (Hartz, 1993). To cooperate with *tao*, one does nothing strained, artificial, or unnatural.

Taoism has no founder or central figure like Jesus, Buddha, Muhammed, or Confucius. Instead, it claims a number of teachers or masters. The philosophy and mystical beliefs can be found in the Tao Te Ching (Classic Way and It Power), a text dating from about the 3rd century B.C.E. and attributed to Lao-tzu. Another set of writings, the Chuang-tzu, is a book of parables and allegories dating from a similar period as the Tao Te Ching, but attributed to Chuang-tzu.

Rituals and Practices   Taoists believe that a healthy body is part of achieving a spiritual state. Many nutritional and medicinal practices, including acupuncture, can be traced to the Taoists (Hartz, 1993). Taoists suggest balance in their approach to diet. In addition, exercise is integral to Taoist practice. T'ai chi ch'uan, the ancient Chinese form of exercise developed in conjunction with Taoist thought. Moreover, meditation, often associated with Buddhism or Hinduism was in practice in China long before these religions made their debut there. In Taoist meditation, the goal is to come into harmony with the ultimate reality of the universe by doing nothing. Because

Taoists seek balance and harmony in life, the concepts of yin and yang (the interaction between opposite forces) is present in their thought (Overmyer, 1993).

Although Taoism is more of a way of life and a moral philosophy than a religion with a deity and worship, it has influenced many Asians as well as contemporary Americans. Counselors should note the obvious ways in which Taoist thinking has been incorporated into New Age spirituality, a topic discussed later in this chapter.

Shinto

Shinto is the native religion of Japan. It developed in prehistoric times on the Japanese islands (Hartz, 1997). The vast majority of Japanese are followers of Shinto. In fact, in 1990, the Keizai Koho Center in Tokyo estimated the number of Shinto followers to be roughly 112 million. More than 75% of those reported that they follow Buddhism as well (Hartz, 1997).

During the early period, Shinto was without a name and had no fixed dogma, moral doctrine, or sacred writings. A pantheon of spirits, or *kami*, was worshipped. Most of these deities were related to the natural world such as the sky, earth, heavenly bodies, and storms (Watts, 1993). The deities are not endowed with special qualities that distinguish them from humans. In fact, all things may have spirit—rocks, trees, and dust as well as human beings (Earhart, 1993). As a result, Shinto followers have respect for the natural world because anything could be invested with spirit (kami) (Hartz, 1997).

There is no founder of Shinto and no central figure. Like Taoism and Native American religions that had prehistoric origins, Shinto followers revere the spirits that are manifest in many things. For Shinto followers, there is no central spirit like the Tao or the Great Spirit (Hartz, 1997). In addition, Shinto has no fixed doctrine, scripture, or holy book; however, there are ancient prayers that were part of the oral tradition before being written down.

Shinto focuses on simplicity and cleanliness as signs of inner goodness. Physical and spiritual purity are emphasized. Followers of Shinto are encouraged to be grateful for their blessings, bestowed by the kami; however, how they meet the obligation of gratitude is up to the individual (Hartz, 1997).

Shinto worship is more individual than corporate. Some Shinto followers worship daily, others only at festival time. Regardless of the regularity of their worship, Shinto believers engage in purification rituals including handwashing (Hartz, 1997). Worship occurs outside the shrine rather than inside. Worshippers often bring offerings of food or coins for the kami. These offerings are signs of gratitude, not forms of sacrifice (Hartz, 1997). Worshippers write prayers on slips of paper and leave them nearby.

Shinto is embedded in Japanese culture. Regardless of whether or not they believe in kami, Japanese attempt to live in the Shinto way in harmony with nature and the spiritual sources therein. Shinto invites people to return to their spiritual roots as it gives its followers a sense of the sacred and a will to practice gratitude (Hartz, 1997).

SPIRITUAL TRADITIONS

In Chapter 1, I distinguished between "religion" and "spirituality," suggesting that religions were characterized by an organizational structure, doctrine, ritual, authoritative leadership, and a set of clearly defined traditions. "Spirituality" is concerned with persons' search for meaning, purpose, and value in life. When it comes to discussing contemporary spirituality, one is faced with the myriad of different belief systems and practices that seem to defy both labeling and categorization. However, it is important to present information that helps counselors organize their thinking about the content and experience of modern-day spiritualities.

Ironically, one unifying factor associated with present-day "spirituality" is its diversity. One person might practice Zen Buddhism, attend workshops on astrology, and consult a channeler; another might focus on the Christian-based "Course in Miracles," (1992), privately worship a goddess, and engage in some form of meditation. These varieties of practices differ from person to person, and it is impossible and unwise to make assumptions about someone's spiritual practices based on limited information.

It is possible to claim, however, that one of the major themes in contemporary spirituality is the use of self as the final authority (Bloch, 1998). Thus, each person must find his or her own spiritual path. Persons who align themselves with the spiritual movements of the day are not prone to respond to dogmatic claims that any one approach is the "best" or "only" means of obtaining spiritual growth or depth (Bloch, 1998).

Another characteristic of modern spiritualists is their solidarity and community in the midst of striking individuality. Even though there is a wide continuum of belief and practice, there is also a kinship among persons who have chosen countercultural or noninstitutional means of pursuing spiritual direction.

Another aspect of modern spiritualists is related to the paradigm shift that has occurred in contemporary philosophy. The absolutist notions that undergirded social institutions and the positivist approach to epistemology have been questioned by some and abandoned by others. In an effort to flee from the rationalized institutional structures of religion, some people have taken on what Bloch (1998) calls "a consumerist and personal approach to acquisition of religious or spiritualized information" (p. 9). Bloch maintained that such persons seek a variety of spiritual experiences based on "a desire to reduce social uncertainty by seeking compatibility across different knowledge claims, rather than having to select one at the absolute social cost of another" (p. 9). Thus, it is not uncommon for contemporary spiritualists to embrace multiple belief systems that may include some contradictory material.

New Age Spirituality

New Age spirituality is better described than defined. It is by no means a unified system of belief or practice. Instead, it encompasses a wide variety of ideas, activities, and rituals. According to Burrows (1986), the new Age movement emerged from the counterculture of the 1960s when many persons sought inspiration in ancient traditions of Eastern mysticism and Western occultism. He described the movement in this way:

> The term New Age suggested itself because of the millenial spirit of many of the traditions—and because of the dawn of the Aquarian Age at the close of the century. The counterculture's size and radical disaffection with the cultural mainstream reinforced the sense that something novel and revolutionary was underway. And that sense of the imminent culmination of humanity's evolution remains a hallmark of New Age enthusiasms. (p. 17)

The New Age movement holds to a holistic and organic worldview wherein the sciences are considered sources of "the unity aspect within the physical reality" (Frost, 1992, p. i). The New Age movement is concerned with the transformation of consciousness. It is open to altered states of consciousness over against the mechanistic worldview of science. It is interested in the integration of the paranormal (Frost, 1992). In an effort to explain some of the aspects of the New Age movement, Jack (1990) provided these definitions:

> 1. A movement of emerging planetary consciousness devoted to making earth a healthier, happier, and more peaceful place to live based on respect for humanity's diverse traditional ways of life in harmony with the environment; 2. Holistic community in general, including practitioners of yoga, meditation, natural foods, spiritual development, humanistic psychology, environmental and peace activities, psychic arts and science. (p. 2)

One of the hallmarks of New Age spirituality is its focus on holistic medicine and alternative methods of healing body, mind, and spirit. Among New Agers, there is an interest in the archaic tradition of the Shaman and in Native American practices. Homeopathy is also an important feature of the New Age movement. Specially trained persons knowledgeable about herbs, essential oils, vitamins, and minerals prescribe "natural" remedies for a host of ailments.

A significant belief among espousers of the New Age movement is that the spirit of the whole is in everything and everyone. To experience healing, individuals get in touch with holistic energy and learn to harness it, whether it is called "Chi" (Chinese) "Ki" (Japanese), or "Prana" (yogi) (Frost, 1992). Among the forays into the notion of bioenergy are acupuncture, reflexology (the theory that holds that the bottom of the foot is divided into areas that correspond to all the other body parts), and iridology (looking into the eye to determine the overall health of the body). In addition, auras or electromagnetic color fields are read to determine what kinds of interventions (massage, scent or color) might be needed to improve one's well-being. Cymatic therapy is often employed: Certain vibrations are beamed into various areas of the body to put them back in harmony with each other (Frost, 1992). In addition, other body therapies are often employed such as rolfing, yoga, and reiki (Chandler, 1988).

Seekers attached to the New Age movement are inspired by the awareness of mystery. As a result, there is a renewed interest in the mystical traditions inherent in Christianity, Kabbalah, Quakers, Shinto, Taoism, Zen

Buddhism, and others (Guiley, 1991). In addition, explanations for mysterious phenomena are sought through various techniques such as alchemy, astrology, magic, palmistry, transcendental meditation (Guiley, 1991). A growing interest has developed among New Agers in apparitions, déjà vu, exorcism, firewalking, hauntings, levitation, poltergeists, near death experiences, and many, many others. Certain places on the earth have taken on special significance for participants in the New Age movement. Some of these are ashrams, Stonehenge, Mt. St. Helens, and Native American sacred spaces.

It would be nearly impossible to list all the books that have influenced the New Age movement. However, some notable books are Ferguson's (1980) *The Aquarian Conspiracy: Personal and Social Transformation in the 1980s* addresses the breakthroughs in human consciousness that lead to a deeper appreciation of life. Zukav's (1989) *The Seat of the Soul* uses the karma doctrine and advocates liberating oneself from the bodily realm. In addition, Campbell's books (1968; 1971; 1986; 1988) on mythology have inspired much writing and dialogue within and outside the New Age movement. Certainly Schucman's (1992) best seller, *A Course in Miracles* should be included in the seminal works of the New Age movement. In it, she professes to be recording the words of an inaudible voice that dictated to her for seven years (1965–1972).

A vast panoply of organizations has been identified with New Age during the past 30 years, including Transcendental Meditation Program, Hare Krishna Consciousness, Scientology, Ehrhard Seminars Training (EST), Enckankar, Bahai, the Unification Church, and others (Chandler, 1988).

The New Age movement has been associated with a political agenda focused on environmental and ecological concerns and world peace. Also included in its concerns are zero population growth and solar energy (Frost, 1992). Moreover, many feminists, disenchanted with the patriarchy of established religions have found a place of acceptance, comfort, and activism within the New Age movement (Bloch, 1998).

In his qualitative study of 22 persons who professed involvement with the New Age movement, Bloch (1998) discovered several themes common to the experiences of those he interviewed. These prevailing themes included (a) an emphasis on self, self-autonomy, and self-as-authority; (b) a sense of being "born different" from other people to a supernatural extent; (c) moral and religious conflict with mainline religious bodies; (d) a feeling of being spiritually empowered; (e) a resistance to labels; (f) the importance of an alternative spiritual community; and (g) a sense that other social opportunities were less viable for them (Frost, 1992). When asked about their spiritual practices, respondents mentioned the following: psychic experiences (such as dreams, out-of-body, healing), magic (Shamanism, Kabbalism), Eastern spirituality (Zen, Hinduism, yoga), Native American tools and rituals, other tools and rituals (tarot, runes, astrology), and meditation (Bloch, 1998).

In summary, the New Age movement is broad and difficult to define. Guiley (1991) is helpful when she writes,

New Age is a controversial term applied to a spiritual and social movement encompassing a broad range of interest in religion, philosophy, mysticism, health, psychology, parapsychology, ecology, and the occult . . . It is virtually impossible to define precisely what constitutes "New Age" . . . and much of what is called" New Age," is not new, but a renewed cycle of interest and discovery. (p. 403)

Wicca and Neo-Paganism

Some would argue that Wicca (said to be an early Anglo-Saxon word for witchcraft) and Neo-Pagan practices fall within the realm of New Age spirituality. Certainly, in the last half of the 20th century there has been a revival of pre-Christian paganism in the United States and Europe (Ellwood, 1993). Witchcraft, however, is a very old religion. It has been practiced in many forms throughout the centuries. In Europe and North America, thousands of people have been executed for practicing witchcraft (Grist & Grist, 2000). Most notable were the Salem witch trials that occurred in Salem, Massachusetts, in the 17th century. Until 1951, it was illegal to practice witchcraft in the United Kingdom. The last case involved Helen Duncan, a spirit medium, who was imprisoned during World War II (Grist & Grist, 2000).

Modern witchcraft or Wicca was inspired by the writings of Gerald Gardner. In *Witchcraft Today* (1955), Gardner claims he was initiated into a Wiccan coven by a surviving witch who taught him the lore and rituals of English witches (Grist & Grist, 2000). Gardnerian witchcraft spread to the United States during the 1960s when the cultural climate was ripe for its emphasis on nature, colorful rituals, love of fantasy, and challenge to conventional religions (Ellwood, 1993).

Basic Wiccan Beliefs   Wicca is a religion grounded in the rhythms and cycles of nature. Within it is a respect for life, a celebration of the magical and numinous, and an emphasis on personal experience (Grist & Grist, 2000). Most Wiccans believe that the divine is both male and female. Some members hold to a single god or goddess, but many others worship a variety of gods from the Greek, Roman, Celtic, Nordic, Egyptian, Aztec, and other pantheons (Grist & Grist, 2000). Wiccans do not believe in harming anyone, nor do they practice "black magic." They believe that they do not have the right to cast spells on persons without their consent. Moreover, Wiccans believe that every act has consequences and that whatever one does, it will affect him or her in some way (Grist, & Grist, 2000).

Wiccans focus on the four elements of nature: air, fire, water, earth. Each element is assigned a directional point. Air is to the east, fire to the south, water to the west, and earth to the north. Each element is also assigned a color: Air is blue, fire is red, water is green, and earth is yellow, black brown, or other earth tone (Grist & Grist, 2000). Many correspondences such as these in the Wiccan religion are central in the practice of magic and spellcraft. A fifth element, or spirit, manifests through the other four. Wiccans refer to the great spirit as Dryghten, the Anglo-Saxon word meaning *lord*. At initiation, Wiccans take a spirit name that is connected to one's hopes for oneself (Grist & Grist, 2000).

Wiccans usually gather in small groups called covens, although it is acceptable to be a solitary Wiccan. Covens meet regularly for festivals and other ritual activities. There is an air of secrecy around the coven and its membership because of continuing persecution and the need for protection.

Entering the Wiccan religion involves being open to mystery and self-searching. It is not a religion that proselytizes, so those who wish to join must ask to do so (Grist & Grist, 2000). Traditionally, a year and a day must pass between asking for membership and initiation. The initiation process involves three degrees. The first is the initiation of the personality, the second is the initiation of the spirit, and the third is becoming the god or goddess.

A summary of Wiccan beliefs developed by the Council of American Witches is as follows (as cited in RavenWolf, 2000, pp. 6–7):

1. We practice rites to attune ourselves with the natural rhythm of life forces marked by the phases of the Moon and the seasonal quarters and cross-quarters.
2. We recognize that our intelligence gives us a unique responsibility toward our environment. We seek to live in harmony with Nature, in ecological balance offering fulfillment to life and consciousness within an evolutionary concept.
3. We acknowledge a depth of power far greater than is apparent to the average person. Because it is far greater than ordinary, it is sometimes called "supernatural," but we see it as lying within that which is naturally potential to all.
4. We conceive of the Creative Power in the Universe as manifesting through polarity—as masculine and feminine—and that this same Creative Power lives in all people, and functions through the interaction of the masculine and feminine. We value neither above the other, knowing each to be supportive of the other. We value sexuality as pleasure, as the symbol and embodiment of Life, and as one of the sources of energies used in magickal [sic] practice and religious worship.
5. We recognize both outer worlds and inner, or psychological worlds—sometimes known as the Spiritual Word, the Collective Unconscious, the Inner Planes, and we see in the interaction of these two dimensions the basis for paranormal phenomena and magickal exercises. We neglect neither dimension for the other, seeing both as necessary for our fulfillment.
6. We do not recognize any authoritarian hierarchy, but do honor those who teach, respect those who share their greater knowledge and wisdom, and acknowledge those who have courageously given of themselves in leadership.
7. We see religion, magick, and wisdom-in-living as being united in the way one views the world and lives within it—a world view and philosophy of life, which we identify as Witchcraft or the Wiccan Way.

8. Calling oneself "Witch" does not make a Witch—but neither does heredity itself, or the collecting of titles, degrees, and initiations. A Witch seeks to control the forces within him/herself that make life possible in order to live wisely and well, without harm to others, and in harmony with Nature.

9. We acknowledge that it is the affirmation and fulfillment of life, in a continuation of evolution and development of consciousness, that gives meaning to the Universe we know, and to our personal role within it.

10. Our only animosity toward Christianity, or toward any other religion or philosophy-of-life, is to the extent that its institutions have claimed to be "the one true right and only way" and have sought to deny freedom to others and to suppress other ways of religious practices and belief.

11. As American Witches, we are not threatened by debates on the history of the Craft, the origins of various terms, the legitimacy of various aspects of different traditions. We are concerned with our present, and our future.

12. We do not accept the concept of "absolute evil," nor do we worship any entity known as "Satan" or "the Devil" as defined by Christian Tradition. We do not seek power through the suffering of others, nor do we accept the concept that personal benefits can only be derived by denial to another.

13. We work within Nature for that which is contributory to our health and well-being.

Rituals and Practices   Wiccans celebrate the wheel of the year that offers a festival every six weeks. These seasons are Candlemas (February 1–2), Spring Equinox (February 21–22), Beltane (April 30–May 1), Midsummer Solstice (June 21–22), Lammas (July 31–August 1), Autumn Equinox (September 21–22), and Samhain/Halloween (October 31–November 1) (Grist & Grist, 2000). Each of these festivals has special ceremonies. Some typical rituals include opening the circle in preparation for a ritual, raising energy through a circle dance or mental activity, drawing down the moon in which the gods or goddess are invoked, charging in which the energy from a god or goddess is invoked in one of the coven members, the Great Rite, either an actual or symbolic engagement in sexual intercourse, making magic which entails using energy for healing or empowerment, and feasting with cake and wine (Grist & Grist, 2000).

In summary, Wicca and Neo-Pagan spirituality are ways of connecting with a Higher Power that appeal to many persons who are not interested in traditional religions. Some may be involved in Wicca as a means of expressing their connection to the New Age movement. Some might identify themselves both as Wiccan and as members of some other religion. For others, Wicca is their only foray into spirituality or religion. Secrecy surrounds the practice of Wicca religion, and, therefore, clients who are involved in this type of spirituality might not readily reveal this information to their counselors. Clients who are Wiccan might need to be convinced that their counselors are open to Wiccan spirituality and that disclosing their involvement in a coven is a safe thing to do.

CASE EXAMPLES
Mary Elizabeth

Mary Elizabeth, a 45-year-old, Caucasian Roman Catholic requested counseling because she was contemplating divorcing Paul, her husband of 22 years. Mary Elizabeth reported that there was some domestic violence involved but that Paul never seriously injured her. Mary Elizabeth told Bart, her counselor, that she could not bring herself to file for divorce because in the eyes of the Church, divorce is a sin. If she were to find someone else, she would not be permitted to remarry in the Church. Mary Elizabeth indicated that she had always been a devout Catholic and had raised her four children in the church. She said that much of her social life revolved around church activities and relationships. She reported that if she were to divorce Paul, she would lose not only her marital status but her spiritual and social support as well.

Discussion Questions
1. What do you see as the major issues with which Mary Elizabeth must deal?
2. How does Mary Elizabeth's religion (Roman Catholic) influence the ways she thinks about her alternatives?
3. How would you work with Mary Elizabeth given that the teachings of her church are contributing to her difficulty in deciding whether or not to divorce her husband?
4. Using information from Chapter 2 on models of faith development, which model seems to fit well for working with Mary Elizabeth? Which stage does she appear to be in?
5. What resources in the community or elsewhere might be useful in working with Mary Elizabeth?
6. What issues would emerge for you personally in working with Mary Elizabeth? How do you think these issues would affect your counseling relationship or therapeutic effectiveness?

Ibrahim

Ibrahim is a 33-year-old Muslim immigrant from Jordan. He is married and has five children. His supervisor referred him to the company's employee assistance counselor, Carla, because he thought Ibrahim's usual high quality work performance was slipping into unacceptable levels of productivity. Reluctantly, Ibrahim agreed to see a counselor. When he arrived at Carla's office, his brother, his brother's wife and two children, his wife, and two of his five children accompanied him. When asked about his symptoms, he reported feeling tired and lethargic. He said he had lost his appetite and found it difficult to concentrate at work. Ibrahim volunteered that he was skeptical of mental health services and reported that he prayed to Allah for all his needs. Ibrahim also indicated that his nuclear and extended family members would all want to be involved in any decisions made about his health or treatment.

Discussion Questions

1. What do you see as the major issues with which Ibrahim must deal?
2. Which, if any, of the faith development models from Chapter 2 seem to apply to Ibrahim? In which stage of which model would you place him?
3. What treatment approaches do you think might be helpful for Ibrahim?
4. How should Carla handle the fact that Ibrahim has brought a family entourage with him to counseling?
5. If you were his counselor, what questions would you ask Ibrahim so you could gain a deeper understanding of the importance of Islam for him and how it impacts his daily life?
6. How could you draw on Ibrahim's religious resources to fortify your treatment interventions?
7. What issues would emerge for you personally in working with Ibrahim? How do you think these issues would affect your counseling relationship or therapeutic effectiveness?

Raya

Raya is a 27-year-old Caucasian who began practicing Mahayan Buddhism during college. She became immersed in her religious practices and would not let anything, including relationships, interfere with her hours of meditation. Raya's boyfriend, Brian, appreciated Raya's calm and contemplative personality, but he resented the time she spent meditating and reading spiritual literature. He and Raya sought counseling from Jeremy to improve their relationship. Once in counseling, Brian complained that Raya had become so disciplined about her vegetarianism, meditation, and abstinence from alcohol and caffeine that she was "not much fun to be with." Raya acknowledged her devotion to Buddhist ways and reported that she felt torn between Brian's demands and those of her religion. She offered that sometimes she was "compulsive" in her attempts to obtain perfection, and that she did not tolerate failures in herself nor in others. Brian revealed that he cared for Raya and wanted to be "at the head of her parade." Instead, he said he felt like he was "bringing up the rear." Brian reported that he had "dabbled" in Buddhism, but could not commit to it in the ways that seemed important to Raya.

Discussion Questions

1. What are the clinical issues that Raya and Brian are facing?
2. How do you think that issues of religion are affecting this couple's relationship?
3. What do you know about the central beliefs of Buddhism that might be helpful to Jeremy in counseling Raya and Brian?
4. If you were counseling Raya and Brian, what questions would you ask them about the role of religion in their relationship? What other questions would you ask to help you uncover the issues that are keeping them stuck?

5. What resources would you recommend for Jeremy in counseling this couple?
6. What issues would emerge for you personally in working with Raya and Brian? How do you think these issues would affect your counseling relationship or therapeutic effectiveness?

Sharma

Sharma is a 23-year-old graduate student from India. She has been living in England since she began college at age 18. Sharma was raised a Hindu and has maintained a commitment to her religion despite having let some of her practices such as meditation "slide" while she has been in school. Sharma sought counseling in the University's counseling center because she was feeling pressured by her parents to return to India and marry a husband whom her family had chosen for her. Although Sharma had dated very little during her stay in England, there were several male students who were interested in her and for whom she had affection. Sharma told her counselor, Janelle, that she felt torn between Western ways of dating and marriage and those of her family and tradition. She was anxious to explore relationships of her own choosing, but she was frightened of the sexualized culture in which she found herself and longed for the safety of home and the way of life she had always known.

Discussion Questions
1. What are the central issues Sharma is facing?
2. How could Janelle use some of the principles of Hinduism to work with Sharma's dilemma?
3. What questions would you ask Sharma if you were her counselor?
4. What do you think is the impact of Sharma's bicultural experience on her current situation?
5. What resources would you suggest for Janelle in working with Sharma?
6. What issues would emerge for you personally in working with Sharma? How do you think these issues would affect your counseling relationship or therapeutic effectiveness?

Thomas

Thomas is a 53-year-old Caucasian male who has been divorced from Vicky for seven years. He sought counseling with Ben because he was feeling "burned out" in his career and was seeking a new direction. During the intake session, Thomas reported that he was interested in a holistic approach to counseling and that he hoped that Ben would be sensitive to his spiritual leanings. When asked about the nature of his spirituality, Thomas indicated that he had rejected the Protestant Christianity of his parents and had found himself drawn to Eastern traditions. Moreover, Thomas revealed that he had had paranormal experiences that he considered both "psychic" and "spiritual." He said that he would like to tap into his spiritual power in hopes that it would help him find a new career path.

Discussion Questions

1. How would you frame Thomas' problem?
2. What do you think Ben needs to know to help him work effectively with Thomas?
3. What questions would you ask Thomas if you were his counselor?
4. How could you appropriate Thomas' spirituality in service of his therapy?
5. What resources could Ben tap into that could assist him in counseling Thomas?
6. What issues would emerge for you personally in working with Thomas? How do you think these issues would affect your counseling relationship or therapeutic effectiveness?

SUGGESTED ACTIVITIES

Use a Fishbowl Role-Play with These Cases

Consider having some of your classmates play the roles of the clients and counselors in the cases just described. If the logistics of the room allow for it, place the "clients" and "counselors" in the center of the room in the "fishbowl" and the remaining students in a circle around them. Have different students role-play the "clients" and "counselors." Students observing from the outside circle should use their notes from the "Discussion Questions" sections to organize their thinking about the cases. They should also be prepared to play the role of the counselor if the current counselor needs assistance or wants to rotate out of the role. After about 10 minutes of counseling, the instructor may ask the "clients" and "counselors" how they think their session is going. Then, students in the outside ring may offer observations and alternative directions for the "counselors" to take during the remainder of the session. Also, new "counselors" may be substituted after the break.

Visit a Place of Worship That Is the Most Different from Your Own Tradition

Research the presence of various world religions in your community. Find out what kinds of activities, worship opportunities, and services are offered. Attend at least one of these events and answer the following questions:

1. What was the most surprising aspect of your experience with another religion?
2. What occurred that you had expected?
3. What new understandings did you gain about this religion after having this experience?

4. What did you learn from this visit that could help you in counseling someone from this religion?
5. What aspects of the experience made you feel uncomfortable? What do you think was the source of this discomfort?
6. What aspects of the experience were comfortable for you? To what do you attribute your comfort?

Interview a Leader from a Religious or Spiritual Tradition

Select a religion or spiritual tradition about which you know little or feel uncomfortable. Arrange to conduct a short interview with a leader in this tradition. Consider using the following questions as guidelines for your interview:

1. If you had to describe in three to four sentences the essence of your religion or spiritual tradition, what would you say?
2. What do you think is the strength of your religion or spiritual tradition?
3. What is your tradition's position on these social issues: abortion, premarital sex, divorce, alcohol use, homosexuality, or others?
4. How does your tradition view counseling and other mental health services?
5. What do you think counselors need to know about your tradition to better serve people who share this religious or spiritual orientation?

Invite a Speaker

If your institution has a religion department, consider inviting a member of that faculty whose specialty is world religions to speak to your class. Consider having class members write their questions about various religions on slips of paper before the speaker's visit. Ask the speaker to address the questions generated by class members.

SUPPLEMENTAL READINGS

World Religions

Armstrong, K. (1993). *A history of God.* New York: Knopf. This book is a scholarly approach to "the 4000 year quest of Judaism, Christianity, and Islam." It is a comprehensive (more than 400 pages) review of these monotheistic religions.

Earhart, H. B. (1993). (Ed.). *Religions and traditions of the world.* San Francisco: HarperSanFrancisco. This large (more than 1000 pages) edited volume contains detailed information about the major world religions. The data is well-researched, placed in its historical context, and readable.

Pagels, E. H. (1981). *The gnostic gospels.* New York: Vintage Books. In this book, the author explores the gnostic tradition within Christianity, both from an historical and contemporary perspective.

Smith, H. (1958). *The religions of man.* New York: New American Library. Huston Smith is a well-known writer in the area of world religions. This book is his classic treatise on the subject. Though dated, in this book the author provides readers with a vibrant sense of the major religions.

New Age

Bloch, J. (1998). *New spirituality, self, and belonging: How new agers and neo-pagans talk about themselves*. Westport, CT: Praeger. This book is one in a recent series entitled, "Religion in the Age of Transformation." In it, Jon Bloch reports the results of his qualitative study of 22 adults who called themselves New Agers or Neo-Pagans. This draws out the themes that emerged and links them to current sociological theory.

Chandler, R. (1988). *Understanding the new age*. Dallas, TX: Word Publishing. For the first two thirds of this book, Chandler provides a comprehensive look at persons, practices, and ideas related to the New Age movement. He discusses new age business including some of the journals, centers, and products available. The final third of the book is Chandler's personal treatise written from his traditional, orthodox Christian perspective.

Frost, W. P. (1992). *What is the new age? Defining the third millennium consciousness*. Lewiston, NY: Edwin Mellen Press. In this book, William Frost presents an in-depth coverage of the new age phenomena from a variety of perspectives. He draws in theory from across disciplines to help the reader understand the place of the new age movement among religious traditions and psychological, philosophical, and sociological theories.

Lesser, E. (1999). *The seeker's guide: Making your life a spiritual adventure*. New York: Villard. In this book, the author provides readers with guidelines for finding meaning in their lives. She analyzes the New Age movement, making an appropriate critique of its pitfalls and liabilities.

Needleman, J. (1970). *The new religions*. Garden City, NY: Doubleday. In this book, world religion professor, Jacob Needleman develops a phenomenological approach to the new age movement and acknowledges that he himself is a seeker. In this well-researched, scholarly book, he analyzes various Eastern traditions and their impact on the modern new age orientation. He deals even-handedly with various spiritualities, including the occult.

Wicca

Adler, M. (1986). *Drawing down the moon*. New York: Beacon Press. This book is one of the most comprehensive modern texts on witchcraft today.

Grist, T. & Grist, A. (2000). *The illustrated guide to Wicca*. New York: Godsfield Press. This easily read book is a handbook for the uninitiated to understand the Wiccan religion. It is straightforward and includes a number of rituals and spells.

RavenWolf, S. (2000). *To ride a silver broomstick: New generation witchcraft*. St. Paul, MN: Llewellyn. Silver RavenWolf is a member of the Wiccan Priesthood. Her guidebook for aspiring witches includes how-tos for spell-casting, conducting rituals, divinations, and celebrations. Her down-to-earth style and humor make the book fascinating reading.

ASSESSING RELIGIOUS AND SPIRITUAL BELIEFS AND VALUES

CHAPTER 4

INTRODUCTION

The moment a client walks into your office, you have already begun the process of appraisal. Whether you are aware of it or not, you are making judgments about the client based on his or her appearance, gender, race, age, tone of voice, manner of dress, affect, interpersonal style, and other attributes. As we begin to work with clients, we are constantly assessing who they are as people, what their problems are, how severe their distress is as a result of those problems, what resources they bring to their situation, and which interventions might be most suitable to help them address their issues and concerns. In this chapter, I focus on more formal methods of assessment, including global approaches and those associated specifically with religious and spiritual issues. I present information regarding the purposes and principles of assessment, various types of clients and kinds of religious or spiritual problems, and multiple assessment methods. In addition, I introduce and describe specific paper-and-pencil instruments and review their usefulness in counseling. Finally, I devote a section of this chapter to the characteristics of unhealthy religion or spirituality and suggest how some cults can exemplify such pathology.

PURPOSES OF ASSESSMENT
To Understand Worldview and Context

It is important to conduct assessments when working in the area of spirituality and counseling for several reasons. First, it is important *to understand clients' worldviews and the context in which they live.* Clients come to us from a variety of backgrounds with an array of religious and spiritual beliefs that might or might not be central to the way they conduct their lives. To understand how clients appropriate their religious/spiritual beliefs, to grasp the degree of impact their beliefs have on their behaviors, and to identify the cultural milieu that surrounds such beliefs and practices, counselors must inquire about these dimensions through an assessment process. What is expressly challenging about working with clients' religious and spiritual beliefs is precisely what makes assessment so crucial: the diversity of beliefs and the peculiar ways these beliefs present themselves both between and within religious or spiritual traditions. For example, Madeline, a 38-year-old Caucasian identified herself as a Christian when she came to counseling. When asked about her beliefs she responded, "Oh, I'm not really sure what I believe. I was raised a Lutheran, but to be honest, I don't know how that is any different from a Baptist, a Presbyterian, or a Methodist. I just think of myself as a Christian. I haven't really thought about *what* I believe about God or Jesus or the Bible . . ." Her counselor asked Madeline how her religion affected her daily life, and Madeline said, apologetically, "I guess it really doesn't make a big difference . . . I try to be a good person and follow the Golden Rule, but that's about it." On the other hand, Glenn, a 40-year-old Caucasian client also claimed to be a Christian. When asked about his belief system, he announced he was a "born-again Christian." His counselor asked Glenn to explain what the term "born-again Christian" meant to him. Glenn answered, "It means that I have accepted Jesus Christ as my personal savior and that I am striving to live my life according to his teachings." Glenn went on to say that his "born again" experience led to a total reordering of his lifestyle, including his abandoning drinking alcohol and smoking and his committing 10% of his income to his local church. These clients were similar in age, race, and religious affiliation, but they reported vastly different belief systems and religious experiences. Whereas one (Madeline) was associated with Christianity only nominally, the other (Glenn) was an enthusiastically committed Christian whose daily activities and life orientation has undergone major transformation because of his new-found faith. Thus, one reason we engage in an assessment process with our clients is to gather relevant data regarding their perspectives and practices so that we do not make faulty assumptions about how their religious or spiritual beliefs function in their lives. By learning about how our clients see the world and their place in it, we can become more empathic and less biased in our work with them.

Another important aspect of clients' context is that of their faith community (Gorsuch & Miller, 1999). Some clients might think that they are unwelcome in their church, synagogue, mosque, or other spiritual group because of their life situation (e.g., divorce, remarriage, gay, lesbian, bisexual or trans-gendered orientation). For others, their problems could be barriers to their attendance or participation in their community of faith (Gorsuch & Miller, 1999). In the first case, it could be critical for counselors to help clients evaluate whether or not their existing faith community is currently a good fit for them or if they need to search for a group better suited to their circumstances. In the second case, counselors can assist clients in regaining entry into their faith community or can consider increased participation as one mark of the success of treatment (Gorsuch & Miller, 1999).

Evaluating clients' understanding of their religious traditions and doctrines can be an important aspect of assessing context. Sometimes clients are distressed because they have misunderstood the meaning of certain religious beliefs or practices and might feel guilty for holding views that they think are contrary to their tradition. Others are simple uninformed or confused about what their particular religious community believes and values. Under these circumstances, and with the permission of the client, consultation with clergy or other religious or spiritual leaders could provide knowledge and insight for both the client and the counselor (Gorsuch & Miller, 1999; Kelly, 1995; Richards & Bergin, 1997).

To Facilitate Client Self-Exploration

Many clients come to counseling with little sense of the content of their religious or spiritual beliefs and how those beliefs shape their thoughts, feelings, and behaviors. Some clients enter counseling because they experience a crisis of meaning and must grapple with questions regarding the purpose of their lives and what they most value. Assessing clients' history, beliefs, values, and religious and spiritual practices can enable clients to be proactive in owning or changing their perspectives, making decisions, and taking charge of their life directions (Campbell, 1990). Using assessment results by integrating them into a holistic picture of the client's world can stimulate clients to take a fresh view of their problems and to consider alternative ways of addressing them (Goldman, 1990).

Humberto, a 45-year-old Hispanic male came to counseling after the tragic death of his wife and two children in an automobile accident. Humberto was devastated by the loss of his family and felt he had no place to turn. His counselor, Miranda, helped Humberto explore the sources of support and strength in his life. She asked him about his religious or spiritual connections and their significance. Humberto reported that in the past 20 years he had been totally consumed by the necessity of providing for his family. He had worked two jobs and had often fallen into bed exhausted without even eating a meal or interacting with his family. As a result of his interview with Miranda and completing some instruments designed to measure religious and spiritual health, Humberto discovered that he had a deep faith whose resources he had forgotten. He vowed to attend worship at a Spanish-speaking Roman Catholic church, the tradition of his extended family for generations. Miranda's assessment became the vehicle for Humberto to re-discover his religious roots and, in turn, he began to view his grief as a wake-up call to readjust his values and his lifestyle.

To Assist in Diagnosis

Malony (1985) suggested that assessing the religious and spiritual domain could assist counselors in determining how spirituality might be related to clients' presenting problems. By using various forms of assessment, counselors may be able to determine the degree to which clients' religious and spiritual beliefs are contributing to or maintaining their distress (Worthington, 1989). For example, Jill, a 23-year-old graduate student sought counseling for depression. After taking a personal history and inquiring about Jill's religious/spiritual beliefs, her counselor Derek gained special insight into Jill's situation. Jill reported that she had been a devout Mormon all her life. She had attended church, had been involved in family activities, had taken on mission work as prescribed by her religion, but was feeling guilty because she had lapsed in some of her religious activities during her rigorous course of graduate study. Derek helped Jill to see that her depression was brought on partly by her belief that she needed to be perfect in everything, especially in her religious duties. When she could not meet those self-imposed demands, Jill became depressed. In this case, had Derek not completed an assessment that included Jill's religious beliefs, he might not have been able to pinpoint a contributing factor to her distress.

To Explore Religion and Spirituality as Client Resources

A growing body of literature points to religion and spirituality as protective factors for persons' physical and mental health (Miller & Thoresen, 1999). Researchers have shown that spiritual and religious involvement is predictive of later health outcomes across various domains including physical (Levin, 1994), mental (Bergin, 1983; Larson, Pattison, Blazer, Omran, & Kaplan, 1986; Larson et al., 1992), and substance use disorders (Gorsuch, 1995). Moreover, religious and spiritual communities can be the source of support for clients (Duncan, Eddy & Haney, 1981; Koltko, 1990; Pargament et al., 1987; Pargament, Silverman, Johnson, Echemendia, & Snyder, 1983) because they can provide a sense of belonging, safety, purpose, structure, and opportunities for giving and receiving service (Richards & Bergin, 1997). Assessing clients' potential for garnering social and spiritual support and other services from faith communities provides counselors with valuable information about other resources that could be tapped on behalf of their clients' well-being.

To Ascertain the Degree of Health or Pathology in Clients' Belief Systems

Religion and spirituality can be associated with improved physical health, emotional well-being, and social adjustment (Batson, Schoenrade, & Ventis, 1993; Bergin, Masters, & Richards, 1987; Gartner, Larson, & Allen, 1991; Payne, Bergin, Bielema, & Jenkins, 1991; Richards, 1991). However, it is well known among clinicians that religion and spirituality are also likely to present themselves in unhealthy or pathological forms (Galanter, 1996; Lovinger, 1984, 1996; Meadow & Kahoe, 1984; Meissner, 1996; Pruyser, 1971). According to Richards and Bergin (1997), some examples of religious activity that could be considered unhealthy include demonic possession, obsessive preoccupation with one's sinfulness, ecstasy or frenzy, a pattern of denominational shifting, spiritual depression, speaking in tongues in settings where this practice is not valued, sudden conversion, and panic with religious themes. In addition, Meadow and Kahoe (1984) pointed to other religious experiences including delusions, compulsions, and masochism in their list of unhealthy or pathological religious behavior. (A more detailed discussion of the characteristics of healthy and unhealthy religion is found later in this chapter.)

To Uncover Religious and Spiritual Problems

Richards and Bergin (1997) argued that sometimes clients' religious and spiritual concerns or doubts cause their psychological distress. Comprehensive assessment of the relationship between clients' emotional issues and their spiritual beliefs or experiences (or the lack thereof) can provide clues for deeper exploration. For example, some clients who have low self-esteem and are haunted by shame and guilt might also question their spiritual nature and their God-given self-worth. Others who experienced abuse or abandonment by parents or caregivers might question the notion of a providential and loving God.

Jacob, a 56-year-old Jew, sought counseling with Sarah because of his unrelenting grief after the death of his wife, Deborah, in an automobile accident. In addition to the terrible guilt he felt for having been the driver in the fatal crash, Jacob also felt alienated from God. He told Sarah that he had been a faithful Jew his entire life, had attended synagogue regularly, not just during holy days and festivals, and that he had given substantial sums of money to local Jewish charities. Jacob kept wondering why God would punish him so horrendously. In this case, Sarah's assessment of Jacob's doubt and his understanding of God's character became a means for Jacob to redefine his faith.

Turner, Lukoff, Barnhouse, and Lu (1995) noted several other spiritual problems that should be assessed. Counselors who are aware of these religious issues could be successful in helping their clients reevaluate their belief systems to mitigate their distress.

One common religious problem is *changing denominations or conversion to a new faith*. Such a move brings with it some inevitable loss regardless of whether or not the change was voluntary. Counselors might want to help clients grieve lost traditions or practices that have been meaningful.

Intensification of practices or adherence to beliefs can cause distress in some clients. It is important for counselors to consider the purpose of such intensification and how that change is connected to areas of clients' distress.

Conditional love is another potential spiritual problem. Most religious doctrine holds that God's love is freely and graciously given. However, some clients come to believe that they are not chosen to receive God's love. Because of this belief, they feel isolated and rejected by the Supreme Being.

Instant peace is the notion that because of their faith people should immediately feel peace in the face of suffering or tragedy. Helping clients realize that coming to terms with trauma can be a long process rather than an instantaneous one can relieve their guilt.

Some clients are involved with religions that *guarantee healing*. They purport that if believers have enough faith or pray hard enough they can effect healing in themselves or others. When this benefit does not occur, clients can be thrown into a faith crisis. Faiver, Ingersoll, O'Brien, & McNally (2001) pointed out that there is a difference between healing and cure. Some people can be healed of anger, resentment, or frustration without being cured of their infirmities. Counselors can assist clients in making this distinction.

Imperfect clergy pose another religious problem for some clients. Despite their ordination, not all clergy are trustworthy or inspired by God. Sometimes clients present for counseling because they are experiencing a conflict between their own understanding of their faith and that presented by a particular clergyperson. Counselors may be called on to help clients evaluate the genuineness and trustworthiness of their religious leaders.

Emphasis on monetary rewards is a hallmark of some religions. Some clients have come to believe that if they have faith in God they will be rewarded with material blessings. Moreover, some have been told that if they give a certain amount of their income to their church or religious organization they will be guaranteed to get that much or more in return. Counselors might need to help clients realize that a cultivated spirituality may provide blessings, but does not necessarily guarantee fiscal prosperity.

Other religions preach *"salvation by works"* meaning that if believers have faith, engage in good deeds, meet others' needs (even when doing so endangers health or safety), contribute financially, and serve unrelentingly in any capacity then they will attain enlightenment or will go to heaven. This religious orientation can become an extreme burden for some clients, contributing to their overall distress. Helping clients examine their beliefs in this area can be an important task for counselors.

Irrational submission is a tenet of some religions. Because of this belief, some clients accept without scrutiny the dictates of their religious leaders. Again, such an approach to religion can create serious conflict in believers who are attempting to be faithful. Counselors can assist such clients in critically evaluating their religious leadership and asking themselves if they are really required to submit to such leadership unconditionally.

Related to irrational submission is the religious problem of *passivity*. Some clients are led to believe that they must not take initiative in solving their problems because they are to wait for God to take care of their dilemmas. Such passivity can create or exacerbate depression. By helping clients affirm their God-given human agency, counselors can address this religious difficulty.

Textual exclusivity refers to the belief that unless an issue is discussed in the authoritative writings of a religion, it is irrelevant. Sometimes clients become immobilized in their attempts to find solutions to their problems because the particular problems are not addressed in their scriptures. Counselors can help clients understand the historical context of their authoritative writings and understand that although scriptures can provide inspiration they do not tell us everything about everything.

Another problem encountered by some clients is the belief that *God will provide the perfect mate*. This notion may include the idea that someone has already been chosen for each person by God. Or, it could mean that believers must suspend their ability to choose a mate to wait for God to select one for them. Some clients may present for counseling because they are uncertain whether a particular relationship is the one destined for them. Again, counselors might have to help clients understand how their freedom of choice can be exercised in the context of the type of relationship they believe God would like them to have.

The *Pollyanna perspective* refers to the idea that everything that happens to us is good. Nothing could be further from the truth; however, clients who hold this belief might be distressed by trying to make sense of untimely deaths and other tragedies. Counselors might be called to assist clients in acknowledging that life has its polarities, including good and evil. The Pollyanna perspective also provides a good excuse for not confronting the negative aspects of one's own life (Faiver et al., 2001).

Another religious problem has been called "bullet-proof faith." Clients who hold this belief contend that if they have a strong enough faith, they can be insulated from pain and suffering. Many world religions indicate much to the contrary. Indeed, the whole focus of Job's story in the Bible is to have readers reflect on the suffering incurred by a man of faith. Counselors might have the opportunity to help clients explore the ways that faith could facilitate their coping with pain and suffering rather than avoiding it.

To Determine Appropriate Interventions

Another reason for conducting religious and spiritual assessment is to gather data that will assist in treatment planning and in selecting appropriate interventions (Gorsuch & Miller, 1999; Malony, 1985; Richards & Bergin, 1997). Careful assessment of clients' religious and spiritual beliefs helps counselors make judgments regarding which aspects of clients' religion or spirituality could be used as resources in treatment and which ones could be contributing to the problem. Furthermore, assessing clients' religious and spiritual perspectives enables counselors to decide whether or not to use interventions that are uniquely religious or spiritual (such as prayer, meditation, forgiveness). Assessment results also provide counselors with information so that they can determine if using spiritual interventions might be contraindicated (as with clients who are psychotic, delusional, or obsessive-compulsive) (Richards & Bergin, 1997).

ASPECTS OF ASSESSMENT

When beginning religious and spiritual assessment, it is important to consider how to approach the task and what areas of clients' lives should be explored. At first, it is helpful to conduct a general assessment of clients' functioning, their understanding of the problem, what solutions they have attempted, and whether or not religious or spiritual issues appear to be germane to the presenting problem. When clients' worldviews or their problems seem related to spirituality or religion, then it becomes necessary to inquire further about these connections. Because religion and spirituality are complex and multifaceted constructs, Richards and Bergin (1997) listed nine dimensions of religiosity that ought to be investigated when conducting a thorough assessment in the religious or spiritual domain. These areas include: (a) worldview, (b) religious affiliation, (c) level of orthodoxy, (d) religious problem solving, (e) spiritual identity, (f) image of God, (g) value-lifestyle congruence, (h) doctrinal knowledge, and (i) religious and spiritual health and maturity.

Worldview

In assessing clients' worldviews, it is important to determine whether or not their belief systems are theistic and include some kind of deity or Higher Power. In addition, it is critical to understand how clients see the nature of the world, their place in it, the existence of evil, and how much free will they have in determining their destiny. Counselors should try to ascertain if clients hold Western or Eastern perspectives and how those views translate into daily life. Richards and Bergin (1997) suggest asking the following questions:

> How did human beings come to exist? Is there a Supreme Being or Creator? What is the purpose of life? How should people live their lives to find happiness and peace? What is moral and ethical? Why is there suffering, grief, and pain? Is there life after death? (p. 176)

Religious Affiliation

Although discovering clients' religious affiliations or the traditions of their families of origin doesn't tell counselors everything about clients' religious and spiritual orientation, it does provide some helpful information for further exploration. Knowing that Brent was raised as a Southern Baptist but later became a Buddhist helps his counselor consider ways in which both religious identities could continue to influence his worldview and his current difficulties. Moreover, discovering that clients have had no religious training or experience reminds counselors (especially those with a religious or spiritual perspective) not to make assumptions about clients' backgrounds or beliefs.

Level of Orthodoxy

Clients' level of orthodoxy refers to how closely their belief systems and behaviors are aligned with the traditions and doctrines of their religions. When inquiring about how clients' actual beliefs and practices are related to their religious traditions counselors might discover a variety of answers. Carolyn, for example, indicated that she was raised a Catholic, but that she hasn't attended church for the past 15 years and that she "never did believe any of it anyway." This response is quite different from Colin's emphatic answer: "I've been a Lutheran all my life and I try very hard to live my life in accordance with my church's doctrine." Knowing clients' level of orthodoxy can be useful because the more religiously orthodox the clients are, the more likely they will want to work with counselors who share their religious persuasions (Worthington, 1988). Also, clients who are religiously orthodox are more likely to view their spirituality or religion as relevant to their psychological concerns (Richards & Bergin, 1997). Further, clients who are not terribly orthodox in their beliefs or behavior are most likely to hold negative views of religion. Such clients might not be receptive to the use of religious or spiritual interventions or to counselors making links between their presenting problems and their religious affiliation.

Approach to Religious Problem-Solving

It is helpful for counselors to know how clients approach solutions to their problems. Pargament (1996) suggested three ways religious clients tend to deal with their difficulties. First are persons who are self-directing. They approach their problems with the understanding that it is up to them to take the lead in finding solutions. They might rely on God or a Higher Power to provide them support and strength as they take the initiative in problem-solving. Second are those who defer to God, whose responsibility it is to render solutions to their problems. Third are those who view problem-solving as collaborative; that is, persons are partners with God in joint problem-solving efforts. Counselors who assess the problem-solving style of their clients might be helped in determining the types of interventions that would be appropriate with various kinds of clients. It follows that self-directing clients might not be open to particular religious interventions, whereas deferring clients might defer to the counselors as well as to God (Richards & Bergin, 1997). Collaborative problem-solvers may be the most receptive to using spiritual or religious interventions in psychotherapy (Richards & Bergin, 1997).

Spiritual Identity

Spiritual identity is concerned with how clients perceive themselves in relation to God and the universe. Some clients believe that a loving God created them and imbued them with self-worth. These clients typically hold that God providentially cares for them. Other clients do not have a theistic worldview, nor do they necessarily believe that they have any particular worth or purpose. According to Richards and Bergin (1997), clients who have positive self-esteem rooted in their religious and spiritual beliefs are better able to cope with their problems than are those who do not.

God Image

Assessing clients' God image means that counselors inquire not only about a belief in God but also about what kind of God clients believe in. It is important to know if a client's God is loving, benevolent, merciful, forgiving, involved, and accessible or if her God is vengeful, aloof, punishing, or impersonal (Benson & Spilka, 1973). How people conceive of God shapes their relationships with other people, is related to the hopefulness they feel about their lives in general and the outcome of counseling in particular, and is a clue for counselors about how self-worth might or might not be internalized.

Value-Lifestyle Congruence

The congruence between values and lifestyle indicates that clients are behaving in ways that are consistent with their professed values, whether they are ethical, moral, religious, or spiritual values. When people are able to live in ways that conform to their beliefs, they are better functioning and healthier psychologically. Assessing the relationship between values and lifestyle is an important aspect of religious and spiritual appraisal. When clients' behavior is incongruent with their values, there is more likelihood of interpersonal conflict as well as guilt and anxiety that issue from not living up to standards they claim they hold (Richards & Bergin, 1997).

Chloe, a 25-year-old law student sought counseling with Kenneth because pervasive guilt and anxiety immobilized her. Chloe reported that she had been raised in a Pentecostal-Holiness Christian tradition that forbade drinking, smoking, premarital sex, and dancing. Although she claimed she had rejected the teachings of her religion and that she no longer attended worship in any setting, she was unable to disengage from the behavioral standards that were part of her past. Chloe told Kenneth that she was living a "party lifestyle," and despite the demands of law school, she was out every night until 2:00 A.M. drinking, smoking marijuana, and dancing. She confessed that she had been in a series of unfulfilling sexual relationships that she believed were to blame for her intense guilt and shame. Kenneth helped Chloe to understand that even though she thought she had abandoned her religious values, they were still strong enough to induce significant guilt when she violated them. Through the process of counseling, Kenneth helped Chloe come to a critical decision-point regarding both her values and lifestyle. Ultimately, she was able to alter the severity of her values and to change her lifestyle enough to attain congruence between the two. As a result, Chloe became less guilt-ridden and more content.

Doctrinal Knowledge

One of the most challenging aspects of working with clients' religious and spiritual beliefs is the complexity of religious doctrines and the variety of ways that clients construe them. It is not uncommon for clients to be active members of churches, synagogues, or mosques, yet to possess incomplete or incorrect information about their religious doctrines. Such misinformation often creates dissonance for clients in their values and lifestyle congruence. Thus, counselors working with religious clients must help them examine the tenets of their religion that could be contributing to their distress. Obviously, how doctrinal misinformation affects clients depends on the religion, the doctrine, the client, and the interaction between them. Richards and Bergin (1997) argued that counselors who are well-versed in the tenets of their clients' religion will be best able to help these clients sort through, examine, and modify their beliefs. Of course, not all counselors are prepared to engage in theological or doctrinal conversations with their clients. When counselors do not feel competent in this area, it is appropriate for them to consult with clergy in their communities to get assistance.

Religious and Spiritual Health and Maturity

Much has been written about the difficulties associated with separating healthy and mature religion and spirituality from that which is unhealthy or immature (Allport, 1950; Allport & Ross, 1967; Chandler, Holden, & Kolander, 1992; Ellison, 1983; Malony, 1985). Allport began by suggesting that persons whose religious sentiments were intrinsically motivated were healthier than were those whose religious sentiments were externally motivated. Allport and Ross (1967) described people with an intrinsic religious orientation as those who

> find their master motive in religion. Other needs, strong as they may be, are regarded as of less ultimate significance, and they are, so far as possible, brought into harmony with the religious beliefs and prescriptions. Having embraced a creed, the individual endeavors to internalize it and follow it fully. It is in this sense that he *lives* his religion. (p. 434)

In addition, they described persons whose religious orientation was extrinsic as persons

> who use religion for their own ends . . . Persons with this orientation may find religion useful in a variety of ways—to provide security and society, sociability and distraction, status and self-justification. The embraced creed is lightly held or else

selectively shaped to fit more primary needs . . . The extrinsic type turns to God, but without turning away from self . . . (p. 434)

Although these distinctions are neither perfect nor comprehensive, they do provide counselors with a starting point for assessing what type of role religion plays in the lives of clients. Clients whose religion is expressed intrinsically tend to be healthier psychologically and experience less incongruence between their beliefs and their lifestyles. In contrast, clients whose religion is primarily extrinsic may find less consistency between their professed values and their actual behaviors. These clients could benefit from examining their faith so they can integrate it better with their lifestyles.

ASSESSMENT METHODS

Having identified some reasons for conducting religious and spiritual assessments and having noted a variety of topics that might be considered appropriate client aspects to assess, now we turn the methods by which we conduct these appraisals. One central principle of assessment in general is to approach the task through multiple methods (Cromwell & Peterson, 1983). This approach suggests that it is impossible to gain a thorough picture of our clients by having them complete an intake form or by simply administering a paper-and-pencil inventory. In essence, engaging in the assessment process is like looking through a collection of lenses until clients' situations come into clear focus. When counselors assess clients' religious and spiritual worlds, they are seeking to better understand their clients' worldviews and how those perspectives are related to clients' presenting problems. It is essential then, to use assessment methods that assist us in obtaining the most complete picture of our clients' worlds. In the following section, I introduce assessment methods including the intake form and the clinical interview, including family history, and I list a battery of paper-and-pencil instruments designed to measure various aspects of religion and spirituality.

Intake Forms

Intake forms are an expedient means for gathering information from clients at the beginning of the counseling process. Clients are asked to complete forms that ask for demographic data as well as a description of the problem, problem solving approaches that have been tried, previous counseling experiences, medical history, substance use, family background, abuse issues, and other information the counselor deems important. Intake forms vary based on the counseling setting. Some community agencies require very detailed intake forms, including the results of mental status exams and other assessments. Some private practitioners use rudimentary intake forms and gather the remaining information in a clinical interview. Regardless of the level of detail, it is helpful to include some questions about religion and spirituality on the intake form. Faiver and O'Brien (1993) developed a form that helps counselors assess clients' religious beliefs. They urge counselors to have clients provide information about their relevant religious history, denomination, faith of origin, current denomination or faith, role of faith in their life, including conflicts and supports. Kelly (1995) suggested including religion and spiritual practices on a checklist of possible problem areas or concerns that clients bring to counseling. In addition, other areas to be explored are (1) family of origin's religion, (2) client's current religion, (3) membership in a religious community, (4) degree of participation in a religious community, and (5) satisfaction with religious or spiritual practices. In addition, Richards and Bergin (1997) also include questions about religion and spirituality on their intake forms. They employ questions such as

> Do you believe in a Supreme Being? Do you believe you can experience spiritual guidance? Are you aware of any religious or spiritual resources in your life that could be used to help you overcome your problems? Do you believe that religious or spiritual influences have hurt you or contributed to some of your problems? Would you like your counselor to consult with your religious leader if it appears this could be helpful to you? Are you willing to consider trying religious or spiritual suggestions from your counselor if it appears that they could be helpful to you? (p. 193)

Richards and Bergin (1997) also ask clients to elaborate on these questions if they choose to do so. Clients who are not interested in having religion and spirituality addressed in counseling do not complete the more detailed intake questions just listed.

When religious and spiritual issues are present in the initial contact clients have with their counselors, clients learn that their counselors are open to discussing religion and spirituality with them. Moreover, when clients choose to provide significant information about their religious or spiritual background, their experiences, or the ways in which they believe their spirituality intersects with their difficulties or provides them coping resources, then counselors have a greater understanding of the whole person. Counselors also have some openings for following up client responses in a clinical interview or later in the counseling process.

The Clinical Interview

The clinical interview provides an opportunity for counselors to discuss clients' situations with them face to face. Intake forms are often completed during clinical interviews such that the two assessment modalities are combined. In other cases, clients fill out a brief intake form before the initial counseling session, and in the clinical interview, the counselor follows up on the intake information or probes further areas that might be related to clients' presenting problems.

In conducting the clinical interview, counselors may inquire about clients' religious and spiritual background, their belief systems, and the spiritual resources available to them from their religious or spiritual heritage (Yost,

1986). In addition, counselors may ask clients to reflect on what is important to them in the context of their presented distress. In this way, counselors can help clients review and possibly adapt their value systems such that their beliefs and behaviors become more congruent. Questions from the intake form suggested earlier can be used in a clinical interview. In addition, Stoll (1979) suggested using questions regarding clients' sense of hope. It is often helpful to ask, "What is your source of strength and hope? What helps you the most when you feel afraid or need special help?" (p. 1575). Spiritual practice is another domain to probe. Stoll's (1979) questions in this area are the following: "Are there any religious [or spiritual] practices that are important to you? Has being sick [discouraged, worried upset, distressed] made any difference in your practice of praying? Your religious [or spiritual] practices? What religious [spiritual, inspirational] books or symbols are helpful to you?" (pp. 1576–1577). Gorsuch and Miller (1999) suggested exploring clients' sense of meaning or purpose in life. Some possible questions are these: "What things are most important to you? What gives your life purpose or meaning?" (p. 52). One advantage of having a conversation with clients about their religious and spiritual persuasions and experiences is that counselors can ask follow-up questions and can assist clients in making connections between their spiritual perspectives and their current difficulties. Another advantage to the clinical interview is that few assessment instruments are reliable, valid, and standardized for use in clinical settings (Richards & Bergin, 1997). A disadvantage to the clinical interview is that it is more time-consuming, and clients could feel that counselors are dwelling too long on the religious and spiritual aspects of their problems.

The Spiritual Genogram

The spiritual genogram is an assessment approach (Frame, 2000) used by counselors to obtain a broad picture of a family's religious and spiritual background. The spiritual genogram could be constructed by clients as a homework assignment and used in a subsequent counseling session to enhance the clinical interview.

A genogram is a map of several generations of a family. It includes family structure and composition, using symbols to depict who is in the family and biological and legal relationships to one another (McGoldrick, Gerson, & Shellenberger, 1996). Other demographic information is included, such as births, marriages, divorces, and deaths. Family members' notions about nature of their family relationships are also included. For example, disengagement, enmeshment, conflict, and alliances might be designated to give a richer depth to the family diagram (Friedman, Rohrbaugh, & Krakauer, 1988). The genogram has been especially useful in helping clients learn about the transmission of family patterns across generations and to reduce emotional reactivity in therapy (Kuehl, 1995). Used specifically to identify spiritual and religious issues, the spiritual genogram provides clinicians with a tool for assessing the ways in which clients' religious/spiritual heritage continues to affect their current beliefs and practices.

Using the spiritual genogram involves four steps: (1) creation of the spiritual genogram, (2) questions for further reflection, (3) connection with one's family of origin, and (4) integration into the global therapeutic endeavor. First, therapists instruct clients about how to capture the family structure by drawing a three-generational genogram, including as much information as possible about family members. Using the symbols offered by McGoldrick, Gerson, and Shellenberger (1996), significant events and their dates such as births, marriages, divorces, remarriages, and deaths are included. Gender of each person is indicated, as well as information about adoption, stillbirth, abortion, twins, unmarried couples, and the quality of family relationships.

In the spiritual genogram, religious/spiritual traditions are indicated by a variety of colors (Lewis, 1989). For example, Roman Catholics may be drawn in red, Protestants in orange, Jews in blue, Muslims in black, Mormons in gray, Buddhists in yellow, Unitarians in purple, agnostic or atheist in pink, personal spirituality in green, and no religious/spiritual affiliation in brown. If religious/spiritual heritage is unknown, no color is added.

The color-coding on the spiritual genogram indicates interreligious marriages and reveals the variety of religious backgrounds that influence clients. Some couple or family conflicts previously outside the clients' awareness can be readily apparent when the religious/spiritual history is depicted in color on the genogram. Sources of attitudes, morals, values, and beliefs are also uncovered and can be addressed within the full scope of therapy.

Important events occurring in the religious life of family members should be noted on the genogram. For example, baptisms, first communions, confirmations, bar and bat mitzvahs, and other rituals and rites of passage may be included. If family members were highly involved in their religious congregations, significant events in the religious community can be added. These events could include building projects; death of a well-loved priest; a congregational relocation; sexual misconduct of a clergy member leading to dismissal; the closing of a church, synagogue, mosque, or other religious center; changing racial/ethnic/class composition in the congregation; or other important events. (See Figure 4.1 for an example of a spiritual genogram.)

To indicate that particular family members left a religious/spiritual organization or movement, square brackets ([ ]) are placed around these persons on the genogram. If family members converted to other religions or joined other types of churches, synagogues, or mosques, clients add another layer of color around the family member's symbol, indicating the nature of the change. Dates for leaving and joining religious organizations should be indicated. This aspect of the genograms reveals the stability or fluidity of religious/spiritual affiliation.

The symbol ⇌ illustrates religious or spiritual closeness between family members. For example, a large, extended Southern Baptist family in which all members attend church together several times a week could be represented in this way. For this family, religion provides a bond that connects family members across generations. Or, perhaps the absence of any identified religion or spiritual practice is the foundation of another family. Conflict

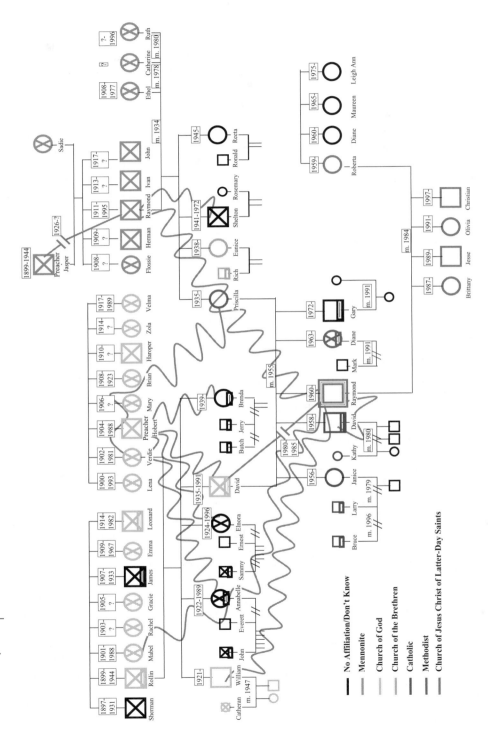

FIGURE 4.1 | SPIRITUAL GENOGRAM EXAMPLE

No Affiliation/Don't Know
Mennonite
Church of God
Church of the Brethren
Catholic
Methodist
Church of Jesus Christ of Latter-Day Saints

between family members that has religious or spiritual roots is depicted by the symbol ᙗᙗᙗᙗᙗ . Perhaps such conflict between a father and son occurred when the son married outside of his religion. Or, perhaps a daughter and her husband have disagreements over the new baby's circumcision because of differing traditions around this religious practice. Representation of religious conflicts on the genogram often reveals that other, more obvious discord is grounded in religious or spiritual friction or disagreement. Counselors ask clients to describe the religious/spiritual antagonism or conflict, and to note the specifics on their genograms. When a divergence of beliefs or moral values is the source of the problem, those are recorded as well. Counselors then inquire about the extent to which these conflicts are being maintained in their current couple or family relationships.

When the standard genogram has been constructed, the counselor is now ready to explore further the role and function of religion and spirituality in couples and families. Such exploration may be accomplished through a homework assignment in which both partners (or an entire family) write the answers to the following questions. Responses to these questions might assist clients in discovering how religious or spiritual beliefs, experiences, rituals, and practices are connected to their therapeutic issues. In addition, the questions could help clients "externalize" religious issues and thus reduce emotional reactivity in their relationships.

1. What role, if any, did religion/spirituality play in your family of origin? What role does it play now?
2. What specific religious/spiritual beliefs are most important for you now? How are they a source of connection or conflict between you and other family members?
3. How is gender viewed in your religious/spiritual tradition? Ethnicity? Sexual orientation? How have these beliefs affected you and your extended family?
4. What patterns emerge for you as you study your genogram? How are you currently maintaining or diverting from those patterns?
5. How does your religious/spiritual history connect with your current distress, or with the problem you presented for counseling? What new insights or solutions occur to you based on the discoveries made through the genogram? (Frame, 2000).

When clients return for the following session, they are invited to share their insights with the counselor and the family members. Occasionally symbols, lines, and colors are modified to reflect new information that emerged during the reflection process. When more information is needed, clients are encouraged to connect with members of their family of origin.

In many cases, such contacts enable clients to retrieve vital information from the past and to renegotiate relationships in the present (Bowen, 1978; Framo, 1976; Williamson, 1981). In this step, clients are able to request information from parents, siblings, aunts, uncles, and cousins to clarify religious or spiritual events and meanings construed by the family. A private, face-to-face contact between clients and their family members is recommended (Hof & Berman, 1986). When the clients reassemble with the therapist for another session, insights, observations, and new information is added to the genogram.

The following questions may be helpful to clients wishing to explore religious or spiritual issues in their families of origin:

1. How important do you think religion/spirituality was in our family?
2. How do you think your experience of the religious/spiritual atmosphere was similar to or different from mine?
3. Which members of our extended family seem to have had the most power when it came to religion/spirituality? Which ones had the least? How do you think the use of power relative to religion/spirituality affected our family and our relationships with one another?
4. How difficult do you think it has been or would be for family members to seek a different spiritual or religious path than the one with which we were raised? Who in our family would be supportive and why? Who would not be supportive and why?
5. How do you think religion/spirituality has been a source of strength and coping for our family? How do you think it has interfered in our family's relationships? (Frame, 2000).

When the religious/spiritual genogram is fully constructed, the counselor asks the clients questions such as, "How has this process provided insight into your current problem?" and "What have you learned about yourselves and each other that can be used to address your marital or family difficulties?" At this stage in the counseling process, the counselor helps clients to make connections between past beliefs, experiences, and family of origin issues and their current problems. One result is that clients often develop a greater objectivity and appreciation for the ways in which they have been shaped (consciously or unconsciously) by the role of religion and spirituality in their families. They are often able to move beyond blaming each other into seeking solutions for current dilemmas.

Paper-and-Pencil Instruments

Using written measures in the assessment process is sometimes appropriate when counselors want to obtain more specific information about a particular area of client functioning. It is important, however, to be certain that administering a paper-and-pencil instrument will result in improving one's understanding of the client's world and circumstances and that the results will contribute to designing and implementing effective treatment plans. When selecting written measures, it is critical that they conform to acceptable standards of reliability and validity and that the norms have been established for the population to which one's client belongs. It is not appropriate to administer an assessment instrument to a 70-year-old Asian American if the instrument has not been normed on Asian Americans or older persons. To do so would mean that the results might not be valid for that person. When the instruments being used conform to acceptable measurement principles and when their results will serve the clients' best interest, paper-and-pencil measures can be useful tools in the counseling process. We turn now to some specific instruments that counselors could consider incorporating in their practice.

Several inventories of a general nature include a few items pertaining to religion or spirituality. Some of these include the *Family Environment Scale* (Moos & Moos, 1981), the *Mooney Problem Checklist-C* (Mooney, 1950), the *Campbell Interest and Skill Survey* (Campbell, 1992), and the *Family Crisis-Oriented Personal Evaluation Scales* (F-COPES) (McCubbin & Thompson, 1991). Another group of instruments falls into the category of measures of wellness. These measures also include spirituality as an aspect of wellness or holistic functioning. Some examples are the following: *The Life Assessment Questionnaire* (DeStefano & Richardson, 1992; National Wellness Institute, 1983; Palombi, 1992), the *Wellness Inventory* (Palombi, 1992; Travis, 1981), the *Holistic Living Inventory* (Stoudenmire, Batman, Pavlov, & Temple, 1985, 1986), and the *Wellness Evaluation of Lifestyle* (Witmer, Sweeney, & Myers, 1994). Although these and other instruments like them include items related to religion or spirituality, they are focused on broader constructs. The results of these assessments could be useful to counselors in suggesting the need to explore further clients' spirituality.

A growing number of instruments, however, have been developed to measure various aspects of spirituality. Several of these instruments are described here:

- *The Spiritual Assessment Inventory* (SAI) (Hall & Edwards, 1996) is a 43-item measure of spiritual maturity based on a Judeo-Christian theological perspective and object relations theory (Stanard, Sandhu, & Painter, 2000). Five aspects of spiritual maturity are measured: awareness, quality (including instability, grandiosity, and realistic acceptance) and defensiveness/disappointment. Respondents select answers on a continuum from 1 (*not true about me*) to 5 (*true about me*). All the scales except Grandiosity have good reliability, and construct validity was demonstrated by correlating the SAI with the Bell Object Relations Inventory (BORI) (Stanard, Sandhu, & Painter, 2000).
- *The Index of Core Spiritual Experiences* (INSPIRIT) (Kass, Friedman, Leserman, Zuttermeister, & Benson, 1991) is a 7-item instrument that measures experiences that convince the respondent that God exists and a perception that God dwells in the individual (Stanard, Sandhu, & Painter, 2000). Questions 1 through 6 have different response options for each item. There are 13 parts to question 7. The first 12 parts are scored from 1 (*I have never had this experience*) to 4 (*convinces me of God's existence*). There is also an open-ended question in which persons list other spiritual experiences (Kass et al., 1991). INSPIRIT boasts high internal consistency reliability at .90 using Cronbach's alpha coefficient. Concurrent validity was demonstrated between INSPIRIT and Religious

Orientation Inventory (ROI), the Medical Symptom Checklist (MSCL), and the Inventory of Positive Psychological Attitudes to Life (IPPA) (Stanard, Sandhu, & Painter, 2000).

- *The Spiritual Well-Being Scale* (SWBS) (Ellison, 1983) is a 20-item instrument that measures both religious well-being and existential well-being. The former is related to the respondents' concept of God, and the latter is concerned with life purpose and satisfaction apart from religion (Stanard, Sandhu, & Painter, 2000). Six possible responses to item statements range from strongly agree to strongly disagree. The SWBS demonstrates strong test-retest reliability and concurrent validity. Concurrent validity was established by correlating the SWBS with the UCLA Loneliness Scale and the Purpose in Life Test, Intrinsic Religious Orientation, and self-esteem (Stanard, Sandhu, & Painter, 2000). Some difficulties with this instrument are its lack of norms and its ceiling effects (not being able to measure clinically significant scores above the mean) (Ledbetter, Smith, Vosler-Hunter, & Fischer, 1991). This instrument has been well-researched, and its results could provide useful information for clients who affirm a belief in God.

- *The Spiritual Health Inventory* (SHI) (Veach & Chappel, 1992) is an 18-item scale in which respondents select the degree of agreement or disagreement with the each item statement. Six possible responses range from strongly agree to strongly disagree. The inventory is based on a concept of well-being that includes biological, psychological, social, and spiritual dimensions (Stanard, Sandhu, & Painter, 2000). This instrument is used to measure the spiritual aspects of well-being. Other instruments measure the other dimensions (Veach & Chappel, 1992). Four factors emerged from a factor analysis: Personal Spiritual Experience (belief in and experience of a Higher Power), Spiritual Well-Being (benefits from having an active relationship with a Higher Power), Sense of Harmony (feeling harmony as a result of spiritual beliefs), and Personal Helplessness (lack of self-efficacy). Initial validation studies indicate some positive correlations with physical and mental health, but more research needs to be conducted in this area (Stanard, Sandhu, & Painter, 2000).

- *The Spirituality Scale* (Jagers & Smith, 1996) is a 20-item measure that assesses spirituality from an Afrocultural perspective. According to Jagers and Smith (1996), spirituality pervades African American experience and extends beyond church attendance or formal religious activities. African American spirituality is more centered in worldview and sense of African identity. Respondents are asked to select from six choices, from 1 (*completely false*) to 6 (*completely true*). Jagers and Smith (1996) have reported good internal consistency and test-retest reliabilities as well as construct validity. Evidence also indicates that this instrument discriminates between African American and Caucasian respondents and could thus be considered an appropriate measure of the construct of Afrocultural spirituality (Stanard, Sandhu, & Painter, 2000).

- *The Spirituality Assessment Scale* (SAS) (Howden, 1992) is a 28-item scale that requires respondents to rate the various statements from 1 (*strongly disagree)* to 6 (*strongly agree).* This instrument has strong theoretical underpinnings in psychology, sociology, theology, philosophy, and nursing (Stanard, Sandhu, & Painter, 2000). This instrument measures four major concepts: Unifying Interconnectedness, Purpose and Meaning in Life, Innerness or Inner Resources, and Transcendence (Howden, 1992). The SAS has good internal consistency and high face validity. One strength is that its spiritual construct is not linked to any particular religion (Stanard, Sandhu, & Painter, 2000).

- *The Human Spirituality Scale* (HSS) (Wheat, 1991) is a 20-item, five-point Likert-type instrument that measures three content dimensions of spirituality: (a) larger context or structure in which to view one's life, (b) an awareness of life itself and other living things, and (c) a reverent compassion for the welfare of others (Wheat, 1991). Cronbach's alpha reliability coefficient of .89 was reported by Wheat (1991) for the HSS. Accordingly, a panel of expert raters determined content validity, and construct validity was demonstrated through a series of factor analyses. This instrument shows promise for measuring spirituality that is not necessarily theistic.

According to Gorsuch and Miller (1999), the National Institute on Aging and the Fetzer Institute were collaborating to develop a core instrument to measure the constructs of religiousness and spirituality that are related to healthy outcomes. The preliminary work included a 40-item instrument with items such as "religious preference of affiliation, spiritual experiences, organizational religiousness, private spiritual practices, religious social support, religious coping, beliefs and values, commitment, forgiveness, meaning, and overall self-rankings" (Gorsuch & Miller, 1999).

See Table 4.1 for a summary of paper-and-pencil inventories.

Although several instruments have been developed to measure various aspects of religion or spirituality, there are two major challenges in this area. The first is that of measuring spirituality apart from religion. Relatedly, many of the instruments that measure either religion or spirituality or both do so from a Christian or at least a theistic perspective. What is lacking are reliable and valid measures that are oriented toward spirituality that is grounded in other religions and worldviews and that do not presume the existence of God. A second area of concern is whether measures are ethnically and culturally sensitive. Many existing measures have not been normed on diverse populations. Moreover, research on the *Spirituality Scale* (Jagers & Smith, 1996) suggests that some ethnic groups have a unique confluence of culture and spirituality that might not be evident in results obtained by using certain instruments.

TABLE 4.1 | PAPER-AND-PENCIL INVENTORIES

Instruments That Contain a Few Items Related to Religion or Spirituality	Instruments That Include Spirituality as an Aspect of Wellness	Instruments Focused Specifically on Spirituality
Family Environmental Scale (Moos & Moos, 1981)	*The Life Assessment Questionnaire* (DeStefano & Richardson, 1992; National Wellness Institute, 1983; Palombi, 1992)	*The Spiritual Assessment Inventory* (Hall & Edwards, 1996)
Mooney Problem Checklist-C (Mooney, 1950)		*The Index of Core Spiritual Experiences* (INSPIRIT) (Kass, Friedman, Leserman, Zuttermeister, & Benson, 1991)
Campbell Interest and Skill Survey (D. Campbell, 1992)	*The Wellness Inventory* (Palombi, 1992; Travis, 1981)	
Family Crisis-Oriented Personal Evaluation Scales (F-COPES), (McCubbin & Thompson, 1991)	*The Holistic Living Inventory* (Stoudenmire, Batman, Pavlov, & Temple, 1985, 1986)	*The Spiritual Well-Being Scale* (Ellison, 1983)
		The Spiritual Health Inventory (Veach & Chappel, 1992)
	The Wellness Evaluation of Lifestyle (Witmer, Sweeney, & Myers, 1994)	*The Spirituality Scale* (Jagers & Smith, 1996)
		The Spirituality Assessment Scale (Howden, 1992)
		The Human Spirituality Scale (Wheat, 1991)

ASSESSING HARMFUL OR PATHOLOGICAL RELIGION OR SPIRITUALITY

Although there is considerable research about the positive benefits of religion and spirituality (Bergin, 1983, 1991; Gartner, Larson, & Allen, 1991; Pargament & Park, 1995), there is also concern about their deleterious effects. Therefore, as counselors assess their clients' religious and spiritual leanings, counselors should consider whether religion or spirituality is contributing to their clients' positive mental health.

The difficulty of evaluating the "health" of clients' religious or spiritual beliefs or practices is in selecting a set of criteria to use in making such a determination. Meissner (1996) has pointed out the futility of attempting to judge the quality of spirituality or religiosity based on the objective truth of a certain set of beliefs. What is more critical is how a belief system affects clients' lives and functioning. If, for example, a client believes in reincarnation and thus becomes a strict vegetarian, the belief itself is not necessarily the subject of scrutiny. The question is whether the belief and the corresponding practice (vegetarianism) issue in a positive or negative life experience for the client. In another instance, if a client believes she is going to spend eternity in hell because of her various sins, it is possible for the clinician to focus more on the client's neurotic use of the belief system (as a vehicle for unconscious guilt motives) (Meissner, 1991) than on the veracity of a belief in hellfire and damnation.

Some cases appear to be more readily diagnosable relative to religious or spiritual health or pathology. Religious paranoia, delusions, or hallucinations associated with actively psychotic clients may be considered unhealthy, despite the theory that in some way these religious manifestations are connected to the client's own personality structure and self-system. Counselors are mindful that a psychotic client claiming to be the Buddha or the Virgin Mary is exhibiting religious delusions. Nevertheless, counselors working with clients with thought-disorders must enter the clients' worlds and try to understand how the paranoia or delusions function.

Assessing the health of other religious or spiritual manifestations is not so easy when the impact of a belief system on a client or client family is unclear. Clinebell (1984) developed a set of criteria by which to evaluate whether or not people's religion enhances or diminishes human wholeness in all aspects of their lives. I have paraphrased Clinebell's criteria here:

Do the religious or (spiritual) beliefs, attitudes, and practices of persons . . .

- give people meaning, hope, and trust in the face of life's tragedies?
- provide creative values and ethical sensitivities for personally and socially responsible living?
- nurture the transcendent aspects of people's lives?
- inspire reverence and love of life and nature?
- provide for renewal of a sense of trust and belonging in the universe?
- bring inner growth and enrichment from peak experiences?
- offer growth-enabling community of caring?
- build bridges with people of different values and faith systems?
- improve love and self-acceptance rather than fear and guilt?
- foster self-esteem and a contribution of their strengths toward constructive living?
- stimulate inner freedom and autonomy?
- enable them to develop deep relationships of mutual growth?
- encourage sex and assertiveness and their use in affirming rather than repressive ways?
- foster realistic hope by encouraging the facing of reality rather than the denial of it?
- enable them to move from appropriate guilt to reconciliation with self, others, and God?
- encourage lifelong development of beliefs and values that keeps step with their intellectual growth?
- provide means of keeping in touch with the creative resources of the unconscious through myth, symbol, and ritual?

- create in them awareness of damaging institutional practices and encourage them to work toward overturning corporate repression.
- encourage people to balance the rational and emotional aspects of their personalities and their religion?
- provide trust, hope, and meaning in the face of inevitable loss and make them more aware of life's preciousness?
- encourage the celebration of the goodness of life and foster a commitment to living creatively in response to such a gift? (p. 118–119).

| CASE | YOLANDA |

Yolanda, a 25-year-old graduate student sought counseling because she was "feeling trapped in some relationships" that she considered detrimental to her well-being. When asked to describe her situation, Yolanda told her counselor, Jason, that she had been attending a prayer group in the home of a couple in their 40s. She had met Alicia through her work in an insurance office and been drawn to her because of "her strong faith and sense of what was right and wrong." After having attended the prayer meetings for about six months, Yolanda said she felt like she was being judged and that she had to conform to the expectations of the leaders, Alicia and Bill, or else "something bad would happen to me." Yolanda told Jason that she thought religion was supposed to "build you up and make you feel stronger," but she confided that she often felt fearful, guilty, and anxious. Yolanda also indicated that Alicia and Bill were very controlling, demanded allegiance to them and to their "rules for Godly living." Jason helped Yolanda to see that the religion she had adopted shared many of the characteristics Clinebell (1984) listed as unhealthy. Over time, Yolanda became strong enough to separate herself from Alicia and Bill and to seek a religious experience that was more growth-oriented, nurturing, and affirming.

Richards and Bergin (1997) adapted Bergin's (1993) work on adaptive versus maladaptive values and lifestyles, including religion and spirituality. Their schema includes dimensions of what they consider healthy or unhealthy. The adaptive lifestyles and values are intrinsic rather than extrinsic. Those for whom religion (spirituality) is intrinsic are authentic people whose faith is lived and whose behaviors and values are congruent. Those for whom religion (spirituality) is extrinsic are often using religion as a means of gaining something else. Religion or spirituality is not an integrated aspect of the self. Adaptive religion is growing, creative, and experiential and enables people to make sense of the ambiguous and paradoxical aspects of life. Maladaptive religion, on the other hand, is more perfectionistic. Its followers tend to be overcontrolled and anxious. They can be self-punitive and become stagnant in their practices. Healthy religion is evidenced by its openness to reform, renewal, and change. Those for whom religion is healthy tend to be more egalitarian and tolerant of differences. Unhealthy religion is authoritarian, rigid, dogmatic, absolutist, intolerant, and controlling. Adaptive religion has a social dimension that involves networking and the establishment of cooperative, kinship-type relationships. Maladaptive religion is narcissistic, and competitive. It can involve manipulation and deception. Healthy religion is nurturing, caring, protective, empathic, and issues in caring. Unhealthy religion is aggressive, abusive, violent, power-seeking, and insensitive. Adaptive religion is reconciling and forgiving, and those who embrace it aim at open problem-solving. Maladaptive religion is dependent, submissive, passive aggressive, and conflict-avoidant. Healthy religion is inspiring and prophetic. When it includes mysticism, that element is grounded in reality. Unhealthy religion is hyperspiritual and might involve the occult or evil. Its mystical aspects do not evidence good reality testing (Richards & Bergin, 1997, p. 189).

CASE | DIANA

Diana, a 34-year-old Caucasian, began practicing Buddhism when she was in college. She attended lectures, workshops, and retreats and took seriously the tenets of her faith. Diana came to counseling to "work through her anger at her father for abandoning the family when she was a child." Her counselor, Martin, asked Diana about her religious beliefs and practices. He found that her religion was well-integrated into her daily life. She experienced meditation as a powerful force for renewal, and her connection with others in her faith circle provided her with significant social support. Martin concluded that Diana's religion was a healthy aspect of her life and a resource on which she could draw while she faced the difficult issues in her past.

CULTS

Cult Characteristics

In the past four decades—since the rise of Scientology, Divine Light Mission and Hare Krishna in the 1960s to the Jonestown massacre in the 1970s to the Waco tragedy of the 1990s—religious cults have attracted the attention of the media, college students, religious leaders, parents, and mental health service providers. Although a comprehensive treatment of the subject is beyond the scope of this book, it is important to address the cult phenomenon in the context of the intersection of religion and spirituality and psychotherapy.

It is difficult, if not impossible, to offer a cogent definition of cults because of the significant differences among them in structure, organization, authority, and function (Collins, 1991). There are at least 10 different types of cults: (a) neo-Christian religious, (b) Hindu and Eastern religious, (c) occult and satanic, (d) spiritualist, (e) Zen and other Sino-Japanese philosophical-mystical, (f) racial, (g) flying saucer and other outer-space phenomena, (h) psychology or psychotherapeutic, (i) political, and (j) self-help, self-improvement, and lifestyle systems (Singer & Lalich, 1995, pp. 13–14). Given such a range of cultic varieties, it is easy to understand why definition is elusive. Nevertheless, we can suggest some general characteristics that are common across various types of cults. First, cults have an authoritarian structure. The leaders of cults are regarded as the absolute authority in all matters. These leaders might delegate some responsibilities to others, but ultimately, the leaders have the final say about everything. Sometimes the cult's authority is evidenced by a formal, hierarchical organization. Other times, the authority comes from the leader's personal charisma (Collins, 1991; Singer & Lalich, 1995). Cults also appear to be innovative and exclusive. Their leaders claim to bring some new knowledge, practice, or wisdom that is the cure-all for life's problems. Another aspect of the authoritarian structure is that cult leaders claim that their members are "chosen" or "special" and that they are somehow superior to other people who are outside of the cult (Singer & Lalich, 1995). Cults also tend to have a double standard when it comes to ethical requirements. Members are encouraged to be open and honest and to disclose everything to the leader, but simultaneously deceive and manipulate nonmembers (Singer & Lalich, 1995).

Second, cult leaders are considered charismatic or even divine. Such leaders might claim to have special knowledge or a divine mission. Many have the personal charm to attract members, to convince them to cut themselves off from their family members and other outside relationships, and to take control of members' possessions, finances, and lives. Cult leaders often center veneration on themselves (Singer & Lalich, 1995). In some cases, spouses are required to separate and parents give over their children as a test of loyalty and commitment to the leader (Singer & Lalich, 1995).

Third, cult members are encouraged to conform to group norms. In many cases, cult members dress alike, think alike, and talk alike (Collins, 1991). In most cults, the leader scrutinizes all the details of everyday life. Codes of conduct are implemented, including dress codes, food restrictions, sexual practices, financial arrangements, and child-rearing (Galanter, 1996; Singer & Lalich, 1995). Such social control is possible because of the powerful influence of the forces of group cohesiveness, shared belief, altered consciousness, codes of conduct, and a charismatic leader's appeal (Galanter, 1996).

Fourth, cult members engage in shared beliefs, experiences, and practices. Some of these experiences are related to states of altered consciousness that are achieved through a variety of means such as meditation, drug usage, and intense group experiences. In the context of a powerfully charismatic leader, engaging in these practices develops strong affiliations between members and group identity formation (Galanter, 1996).

Fifth, many cult members are involved in communal living arrangements. This communal living approach forges the bonds of affiliation, leads many members to refer to each other as family, and creates clear boundaries between the cult and outsiders. Communal living also assists in maintaining affiliation and reinforces ongoing participation in the cult (Galanter, 1996).

Sixth, many cults require renunciation of the world (Collins, 1991). This regulation grows out of cult leaders' beliefs that they are gifted with the truth and that all other religions, beliefs, groups, and secular society are deluded, evil, or corrupt. Agreeing to reject the world's standards is often a prerequisite for membership and attaining the purity associated with the cult's mission or goals (Collins, 1991).

Seventh, many cults operate through a system of persuasion and thought control. In many cases, leaders intentionally engage in coordinated, planful efforts to take control of others so others will join, stay, and obey (Singer & Lalich, 1995). This process of thought and behavioral control can involve the lack of tolerance for diverse opinions, the threat of physical harm if one strays from the beliefs or routines, the threat of spiritual and mystical punishment for disobedience, the induction of psychological stress and guilt in converts for their prior ways of thinking, continual sensory overload with cultic propaganda, deprivation of sleep and food, and isolation from family members and others outside the cult (Collins, 1991). In addition, cult leaders might resort to the use of trance and hypnosis, trickery, the revision of one's personal history, peer pressure, and modeling and emotional manipulation to keep their members loyal to them and their causes (Lifton, 1961; Singer & Lalich, 1995).

Member Characteristics

There is the notion that normal people are not susceptible to cults and that only a person who was psychologically disturbed would be attracted to such a leader or organization. Unfortunately, such ideas are unfounded. Although some researchers found some psychological distress in young persons before they joined cults (Etemad, 1978; Levine & Salter, 1976), many cult inductees were undergoing normal transitions from adolescence to young adulthood (Nicholi, 1974). Some cult members reported coming from troubled families (Deutsch, 1975; Nicholi, 1974) or overly enmeshed families (Minuchin, Montalvo, & Guerney, 1967), but most cult members are not experiencing psychological distress. Most come from middle- and upper-middle-class families that are fairly well educated (Galanter & Buckley, 1978; Galanter, Rabkin, Rabkin, & Deutsch, 1979; Singer & Lalich, 1995).

Many adult cult joiners have undergone similar challenges to those of adolescents. They might have felt isolated from family and friends, felt insecure about their jobs or financial futures, experienced a loss of respect of authority figures, wandered away from their earlier religious ties, or sensed a loss of meaning in their lives. These realities make adults vulnerable to the approaches of cult leaders offering freedom from worries, inner peace, or some form of transcendent experience of Ultimate Reality.

Some people are more open to the lures of cult recruiters at particular times in their lives. Persons who have suffered losses, who are experiencing mild depression, or who are undergoing transitions in work, relationships, education, or geographical location are more susceptible to the attraction of cults. Although some people believe that cult-joiners were seeking out these groups from the beginning, most former cult members reported that they were looking for companionship, affiliation, and a way to serve others (Singer & Lalich, 1995).

What Keeps People from Leaving Cults

To people not involved in cults it seems preposterous that those who join them do not simply leave when they become disillusioned with the mission or disappointed in the leader. According to Singer and Lalich (1995), however, there are several reasons why cult members do not walk away from their groups. All these reasons have to do with the coercive psychological and social influences of the cult. First, cult members are unable to leave because of the shared beliefs that have created the bond between them and their compatriots. Second, they are loyal to the group and its leader and typically follow through on their commitments. Third, they trust in the leader and other authority figures, and they may be punished for raising doubt or questioning the process or experience. Fourth, peer pressure and lack of information keep people from leaving. Members are led to believe that there is something wrong with them if they speak out against the leader or any of the group's practices. In some cults, those who raise questions are belittled and isolated from the group. In addition, little information is made available to group members, and sometimes what they do know is inaccurate. Having little contact with the outside world also contributes to cult members' reluctance to leave. Fifth, exhaustion and confusion contribute the cult members' immobilization and inability to act. In some cults, members are expected to labor long hours with no time off, no recreational opportunities, and no intimate relationships. As a result, they lose sight of what has been important to them and become confused about who they are and what they really want. Sixth, people tend not to leave cults because they have been separated from the past. They have little or no contact with family and friends outside the cult. Their worlds have been reduced so that they rarely encounter persons who are not associated with the cult. They have no idea how they would function outside of the group. Seventh, people do not leave cults because they are afraid they might be stalked, punished, ostracized, or harmed in other ways if they defect. Because of the possible outcomes of leaving, cult members are often terrorized into staying. Finally, it is difficult for cult members to leave because of the guilt they might feel for having participated and committed themselves totally to the group. The shame associated with some cult activities might keep people from leaving. Singer & Lalich (1995) claimed that cult members' experience "enforced dependency" (p. 277). They suggested that cult members start out as autonomous individuals and later realize that they are completely dependent on the cult for all their social, family, and self-image needs and, ultimately, for their survival. Because of this type of dependency, cult members believe they would not be able to function outside the group.

Former Cult Members' Psychological Issues

Despite the difficulty in leaving just described, some cult members do find their way out, by coming to terms with the reality of the cult's deception, by getting physically and emotionally depleted, by getting angry, by getting thrown out by the cult leader, or by getting counseled out by relatives, friends, or mental health providers (Singer & Lalich, 1995). Regardless of how cult-members exit from their groups, most experience some psychological effects of leaving. Some examples are "relaxation-induced anxiety and tics, panic attacks, cognitive inefficiencies, dissociative states, recurring bizarre content, worrying over the reality of 'past lives.'" (Singer & Lalich, 1995, pp. 299–300). These side effects tend to be associated with cults that relied on techniques such as meditation, trance states, past-lives regression, and hyperventilation. Groups that relied on intimidation and other intense aversive emotional arousal techniques had former members who exhibited "guilt, shame, self-blaming attitudes, fears and paranoia, excessive doubts and panic attacks" (Singer & Lalich, 1995, p. 300). Regardless of the cult's approach, many former cult members reported "depression and a sense of alienation, loneliness, low self-esteem and low self-confidence, phobic-like construction of social contacts, fear of joining groups or making commitments, distrust of professional services, distrust of self in making good choices, problems in reactivating a value system to live by" (Singer & Lalich, 1995, p. 301). Indeed, some of these symptoms parallel what would be labeled Post Traumatic Stress Disorder (PTSD) in the *Diagnostic and Statistical Manual of Mental Disorders* (*DSM-IV*) (APA, 1994).

Treatment Issues for Former Cult Members

There is some controversy about appropriate interventions for persons who have left cults. Obviously, treatments need to be tailored to the presenting problems and symptoms, and clinicians must assess clients' mental functioning and note the adaptive as well as maladaptive aspects of group experience (Galanter, 1996). Deprogramming, a term that became popular during the 1970s, has come to refer to the involuntary treatment of cult members via forceful methods such as kidnapping. Current terminology concerning therapy with former cult members is "exit counseling" (Singer & Lalich, 1995).

Some issues that counselors must help former cult members face are addressing practical concerns related to daily living, psychological and emotional pangs that can be agonizing, developing new social networks and repairing old personal relationships if possible, and examining the philosophical and attitudinal perspectives adopted during their cult experiences (Singer & Lalich, 1995).

CASE EXAMPLES

Carlotta

Carlotta is a 62-year-old single female who sought counseling because she was unsure about moving in with Roland, who was 68. Carlotta told her counselor, Kathleen, she had never been married and had never been involved in a serious relationship with a man. She indicated that she was afraid to live with Roland for a variety of reasons, but mainly she was worried about "falling into sin." Kathleen asked Carlotta to explain what she meant by "falling into sin," and Carlotta said that she was a very religious person and that she had always been taught that sex outside of marriage was a sin. Even though she was attracted to Roland, she did not want to disobey God's law. Moreover, Carlotta indicated that she kept daily routines that included at least two hours of prayer and meditation. She stated that she was concerned that having another person so intimately involved in her life would mean that she might become lax in her efforts to serve others and that she might not be able to do everything she thought God was calling her to do.

Discussion Questions
1. If you were Carlotta's counselor, what questions would you ask her to help you understand her religious worldview?
2. What types of assessment methods would you use to clarify Carlotta's situation?
3. Which of the faith development models in Chapter 2 apply to Carlotta's case? In which stage of which model does she appear to fit?
4. Do you think Carlotta's religious lifestyle is healthy or unhealthy or some of both? What data lead you to this conclusion?
5. What counseling intervention would you consider using with Carlotta?
6. How would you know if your techniques were effective?
7. What personal issues does Carlotta's situation raise for you? How might these issues assist you or interfere with your counseling effectiveness?

Alexander

Alex is a 29-year-old male who is a software engineer for a computer company on the West Coast. He moved to California from Iowa six months ago. Recently, Julian, a counselor with the company's employee assistance program received a telephone call from Christine and Bruce, Alex's parents. They wanted Julian to talk with their son about his obsession with a spiritual group with which he had recently become involved. Christine and Bruce reported that Alex, who once was very communicative with his parents, had stopped calling them and acted very "distant" when they contacted him. In addition, Bruce said that Alex had given up his traditional, tailored wardrobe for robes and now exists on a diet of beans, rice, and seaweed. Christine was worried that Alex's lucrative salary was going to support his spiritual group's activities and that he was being entrapped in something manipulative and exploitative.

Discussion Questions
1. How do you think Julian should handle the telephone call he received from Bruce and Christine?
2. If Julian does meet with Alex, what questions do you think he should ask?
3. What other interventions would you advise Julian to employ?

4. From the information available, do you think Alex is involved in a cult? If so, what action would you take?
5. What is your personal reaction to Alex's situation and his parents' telephone call?
6. What resources would you need to assist you in working with this case?

Gail

Gail, 41, a Caucasian accountant, and her African American partner, Sally, 48, sought counseling with Nancy because they were experiencing significant conflict over the role of religion in their relationship. Gail told Nancy that she had been raised in a home where religion was eschewed in favor of intellectual and recreational pursuits. Sally indicated that she had been involved in a Christian denomination that had supported her medical career, affirmed her sexual orientation, embraced ethnic diversity, and offered her inspiration and opportunities for personal growth and community service. Gail and Sally indicated that the tension between them had grown because Gail wanted to spend Sunday mornings hiking or skiing but Sally was committed to attending worship services at her church. Gail claimed that "just being outside was a spiritual experience" for her. She maintained that she did not need to be sitting inside a church on a nice day. Because they had so little leisure time available, each woman wanted the other to spend that time with her. Gail begged Sally to skip church and head for the hills. Sally pressured Gail into attending worship and getting involved volunteering in the inner-city soup kitchen. Both Gail and Sally hoped Nancy could help them understand the underlying dynamics in their relationship and how they could manage the "religion issue" that caused turmoil in their relationship.

Discussion Questions
1. How would you frame Gail and Sally's problem?
2. What additional information would you like to gather from Gail and Sally about religion or spirituality in their lives?
3. How would you go about assessing the quality of religion or spirituality that each woman presents?
4. What role do you think religion is playing in Gail and Sally's relationship?
5. What interventions would you use if you were working with this couple?
6. What personal issues does this case raise for you? What countertransference concerns might get in the way of your effectiveness as a counselor with Gail and Sally?

SUGGESTED ACTIVITIES
Develop an Intake Form

Review some existing intake forms that might be available in your university counseling center, a community mental health center, or a private practice or a sample your instructor may provide. Using these examples as a guide, write your own intake form, including questions regarding religion and spirituality, that you believe are appropriate. Share your form with your classmates.

Conduct a Clinical Interview

Interview a fellow student, friend, or family member about his or her religious or spiritual background. Use the questions suggested in this chapter, brainstorm additional questions with other class members, or create your own questions. Write a brief summary report of your findings.

Complete Your Own Spiritual Genogram

Using the instructions provided in this chapter, create your own spiritual genogram. Gather information for at least three generations. Be sure to color-code the genogram, include a legend explaining symbols and colors. Consider using Genograms in Family Assessment (McGoldrick, Gerson, & Shellenberger, 1996) for details on appropriate symbols. Answer the questions listed in the section describing spiritual genograms. Share your genogram with a fellow classmate.

Complete a Paper-and-Pencil Inventory

Using the information provided in this chapter, go to your library and obtain a copy of one of the paper-and-pencil inventories that measures an aspect of religion or spirituality. Complete and score the inventory. Share the results with class members if you choose to do so.

Invite a Speaker

Ask your instructor to consider inviting a speaker to class who is knowledgeable about cults and other charismatic groups. Perhaps someone in your community has experience with exit counseling and could share expertise in this area.

SUPPLEMENTAL READING

Galanter, M. (1996). Cults and charismatic groups. In E. Shafranske (Ed.), *Religion and the clinical practice of psychology* (pp. 269–296). Washington, DC: American Psychological Association. In this chapter, Galanter, an expert on charismatic groups, presents research findings and characteristics of cultic organizations.

Kelly, E. W., Jr. (1995). Assessing the Spiritual/Religious Dimension in Counseling. In E. W. Kelly, Jr. *Spirituality and religion in counseling and psychotherapy* (pp. 131–187). Alexandria, VA: American Counseling Association. In this chapter, Kelly provides his own typology of types of clients and kinds of religious/spiritual problems that will appear in counseling. He also includes, in their entirety, some instruments cited in this chapter.

Meissner, W. W. (1996). The pathology of beliefs and the beliefs of pathology (pp. 241–267). In E. P. Shafranske (Ed.), *Religion and the clinical practice of psychology*. Washington, DC: American Psychological Association. In this chapter, Meissner provides an in-depth treatment of the issues of pathology in religion. The chapter is rooted in theological concepts and Christian doctrine but, nevertheless, provides interesting philosophical and psychological perspectives.

Richards, P. S., & Bergin, A. E. (1997). "Religious and spiritual assessment." In P. S. Richards & A. E. Bergin, *A spiritual strategy for counseling and psychotherapy* (pp. 171–199). Washington, DC: American Psychological Association. In this chapter, Richards and Bergin provide comprehensive treatment of assessment issues regarding religion and spirituality. They include sample intake forms, interview questions, and a detailed explanation of their criteria related to healthy and unhealthy forms of religion and spirituality.

Singer, M. T., & Lalich, J. (1995). *Cults in our midst*. San Francisco: Jossey-Bass. This book is one of the best authorities on cults. The authors take the perspective that cult experiences are harmful and members should be counseled out of them. The book contains several useful charts that illustrate the process of thought reform or brainwashing as well as the steps needed for clients' recovery from cult-induced psychological damage.

THE INTERSECTION OF RELIGION, SPIRITUALITY, ETHNICITY, AND CULTURE

CHAPTER 5

INTRODUCTION

In this chapter, I focus on the many ways that religion and spirituality are bound up with ethnicity and culture. By "ethnicity," I mean the "common ancestry through which individuals have evolved shared customs and values" (McGoldrick & Giordano, 1996, p. 1). Ethnicity has to do with a sense of "peoplehood" resulting from the combination of race, religion, geography, and cultural history. By "culture," I mean "the commonalities around which people have developed values, norms, family lifestyles, social roles, and behaviors in response to historical, political, economic, and social realities (Christensen, 1989, p. 275). In short, culture gathers all the aspects of one's life, including religion and spirituality, that give persons meaning, significance, and grounding in who they are and how they choose to live. Counselors must recognize that religion and spirituality cannot be compartmentalized and dealt with apart from clients' ethnicity and culture. Religion and spirituality shape and are shaped by ethnicity and culture.

It is also critical to realize that every person regardless of skin color has an ethnicity. This concept has been difficult for some white Americans to grasp because they are used to being the standard against which all other racial groups are compared. White Americans have tended to believe that "ethnicity" referred to characteristics of people *different* from them, and that "Americans" were those of European ancestry (Tataki, 1993). White Americans must begin to get in touch with the multifaceted roots of their ancestry and come to grips with the ways in which their ethnicity and culture affect their values, beliefs, relationships, and behaviors.

Addressing the interrelationship between religion/spirituality, ethnicity, and culture involves the challenge of providing helpful information about some of the major ethnic groups in America without becoming stereotypical or patronizing. Counselors need to understand that each client, even though belonging to a particular ethnic group, culture, or religion, might or might not share the characteristics attributed to that group. For example, Latino families are tremendously diverse, and knowing a client's nationality will be far more useful in understanding the client's culture than would simply the fact that he or she has been labeled "Latino" or "Hispanic."

Another major factor in addressing ethnicity and culture and their interaction with religion/spirituality is the client's level of acculturation, or the degree to which clients have appropriated the values, beliefs, lifestyles, and behaviors of the dominant culture. Clients who are less acculturated will tend to rely more on the beliefs and practices of their ancestors than will those of the dominant culture. Similarly, clients who see themselves as bicultural will feel comfortable with the ways of both their culture of origin and the dominant culture. Clients who are highly acculturated will most likely have adopted most of the dominant culture's values, beliefs, and practices. Paniagua (1994) suggested that generation, preferred language, and social interaction with members of one's own racial-ethnic group compared with interaction with members of other groups could be considered clues about clients' acculturation levels.

Another significant element that must be considered when working with clients of diverse racial-ethic backgrounds is the affect of class. Class distinctions are often at the root of conflict between ethnic groups or among members of less powerful groups among themselves (McGoldrick & Giordano, 1996). As McGoldrick and Giordano point out, ethnic differences wane among the most educated and upwardly mobile members of society who tend to dissociate themselves from their ethnic origins. These individuals might also withdraw from their religious affiliations and either gravitate toward different ones or abandon them altogether. As a result, various segments or generations in families can experience difficulties related to class differences.

General characteristics of various ethnic groups could provide some rudimentary keys to understanding a client's context; however, individual differences are always to be expected. It is neither possible nor desirable to pigeonhole clients of various racial, ethnic, religious, or spiritual groups to make them conform to some preconceived notion about their identity and lifestyle. What is more helpful to clients is for counselors to take the initiative to become informed about clients' heritage. Counselors should also inquire about how clients see themselves relative to their acculturation level, their sense of ethnic identity, and their interest in how these aspects of their lives intersect with the therapeutic process.

In this chapter, I present information about the general characteristics of five groups: European and Anglo Americans, African Americans, Latinos, Asian Americans, and Native Americans. These groups were selected because they compose the largest percentage of the U.S. population. There are, of course, other groups and subgroups whose ethnic and cultural backgrounds contribute to the diversity of the population. Thus, one limitation of such a chapter is not being able to be comprehensive enough to include every type of person or to represent every cultural milieu. Another limitation is the challenge of including general information that could be contradicted by individual differences. I acknowledge these limitations but hope that the content provided will still be helpful to readers.

In this chapter, I include data about religion and spirituality as well as indigenous healing traditions that could be significant for counselors working with a diverse clientele. I suggest that counselors collaborate with indigenous healers or religious leaders when doing so could benefit the client.

EUROPEAN AMERICANS AND ANGLO AMERICANS

Whites constitute nearly 80% of the U.S. population of 250 million (Giordano & McGoldrick, 1996). These persons include all those of European heritage. Although they come from nearly every country in Europe, these persons tend to be overlooked when the topic of "cultural diversity" surfaces (Roberts, 1995). Because many of them have been in the United States for three or more generations, they are likely to think of themselves as "Americans," rather than to focus on their European ancestry. Moreover, the similarity of race, religion, and language has provided white Americans with the privilege of choosing to accept or reject their ethnic identities—a choice that other racial and ethnic groups do not have (Giordano & McGoldrick, 1996). Nearly one-fourth of all Americans are descendents of English colonists whose names appeared in the first census data from 1790 (McGill & Pearce, 1996). The term, "Anglo-American" has been used to distinguish these Americans from those of other European descent. Anglo Americans have intermarried with descendents from other European immigrants, which suggests that another one-fourth of Americans have direct contact with Anglo American values (Allen, 1989). Interestingly, historical accounts reveal that Anglo Americans had difficulty accepting European immigrants and judged them as intellectually and culturally inferior (Banks, 1991; Perlmutter, 1992; Thernstrom, Orlov, & Handlin, 1980). Despite these differences, whites tend to be considered homogeneous, and the younger generation might not think of them as otherwise.

Values

There are differences in values between European and Anglo Americans based on their countries of origin; however, most whites have been influenced significantly by western ideals and by Judeo-Christian beliefs. A hallmark of

European/Anglo American values is rugged individualism. In fact, most believe that life struggles are centered in the self and that most problems can be overcome if enough individual effort is exerted. Indeed, any type of failure may be ascribed to personal weakness (Pearce & Friedman, 1980). Relatedly, independence is highly valued. People are expected to be strong, or at least project an air of strength and control. The mark of a young person's success is separating from the family of origin and becoming self-reliant and responsible to the degree that he or she might be perceived as self-centered by people from other cultures (McGill & Pearce, 1996). Furthermore, McGoldrick & Rohrbaugh (1987) found that Anglo Americans were less likely than other European Americans were to support the notion that it is important to lend assistance to other family members who needed it, regardless of the demand on one's time and energy.

Among many Anglo Americans, emotional restraint is highly valued. They are unlikely to behave boisterously in public, or disclose too much personal information for fear of burdening others (McGill & Pearce, 1996). When it comes to pain and suffering, Anglo Americans tend to suffer in silence and to criticize those who complain about their troubles. Anglo Americans tend to avoid open conflict, especially in public, and will try to solve problems through insight and reason using an emotionally controlled approach.

The quintessential value for European/Anglo Americans is hard work. For them, work is the key to success, independence, and a secure future. This notion of hard work grows out of the Protestant work ethic in general and specifically from the Calvinist belief that success, won by hard work, was evidence of both virtue and predestined salvation (McGill & Pearce, 1996). As a result, European/Anglo Americans often reframe many aspects of their lives in terms of work. They "work on" their relationships, "work" for a living, and "work on" their family lives. Some even turn their recreation into work, focusing on competition, achievement, and success.

One negative aspect of such an emphasis on work and success has to do with the affect of class. Because in America there has been the notion that economic prosperity was available to everyone, not to attain it is suspect (Rubin, 1976). Thus, poor whites feel simultaneously oppressed by their poverty and guilty about it, attributing their lack of economic success to personal inadequacy and inferiority. Middle-class whites look at the wealthy among them and believe they themselves have not done as well as they could have. Upper-class whites are afraid of losing what they have attained because of their personal failures (McGill & Pearce, 1996).

European and Anglo Americans are future-oriented. They see unlimited opportunities to "get ahead" through dedication and work. They tend to be optimistic compared with some other ethnic groups whose nature it is to expect trouble.

Even though many whites have strong ties to their families of origin, the value of independence can result in a kind of isolation among family members. Adult children are expected to move into their own homes, take jobs, and take care of themselves and their children. If they do not conform to this value, then parents often feel that they have failed to raise responsible children. The same value of self-sufficiency leads elder family members to lose self-esteem if they can no longer live independently. They fear becoming a burden to their children (McGill & Pearce, 1996).

Religion and Spirituality

Religion and spirituality are highly valued among white Americans. In fact, in a 1994 poll, 93% of Americans said they believed in a God who was personally involved in people's lives (Sheler, 1994). White Americans also hold dear the principle of separation of church and state and value the freedom to choose their own religion or to choose not to engage in any religious or spiritual practices at all.

Diversity is one major characteristic of religion and spirituality among white Americans. Actually, religion is the place in American culture where the various white ethnicities are the most visible. Moreover, groups such as Irish Catholics, French Canadians, Scottish Presbyterians, Finnish Lutherans, German Jews, Armenians, and Eastern European Jews, and Greek Orthodox are examples of how religion and ethnicity have forged strong bonds (Gordon, 1964; Greeley, 1969, 1974; Thernstrom et al., 1980). In addition, certain religions are influenced greatly by ethnic diversity. For example, Irish Catholics, Polish Catholics, and Italian Catholics share the same religion but express it very differently. For example:

> For the Irish, the Church is primary; other values, such as family, are secondary. For Italians, the family always come first and everything else, including the Church, is secondary . . . For Poles there is no separation between church and family, but Polish religiosity is tangible and physical, not intellectual or ascetic, as it may be for the Irish. (Giordano & McGoldrick, 1996, p. 436)

In addition to the ethnic variety within one specific religion or denomination, regionalism plays a role in creating further diversity in religious and spiritual expression. For example, Southern Baptists tend to ascribe to Biblical literalism, require strict observance of moral codes of conduct, and take more conservative positions on social issues than do American Baptists of the North and Midwest.

Some European/Anglo Americans are not particularly influenced by their ethnic heritage in their religion and spirituality. Those who are religious might choose their religious affiliation based on other factors such as theological beliefs, personality of the religious leader, proximity to their homes, type of programming available for their children, engagement in political or social activism, or the participation of family members and friends. Other European/Anglo Americans reject the religious background of their families of origin and prefer to practice their own brand of spirituality or to ignore religion and spirituality altogether.

| CASE | SUSAN AND DOUG |

Susan, 48, and her husband, Doug, 52, a Caucasian couple, sought counseling from Don because of a growing dissatisfaction in their relationship. Susan reported that although daily activities continued without quarrels, she suspected their problems centered around conflict over Doug's long work hours, her own sense of being depleted from working full time and caring for their three children, and their isolation from extended family members. Susan indicated that she thought that she and Doug "would have made it by now," given that throughout their 20-year marriage, they had both worked full-time, with one or the other sometimes holding down two jobs. Doug, though not as verbal as Susan, concurred with her analysis of their situation and indicated that he felt that he had disappointed himself, his parents, and God by not earning the income he had once hoped to attain.

The couple's counselor, Don, was able to connect with Susan and Doug's pain by empathizing with them. Don also raised the issue of their values of hard work, success, and how those were linked with their understanding of God's blessing. Don had Susan and Doug look to their Anglo American heritage as the source of their beliefs and values. Both Doug and Susan agreed that they had bought into the "American Dream" and had blamed themselves and each other when that dream did not materialize in financial success. Don asked Susan and Doug to probe their ethnic background for clues to their distress, and both were surprised to discover that they had been raised to believe that "God helps those who help themselves" and that material success was a sign of God's favor. By helping this couple understand the ethnic, cultural, and religious context of their situation, Don was able to help mitigate their guilt and shame. Rather than focusing on Susan and Doug's excessive workload, Don enabled them to examine their values and to begin the process of claiming a new set of meanings for their relationship and their family. Both Doug and Susan offered that they had felt trapped by their unquestioning acceptance of the notion that success was measured by financial strength. They realized that they had sacrificed their relationship with each other, their children, and their extended family members to pursue a value that ultimately was not that important to them. As a result of re-ordering their priorities, both Susan and Doug were able to reduce their workloads, enjoy more leisure time as a couple and family, and seek another faith community in which their new values were affirmed.

In this case, the clients entered counseling unaware of their ethnicity and the cultural values that contributed to their distress. Because they had simply accepted the ideas of independence, hard work, and achievement as givens, they had never considered the possibility of choosing other priorities that would give their lives meaning. By bringing their ethnic and religious heritage into their awareness, Susan and Doug were able to acknowledge their ancestry, to release themselves from crippling blame and self-effacement, and to consciously select a different way of ordering their lives that resulted in greater marital satisfaction.

AFRICAN AMERICANS

About 12% of the U.S. population is composed of African Americans who, until recently, lived in the South. However, between 1940 and 1970, more than 1.5 million African Americans migrated northward and westward (Hines & Boyd-Franklin, 1996). Currently, more than 84% reside in urban areas (Henderson, 1994).

In addition to African Americans whose ancestors were brought to the United States as slave labor, other African Americans include those who immigrated from Haiti, Jamaica, and other West Indian islands. Although they share skin color, their nationalities, values, and customs can be very different. Often, it has been necessary for all African Americans to present a united front while addressing racism, but some groups have polarized around issues such as immigration (Brice-Baker, 1996). Counselors must know the background of their African American clients and not assume that their context is the same based on race.

Values

Many African Americans share a common bond through their unique history or African ethnicity and centuries of forced migration, enslavement, and subsequent discrimination and victimization (Boyd-Franklin, 1989). As a result of these experiences, survival of their people is a central value (Nobles, 1980). A concern for liberation and social justice is also a theme among African Americans (Frame & Williams, 1996). In addition, the African American ethos is characterized by a strong sense of communalism in which strong kinship ties reach beyond bloodlines and into a rich network of extended family members and friends (Collins, 1990; Hill, 1972; Nobles, 1980). What to some white Americans might look like enmeshment is instead a healthy collective identity (Helms & Cook, 1999). African Americans, then, understand themselves in the context of community. Their view of self is, "I am because we are; and because we are, therefore, I am" (Mbiti, 1969, p. 108). Included in such a community are not only people but also animals, plants, objects, ancestors, and even those who are yet unborn. As long as ancestors are remembered, they are considered "living dead" (Fukuyama & Sevig, 1999).

Traditionally, African Americans have placed a high value on work and educational achievement as the key to success and the ticket out of poverty (Hill, 1972; Billingsley, 1992; Staples, 1994). Although many whites perceive that African Americans do not work and rely on welfare for their survival, an overwhelming majority of African Americans do work, sometimes holding down more than one job (Hines & Boyd-Franklin, 1996). African American parents hope that their children will do better economically than they did. However, because they value good character and individual worth, they are pleased when their children can be self-supporting. Those who do not become professionals may win as much parental approval as those who do (Hines & Boyd-Franklin, 1996).

African Americans who become successful often believe they are expected to "give back" to the community and family members (Hines & Boyd-Franklin, 1996). This value comes from the notion that individual well-being is connected to collective welfare.

Other African American values include interdependence, psychological connection, a deep appreciation for the oral tradition, and a fluid time perception (White, 1984).

Religion and Spirituality

For African Americans, spirituality and identity are inseparable. Religion is not compartmentalized into a set of beliefs, doctrine, or dogma. Instead, it is in the life and breath of most African Americans, whether or not they are involved in organized religion (Cook & Wiley, 2000). Some African Americans believe that spirit may be found in everything. Religion and spirituality are considered major strengths for African Americans, which contributed to their resiliency, their survival of slavery, and their ability to overcome present struggles (Billingsley, 1968; Boyd-Franklin, 1989; Comas-Diaz & Griffith, 1988; Knox, 1985). For many African Americans, spirituality dominates their thinking and is integrally related to their sense of security, adjustment, identity development, behavior, and problem-solving ability (Indowu, 1992). When they find themselves in a crisis or particularly stressed, many African Americans seek solace and strength in their religious and spiritual practices (Mbiti, 1969).

The Black Church   Perhaps the most visible expression of religion and spirituality among African Americans is found in the Black Church. Indeed, the Black Church is the only institution in America that is under the sole ownership and control of the African American community (Cook, 1993; Moore, 1991). Although some African American congregations belong to predominantly white denominations, the independent African American churches include Methodist, Pentecostal, and Baptist denominations: African Methodist Episcopal (AME), African Methodist Episcopal Zion (AMEZ), Christian Methodist Episcopal (CME), Church of God in Christ (COGIC), National Baptist Convention of America, Inc. (NBCA), National Baptist Convention, U.S.A., Inc. (NBC), National Missionary Baptist Convention of America (NMDC), and Progressive National Baptist Convention, Inc. (PNBC) (Cook & Wiley, 2000).

Often functioning as the central institution in African American neighborhoods and lives, the Church provides a place for worship, prayer, catharsis in the midst of suffering, and validation of life experiences (Eugene, 1995). The Church also functions as a place of political activism and education, a refuge from the hostility of discrimination, an opportunity to achieve status, and a place to call home (Boyd-Franklin & Lockwood, 1999). Nye (1993) described six subthemes of the African American Church's function:

(a) *expressive function* as an outlet for one's deepest emotions, (b) *status function* where recognition could be attained through leadership, (c) *meaning function* where one can attain order and understanding for life, (d) *refuge function* providing a haven from a hostile world, (e) *cathartic function* such that pent-up emotions and frustrations can be released, (f) *other-worldly function* that provides guidance and fulfillment in the afterlife. (p. 105)

To this list, Boyd-Franklin & Lockwood (1999) added two additional functions: *the social function* that provides fellowship and some insulation for adolescents dealing with peer pressure, drugs, alcohol, and sexual activity and the *child-rearing function* that provides support for parents, including child care.

Worship Practices   The focus of worship in most African American churches is on God who, through Jesus Christ, enters into a personal relationship with believers, reconciles, liberates, heals, and guides (Cook & Wiley, 2000). There is an emphasis on God's "healing presence in life despite suffering and pain" (Wimberly, 1991, p. 16). Worship in African American churches is spirited, emotional, and expressive. It often includes "involuntary acts of praise" (Mitchell & Mitchell, 1989, p. 105). In addition, clapping, dancing, and shouting are common in African American worship, which results in spiritual uplifting and an indwelling sense of hope in the worshipper. Black spirituality involves "the senses, the emotions, and the limbs as well" (Mitchell & Mitchell, 1989, p. 105). There is the expectation that upon leaving a worship service, participants are empowered to manage the demands of daily life.

Other Spiritual Traditions and Practices   The Black Church has been the focus of African American religion, but it is certainly not the only means through which spirituality is experienced and expressed. Music is a universal medium of black spirituality. Typical patterns of oral expression are found in much African American music, including improvisation, call and response sequences, and use of metaphor, imagery, and symbolism (Jones, 1993). Particular musical types such as blues, jazz, soul music, R & B, rap, and hip-hop embody symbolism, metaphor, and call and response patterns as well as spiritual resistance to exploitation (Rose, 1994). Their tradition is rooted in the communal expression of liberation and racial solidarity and, as such, serves significant spiritual functions.

Folktales, stories, proverbs, and short sayings drawn from the oral tradition also serve as vehicles for African American spirituality. These forms of expression often build on Christian symbolism, providing transformation, power, comfort, and guidance (Boyd-Franklin, 1989).

Spiritism is also common among African Americans. This concept includes the notion that the universe has many spirits created by God that exist on a level between God and humans (Mbiti, 1991). Some of these spirits are related to nature and the sky (sun, moon, stars, rain, wind, thunder, lightning) or to the earth (hills, mountains, rocks, trees, water). Although all

African Americans do not hold these beliefs, those who do find that they help explain the mysteries of the world. In addition, some African Americans believe in human spirits of those who died long ago (ghosts) and those who died recently (living dead) (Cook & Wiley, 2000).

Non-Christian forms of spirituality also exist within the African American community. Worship of gods and goddess (*orishas*) linked to West African ancestry and heritage is found in Santeria and originated in the Caribbean (Gonzalez-Wippler, 1992). The customs in Santeria included saint worship, feasts, festivals, rituals, offerings, and sacrifices. Voodoo is another system prevalent among African Americans, especially in New Orleans (Teish, 1985). Voodoo is based on an earth religion that involves worship of ancestors and gods and goddesses. It also includes magic and rituals of every day life. African American spirituality is rich and varied and often shapes identity and purpose for its proponents.

Counseling Issues

One thing that counselors should know about African American clients is that for many the psychic and the spirit are one (Knox, 1985; Mbiti, 1970; Nobles, 1980) and psychological pain may be expressed in spiritual terms. In addition, those for whom religion is central may mistrust counselors who are neutral or who ignore the centrality of their clients' spiritual orientation (Boyd-Franklin & Lockwood, 1999). For them to seek psychotherapy could even be construed as a lack of faith (Hines & Boyd-Franklin, 1996). Further, some African American clients perceive counseling to be for persons who are certifiably "crazy" and or "sick," and they might not want to be categorized as such. In addition, given the oppression many African Americans have suffered over the decades, some could be suspicious of psychotherapy because of its potential to lead to misdiagnosis.

Counselors who aim to be effective with African American clients, especially counselors of other ethnic backgrounds, must do an exceptional job of joining with their clients, dispelling their myths about counseling, communicating empathy, and assuring them that counseling can produce immediate results (Aponte, 1994). In addition to forging trustworthy connections with African American clients, it might be important for non-African American counselors to discuss issues of race and ethnic difference that could affect the therapeutic relationship and counseling outcomes (Hines & Boyd-Franklin, 1996). Non-African American counselors could attend religious services in a Black church to increase their visceral awareness of how religion and spirituality are manifest in this community (Constantine, Lewis, Conner, & Sanchez, 2000). Similarly, counselors need to consider the whole context in which their African American clients find themselves. This requirement includes acknowledging their clients' strengths as well as the multiple systems (educational, social service, judicial, economic, political, and environmental) that can affect their lives (Aponte, 1994; Boyd-Franklin, 1989). Another crucial piece of advice for counselors working with African American clients is to not underestimate the power of the client's church to provide various kinds of support. Further, African American clergy can become influential allies for counselors and might be able to assist in the therapeutic process by giving it their blessing or by lending their spiritual and cultural expertise through consultation.

Religious and Spiritual Strategies

Although a host of psychotherapeutic interventions could be useful with African American clients, some that have a specific religious or spiritual dimension may be especially effective. First, the use of metaphor draws on the oral tradition of storytelling central to African American culture and spirituality. This technique, combined with narrative therapy (Parry & Doan, 1994; White & Epston, 1990) could assist clients in authoring new stories for their lives. Moreover, for counselors who feel competent in this area, drawing on the Biblical narrative for stories that suggest hope and affirmation can be a source of both comfort and motivation for change (Mitchell & Lewter, 1986; Robertson, 1990).

Capitalizing on the importance of music as a means of spiritual expression in African American culture, counselors may draw on the large and varied musical repertoire whose lyrics are often liberating. Asking clients to bring into the session music that has particular spiritual meaning for them could provide a language for expressing their psychological pain while opening a door for them toward change.

Using the strong sense of communalism and kinship bonds provides counselors with the opportunity to help clients garner social and spiritual support for their lives' challenges. Members of clients' "church family" (Boyd-Franklin & Lockwood, 1999) might be called to participate in the counseling process in various ways that communicate strength and support. Moreover, creating counseling groups that focus specifically on the intersection of psychotherapy and spirituality might be effective for African American clients, especially women (Williams, Frame, & Green, 1999).

Capturing the spiritual dimension of social action can be a means by which counselors enable African American clients to overcome the barriers that are creating difficulty for them. Counselors may make use of the African American tradition unifying personal transformation and social action as a resource for behavioral change (Frame & Williams, 1996).

CASE | LATOYA

LaToya is an 18-year-old African American woman with a 2-year-old daughter, Sherita. LaToya was referred to counseling by Social Services because of the stress of being a single parent and having difficulty holding down a job. LaToya began working with her counselor, Shaun, to address these difficulties. When asked about her family, LaToya revealed that she was living with her grandmother, Eva Mae, who occasionally provided childcare "when she was up to it." LaToya indicated that her mother had a drug problem and had been in and out of jail and halfway houses for years. LaToya said she had two sisters and some aunts and cousins nearby who checked on her and "would take the baby when I need a break or have to work." Shaun inquired about sources of social support, including religious or spiritual connections. LaToya responded that she had been involved in an African American Episcopal Church (AME) as a child and that her grandmother was still very active, though she herself had stopped attending at around age 14. She reported that she had enjoyed singing in the church choir during her earlier years "before the baby."

Shaun began working with LaToya to identify her personal and family strengths. Slowly, LaToya was able to acknowledge and appreciate the women in her family who were, for the most part, courageous, competent, energetic, and unassailable people who could be role models for her. In addition, LaToya was able to claim her intelligence and her dedication to Sherita as personal strengths.

In other work, Shaun drew upon the musical tradition of the spirituals to connect LaToya with her ancestors' struggles and to inspire her in her own. He was able to use the metaphor of "slavery" to describe LaToya's sense of being trapped in systems that seemed to impede her progress and "liberation" to capture her dream of breaking free from the bonds that "kept her down." Eventually with LaToya's permission, Shaun consulted with the pastor of her church, Rev. Johnson, about the resources that might be available to her through the church and wider community. LaToya learned of an affordable child-care program, a tutoring program for the General Education Degree (GED), and a job-line, all coordinated by members of her church. In this case, Shaun was able to discover religious and spiritual resources within his client's community that helped support her in achieving her goals. He was able to use her spiritual traditions and language to help LaToya reframe her situation and to make a commitment to change.

LATINOS/LATINAS

The fastest growing segment of the American population in the last two decades has been among Latinos. According to the U.S. Census Bureau (1998), the 29 million Latinos who currently live in the United States will grow to more than 62 million by 2020 and perhaps more than 133 million by 2050. These figures do not include the thousands of undocumented Latinos that are in the United States. Despite their increasing numbers, however, Latinos have not fared well within economic, educational, legal, or social systems.

One of the most important aspects of working with Latinos is to acknowledge their diversity. The three largest Latino groups in the United States are Mexicans, Puerto Ricans, and Cubans (Garcia-Preto, 1996a). Each of these nationalities has its own values, cultural traditions, religious and spiritual practices, and indigenous healers. Recently, there has also been a large influx of persons from Central America and some from South America, including Brazilians. To blend them together arbitrarily is to do a major disservice to all involved. However, it is possible to provide a thumbnail sketch regarding some general values and religious and spiritual traditions that are associated with these diverse peoples.

Many counselors wonder what the correct terminology is when referring to people of Mexican, Puerto Rican, Cuban, and Central and South American descent. The two most prevalent terms are "Hispanic" and "Latino/a." These terms developed as a result of white Americans' looking at people who were mostly Roman Catholic and shared a common language, dark skin color, and a history of conquest and colonization and assuming them to be a homogeneous group (Garcia-Preto, 1996a). What is difficult about these labels is that they both mask the nationalities and conceal the identities of the people they are intended to describe. Further, they are terms that the people themselves would never use in self-description. Nevertheless, the U.S. Census has used the term "Hispanic" despite some critics' concern that it is an English word that has no gender like "Latino and Latina" do and that it is a politically conservative appellation (Garcia-Preto, 1996a). "Latino/a" tends be considered a more progressive label (Gonzalez, 1992), but some resist it because it "refers to an even older empire, the one that took over Spain" (Garcia-Preto, 1996a, p. 142). In this book, I am using the term "Latino/a" when making general statements about these very diverse people.

Values

Despite the diversity of country and customs, they share some value-oriented commonalities. First is the emphasis on *familismo*—family unity, family well-being, and family name (Sabogal, Marin, Otero-Sabogal, Marin, & Perez-Stable, 1987). The survival and welfare of the family group supersedes individual desires (Bernal, 1982; Queralt, 1984). Among Latino families, there is an immeasurable sense of commitment, loyalty, responsibility, and obligation. Those who have resources and strength are expected to care for those who are needy. There is a wealth of support available within Latino families, and large extended kinship networks function at times as safety nets for their members. Godparents (*compadres*) have familial obligations of nurture, economic help, and personal guidance (Garcia-Preto, 1996a). In addition, in some cases children are placed with persons inside the family web when there is a crisis. *Hijos de crianza* is the term for this practice of caring for children as if they were their own (Garcia-Preto, 1996a).

There is a closeness in Latino families that is sometimes mistaken for enmeshment, overprotection, or pathology by white therapists (Zea, Mason, Murguia, 2000). This family connection is one that encourages adolescents to stay in the family home until marriage and is evidenced by a relaxed approach toward children's becoming independent and self-reliant (Falicov, 1996).

Respect for authority is another central value among many Latinos. In some cases, this value keeps them from being assertive and asking for help when they need it. In addition, deferring to authority may put Latinos in precarious positions when they are facing discrimination or other oppressive circumstances. For example, some Latinos might not confront racial slurs from supervisors because culturally they are expected to defer to authority despite the personal price they must endure from such epithets. Closely related to respect for authority is the value of personalism (Garcia-Preto, 1996a), which concerns the dignity and worth of individuals and the qualities that make them unique. Moreover, the value of *respeto* or personal respect in interpersonal relationships is critical to most Latinos (Marin, 1992).

Many Latinos have a sense of cultural fatalism that includes the tendency to approach life with a kind of resignation toward what is perceived as inevitable. This cultural fatalism includes religiosity as a strong belief in God and in prescribed forms of worship, a belief in folk healing, and a tendency toward viewing physical and emotional well-being as unified (Comas-Diaz, 1993).

The notions of *machismo* and *marianismo* are how Latinos ascribe certain gender-related qualities and roles. *Machismo* does not simply connote a type of self-aggrandizement but also includes the notion of a father's responsibility for his family, including his devotion to his children (Falicov, 1996). *Marianismo* is a term taken from the cult of the Virgin Mary in which women are capable of tolerating any kind of suffering doled out by men because they (women) are considered morally and spiritually superior (Garcia-Preto, 1996b). In both cases, there is a special sense of the contribution each gender makes to the other and to the family at large.

Spirituality and Religion

Indigenous Spirituality   One hallmark of the Latino experience in the United States has been that of migration. Many Latinos left family members, familiar surroundings, cultural values, and practices to escape oppression or to build a better life. Part of their migration history, however, has created significant upheavals for many Latinos especially during life transitions and major life cycle events (Falicov, 1996). During these times, Latinos have a tendency to seek comfort and support by turning to folk practices and magical beliefs that cement their ties to ancestors and to their heritage. Such a practice has been called "ideological ethnicity" (Harwood, 1981).

Many Latinos believe in the supernatural and claim that some chronic problems they experience are a result of *mal puesto or brujeria* (bewitchment). *Mal puesto* can be the explanation for infertility or mental illness, including schizophrenia (Falicov, 1999). Relationship difficulties are often attributed to *brujeria* and the notion that one of the parties in a conflict may have hired someone to put a hex on someone else (Falicov, 1999). In addition, because of the co-mingling of indigenous practices and those brought by European colonists, many Latinos believe in white and black witches. The white witches are consulted for protection, success, luck, or romance, whereas black witches are sought when one wishes harm to a rival or to put an evil spell on someone for revenge (Falicov, 1999).

In addition to the witches, a more prominent folk healer among Latinos is the *curandero*. *Curanderos* are not a homogeneous group but, rather, tend to develop specialties in addressing particular problems or in using certain healing interventions. Their approach uses a variety of media including herbal remedies, massage, incantations, sweating, prayer, consultation with the spirit world, and various cleansing rituals (Fabrega & Manning, 1973; Gafner & Duckett, 1992). *Curanderismo* focuses on harmony between individuals, families, communities, and the environment (Foster, 1960). *Curanderismo* has a multidimensional aspect that emphasizes the union of the physical, emotional, spiritual, social, natural, and supernatural aspects of existence. *Curanderos* have three levels of healing: (a) the material, (b) the mental, and (c) the spiritual (Trotter & Chavira, 1981). The material level involves using objects such as herbal remedies, candles, and rituals that are presumed to contain healing powers. The mental level involves having the *curandero* transmit mental energy to the person suffering the illness or difficulty. The spiritual level requires the *curandero* to enter a trance and become the vehicle for spirituality power to emerge and heal (Zea, Mason, Murguia, 2000). *Curanderos* are often known for creating a pleasing, welcoming, warm environment and are known to invite family members to participate in the healing process (Falicov, 1999). Although they do not see themselves as alternatives to Western medicine, they are aware that many of their constituents choose to combine their approaches to health care so they can use both systems (Applewhite, 1995; Mull & Mull, 1983).

Espiritistas (spiritualists) are also among the indigenous healers available to Latinos. These persons are believed to have the ability to communicate with the spirits and to access their power for healing. *Espiritismo* (spiritualism) is the belief in a world of good and evil spirits that influence human behavior (Delgado, 1978; Falicov, 1999). Those who practice spiritualism believe it is possible to increase one's protection by doing good deeds and to decrease it by doing evil (Falicov, 1999). Some writers (Fanon, 1967; Lechner, 1992) believe that *espiritismo* provides its believers with a way to manage their anger at colonization and to deal with their feelings of powerlessness by placing themselves under the protection of the spirits.

Santeria, mentioned earlier in connection with indigenous African spirituality, is prevalent among Cubans, some Puerto Ricans, and others from the Caribbean. It is known as *lucumi* in Cuba and *macumba* in Brazil (Falicov, 1999). *Santeros* are priests and priestesses who are consulted for healing, divination, and rituals. They may predict the future, treat spirit possession, or be proprietors of shops that offer herbs, candles, and other ritual objects (Boswell & Curtis, 1984; Bernal & Gutierrez, 1988; Comas-Diaz, 1989).

Religious Expression

In addition to the spiritual practices just described, Roman Catholicism is a vital religious force for almost all Latinos. Although there are some differences in the way Catholicism is practiced in various Latino cultures, its Christian concepts of an omnipotent God, eternal life, heaven and hell, and guilt and shame all contribute to how many Latinos view themselves and make meaning of their lives. Because there are magical aspects to Catholicism

(Falicov, 1999), these beliefs are well-suited to the indigenous spirituality that was in existence long before the Spanish colonists brought their religion to the Americas. The belief in miracles, propitiatory rituals, promises, and prayers shapes much of Latino religious life. Devotional materials, icons, statues of the Virgin Mary, or other holy items are often prominently displayed in homes, cars, and places of business. In many cases, church involvement is a major source of social and community support for Latino families.

In a discussion of religion among Latinos, it is important to note that there are other religions present besides Roman Catholicism. Missionary efforts in Latin America resulted in the presence of many mainline Protestant denominations, Pentecostals, Jehovah's Witnesses, various types of evangelical fundamentalist groups (Falicov, 1999). Further, many Latinos are Jewish. Nevertheless, one cannot ignore the profound influence that the Roman Catholic Church has exerted on Latino people.

What should be abundantly clear is that diversity is a theme that sounds loud and clear when working with Latinos. Counselors should be especially careful about making assumptions regarding ethnicity, nationality, values, religion, and spirituality and how their Latino clients express those dimensions.

Working with Indigenous Healers   Given that Latino spirituality is infused with a variety of indigenous healers including witches, *curanderos, santeros,* and *espiritistas,* it is important for counselors to know how to interface with them. Relatedly, these healers provide services that are similar in many ways to those provided by mental health clinicians, but they might be more effective because they incorporate cultural values and expectations (Harwood, 1981).

Lee and Armstrong (1995) offered guidelines for counselors who contemplate developing consultative relationships with traditional healers. First, Lee and Armstrong suggest encouraging clients to explore their worldviews and belief systems and to share the ways in which traditional healers are important in clients' lives. By inviting clients to tell their cultural and spiritual stories, counselors help validate clients' belief systems. Second, counselors must suspend their own cultural beliefs before they can truly appreciate and respect clients' beliefs in the role and function of traditional healers. Third, if it appears to the counselor that a client might benefit from the services of a traditional healer, the counselor might have to rely on the client to locate an appropriate source. Fourth, when a traditional healer has been located, it is important for counselors to communicate with that healer. Both the counselor and the healer need to know the other's perspective, role, and contribution to the client's well-being. Even if the counselor doesn't agree with the healer's assumptions or methods, it is important to realize that because this person has authority and healing power in the eyes of the client, he or she may be able to provide the help that is needed. Fifth, counselors must be willing to forge treatment alliances with traditional healers to best serve clients' needs. What is critical in this partnership is the establishment of appropriate boundaries around Western psychological practices and the shamanic tradition. Sixth, to better understand the rituals and practices of traditional healers, counselors might have to participate in the ceremonies or other activities that are engaged in on behalf of the client. Finally, establishing a referral network with traditional healers could help enhance credibility in diverse communities. Such referral systems could provide clients access to their cultural traditions and could offer traditional healers avenues of contact with mental health practitioners.

CASE | GUILLERMO

Guillermo is a 49-year-old construction worker who suffered a serious back injury on the job and spent two weeks in the hospital. He is currently in a rehabilitation center for intensive physical therapy. As part of his treatment, Guillermo has been referred to the career transition center for counseling. Jackie, the counselor at the career transition center noted that Guillermo was depressed and anxious. In the first session, Jackie asked Guillermo to describe his situation. He reported that as a result of his fall at work he was experiencing *susto* (a deep fear as a result of a traumatic incident) and *mareo* ("a form of dizziness or simple anxiety and nervousness") (Falicov, 1999, p. 107). Jackie had no idea what Guillermo meant by these terms and asked him to help her understand his situation. Guillermo continued to talk about his emotional distress in physical terms referring to headaches and dizzy spells. Jackie spent the rest of the first session engaging Guillermo with warmth and *personalismo* (an approach that includes self-disclosure and interpersonal relationships) (Bean, Perry, & Bedell, 2001). She empathized with Guillermo's circumstances, learned about his family and cultural context, and assured him that she would work hard to assist him in eliminating his distress and obtaining a new job that would make use of his skills without exacerbating his injuries and disabilities.

After the session, Jackie spoke with her supervisor, David, and asked for help in understanding Guillermo's Mexican background and the terms he used to describe his problems. David was also perplexed, but suggested the two of them ask to meet with Pedro, a colleague in the center who was also of Mexican descent. Pedro was pleased that his Caucasian colleagues cared enough about Guillermo's cultural background and beliefs to seek consultation with him. He was able to provide them with resources that described Latino traditions and indigenous healing practices.

In the next session, Jackie told Guillermo that she had consulted with Pedro about his (Guillermo's) situation and had learned a little bit about traditional healers in Mexican culture. She told Guillermo that she was open to working alongside other helpers and asked him what he thought would be helpful to him in making his career transition and in addressing the problems of *susto* and *mareo*. Guillermo indicated that "if he were at home [Mexico] he would see the *curandera*." Jackie asked Guillermo if he knew of a *curandera* in his community. Guillermo said he had visited one on a previous occasion and gave Jackie the *curandera's* name and permission to contact her. After a telephone consultation and a brief face-to-face meeting, Jackie and Rosario (the *curandera*) began working together with Guillermo. Rosario used traditional herbal approaches to dealing with *susto* and *mareo* while Jackie collected Spanish language information about career options and training programs. By combining their resources and perspectives, Jackie and Rosario were able to assist Guillermo in eliminating his anxiety and depression and in moving toward a new work situation.

ASIAN AMERICANS

Asian Americans, also, are a highly diverse group of people who hail from China, Japan, Korea, the Philippines, Southeast Asia, Asian India, and the Pacific Islands (Tan & Dong, 2000). More than 50 groups who speak more than 30 languages are included among these people (Sue, Nakamura, Chung, & Yee-Bradbury, 1994). Within the various languages, there are sometimes many dialects (E. Lee, 1996a). Of the Asian American population, Chinese constitute 23%, Pilipino 19%, Japanese 12%, Asian Indian 11%, Korean 11%, and Vietnamese 9%. Thai and Hmong people constitute fewer than 2% of the Asian American population (E. Lee, 1996a).

Learning about the diversity between and among Asian Americans is paramount for counselors to be effective in working with this population. Asian Americans come from different countries with their own particular cultural values, beliefs, and practices, and the circumstances of their being in the United States and their level of acculturation deeply impact their life experiences and their openness to counseling. For many Asian Americans, their family's presence in the United States is marked by immigration challenges, oppression, war trauma, and refugee status (E. Lee, 1996a). These aspects of Asian Americans' lives might be intimately related to the problems that bring them to counseling.

Values

Contrary to the individualism espoused by Western cultures, collectivism is the major orientation of Asian American people (Ho, 1985; Moy, 1992). This sense of group identification is most evident in the significance most Asian Americans place on the family unit. Individual family members are viewed as products of many generations—a concept that is undergirded by rituals that include ancestor worship, family celebrations, funeral ceremonies, and genealogical records (E. Lee, 1996a). Whatever family members do reflects on themselves, the extended family, and the ancestors (Shon & Ja, 1982). Thus, individuals are expected to behave in ways that honor the family name and protect it from shame (Sodowsky, Kwan, & Pannu, 1995). Filial piety (the duty to honor and obey parents), especially that of the eldest son, is an important value for most Asian Americans (Matsui, 1996). Failure to meet these obligations (which often involve caring for the needs of family members), including those to elderly parents, often results in feelings of shame, guilt, and alienation (Uba, 1994).

Hierarchy and status organize most social relationships among Asian Americans. Prescribed roles, codes of behavior, and language usage reflect one's status in the family or society (Moy, 1992; Sodowsky, Kwan, & Pannu, 1995). In extrafamilial relationships, the same hierarchical pattern holds. Moreover, those with the most seniority as a result of age and male gender are considered to hold the most power and authority in the relationship (Sodowsky, Kwan, & Pannu, 1995).

Traditionally, Asians have placed high value on deference, controlled and indirect communication, and restrained emotions to maintain social harmony (Matsui, 1996; Moy, 1992; Uba, 1994). In addition, they tend to be loyal and selfless toward others and are intentional about anticipating others' needs (Uba, 1994). As a result of the influence of many Eastern religions such as Buddhism, Hinduism, Confucianism, Taoism, and shamanism, many Asian Americans have come to value the personality traits of silence, nonconfrontation, modesty, humility, simplicity, self control, patience, and humility (Sodowsky, Kwan, & Pannu, 1995). Concomitantly, physical expression of affection may also be rare if it occurs at all (Tan & Dong, 2000).

Spirituality and Religion

Among Chinese Americans and other Asian groups, indigenous healing practices abound. The most common ones are herbal medicine, acupuncture, and massage. Fortune telling may also be used to prevent "bad spirits" (E. Lee, 1996b). In addition, traditional Asian ethnic groups often hold the belief in animism (spirits within objects) (Piercy, Soekandar, & Limansubroto, 1996). Relatedly, many Asians hold to the notion of a spirit world and recognize a panoply of gods that rule the universe (Hopfe, 1983). They might believe in a supernatural realm (Tan, 1991) and might worship dead ancestors who are viewed as connections to the spirit world (Tan & Dong, 2000).

The Influence of Eastern Religions   Asian Americans' diverse religious background means that they have been influenced by a variety of Eastern spiritual ideas, most notably those of Confucianism, Taoism, Buddhism, and Hinduism. (See Chapter 3 for a detailed treatment of these religions). Originating in China, Confucianism emphasized harmony and order in the social world (Hopfe, 1983). Confucianism is also the foundation for the patriarchal, hierarchical, and androcentric principles in Asian cultures (Tan & Dong, 2000). The family structure in which the father and the eldest male hold authority is also an outgrowth of Confucian thought (Uba, 1994). Taoism focuses on living harmoniously with nature and with others (Hopfe, 1983). From these ideas comes the tendency for Asian Americans to be indirect in their communication patterns and to avoid confrontation (Tomine, 1991). Shame, guilt, and loss of face are the means by which disapproval is communicated indirectly in Asian cultures (Matsui, 1996). Asian Americans' propensity to meet social injustice and personal distress with passive acceptance is undoubtedly a result of Buddhist influences: Personal suffering is something that is to be "endured quietly" (Tan & Dong, 2000, p. 426). In some schools of Buddhism, one is apt to strive for nondesire as a means of attaining spiritual release (Wenhao, Salomon, & Chay, 1993). Employing the concepts of karma, reincarnation, and compassion may be effective in working with Buddhist and Hindu clients (E. Lee, 1996b). With Indonesian clients, however, one would expect to find a majority practicing their own brand of Islam: more than 90% of Indonesia's population is registered as Muslims (Piercy, Soekandar, & Limansubroto,

1996). Indonesians are not necessarily purists when it comes to practicing Islam. The Hindu ideas of reincarnation and the spiritual notions of animism, however, have influenced Indonesians (Piercy, Soekandar, & Limansubroto, 1996).

The Influence of Christianity   The history of Asians in America has been shaped in part by the missionary efforts of Christian churches. As a result, 33.6% of Asian Americans reported they were members of Protestant churches, 27.1% were Roman Catholic, 19.1% reported no religion, and 7.8% indicated affiliation with Hinduism or Buddhism (Busto, 1996). Many Asian Americans, particularly college students are involved to some degree with conservative, pietistic, or evangelical churches or parachurch groups such as Campus Crusade for Christ, Navigators, and Intervarsity Christian Fellowship (Busto, 1996).

Many of those who reported that they were involved in no religion were raised during the height of the Communist regime and, thus, were not permitted to practice openly any form of religion.

Despite the fact that many Asian Americans have adopted Christianity, traditional religions and values continue to influence them in overt and covert ways. It is critical, then, for counselors to explore with Asian American clients the degree to which they are involved in religion or spirituality and how much they continue their traditional practices.

Asian Americans and Counseling

Researchers have consistently found that Asian Americans underuse mental health services (Brown, Stein, Huang, & Harris, 1973; Sue & Sue, 1974) and that part of the reason for their not seeking these services lies in providers' inability to meet their needs (Chien & Yamamoto, 1982; Sue & Morishima, 1985). It is important to understand, then, that as a result of traditional values and beliefs, many Asian Americans may not seek psychological help. First, many Asian Americans would rather seek help from within the family than to share intimate details of their lives with strangers (E. Lee, 1996a). Second, if they do seek outside assistance, they might present somatic complaints when experiencing emotional or relationship issues (Kleinman, 1982; Marsella, Kinzie, & Gordon, 1973; Tseng, 1975). For example, some clients might complain of headaches, backaches, or chest pains when depressed (E. Lee, 1996b). Such somatization can be the means by which Asian Americans avoid the shame and stigma associated with mental problems. It can also be a reflection of the traditional Asian view of the unity of body, mind, and spirit such that a difficulty in one area might be expressed in another. Third, some Asian Americans (particularly Chinese) could have alternative perceptions of and explanations for their emotional distress than are typical in Western approaches. For example, they might view emotional problems or mental illness as an imbalance of *yin* and *yang* and the interrupted flow of *chi* (energy). Or, they believe their difficulties are the result of some type of spiritual unrest caused by a spirit or ghost (E. Lee, 1996b). Some Asian Americans might consider their emotional distress to be the result of transgressing family rituals in ancestor worship (Lin & Lin, 1981). Mental illness can also be considered *karma* issuing from bad deeds in past lives or punishment from God (E. Lee, 1996b). Because of these perceptions, it is not surprising that many Asian Americans would not seek help via psychotherapy. Moreover, when they do seek mental health treatment, counselors and other clinicians might not understand their religious, spiritual, and cultural worldviews and, thus, might not intervene in helpful ways.

Spiritual and Religious Interventions

When working with Asian Americans, for whom religion or spirituality is central, counselors can use these beliefs in the therapeutic process. Seeking to understand how clients appropriate their belief systems and how they integrate them into daily life is crucial. Being open to consulting with leaders in the cultural or spiritual community can be a means of joining with clients and signifying one's commitment to honoring clients' context.

When working with Asian American Christians, it is essential to discover clients' particular denominations or their perspectives on their faith and how clients incorporate their traditional religions, if at all, and to what extent. For evangelical Asian American Christians, Tan and Dong (2000) suggested taking care not to challenge beliefs early in therapy because the counselor risks shaming or embarrassing the client. It can also be helpful, too (if the counselor feels competent to do so) to work within the clients' belief system and to encourage the use of spiritual resources such as prayer, meditation, or Bible study (Tan & Dong, 2000). Asian Americans who are members of churches might seek support through their congregations or the pastoral care offered by clergy. Counselors could also establish relationships with pastors in Asian American churches to offer reciprocal consultation (Tan & Dong, 2000).

CASE | **KIM**

Kim is a 20-year-old Chinese American who immigrated to the United States when she was 6 years old. She is enrolled in a prestigious university studying to be a concert pianist. Kim has become increasingly frustrated and depressed because despite practicing the piano for six to eight hours a day, she has not been able to win the most competitive contests she has entered. Her piano instructor who noticed that she was not performing to the best of her ability and attributed this lapse to stress referred Kim to the university counseling center.

Kim's counselor, Russ, spent the first session exploring Kim's situation: her family, her immigration experience, her commitment to music, and her involvement in her church. Russ learned that Kim's parents were very traditional, spoke Chinese at home, had a small altar where they honored ancestors, kept Chinese holidays, and socialized only with other Chinese immigrants. On the other hand,

Kim had grown up in the United States, had attended public schools, and had become quite acculturated. She indicated that she had converted to Christianity in high school when she and her friends were involved in a parachurch organization called Young Life. Kim reported that she was a devout Christian, that she attended a weekly bible study in her dormitory, was involved in the Baptist church on campus, and enjoyed accompanying the college choir on the piano and organ.

When asked about her distress, Kim revealed that she felt extremely pressured by her father to "become the greatest pianist in the world." Kim acknowledged that she had a gift for music, but said she "didn't know if she could ever please him." Kim admitted that she was ashamed and embarrassed by her failure to be "the best" and was afraid of bringing dishonor to her family. The more she worried about her failure to succeed, the more depressed she became and the more poorly she performed. Kim said she felt trapped in a "vicious cycle of failure."

Russ helped Kim to see how despite her sense of being quite Westernized, she was still significantly influenced by her traditional values and her father's wishes. Russ asked Kim how her Christian faith could be a resource for managing her stress. Kim replied, "If I would really believe that God loves me and accepts me the way I am, then maybe I could be more gracious toward myself and less demanding." Russ worked with Kim, offering her specific stress-management techniques. He encouraged her to spend time in prayer and meditation, asking both for inner peace and strength to perform at her best. Over the next several weeks, Russ worked with Kim, supporting her as she struggled to assimilate her traditional world with her contemporary one. Toward the end of the counseling process, Kim had altered her professional goal. She said, "I want to be *my* best, not necessarily *the* best pianist." Kim was also able to reframe her music as a means of "honoring my heavenly father and my earthly father."

NATIVE AMERICANS

The terms, "Native American," "American Indian, " and "Alaska Native" refer to diverse peoples who maintain a variety of kinship networks, languages, religious and spiritual practices, ways of life, and connections with the dominant culture (Sutton & Broken Nose, 1996). Currently, Native Americans number approximately two million and are related to over 500 different tribes from 314 reservations (Sutton & Broken Nose, 1996). Thirty-seven percent of American Indians live on tribal land and the other 63% are spread throughout rural and urban areas in the United States (Trujillo, 2000). Of the Native Americans living on reservations, the median ages range from 18.8 years to 26.3 years and those living in Alaska native villages have median ages of 16.8 to 25.0 years.

During the 18th and 19th centuries, the mass genocide of American Indians suggested that they might eventually disappear from North America. However, there has been a steady increase in the Native American population, especially between 1980 and the present (Trujillo, 2000). Based on this level of growth, some evidence indicates that eventually Native Americans may regain their population of some five million estimated to have been in existence at the advent of the European explorers (Snipp, 1989).

All ethnic and cultural groups are quite diverse, and it is impossible and inappropriate to stereotype them in any way. Native American tribes are independent and have their own languages, traditions, customs, and practices. Nevertheless, there is a sense of unity and respect among American Indians based on their common bond as Native Americans, their cultural and historical heritage, the shared experiences and the centrality or religion and spirituality (Beck & Walters, 1977; Trujillo, 2000).

Values

Native Americans gain a sense of identity and relationship, as well as social and emotional well-being within the family and, concomitantly, the tribe (Sutton & Broken Nose, 1996). The extended family is central for Native Americans, but it differs significantly from the connotations in the dominant culture. For example, grandparents may include not only the biological parents of one's parents, but also any persons who function in kinship roles similar to grandparents. Similarly, "parents" may include those who have a sibling relationship to the biological parents (Gunn, 1989). Moreover, once a person marries into a family that person is considered a sister or brother, not a sister-in-law or brother-in-law. There are no distinctions between family of origin and family of marriage (Sutton & Broken Nose, 1996). As with African American and Latino families, the role or relationship determines who is in the family, not necessarily blood.

Among many Native Americans, what is valued in communication is listening and silence. Western Caucasians assume that communication is largely talk and might misunderstand Native Americans' silence and indirectness as a sign of resistance (Attneave, 1982; Sutton & Broken Nose, 1996). Nonverbal communication is also a hallmark of Native American exchanges. Indeed, the entire environment in which one finds oneself speaks volumes to Native Americans.

Another value that Native Americans hold is the notion of time geared to personal and seasonal rhythms (Sutton & Broken Nose, 1996). Instead of having their lives circumscribed by the clock and calendar, Native Americans view time as circular rather than linear. They value allowing important events or rituals to take as much time as is needed. Similarly, they might show up to meetings not "on time" but, rather, "at the right time" for them.

Native Americans' sense of community and their place in it have shaped their value of sharing. Those who give the most to others, the tribe, or community are the most respected. "Giveaways" are customary to mark important life-cycle transitions or to honor others who have provided help or have made important accomplishments (Sutton & Broken Nose, 1996). Many Native Americans have had difficulty maintaining businesses such as restaurants because they feel compelled to give away food to family—and "family" can include almost anyone in the community (Sutton & Broken Nose, 1996).

In addition to gift-giving, interdependence is also highly valued among Native Americans. Each individual is expected to contribute skills, resources, and time to the welfare of the group. The group needs are considered priorities over individual needs (Matheson, 1996).

Spirituality and Religion

Indigenous Native American Spirituality   From aboriginal times to the present, the *Sacred* has been protected and kept a secret (Trujillo, 2000). To proceed in describing Native American spirituality and religion, it is necessary to do so with utmost respect and honor, and to acknowledge that there are aspects of this way of life that will not be revealed in this type of media. These dimensions are to be experienced by those who are legitimate members or practitioners of Native American spirituality.

Religion and spirituality give rise to Native American values and shape how Native Americans function in daily life (Toelken, 1976). There is a sense of the *Sacred* in all life. All of creation, including animals, plants, mountains, trees, water, and sky are considered to embody the *Sacred*. Because of the unifying spiritual dimension in all things, humans are expected to care for other persons and the earth (Matheson, 1996).

By virtue of the belief that there is spirit in all things, there is implicitly a relationship between all things. That relationship ideally is characterized by harmony. Health and wholeness, whether mental, spiritual, physical or social, depends on keeping harmonious relationships with the spirit world (Matheson, 1996).

The circle and corresponding Medicine Wheel are almost a universal symbol in Native American spirituality. The circle represents personal growth as well as the cyclical nature of life and its seasons. It also symbolizes community and a life path (LaDue, 1994). When something traumatic occurs, Native Americans experience being outside the circle and must be brought back in (Fukuyama & Sevig, 1999). North, south, east, and west—the four compass points—are representative of the connections between spirit, nature, body, and mind. Though each tribe might have its own interpretations, in general, "the East represents new beginnings, birth, and envisioning the future; the South symbolizes innocence, trust and a time to build a foundation; the West represents strength and courage; and the North represents wisdom. Health is related to balancing these four directions" (Fukuyama & Sevig, 1999, p. 33). In addition to these common themes in Native American spirituality, Beck and Walters (1977) add other shared views: (a) There is a belief or knowledge about unseen and great powers, deities, and mystery; (b) personal worship is the link between individual, tribe, and the great powers; (c) those knowledgeable about the *Sacred* have the responsibility to teach and guide others in the Native American way of life; (d) a shaman is responsible for sacred knowledge and for using oral tradition to pass this knowledge on to future generations; and (e) being human is part of the *Sacred*, and humanity includes making mistakes.

The shaman is a person in the tribe who has a special relationship with the great powers, the nature elements, and the source of life. The shaman makes use of rituals, ceremonies, and prayers to help tribal members meet their needs and serves in a social rather than personal role (Beck & Walters, 1977; Halifax, 1982). Becoming a shaman requires extensive training, personal life experiences, and the acquisition of wisdom. The shamans have gained an understanding of the *Sacred* such that they can experience the continuous relationship between life and death, a relationship to ancestral spirits, and the ability to mediate these to others (Halifax, 1982).

Sacred moments are spiritual experiences that enable Native Americans to gain access to the great powers. They provide clarity and meaning for connecting with the source of life (Trujillo, 2000). The rituals and ceremonies belonging to Native American peoples are the vehicles by which sacred moments are experienced. For example, the sweltering heat of the sweat lodges is a purification ritual in which persons seek transcendence (Bucko, 1999). In the Sun Dance, participants experience extreme pain that provokes trance states and transformation (Walker, 2000). The vision quests of the Plains Indians enable persons to make contact with the spirit world and to obtain direction and meaning for life (Dugan, 1985). The Huichol Indians in Mexico use peyote cactus in drumming and chanting ceremonies to experience spiritual visions, whereas the Mexican Chinantecs use psilocybin mushrooms to engage in dialogue with the divine (Brown, 2001). All these ceremonies are designed to help participants experience transcendence or a connection to the great powers of the universe.

It is important that counselors become knowledgeable about Native American rituals and traditions, but as Fukuyama and Sevig (1999) rightly caution, it is critical to address the issue of borrowing these practices for exploitation or advocating the use of them because they are fascinating. Western counselors and other healers must honor and respect the people whose traditions these are and refrain from misusing them or stealing them for profit (Kasee, 1995).

Christianity Among Native Americans   The story of Christianity among Native Americans is a two-edged sword. On one hand, Christian missionaries organized some of the most oppressive tactics intended to "civilize" the American Indians and to purge them of their tribal customs, traditions, rituals, and practices. They were responsible for a large-scale attempt to have Native Americans assimilated into mainstream Caucasian culture and were supported by the U.S. government (Tafoya & Del Vecchio, 1996). One of these strategies was to organize boarding schools which American Indian children were required to attend. During these educational experiences, Native American children were forced to speak English, wear Western-style clothing and hairstyles, and give up their indigenous religious practices in favor of Christianity (Szasz, 1988; Tafoya & Del Vecchio, 1996). On the other hand, over the years, the various Christian denominations have come to respect the tribal customs, and some have even supported the incorporation of indigenous practices into Christian worship. Probably the most positive outcome of the Christian movement among Native Americans has been the establishment of the Native American church. It has been described as "the most important pan-Indian movement in this country. It is political, cultural, spiritual, a source of pride, power, and psychological health" (Hammerschlag, 1988, p. 60). Because of the missionary efforts to Christianize the American Indians, there are many different ways religion is expressed among Native Americans. Some have not adopted Christianity at all and continue to practice their own forms of religion and spirituality. Others combine aspects of both indigenous spirituality and Christianity. Still others have abandoned their spiritual traditions and are fully assimilated into Western culture, including Christianity. Others move back and forth between traditional and Christian expressions of spirituality. Some might not acknowledge any spiritual or religious leanings at all. Thus, counselors must not assume their Native American clients practice their own traditions or that they are Christians. It is wise to make religion and spirituality topics that are open for inclusion, but not to press clients before establishing a trusting relationship. To do so may be perceived as overstepping one's boundaries or being disrespectful.

Counseling Issues

Native Americans are more than twice as likely as non–Native American clients not to return to counseling after the first session (Sue, Allen & Conaway, 1981). As a result, they have provided a major challenge to mental health providers. There are several reasons why. First, Native Americans might not be aware of the mental health services that are available to them (Dinges, Trimble, Manson, & Pasquale, 1981). Second, often they do not perceive a difference in an ailing body or a troubled soul. Their holistic worldview involving harmony in body, mind, and spirit means that sometimes counselors who are not culturally competent use strategies that are not consistent with Native American values and beliefs (Trujillo, 2000). Third, some Native Americans fear and mistrust mental health services (Dukepoo, 1980) and have negative attitudes toward mental health providers (Manson & Trimble, 1982). The critical factors determining the success of counseling with Native Americans seem to be counselors being culturally knowledgeable, sensitive, and open to clients' experiences and establishing a climate and relationship of trust. Counselors must work within the cultural parameters and demonstrate a willingness to integrate traditional spiritual and religious beliefs in ways that are meaningful to Native American clients.

CASE | PHILLIP

Phillip is a 27-year-old Cherokee who moved with his parents and extended family members from rural North Carolina to an urban area when he was 13. During adolescence, Phillip did everything to fit in with his mostly Caucasian peers. He rejected everything about his Native American roots and heritage. For about 10 years, Phillip focused on becoming as Westernized as possible. He changed his manner of dress, his values, and his friendships. He excelled academically and won several scholarships to a state university. Phillip majored in business and, on graduation, was offered a good paying job with a paper company. During this time, he also met Kristen, one of the company's attorneys. As Phillip and Kristen's relationship became more serious, Phillip began to consider marriage. About the same time, he was offered a promotion as a vice president of his company. These situations put Phillip into a crisis that made him want to withdraw emotionally from Kristen and kept him from focusing whole-heartedly on his work. Phillip's co-worker, Brad, suggested he seek counseling with Jeff, a well-respected therapist in the community. Hesitantly, Phillip made an appointment with Jeff and indicated he wanted "to understand his reluctance to make a commitment to Kristen and to get more excited about and engaged in his work."

Noting Phillip's apparent discomfort with the counseling setting, Jeff took care to explain the counseling process and to listen empathically to Phillip's story. When Jeff asked about Phillip's family, Phillip choked back tears as he told of his Cherokee heritage, his attempt to dissociate himself from anything Native American, and his goal of being accepted and excelling in the dominant culture. During Jeff's work with Phillip, it became clear that Phillip's difficulty in committing to Kristen was related to a growing sense of inner turmoil and a fragmented identity. He found himself realizing that he needed to reclaim the part of himself that he had denied and tried to abandon. The thought of marriage to a Caucasian made Phillip understand that his family of origin, his extended family, and his heritage were more important to him than he thought. He knew he would have to take some time to work on reshaping who he was and what he wanted. Jeff helped Phillip see that he needed to be honest with Kristen and to invite her into his world if he were to continue in that relationship.

Regarding work, Phillip had a similar awakening. Jeff helped Phillip to see that his lethargy about his new position was related to a sense of betrayal Phillip felt toward his people. Phillip had tried to ignore the fact that his company was logging forests and polluting rivers that his people considered sacred. Phillip acknowledged that to continue in his current position would mean sanctioning the practices that were sacrilegious and that created disharmony in the universe. Phillip told Jeff that the disharmony in his relationship and his work was a signal that he needed to regain balance in his own spirit.

Over the next several months, Jeff committed himself to working with Phillip to learn more about Native American ways in general and Cherokee traditions in particular. Phillip made several visits to North Carolina to be among his relatives and other members of his tribe. Ultimately, Phillip decided he must become a whole person by integrating his past and present before he could move into the future.

CASE EXAMPLES

Jamal and Ellen

Jamal is a 33-year-old African American, married to Ellen, 30, an Anglo American. The couple has been married for five years. They have a 3-year-old son, Jesse. Jamal was raised in the African Methodist Episcopal Church (AME), and Ellen was raised in a Presbyterian church. Both were active in their congregations as youth and met in the choir on their college campus. Even though each of their families of origin had difficulties accepting their interracial marriage, both Jamal's family and Ellen's family have come to love and accept the couple, and they all adore their grandson. Although Jamal and Ellen have faced many challenges in their relationship, they could not work out an agreement on which church to join and how to tend to their child's spiritual needs.

Discussion Questions

1. If you were counseling Jamal and Ellen, how would you conceptualize their problem?
2. What do you think the religious or spiritual issues are?
3. How do you think race, ethnicity, and culture are related to the problem? To the solution(s)?
4. What approach would you take to work with Jamal and Ellen on solving their dilemma?
5. What resources would you seek for assistance?
6. What issues does this case raise for you personally? How does your story intersect with that of Jamal and Ellen? How is it different?

Gabriela

Gabriela is a 47-year-old Latina who was brought to Tanya, the hospital social worker, because the neo-natal floor nurses found her "in a psychotic state, babbling to the Virgin Mary." Gabriela had been visiting her daughter, Emilia, who had just given birth to a daughter whom she had named Natalia. Gabriela's outburst began as she listened to the doctor describe the birth defects that were threatening Natalia's survival. When she arrived in Tanya's office, Gabriela was sobbing, fingering her rosary, and trembling all over. All Gabriela could say was that she was sure Julio and his family had put a curse on Natalia.

Discussion Questions

1. If you were Tanya, what would you do first in working with Gabriela?
2. What would you do in response to the nurses' diagnosis of Gabriela as "psychotic"?
3. What questions would you ask Gabriela in an effort to understand her context?
4. Who else would you invite to participate in your sessions?
5. How would you deal with Gabriela's view that Natalia's birth defects were the result of a curse placed on her by Julio and his family?
6. What do you think would be the most difficult aspect of this case for you?
7. Where would you seek assistance?

Zhi Yi

Zhi Yi is a 10-year-old Asian American boy who was born in the United States to parents who immigrated five years previously. Recently Zhi Yi has been asking to see the school nurse, complaining of headaches and stomachaches. When she could find no evidence of a physical problem, the school nurse referred him to Celeste, the school counselor. Celeste called Zhi Yi's parents and asked them if anything had changed in their son's routine or if he had experienced anything upsetting in recent days or weeks. She learned that Zhi Yi had been invited to attend church with a neighbor and had returned from the experience with great curiosity, but also with some fear. Apparently, Zhi Yi had heard the preacher tell his congregation that they "had to believe in Jesus to have eternal life." Zhi Yi did not understand these ideas and was afraid that because he and his family were not Christians something terrible might happen to them.

Discussion Questions
1. How do you understand Zhi Yi's headaches and stomachaches? What do you think about the way the school nurse responded to Zhi Yi's complaints?
2. How would you formulate the problem Zhi Yi is experiencing?
3. If you were Zhi Yi's counselor, what questions would you ask his parents? What would you ask him?
4. What interventions would you use with him and his parents?
5. What cultural or spiritual issues are involved in this case?
6. What personal issues does this case raise for you? How do you think your own issues would help or hinder your work with Zhi Yi?

Martha

Martha is a 16-year-old high school student and a member of the Lakota Nation. She has been attending school during the week in a midwestern city 60 miles from home. There, she lives with her aunt and uncle. She returns home on the weekends and is heavily involved in the activities of her Native American community.

Martha is a gifted artist and excels in the sciences as well. At a recent college fair at her high school, Martha had the opportunity to speak with Dr. Ralph Simon, a representative of a prestigious university in the Northeast. Dr. Simon encouraged Martha to apply for the pre-medicine program at his university and all but promised her a full academic scholarship and a stipend for living expenses. Martha was excited about the possibilities for her future, but when she shared them with her parents and extended family members, she met with either silence or disapproval. When Martha returned to the city on Monday, her aunt noticed Martha's melancholy mood and tried to get her to talk about what was troubling her. When Martha refused, her aunt made an appointment for Martha to see a counselor at the community mental health center.

Discussion Questions
1. If you were the counselor to whom Martha was assigned, how would you make sense of the situation described to you?
2. How would you begin to work with Martha?
3. If you are not a Native American, what do you think you would need to do to be an effective counselor with Martha? If you are a Native American, how do you think your ethnicity and heritage would help you be effective? How might it hinder you?
4. In working with Martha, who else (if anyone) would you include in the counseling process? What is your rationale for this decision?
5. Martha has not disclosed anything about her religious or spiritual beliefs or practices. Would you explore this area with her? Why or why not? If you chose to approach this topic, how would you do it?
6. What personal issues does this case elicit for you? How do you think these issues could affect your ability to work well with Martha?
7. What resources would you consult for assistance in this case?

SUGGESTED ACTIVITIES

Experience Spiritual or Religious Diversity

If you have access to them in your community, attend a religious service or other ceremony from an ethnic tradition different from your own. Be sure to make appropriate contact with the leaders or some other authority to obtain permission to participate, if needed. Perhaps a small group of classmates would like to attend together. Make plans to share your impressions soon after your experience.

Invite a Speaker

Seek someone from your college/university community or the larger community to speak to your class about some of the rituals, traditions, or practices of various ethnic groups discussed in this chapter. It would be helpful to prepare a list of questions before your guest's visit so that she or he may be prepared to answer them.

Attend a Political Function

For many people, their religious and spiritual commitments issue in political agendas. For example, the civil rights movement was and still is grounded in the religious and spiritual understanding of social justice and liberation. Read community bulletin boards, watch the television, and read the papers about political gatherings, meetings, or rallies that are fueled by religious or spiritual beliefs. Attend one of these functions and write a personal response to it.

Conduct Research

Select one of the traditions or indigenous practices described in this chapter and write a 10–15 page research paper about it. Make a short outline of your findings and share them with your classmates, either through a poster session or other presentation method.

Rent a Video

In recent years, many thought-provoking films have showcased issues of ethnicity, spirituality, and religion. With at least one other person, rent one of these films, watch it, and write a journal entry detailing what you learned from the film, how you reacted to it personally, and what it had to teach you about counseling this particular population. Discuss the film with your viewing partner(s). Some suggestions include *Like Water for Chocolate, Life is Beautiful, My Family, The Joy Luck Club, Yentl, Chariots of Fire, Schindler's List, Perez Family, When We Were Colored, The Education of Little Tree,* and others recommended by classmates or your instructor.

SUPPLEMENTAL READINGS

McGoldrick, M., Giordano, J., & Pearce, J. K. (1996). *Ethnicity and family therapy* (2nd ed.). New York: Guilford Press. This book, like the first edition, contains a wealth of information about a host of ethnically diverse families. The contributors have provided details about culture, history, tradition, religion, and spirituality, as well as helpful suggestions about ways to work effectively with diverse populations. Every counselor should own this book.

Richards, P. S., & Bergin, A. E. (Eds.) (2000). *Handbook of psychotherapy and religious diversity*. Washington, DC: American Psychological Association. The editors of this volume have done an excellent job of collating information not only about the religions and spirituality of ethnic populations, but also about the various world religions. Each chapter contains treatment recommendations and raises issues unique to the population discussed. This book is an extremely useful resource for counselors working with religious and spiritual diversity.

IMPLICIT STRATEGIES FOR WORKING WITH CLIENTS' RELIGIOUS AND SPIRITUAL ISSUES

CHAPTER 6

INTRODUCTION

Until recently, when religious or spiritual issues surfaced in secular counseling, several alternatives occurred other than actually addressing these concerns (Frame, 1996). First, some counselors simply referred clients to clergy, pastoral counselors, or "Christian counselors." Although this option might be appropriate under certain conditions, I believe that doing so without first exploring the nature of clients' beliefs and their possible connection to psychological issues is premature. Second, some counselors, put off by clients' religious or spiritual concerns, attempted to change clients' beliefs. This alternative was rarely effective, created power struggles with clients, and frequently violated the ethical standard of not imposing one's values on one's clients. Third, some counselors chose compromise by dividing up clients' problems and treating those they believed to be psychological in nature and referring the clients to another helper for assistance with religious and spiritual issues. Fourth, some counselors, attempting to approach religious and spiritual issues, but feeling unsure of how to proceed, reframed clients' religious or spiritual concerns in psychological terms. Although this approach might have been useful in some cases, ultimately its purpose was to meet clients on the counselors' terms. Moreover, using this approach often led religious and spiritual clients to mistrust psychology as much as psychology has mistrusted religion (Rayburn, 1985).

In this chapter, I introduce implicit strategies for working with clients' religious and spiritual beliefs that take those beliefs seriously, address them in the context of existing counseling theory, or use them as powerful ancillary supports to the counseling process. With this approach, I invite you to journey on "the road less traveled" (Peck, 1978) in counseling and psychotherapy.

The strategies described earlier are essentially dualistic, either/or approaches. In none of these models does the counselor address the whole person or the multidimensional aspects of clients' problems. What is needed is a point of view that enables counselors to acquire multiple frames of reference when working with clients' religious and spiritual issues (Frame, 1996). The journey begins with taking a refreshing new perspective provided by social constructionist theory.

The social constructionist believes that individuals do not discover reality but, rather, invent it (Watzlawick, Weakland, & Fisch, 1974). Our thoughts and images about reality are subjective creations, rather than objective representations of a reality that exists outside ourselves (Efran, Lukens, & Lukens, 1988). People construct their worldview as a result of interactions with others in a social context, and the "experience, belief systems, values, fears, prejudices, hopes, disappointments, and achievements of the constructor" (Guba & Lincoln, 1989, p. 143) help define that subjective reality. When psychological problems occur, they are the result of a breakdown in one's constructions, a conflict in constructions or are interfering with one's ability to make meaning out of personal experience (Neimeyer, 1995). Thus, counseling is conducted within the client's belief system using techniques that incorporate aspects of a client's worldview (Zinnbauer & Pargament, 2000).

One aspect of counseling from a social constructionist framework involves applying the model to oneself. This notion means asking,

> How do my beliefs and my own thinking about [these clients] organize how I might tend to work with them? How can I step outside my beliefs to work with [these clients]? What will I need to do to keep myself from working against their religious meanings but rather to use their language to construct new meanings? (Frame, 1996, p. 303)

The answers to these questions may signal the counselor that he or she might have to give up some rigidity about the therapeutic enterprise to be effective with clients for whom religion or spirituality are paramount.

Another aspect of working from a social constructionist perspective involves looking at one's own social constructions. It means being willing to give up the position of "expert" to learn from clients about how they construct meanings and what their reality is. A "not knowing" position (Anderson & Goolishian, 1991) helps clients trust themselves and communicates to them that they are the ones who know themselves best (Koch, 1998). Operating from the perspective of "not knowing" rather than "knowing" keeps the counselor from approaching clients with preconceived notions and inflexible styles that preclude discovery and personal growth by both client and counselor (Koch, 1998). When counselors are able to adopt a curious stance toward clients' perspectives, they move toward collaboration in the counseling process and are better able to instill hope (Yalom, 1995) for change and renewal.

In the remainder of this chapter, I present both implicit and explicit approaches to addressing religion and spirituality in counseling (Tan, 1996). The implicit approaches use existing therapeutic models and incorporate clients' beliefs, values, and meaning structure into those frameworks. The explicit approaches use religious or spiritual strategies (such as prayer, meditation, forgiveness) to augment counselors' therapeutic endeavors. It is important to note that the "implicit" and "explicit" approaches are not mutually exclusive poles of intervention. They are, according to Tan (1996), two ends of a continuum.

GRAPPLING WITH THE THORNY ISSUES

Counselor Self-Disclosure

Once counselors commit themselves to addressing clients' religious and spiritual concerns in the context of their therapeutic work, several dilemmas present themselves regularly. First, counselors often wonder how much self-disclosure of their own beliefs is appropriate. Sometimes this question is triggered by clients' inquiries. Many counselors have struggled with how to respond to clients who ask, "Are you a Christian? Have you been born again?" "Do you believe in God?" At the root of these questions is a concern by some religious clients that secular counselors (or any counselors that do not share their particular beliefs) might misunderstand them, not comprehend religious terminology, pathologize their religious or spiritual worldviews, or ignore them altogether, or dismiss their beliefs that divine revelation is a valid source of truth (Worthington & Scott, 1983). In addition, these questions can also be a means by which clients test trust in the therapeutic relationship (Fong & Cox, 1983). Given that secular counselors are not especially religious (Bergin & Jensen, 1990; Goud, 1990; Shafranske & Malony, 1990) and that some counselors have not been trustworthy relative to clients' beliefs, these fears might not be totally unfounded (Genia, 2000).

Nonreligious clients or those who have disaffiliated with their religious or spiritual traditions might worry that counselors may be judgmental about their atypical views or their departure from orthodox beliefs. Others might be concerned that atheist counselors might not provide them with an opportunity to explore alternative religions or spiritualities (Genia, 2000). Still others could fear that counselors who are religious might try to convert them or to encourage in them values that are similar to their own.

There are divergent opinions in the mental health field regarding how to manage clients' curiosity about counselors' personal beliefs. Most psychoanalytic therapists hold that such self-disclosure inhibits clients' autonomy and their opportunity to freely explore their feelings and beliefs, especially in arenas that are morally sensitive (Rizutto, 1993).

Other counselors take an opposing view, arguing that because counseling is not value-free (Bergin, 1991; Corey, 2001), disclosing religious and spiritual values is ethical and assists clients in maintaining autonomy (Bergin, 1991; Presley, 1992). By exposing their values, some counselors argue that clients are not subjected to inadvertent imposition of counselor values and have an opportunity to examine them critically (Genia, 2000).

Kelly (1995) proposed a middle way: deferring or deflecting such questions so that clients are led to explore the meanings implicit in such inquiries. Kelly (1995) noted that direct answers have the potential to alienate clients whose beliefs are different than those of the counselor. In addition, he indicated that direct answers, which reveal counselor-client similarity, could contribute to clients thinking they will be spared the confrontation often associated with the therapeutic process. Moreover, Kelly maintained that such questions regarding counselors' beliefs might mask pain and vulnerability such that a direct answer might protect clients from addressing critical concerns. Kelly (1995) indicated that it might be helpful to respond by saying to clients, "I value your question, especially because it suggests something of importance to you. Rather than respond to it directly, I think it might be helpful if you were to talk a bit more about salvation (or belief in God) and how it's important to you" (p. 193). Another possible response would be, "It sounds like you are concerned that if my beliefs are different from yours that I might try to convince you to change them and that would not be acceptable to you. Or, maybe you are worried that I won't take your religious or spiritual concerns seriously or that it isn't safe to raise these topics in counseling. I want you to know that you can trust me to respect your beliefs and to help you explore the ways in which they may be important in the work we do together." If, however, such responses elicit unrelenting questioning from clients, it is best to give a direct, honest answer than an evasion (Genia, 2000; Kelly, 1995; Lovinger, 1990).

Working with Clients' Religious or Spiritual Authorities

According to Webster's dictionary (1987), one definition for the word *authority* is "the power to influence or command thought, opinion or behavior" (p. 117). We all have various authorities that govern the way we live. Laws, bosses, supervisors, and judges are all examples of authorities that circumscribe our behavior at work and in civil situations. In interpersonal relationships, too, there are authorities such as parents, partners, teachers, and friends whose opinions are important and whose desires and expectations influence us in significant ways. In the religious and spiritual arena, there are also authorities. Some of these include clergy, ecclesiastical leaders such as the Pope, sacred writings such as the Bible, Qur'an (Koran), I Ching, or A Course in Miracles, or even family members whose religious or spiritual beliefs have guided generations.

One challenge of counseling clients who are religiously or spiritually oriented is working with their sacred authorities. In general, I have found that the more significant a religious or spiritual authority is in a client's life, the less power I have as a counselor relative to that authority. For example, clients who view the Bible as the sole directive for life and faith might listen to what a counselor says while screening it through a biblical filter. Thus, counselors' interventions and strategies must conform to these clients' understanding of what is "biblical" to be considered sound or helpful. Moreover, counselors' attempts at addressing psychological problems might be ignored or challenged by clients who perceive counseling approaches to be antithetical to biblical authority.

Another example of the impact of religious or spiritual authorities involves the Roman Catholic couple that is in constant conflict, has extremely divergent values and goals, and yet stays married because divorce is not an acceptable alternative according to Church law. Such a couple is effectively in a double bind. Ironically, to stay together means lifelong misery, anger, and no foreseeable means of obtaining the "abundant life" (John 10:10) the Christian life promises. To get divorced means to reject the authority of the Church, to be severed from their religious community, and to experience guilt, shame, and alienation from the very institution that could provide them with spiritual support. Counselors working with couples caught in such dilemmas must recognize the power of the local priests, church law, and the Pope to influence constituents' behavior. To challenge these authorities directly could lead to clients' premature termination because they see their ecclesiastical leaders as more authoritative than their psychological helpers.

One approach to managing the impact of religious and spiritual authorities is to talk openly with clients about the various authorities that govern their lives. Many times clients have not been fully aware of the authority they have given to the Bible, vegetarianism, meditation, the Pope, or Grandma Jones. After having clients enumerate who or what is authoritative in their lives, counselors could ask them to rank these authorities from most significant to least significant. Such an exercise assists clients in clarifying where they are most influenced and how readily they accept that source of power for directing their lives. Clients who are surprised or embarrassed about their religious or spiritual authorities might be open to a process by which they evaluate the salience of these authorities and consciously choose which ones will be most influential for them. Other clients have their minds made up and are not amenable to discussions centered on the notion of choosing one's authorities. They view religious and spiritual authorities as givens to which they must surrender.

Another approach to dealing with clients' religious and spiritual authorities is to use the authorities themselves as tools in the psychotherapeutic process. For example, in working with clients who submit themselves to biblical authority, counselors might ask clients to gather the biblical texts that speak about their dilemma. In a subsequent session, counselors may review these texts and inquire about their meanings and how these meanings apply to their circumstances. Counselors need not be biblical scholars themselves to work effectively with these sacred texts. In fact, those who are least familiar with them might have fewer of their own interpretations to manage and, thus, might be more open and objective when listening for multiple meanings and perspectives. By taking clients' authorities seriously, counselors are able to reduce client defensiveness, and assist clients in generating new hermeneutics for an old story.

In one case (Frame, 1996), a couple was in conflict over the wife's desire to go back to work and the husband's disdain at such a notion. The husband claimed the story of Adam and Eve (Genesis 1:26–31; Genesis 2:15–25) meant that "women made bad decisions and that men should be in charge of things" (p. 304). The wife was not sure she agreed with her husband's interpretation. The counselor asked the couple, "What would it mean for you to let this story say something different than it has always said?" (Frame, 1996, p. 304). Counselors could then ask clients to generate multiple meanings or may offer some themselves. An example of a new interpretation of this story is found in the exegetical work of Trible (1978), who pointed out,

> Eve . . . Does not discuss the matter with her man. She acts independently, seeking neither his permission nor his advice. At the same time, she is not secretive, deceptive, or withdrawn. In the presence of the man she thinks and decides for herself . . . Throughout this scene the man has remained silent; he does not speak for obedience . . . The contrast that he offers to the woman is not strength or resolve but weakness . . . No patriarchal figure making decisions for his family, he follows his woman without question or comment. (p. 113)

Because of the authority the biblical narrative holds for some clients, using it with an interpretive twist may provide counselors with fresh opportunities for effecting change in their clients.

Another approach to working with religious and spiritual authorities in clients' lives is seeking consultation with religious or spiritual authorities themselves. Cultivating a network of clergy and spiritual guides and directors from various religious and spiritual traditions who are amenable to consulting on difficult cases is extremely helpful. At times, it might be appropriate (with clients' permission) to invite these persons to participate in a counseling session. Their expertise could be invaluable in interpreting beliefs and practices that are important to clients or clearing up doctrinal misunderstandings. When such an alliance is productive and accepted by clients, then counselors can gain more authority as a result of the vicarious sharing of power.

Sometimes, however, despite these attempts at addressing the influence of religious and spiritual authorities, clients are unwilling to reflect on their sources of authority, reject counselors' attempts at working within the authorities or consulting with them, and refuse to open themselves to counselors' strategies and interventions. Under these conditions, it is probably best that a referral is made so that clients who are dependent on religious and spiritual authorities get help in ways they perceive are congruent with their worldviews and belief systems.

Handling Harmful Beliefs or Practices

Most counselors seek to be open to their clients' religious and spiritual beliefs, their worldviews, and their ritually based practices, but sometimes these aspects of clients' lives create serious value-conflicts for counselors. Most counselors would tend to back away from a direct attack on clients' beliefs for fear of violating ethical standards that prohibit imposing one's values on one's clients. However, some religious beliefs or spiritual experiences call for action. For example, clients who claim they hear God telling them to commit a homicide or those for whom child sexual abuse is considered a spiritual practice. Under these circumstances, counselors are required to take protective action for potential victims in compliance with state and federal laws and institutional regulations.

When issues of protection have been addressed, and the client continues in the therapeutic relationship, counselors must decide how to address what they consider harmful, pathological, self-depreciating, or noxious beliefs or practices. Kelly (1995) suggested the use of "invalidating approaches," which are intended to eliminate these beliefs and practices. Although controversy remains regarding whether or not it is ever appropriate to attempt to "annihilate" (Malony, 1993) clients' beliefs, some strategies are offered. Ellis (1989) presented cognitive-behavioral approaches that are aimed at eradicating crooked or irrational ideas. Ellis (1989) contended that clients' distress was not a result of events that happened to them but, rather, was a response to thoughts and beliefs that were irrational. By changing one's thoughts or beliefs, Ellis claimed that one's difficulties could be minimized or eliminated. These methods might or might not be effective. Kelly (1995) noted that noxious and deleterious beliefs could "represent some kind of unhealthy, pathological distortion of a larger, benign system of belief" (p. 195). Dealing with these larger systemic distortions might require what Imbrie (1985) called "untwisting the illusion" from its connection to healthy spirituality and religion. Counselors who work in this way must simultaneously respect clients' religious or spiritual orientations while working on the psychosocial sources of the distortions or illusions (Kelly, 1995). In addition, counselors will want to assist clients in confronting the roots of their difficulties with the goal of ultimately helping them integrate a healthier religious or spiritual perspective into their lives.

IMPLICIT APPROACHES TO RELIGIOUS AND SPIRITUAL ISSUES: THEORETICAL INTEGRATION

Psychoanalytic Approaches

Object Relations   As with most theoretical models of counseling, there are many variations in how they are practiced. Such is the case when it comes to psychoanalytic theory. Freud, the founder of this approach, was known for his diatribes against religion. He believed that religion was a crutch for the fragile ego, which needed a cosmic parent figure for security and protection. Indeed, some practitioners of psychoanalysis continue this perspective in their contemporary work with clients. However, others (Genia, 1995; Rizzuto, 1996; Spero, 1990) have made a place for religion and spirituality in their psychoanalytic work. Essentially, they continue using psychoanalytic techniques such as free association, interpretation, and analysis of transference to help clients gain insight into their dynamic relationships and their current difficulties. However, instead of dismissing religious ideation as wish fulfillment or some other manifestation of neurosis, these counselors take seriously clients' views of and relationships with God. In turn, they are able to use these concepts and experiences as windows into clients' intrapsychic distress.

Rizzutto (1996) made a case for clients' "God representation" (p. 413) and claimed that "the child who is developmentally ready creates the sacred reality, God, (or goddess, or nirvana or Great Spirit or some other name) that its culture has placed there for the young person to find" (p. 415). Rizzutto (1996) defined "representations" as the *means* the mind has to know existing reality. She indicated that

> The God representation is the means the mind has to seek God. Its developmental and dynamic sources are unconscious and not accessible without psychic exploration. God, on the contrary, appears to the believer as the object of conscious belief in an existing being beyond the limits of the mind. (p. 417)

Rizzuto (1996) held that one's representation of God necessarily changes as a result of developmental growth, social shifts, and scientific discoveries. She maintained that these changes must occur for one's concept of God to be believable.

In addition to these notions about how God (or any Higher Power) is conceived, Rizzutto (1996) posited that one's concept of God is dynamically influenced by one's relationship to his or her parents and to one's own self. Thus, it is not uncommon for clients to project onto God issues they have with one or the other parent. For example, one client revealed that her father was a good provider, but moments later spoke of a God who never delivered what she prayed for. Rizzutto (1996) suggested that in such a case, the psychoanalytically oriented counselor might want to explore the client's need to idealize her father and, as a result, to rely on a God who could tolerate her rage and disappointment.

CASE | EMILIO

Emilio is a 35-year-old Latino who was referred to counseling because of a chronic problem with alcohol abuse. During the course of therapy with his counselor, Melinda, Emilio expressed both anger and sadness that his father had abandoned the family in favor of a life of substance abuse and crime. Although Emilio had once considered the priesthood, he dropped out of seminary in his mid-twenties because he "could not serve a God who was absent and did not provide him with the love and care he had expected." In the course of some stormy sessions involving difficult transference issues between Emilio and Melinda, Emilio began to understand that his rejection of God and the priesthood was a means of getting revenge against his father. Furthermore, Emilio discovered that he also feared becoming a "father" himself because he was not sure he could fulfill the role without committing the same kind of betrayals in his church family as he experienced in his biological family. Through Melinda's skillful and patient questioning, listening, and insight into the dynamics of Emilio's religious issues, she was able to create a safe space where he could redirect his anger at his father, thus freeing up God for a new and positive relationship.

Jungian Approach   Carl Jung, trained as a psychoanalyst and a colleague of Freud, parted ways with his mentor to develop "a spiritual approach that places emphasis on being impelled to find meaning in life" (Corey, 2001, p. 82). Jung was not able to support Freud's notion of life being driven by psychological and sexual forces. Jung chose to focus on ongoing human development in contrast to Freud's theory of determinism. For Jung, the primary goal of human existence was to integrate the conscious and unconscious aspects of the self. Part of this process is to acknowledge the dark side of the self, the *shadow,* as Jung called it. Jung posited a deep layer of the unconscious and referred to it as the *collective unconscious,* which he considered "the powerful and controlling repository of ancestral experiences" (Schultz & Schultz, 1998, p. 92). The collective unconscious is composed of universal images across human history known as *archetypes.* The three most important archetypes are the persona, the anima and the animus, and the shadow (Corey, 2001). The *persona* is the social mask that we present for self-protection. The *anima* and *animus* are the psychological and biological aspects of being female and male. These dimensions exist in both genders. The *shadow* represents the negative and socially unacceptable thoughts, feelings, and actions that we reject in ourselves and project onto others (Corey, 2001). Jung believed that through dream analysis, persons could meet the significant archetypes and could integrate the polarities and contradictions within the self.

Jung's approach is spiritual in nature because it opens a pathway for clients to discover and make meaning in their lives. The archetypes function as universal symbols and are evident in the myths and stories of many cultures and eras. For example, according to Van Eenwyk (1996), "snakes have long been symbols of evil or the Devil (the Garden of Eden), healing (the caduceus), resurrection (they shed their skins), the Great Mother (the uroboros)" (p. 469). These images provide the keys for helping clients explore unconscious material and integrate the various parts of themselves into significant wholes. Knowing that experiencing internal chaos is part of being human helps clients normalize the inner turmoil when it happens to them.

CASE | **MELODY**

Melody is a 33-year-old medical equipment salesperson. She sought counseling with April, known in her community as a therapist who worked with dreams. Melody revealed to April that she had been experiencing a series of recurring dreams that were troubling to her. She indicated that she did not understand their meaning and wanted to make sense of them. In one dream, Melody reported that she found herself scuba diving in the ocean, where she encountered sharks and bar-racuda that frightened her, but at the same time the beauty of the fish and the coral reefs under the sea moved her. In another dream, Melody related how she was journeying in the land of the dead. She saw people she knew who had died, famous people from history, and millions of faces she did not recognize. Melody was afraid of the recurring dreams about death and the dead and wondered why they were tormenting her. April shared with Melody the basic tenets of Jungian psychology and the notion of archetypes. April indicated how the journey to the underworld is a prevalent theme in ancient Greek and Roman literature and that these stories (Persephone, Psyche, Orpheus and Eurydice, Inanna) were told about women's ex-perience (O'Hare-Lavin, 2000). Moreover, these archetypes were not necessarily about death, but about a place for learning and "a cauldron for rebirth" (O'Hare-Lavin, 2000, p. 202). April told Melody that the notion of seeds being in the dark earth before germination and embryos developing in a watery womb were promi-nent themes of growth and new life. April said her hunch was that Melody was on the verge of moving into a new life that would necessitate the end [death] of part of her. April warned Melody that the transformation would be both frightening and exhilarating.

Upon learning about these archetypes, Melody said they helped her understand her inner struggle with her religious commitments. Melody said she had tried to be a good Catholic, had attended Mass faithfully, and tried to uphold the doctrine of her church, but that she felt like a hypocrite because she had engaged in premarital intercourse and had had an abortion. In fact, she described herself as "spiritually dead." Melody said she experienced severe inner turmoil because she knew she would be betraying her family if she were to leave the church. However, she was desperately yearning for a spiritual experience that would deepen her faith and would provide a way for her to feel at peace with herself and her beliefs.

In this case, April's knowledge about archetypes and symbols was an effective means to help Melody deal with the spiritual themes in her life. April was able to help Melody attach meaning to the dreams and to forge a path for her own per-sonal and spiritual growth.

Humanistic-Existential Approaches

During the 1960s and 1970s, alternatives to psychoanalytic and behavioral models emerged as a "third force" in psychotherapy (Corey, 2001). Although distinct from each other in particular ways, the humanistic and existential movements had in common a trust in the client to make positive choices for his or her life and a deep appreciation for clients' subjective (phenomenologi-cal) experiences. In addition, there was an emphasis on the freedom and re-sponsibility to make choices, to carve out personal meaning and values, and to do so in the context of interpersonal relationships. These two approaches to counseling, humanism and existentialism, differ in that humanistic coun-selors focus on the potential for clients to become self-actualized and find meaning if they are surrounded by supportive environmental conditions. Ex-istentialist counselors, on the other hand, are more concerned with clients' creating a personal identity and making meaning out of life's circumstances in the face of the anxiety of death and meaninglessness (Corey, 2001). In nontheistic existentialism, the issues of meaning and authenticity are paramount, though deities or concepts such as eternal life are not considered important. In theistic existentialism, these same concerns are significant in both human relationships and in the divine-human encounter. The philosophy behind both humanism and existentialism make each approach compatible with religious and spiritual concerns.

Counselors working from a person-centered perspective (Rogers, 1961, 1967, 1986) can use the concepts of unconditional positive regard and the primacy of the therapeutic relationship when working with clients' religious and spiritual beliefs. The techniques of accurate empathy, reflective listening, and paraphrasing can be invaluable when addressing religious and spiritual material that emerges in counseling.

Brittany, a 19-year-old receptionist came to counseling because she was pregnant and her boyfriend wanted her to have an abortion rather than to deliver and raise their child. Though not active in any religious community, Brittany said to her counselor, "I just believe that God wants me to have this baby and that to have an abortion is to destroy one of God's children." Brittany's counselor, Brandon, responded with empathy saying, "You are feeling torn because your boyfriend wants you to have an abortion and in some ways it makes sense and it would please him. On the other hand, you don't want to do it. You are afraid you would feel guilty for terminating a life that you believe was given to you by God." In this case, and from this theoretical perspective, it makes no difference how Brandon, the counselor, feels about abortion. His focus is on his client's well-being and on helping her explore her feelings and spiritual beliefs in a safe, supportive environment. He believes that she has within her the tools to make a decision that will be right for her. By building a strong therapeutic alliance, clients come to trust that whatever they offer in counseling will be received nonjudgmentally, even their religious and spiritual questions, struggles, and dilemmas.

Open-ended questions constitute another set of techniques belonging to the humanistic-existential domain. Essentially, these questions begin with "who," "what," "when," "where," and, at times, "why." Asking open-ended questions helps clients explore their own thoughts and beliefs and provides them with the opportunity to discover the connections between their feelings, thoughts, and behaviors. Although these techniques are basic to any counselor's repertoire, they are particularly useful when counselors want to assist clients in telling their stories and uncovering the links between religious and spiritual experiences or beliefs and their current dilemmas. Using this approach requires only that counselors be open to hearing clients' responses and are able to receive client data and summarize it in ways that are useful to their clients.

His employer referred Andrew, a 27-year-old Native American, to counseling because Andrew had committed some petty thefts in the office to support his gambling compulsion. Andrew was especially reluctant to enter counseling because he thought counselors "are jerks that mess with your mind." Andrew's counselor, Bonnie, began her work by attempting to join with Andrew and to empathize with him. She stated, "Andrew, I imagine it is uncomfortable for you to be sitting here right now. You've been pacing around and can hardly sit still. I bet just being here makes you nervous." Bonnie's patience and her ability to accurately reflect Andrew's discomfort and suspicions about counseling helped her client to relax. Although initially Andrew had difficulty revealing much information about himself and his problems, Bonnie asked some open-ended questions that became the catalyst for Andrew to explore multiple dimensions of his situation. At one point, Bonnie asked, "What is it about your problem that troubles you the most?" Andrew responded, "It's not the gambling that bothers me so much—lots of people are into it—but the worst thing is that I have disgraced my family and have betrayed the ways of our people. I have become greedy and competitive and am out of touch with the Sacred in my life." Bonnie followed up this response by asking, "What would you have to do to regain the harmony and the Sacred in your life?" In this case, Andrew framed his problem in spiritual terms rather than in addictive ones. By inquiring about how his spirituality was connected to the solution to his problem, Bonnie was honoring her client's worldview, addressing an existential concern, and working within his framework to address his difficulties.

Another form of humanistic counseling is Mahrer's (1996) experiential therapy. In this approach, there are two goals for each session: (1) the client becomes a qualitatively different person and (2) the client becomes free of the bad feels that were significant aspects of the old person (Mahrer, 1996). In experiential therapy, four basic steps are involved in each counseling session. First, the counselor helps clients discover the inner, deeper capacities for experiencing that exist within themselves. This task is accomplished by having clients select a strong feeling and locate the scene or context that captures the feeling. Second, counselors assist clients in welcoming and appreciating the scene and accompanying feelings regardless of their nature and content. For example, a client might experience either the deepening potential for experiencing joy or aggression. Third, counselors enable clients to make a radical shift in how they experience themselves so that they actually become the new being that has been heretofore only potentially accessible. Such a change requires an "existential leap of faith" (Mahrer, 1996, p. 436). Fourth, counselors help clients become new and different people by integrating the potential they have experienced in step three. This goal is accomplished by having clients rehearse in the session new ways of being and apply them in out-of-session experiences. When working with clients using experiential therapy, counselors and clients are aligned, and counselors are free of their own personal religious, spiritual, or transpersonal convictions attitudes and beliefs (Mahrer, 1996). Although it is not designed that way, Mahrer claimed that steps two to four in his approach may be closer to religious or spiritual ways of helping bring about change than the traditional psychotherapeutic ones. Such change, however, is not intended to have clients adopt counselors' religious or spiritual beliefs, nor to have them accept psychotherapeutic, religious, or spiritual insights or understanding of themselves or the world. Although engaging in this type of therapy could involve the risk of changing one's religious or spiritual beliefs or values, such decisions lie within clients and are not imposed by counselors (Mahrer, 1996).

| CASE | KAHLIL |

Kahlil, a 38-year-old business owner came to counseling because of an inability to concentrate, declining interest in sports and other hobbies, and sliding revenues in his yearly sales of fitness equipment. Working within the experiential framework, Wanda, the counselor, asked Kahlil to select a strong feeling and to locate a scene that captured the feeling. Almost immediately, Kahlil began to tremble as he disclosed a deep feeling of guilt for having failed to keep the requirements of Islam, including his neglect of prayer and his nonobservance of Ramadan with its emphasis on fasting. Moreover, he had been guilty of idolatry—placing financial success above his devotion to Allah. Kahlil located himself in a hotel in a distant city where he could be guaranteed anonymity and could attempt to escape from the demands his religion placed on him. His life "on the road" was a means of ignoring and "forgetting" about his religious duties. Wanda helped Kahlil embrace the guilt and look to it as a means of deepening his experiences, regardless of the pain associated with it. As Kahlil struggled with his guilt and feeling of alienation from his faith, Wanda invited him to try on a new self that would result in a radical shift in how he experienced himself. Kahlil said he wanted to become a person for whom his religion was uplifting and inspiring, rather than always feeling like it was an unrelenting demand. He vowed to begin practicing his faith again, but this time he would view it as a response to Allah's love, rather than as drudgery and demand. Over the ensuing weeks, Kahlil began praying again, five times a day, but only on the days he felt like doing so. He was determined to become a person for whom religion was integrated, rather than behaving like it was an accessory to his life.

Gestalt Approaches

Another phenomenological, humanistic, existential, and experiential approach to counseling is found in Gestalt therapy developed by Fritz Perls (1969). One goal of this form of counseling is for clients to integrate the various parts of themselves into a functioning whole (gestalt) and to increase their awareness of themselves in the present moment. Gestalt therapists work with a variety of issues, but one that is particularly relevant for spiritual and religious concerns is "unfinished business." This term refers to feelings from the past that are unexpressed and that have a negative impact on current experiencing and relating (Corey, 2001). Gestalt therapists practice using a large repertoire of techniques called exercises or experiments. These experiments bring out internal conflicts by making the struggle an actual process that occurs in the client in the present moment (Polster, 1987). One such exercise, known as "the empty chair," can be tremendously effective when God is a significant participant in a client's life. In this technique, counselors ask clients to speak to either a polarity in themselves, or to a significant other about whom one is holding unresolved feelings.

CASE | SHAMEKA

Shameka is a 21-year-old African American college student. Her academic advisor referred her to counseling because of her poor performance during the past semester. Shameka told her counselor, Stuart, that she had become depressed earlier in the semester because she was still dealing with unresolved grief related to her father's death three years previously. On the anniversary of his death, she began to feel not only extreme sadness but also anger that frightened her. Although Shameka was able to discuss her grief rationally and intellectually, she was stuck in a vicious cycle of not being able to fully experience her pain nor to move beyond it. Shameka explained that her father had been a traveling evangelist who held tent-revivals across the southeastern United States. She said that often he was gone for months at a time, abandoning his family to "win people to Jesus."

Stuart suggested that Shameka try the empty chair exercise to get in touch with her unresolved feelings about her father's death. In the first session, Shameka chose to speak to her father in the empty chair. She actually screamed and wailed at him, "Why did you have to leave me? How could you claim Jesus was more important than your own family? Now that you're dead, how am I supposed to know whether you ever really loved me?" At Stuart's direction, Shameka changed chairs and sat in the seat previously reserved for her father. When she made the physical move, she spoke in response to the previous accusations as if she were her father: "Shameka, I know you felt alone and abandoned and I'm sorry. But, I told God years ago, before you were born, that he was first in my life. I have been faithful to that commitment even though it cost me my life and my family." Although it was extremely difficult for Shameka to utter those words from her father's perspective, they proved to be helpful to her in experiencing her anger toward him and beginning to let go of it. In a subsequent session, Shameka chose to speak to God in the empty chair. This time her rage was palpable. She both sobbed and shrieked at the deity: "You stole my father from me and made him your slave! How could I love you or serve you or worship you when you have robbed me of the person I cared about most?" Shameka's freedom to explode in anger toward God provided her with permission to experience a full range of emotions related to her father's death. In this case, the empty chair technique became a powerful vehicle for Shameka's releasing pent-up emotions toward both God and her father and for beginning the road to healing.

Cognitive Behavioral Approaches

During the past two decades, cognitive behavioral counselors have made a journey from disdaining religion and spirituality, conceiving the beliefs associated with them as pathological (Ellis, 1980), to appreciating the contribution of religious and spiritual beliefs to clients' cognitive schema (Propst,

1996). Cognitive-behavioral counselors work with clients' thoughts and beliefs seeking to enable a cognitive shift that results in decreasing psychological disturbances. Thus, clients' religious and spiritual beliefs and the worldviews and perceptions that shape their reality are logical foci for the cognitive restructuring that is fundamental to this type of therapy. Basically, the cognitive-behavioral approach first involves acknowledging that thoughts shape feelings and behaviors. Second, clients must recognize their self-defeating thoughts. Third, counselors challenge these thoughts and address the underlying cognitive schemas that are contributing to clients' distress. Fourth, counselors assist clients in modifying their interpersonal assumptions and behaviors.

Propst (1996), working from a Christian perspective, offered several ways in which counselors, working within clients' Christian tradition could use particular religious beliefs to bring about cognitive change. Propst suggested that cognitive therapy can be "a type of spiritual transformation of the mind" (p. 394). She likened cognitive restructuring to the Christian notion of "repentance" based on the Greek word, *metanoia*, meaning to turn around, to change one's mind about the world and the self.

Within Christian circles, Propst (1996) used the theme of self-examination drawn from the mystic tradition to motivate clients to enter counseling and to investigate how their thoughts and beliefs contribute to their emotional difficulties. Once clients are involved in cognitive-behavioral treatment, Propst claimed that several typical beliefs could be addressed within a Christian context. First, some clients come to counseling exhausted and with a feeling of having failed in the effort to be perfect. Cognitive-behavioral counselors can address this perfectionism by reminding clients that no one is perfect and that there are no perfect answers to life's problem. Moreover, a counselor could suggest that experiencing emotional pain is not the same thing as being imperfect and might offer the client the paradoxical biblical concept that power comes out of weakness. The apostle Paul claimed this truth saying, "My grace is sufficient for you, for power is made perfect in weakness. So I will boast all the more gladly of my weaknesses, so that the power of Christ may dwell in me" (New Revised Standard Version, 2 Corinthians 12:10).

For clients who are unassertive or unwilling to move beyond their comfort zones, Propst (1996) proposed that counselors challenge those cognitive constructions by presenting Jesus as the one who suffered for a purpose. This approach is based on the idea that Christian clients will be motivated to model their lives on that of Jesus Christ. Holding him out as a risk-taker suggests that clients might re-order their thinking to align themselves more with their role model. For example, a female client who was painfully shy and lonely had difficulty venturing out from her home or attending social functions because she was afraid of being rejected. Propst (1996) offered her the idea that suffering some discomfort in the pursuit of a greater purpose would be the kind of thing Jesus would have done. Because the cognitive challenge supported the client's belief system, she was motivated to change her thinking and subsequently her behavior.

Another intervention used by Propst (1996) was intended to confront the overfunctioning of a wife and the underfunctioning of her husband in their marital relationship. The couple's belief system had reinforced this interlocking but unsatisfying pattern of interaction. Propst used the Christian concept of the mutuality and reciprocity of the Trinity (Father, Son, and Holy Spirit, the three aspects of God) to challenge this couple's schema. Because the couple accepted the metaphor of the Trinity as a model for their relationship, they were able to change the way they perceived their marriage roles and relationship.

Cognitive-behavioral techniques can be applied to any religious or spiritual tradition if counselors are knowledgeable about clients' religious or spiritual traditions. For example, a counselor working with a Buddhist client experiencing emotional pain because of a broken relationship could challenge the client's notion that he should not be suffering so much. Using the Four Noble Truths that acknowledge suffering and claim that it is a result of desire, attachment, and craving (Lester, 1993), the counselor could confront her client's cognitions within his religious tradition. Relying on several aspects of the Eight-fold path to support cognitive strategies, the counselor could remind her client that the way to end desire and thus suffering involves right opinion, right mindfulness, and right concentration (Wangu, 1993). Even counselors who are not religious can use religiously based cognitive-behavioral interventions effectively. Nonreligious counselors, trained in cognitive-behavioral approaches using religious content were found to be as effective as religious counselors using religiously based cognitive-behavioral therapy (Propst, Ostrom, Watkins, Dean, & Mashburn, 1992).

CASE | LEAH

Leah, a 42-year-old Jewish client, came to counseling because she was experiencing sexual harassment in her workplace. Her boss, Seth, had been making sexual advances toward her for several months. Leah was afraid she would lose her job if she reported the harassment to the authorities in her company. In addition, she was a quiet and withdrawn person who rarely asserted herself in any situation. In the initial intake session, her counselor, Amy, learned that Leah was a devout Jew, attended synagogue regularly, and that her religious community was the basis for her social interactions. Drawing on the Hebrew prophetic tradition, Amy was able to help Leah identify with the prophets who spoke out about social injustice and abuse that characterized their times. By assisting Leah to restructure her thoughts about assertiveness by taking the role of a prophet (Propst, 1996), she became able to challenge her boss' harassment.

Behavioral Approaches

Behavior therapy, based on learning theory, posits that all behavior is learned and thus can be unlearned or relearned. Through the techniques of reinforcement, shaping, modeling, self-monitoring, systematic desensitization, punishment, and extinction (Spiegler & Guevremont, 1998), undesirable behaviors can be eliminated and replaced with more adaptive ones. Behavior therapy has been shown to be effective in reducing or eliminating distress caused by a variety of problems (Spiegler & Guevremont, 1998). It is also being used to increase spiritual practices that are associated with positive mental and physical health (Martin & Booth, 1999).

Martin and Booth (1999) applied the behavioral strategies of *goal setting, self-monitoring* (diary keeping or checklist use) and *contracting* with clients who wish to enhance their spiritual practices in association with other therapeutic aims such as reducing negative feelings or eliminating addictive behaviors. For example, incremental periods of prayer or meditation can be increased to the client's target goal (perhaps an hour) by *shaping* techniques. In this approach, clients are asked to spend two to three minutes in prayer or meditation and to increase the time gradually until they reach their goals. Related to and important in this intervention is *positive reinforcement* for attaining intermittent goals. *Stimulus control* or contextual prompting techniques can be applied such that clients are cued to practice their spiritual disciplines when they are in certain environments. For example, clients might be more apt to read scriptures when doing so is associated with a particular place (favorite chair, sanctuary, sacred space). *Modeling* (Bandura, 1986) can be employed to assist clients in attaining a set of spiritual practices. For example, role models, guides, or mentors can be used with clients who want to incorporate or maintain meditation, yoga, fasting, or some other disciplines. Such an approach can be especially helping for clients recovering from religious environments that were aversive, abusive, or punishing (Martin & Booth, 1999).

Counselors' effectiveness in helping clients attain spiritual qualities such as forgiveness, mindfulness, acceptance, hope, or other virtues may be aided by having them acknowledge the ways in which their desired qualities comprise certain behaviors and cognitions (Martin & Booth, 1999). Thus, clients are better able to see a path toward achieving their desired qualities when they are aware of the thoughts related to these qualities and how they must act to attain them. For example, counselors who assist clients wishing to become more hopeful would coach them in thinking optimistically. In addition, counselors would have clients act as if good things were going to happen to them, thus addressing the behavioral component of hope.

CASE | REID

Reid, a 53-year-old stockbroker was referred to counseling by his physician because of concerns related to stress and the beginning signs of heart disease. Reid told his counselor, Justin, that it was not uncommon for him to work 80 to 90 hours a week, eat meals at his desk or in his car, stay up late tracking his own stocks on the Internet, and awaken exhausted every day. Reid boasted that he had not taken a vacation in three years, nor a day off in four months (except to visit his mother on her deathbed). Reid acknowledged that his lifestyle was unhealthy, but revealed that he became anxious when he was not working. He could not even watch a 30-minute television program without pacing. Justin inquired about Reid's hobbies, social networks, and spiritual resources. Reid indicated that he had once enjoyed both golf and racquetball, but had played neither in nearly a year. He reported that beside his work colleagues, his friendships were with people his wife knew through her contacts at work and in the neighborhood. Reid made it clear to Justin that he was not religious, but he indicated that he was "a spiritual person" who had "lost touch" with that part of himself. In concert with Reid's goal of reducing his stress and workaholism, Justin decided to use behavioral techniques. He wanted to help Reid attain his goal of adding more relaxation and fun into his life, cultivating his spiritual side, and reducing his reliance on work to maintain his self-esteem. Justin began by having Reid plan to play golf or racquetball at least once every 10 days, to invite some friends over for dinner, and to reacquaint himself with meditation. Justin used successive approximations with Reid to help him meet his goals. He had Reid join a meditation group so that Reid would have role models and guides to help him with this spiritual discipline. Justin also suggested that Reid set aside a specific time and place for meditation and that he reward himself every time he was able to keep his meditation appointment. Eventually, Reid introduced enjoyable activities into his life, expanded his social circle, and began exploring spirituality in a new way. In fact, Reid discovered that meditation itself was a means of reducing his anxiety and stress. Later in the counseling process, Reid was able to take "meditation breaks" to ward off his stress and anxiety rather than adding more tasks. In this case, behavioral techniques were applied to the spiritual practice of meditation to enable Reid to manage his addiction to work and to achieve a more balanced lifestyle.

In addition to the classic behavioral techniques just described, Curtis and Davis (1999) offered a means of incorporating spirituality into Lazarus' (1984) multimodal therapy. Lazarus' model involves assessing the BASIC ID (an acronym for the seven different dimensions of clients' lives). In this approach, counselors inquire about clients' behavior (B), affect (A), sensations (S), imagery (I), cognitions (C), interpersonal relationships (I), and drugs and biological factors (D). In addition, counselors explore with their clients the "firing order" (Lazarus, 1984) or sequence in which clients respond to particular events. For example, some clients may respond to anxiety-producing situations by thinking about the anxiety, which leads to imagining a way to escape from the scene, which leads to heart palpitations and rapid breathing, and results in the feeling of anxiety (Curtis & Davis, 1999). Lazarus (1984) suggested addressing this "firing order" of CISA (cognitions, imagery, sensations, and affect) by starting with the first response, that of cognitions. Offering the client a cognitive intervention could be a means of interrupting the pattern of an anxiety response to a particular set of stimuli. In addition to the dimensions assessed using the BASIC ID, Curtis & Davis (1999) added a set of questions intended to ascertain the importance of spirituality in clients' lives. They proposed asking clients routinely if they have any spiritual or religious beliefs. They used closed questions to give clients the freedom to answer negatively without counselor censure. This method of introducing the subject of spirituality conveys to clients that it is an acceptable topic for exploration during counseling. It also gives clients for whom religion or spirituality is not significant an opportunity to bypass this line of questioning. For those who indicate that they have religious or spiritual beliefs, Curtis and Davis (1999) engage their clients as follows:

> (a) Tell me about your spiritual and religious beliefs; (b) What role do your beliefs play in your life? (c) Tell me about any beliefs, rituals, or prayers that you find particularly comforting; (d) Tell me about any of your beliefs that cause anxiety or confusion. (p. 204)

The purpose of asking such questions is to help clients use their religious and spiritual beliefs in dealing with their difficulties and in normalizing their concerns and doubts (Genia, 1994).

CASE | **GERTRUDE**

Gertrude, a 73-year-old former teacher, was brought to counseling by her daughter, Marie, because of Gertrude's fear of driving over bridges. Marie indicated that in the past several months, her mother had refused to drive over the San Francisco Bay Bridge to visit her and her family. Although Marie understood the stress her mother experienced because of the traffic and the bridge's height, she was frustrated by the inconvenience this phobia created for her. Also, she had lost patience with Gertrude's stalwart behavior in the face of this routine activity and wanted her mother to "snap out of it."

Gertrude's counselor, Catalina, used the BASIC ID to assess her client's situation and added the questions concerning spirituality recommended by Curtis and Davis (1999). During the initial interview, Catalina learned that Gertrude was a devout Christian who indicated that she had a strong faith in God. Concomitantly, she discovered that six months previously, Gertrude's best friend of 50 years, Millie, was killed when a semi truck sideswiped her car as she drove across an overpass on a busy interstate highway. Gertrude reported that ever since then she had experienced nightmares and had awakened at night in a cold sweat dreaming about Millie's accident. Catalina asked Gertrude about the sequence of events that occurred when she considered driving across the Bay Bridge. Millie indicated that the first thing that happened was she imagined herself losing control of the car, driving over the edge, and drowning in the Bay. The image of careening off the bridge in her car caused Gertrude to perspire, shake, and become nauseated. In the course of these sensations, Gertrude would recognize the anxiety she felt, but was powerless to stop it. She confided that in response to the escalating anxiety she would take tranquilizers. Catalina decided to begin with imagery since Gertrude's "firing order" was ISAD (imagery, sensations, affect, and drugs). She also decided to make use of Gertrude's professed faith as part of the visualization exercise. First, Catalina had Gertrude contemplate driving over the Bay Bridge. When Gertrude felt the anxiety, Catalina asked her to visualize herself driving over the bridge with Jesus* sitting in the passenger seat beside her. Catalina instructed Gertrude to listen to Jesus saying to her, "Do not be afraid, Gertrude." "When you pass through the waters, I will be with you; and through the rivers, they shall not overwhelm you . . . for I am the Lord your God, the Holy One of Israel, your Savior" (NRSV, Isaiah 43:2–3).

Tapping into the power of Gertrude's religious faith, quoting a familiar passage from the Bible that was particularly related to Gertrude's fear, and helping Gertrude attack the traumatic imagery through substituting an alternative visualization, helped reduce Gertrude's anxiety. By adding relaxation training and successive approximation, Gertrude was able to drive over the bridge within six months of beginning treatment.

*Another religious figure such as Buddha, Mohammed, or Confucius could be substituted for Jesus and the words appropriately altered to reflect that religion's sacred beliefs or texts.

Transpersonal Psychology Approaches

One major aim of transpersonal psychology is the transformation of consciousness (Assagioli, 1993; Walsh & Vaughan, 1993). Approaches designed to achieve this goal are "intended to help people explore levels of energy and awareness beyond or on the other side of the masks and patterns of the personality" (Brown, 2001, p. 104). Spiritual practices from a host of religions have evolved as means of contacting the "Other" and experiencing a deeper awareness of Self. For example, Hindus and Buddhists have practiced yoga and meditation for centuries. Moslem Dervish orders have engaged in howling, whirling, and trance dancing to attain a heightened awareness (Garnett, 2000). Christian mystics have cultivated the disciplines of prayer, fasting, and even self-flagellation to achieve spiritual connection with God (Bobin, 1999; Frohlich, 1994; Romano, 1996). Native American traditions have included purification in sweat lodges (Bucko, 1999) and painful rituals such as the Sun Dance to reach states of increased awareness. Others have experimented with psychoactive substances such as LSD or MDMA (ecstasy) to fulfill their needs for transforming experiences and altered states of consciousness.

Psychosynthesis is one model of working within the realm of transpersonal psychology. Counselors who practice in this way are convinced people have within themselves the intuitive knowledge of a Higher Self, and they work toward integrating the physical, emotional, mental, and spiritual dimensions of personhood through this method (Brown, 2001). Psychosynthesis involves the use of right-hemisphere language such as symbol, myth, metaphor, and images (Watzlawick, 1993) and is often tapped through the arts.

Brown (2001) developed the Creative Explorations of Inner Space (CEIS) process to accomplish the goals of psychosynthesis in 12 steps* described

*These 12 steps are not to be confused with 12-Step Programs that are used to address addiction issues.

here. The interventions are divided into two parts: preparation and exploration. Step 1 involves having clients secure an undisturbed sacred space wherein they can be alone and experience *solitude* in preparation for an inner journey. In Step 2, clients use *relaxation* techniques (including focusing on breathing) to reach a state of calm centeredness. In Step 3, clients engage in *reflective thinking* in which they select a topic of concern, write it on a piece of paper, and then spend 10 minutes writing about it. This activity helps clients focus and concentrate. In Step 4, clients participate in *receptive thinking,* in which they reflect on their reactions to the topic and write down their impressions. They repeat this process twice in hopes of gaining insight and empathy. Steps 1 through 4 are preparatory and the remaining eight steps exploratory. In Step 5, clients undertake *visualization,* and with their eyes closed, they summarize their reflections in one sentence and then in one word. As part of this process, clients then wait for an image to appear that represents the essence of their discovery. They are then instructed to attend to the feelings that emerge as they meditate on the image. In Step 6, clients engage in *mandala art* in which they draw a circle and illustrate the image that came to them in Step 5. Various instruments such as pens, markers, or crayons are used. Creativity is encouraged. In Step 7, clients undergo a *cognitive analysis* of their drawings seeking to understand the feelings, meanings, and symbols attached to their images. This aspect of the process emphasizes the development of reason and understanding. In Step 8, clients participate in an *inner dialogue* in which they question the image they have drawn asking, "What have you come to teach me at this time in my life?" (Brown, 2001, p. 114). In Step 9, clients involve themselves in *symbolic identification or psychodrama* by standing up, and actually "becoming" the image using appropriate sounds or movements. Then they imagine their "normal" selves standing in front of the image, and they are to "give that self a special subvocal message" (Brown, 2001, p. 114). Afterwards they sit down and document what happened for them. In Step 10, clients *integrate* their experiences and participate in *homework* and *strategic planning.* As part of this step, clients write down three steps they will take in the near future in response to their insights. Step 11 involves *closure* in which clients date their mandala and hang it up so it can continue to speak to them. Step 12 involves sharing what happened in the CEIS process with someone who is trusted. Such action helps develop a support network for future transforming work (Brown, 2001).

CASE | MITCHELL

Mitchell is a 39-year-old attorney who was referred to counseling by his wife, Stephanie, who reported that Mitchell had quit his lucrative job saying it was too demanding, unfulfilling, and "robbed him of meaning in his life." Mitchell told Stephanie he wanted to "find out who he really was" and would only consider counseling if the counselor could help him discover his true identity and find something significant to which he could dedicate his life. Stephanie suggested Mitchell see Terry, a counselor known in the community for his work in transpersonal psychology. Because Mitchell had indicated he had a "kind of spiritual yearning," Terry thought that Brown's (2001) CEIS process could be helpful to him. Terry took Mitchell through the 12 steps of CEIS, and Mitchell had a profound experience in the first session. The topic he chose to explore was the lack of meaning in his life, and the image that came to him in step five was that of a desert. His mandala art consisted of a maze of concentric circles drawn in brown. There was no other color at all on his mandala. He realized that the color signified that something inside him had died. The feelings were of grief, sadness, and emptiness. The maze symbolized for Mitchell his sense of wandering through a labyrinth unable to find his way out. The turning point of the session came in response to the question Mitchell asked of his mandala: "What have you come to teach me at this time in my life?" (Brown, 2001, p. 114). The response he heard was this: "Your old Self that was aggressive, competitive, and materialistic has died. You must seek a rebirth through an inner odyssey. You will find a new Self that is more alive and more whole. Focus on the journey, not the destination." In this one session, Mitchell felt affirmed in his decision to leave his job and became willing to be a pilgrim on an unknown road toward discovering his true Self.

This chapter dealt with implicit models (Tan, 1996) of integrating spirituality into counseling. That is, I presented five broad theoretical orientations, provided examples of ways to incorporate spiritual concerns within the existing techniques and strategies associated with each model. I included case examples that illustrated specific ways counselors could work with clients' religious and spiritual issues in the context of their theoretical perspectives. In the next chapter, I turn to the more "explicit" (Tan, 1996) interventions that are essentially religious or spiritual in nature and demonstrate how these, too, can be employed in the therapeutic endeavor.

CASE EXAMPLES

Sonya

Sonya is a 55-year-old Caucasian high school teacher who came to counseling because she "lacked direction and meaning in her life." Sonya told her counselor, Rodney, that her youngest son, Ted, had left for college in the fall and that ever since she could not gain a new focus for her energies. She reported that even though she had always held a full-time teaching job, her three children had been her priority. Now that she was "an empty-nester," she had lost her sense of purpose and "had no personal goals."

Discussion Questions
1. What counseling approach would you take in working with Sonya?
2. How do you think Sonya's presenting problem could be related to spiritual issues?

3. If Sonya were open to considering spirituality as one possible dimension of meaning, how would you go about introducing the concept? What strategies might you employ to assist Sonya in finding direction and purpose for her life?

4. If Sonya were not amenable to a spiritual perspective, what other options would you see in addressing her problem?

5. What personal issues does Sonya's case raise for you? How do you think your own issues can affect your work with Sonya?

Christopher

Christopher is a 30-year-old Asian American graphic artist who sought counseling with Shirley because of his extreme loneliness and inability to form long-term intimate relationships with women. He reported that he had dated numerous women, but that these relationships lasted at most three months. Christopher indicated in his intake interview that he was a spiritual person, but had given up being Catholic when he was in high school. He said he had "dabbled in Buddhism" and was attracted to "New Age" ideas and practices, but did not have clarity about how spirituality was connected to the other aspects of his life. He stated that he was open to exploring spiritual concerns as long as he could find help in his struggle for intimacy.

Discussion Questions

1. What additional information would you want to gather from Christopher regarding his presenting problem? How would this information shape how you would work with him if he were your client?

2. From the information available in this case, how do you think you could use Christopher's spiritual openness to work with his presenting problem?

3. What theoretical perspective seems to be the most appropriate lens for viewing Christopher's case? Why? What other perspectives might be useful?

4. What personal issues does Christopher's case raise for you? How do you think you would react to his problem if you were his counselor?

5. Under what conditions would you consider referring Christopher to another counselor, or spiritual guide?

Joyce

Joyce is a 41-year-old Caucasian vice-president of an advertising firm. She sought counseling because she felt stymied in her career and alienated from her spiritual self. She told her counselor, Ann Marie, that she needed "a new vision of her future" and that she wanted to be intentional about developing her spiritual side.

Ann Marie inquired about Joyce's religious and spiritual background. Joyce revealed that she had been raised in an upper-middle-class home in the

Northeast. She indicated that religion was considered "hogwash" by her parents, who were both well-respected professors at Ivy League institutions. As a result, Joyce said she never had an opportunity to learn about organized religion, except on a few occasions when she would attend church or synagogue with a friend. Joyce said that she had felt "a spiritual spark ignite" when she read *Women Who Run with the Wolves* (Estes, 1997). She said she identified with the archetypes and images that were so powerfully described in that book. She told Ann Marie she wanted to learn more about the metaphors of spirituality and how they might draw her out of her mindset that had been shaped primarily by materialism and success.

Discussion Questions
1. How would you frame Joyce's presenting problem?
2. What theoretical perspective do you think might be the most useful for Joyce's goals?
3. Which model of faith development, including St. John's model, seems to be most useful for working with Joyce? What stage do you think she is in?
4. How would you work with the idea of archetypes, metaphors, and images in helping Joyce gain clarity about her spirituality?
5. How do you think Joyce's disillusionment with her career could be connected to her spiritual search? If you think there is a connection, how would you offer this insight to Joyce?
6. What part of your own spiritual journey makes you feel comfortable with Joyce's newfound insights? What parts of your spiritual journey find you perplexed or out of touch with her discoveries?
7. What additional resources could you call on for assistance in working with Joyce?

SUGGESTED ACTIVITIES

Make a Video

If you have access to a video recorder, make a video of yourself role-playing one of the cases in this chapter. Ask your classmates to review your tape and give you feedback about your work. Review a tape belonging to another classmate and provide feedback to him or her regarding the videotaped role-play.

Invite a Panel of Counselors

After talking with your instructor and classmates, invite several counselors or other mental health service providers from your community to speak to your class about how they integrate spirituality into psychotherapy. Try to have as many different disciplines and theoretical perspectives represented as possible. Develop a list of questions for the panel beforehand and be sure the members have an opportunity to prepare answers to the questions. Select a moderator for the panel who will be certain that the questions are answered and that everyone has plenty of time to speak.

Interview Clergy and Spiritual Leaders

Select some clergy and other spiritual leaders in your community to interview. Ask them how they see the relationship between religion/spirituality and secular counseling. Ask them to describe the kinds of counselors to whom they would consider referring their parishioners or members. Ask them to describe the issues (both spiritual and psychological) that tend to emerge when they are counseling constituents. Ask them what they think about secular counselors integrating religious or spiritual issues into their work.

SUPPLEMENTAL READING

Brown, M. H. (2001). A psychosynthesis twelve step program for transforming consciousness: Creative explorations of inner space. *Counseling and Values, 45,* 103–117. Michael Brown describes the method of psychosynthesis in this article and gives specific suggestions on how to use it in a counseling setting. Counselors interested in learning one approach grounded in transpersonal psychology should read this article.

Murgatroyd, W. (2001). The Buddhist spiritual path: A counselor's reflection on meditation, spirituality and the nature of life. *Counseling and Values, 45,* 94–102. In this article, the Wanpen Murgatroyd describes her spiritual journey from its beginnings in Buddhism through her training in Western approaches to mental health. The article illuminates the Buddhist way and the issues raised from that perspective alongside psychotherapy.

Shafranske, E. P. (Ed.). (1996). *Religion and the clinical practice of psychology.* Washington, DC: American Psychological Association. This edited book is a well-done volume containing several chapters related to integrating spirituality into existing theoretical perspectives. It provides a solid basis for practitioners who are beginning to make these connections.

EXPLICIT RELIGIOUS AND SPIRITUAL STRATEGIES FOR COUNSELING

CHAPTER 7

INTRODUCTION

In addition to using theoretically based counseling interventions when working with clients' religious or spiritual issues, counselors can also employ specific religious or spiritual practices in counseling. This approach is fairly new among secular counselors, is controversial, and may raise ethical questions. Nevertheless, there are times when such strategies are appropriate, are welcomed by the client, do not violate any ethical standards, and result in client improvement. In this section the following strategies will be discussed: (a) prayer and meditation, (b) spiritual journaling, (c) religious and spiritual bibliotherapy, (d) authoritative writings, (e) forgiveness, (f) surrender, and (g) 12-step programs. Although these activities are often used with individual clients, they may be adapted for use with couples and families. Before describing these methods, it is important first to offer some guidelines for using spiritual interventions.

GUIDELINES FOR USING SPIRITUAL INTERVENTIONS

When considering spiritually derived counseling interventions, counselors must have clarity about their own religious or spiritual world-views (Fukuyama & Sevig, 1999). As indicated in Chapter 1, the "person-of-the-therapist" dynamics can have significantly negative impact when counselors are unaware of their issues and inadvertently impose them on their clients. Engaging in thoughtful self-examination, perhaps with another counselor or spiritual leader, could assist counselors in gaining the personal insight they need to proceed in the arena of spiritual strategies. Second, assess clients' religious and spiritual backgrounds before using spiritual interventions (Richards & Bergin, 1997). If clients are not open to religious or spiritual aspects of their difficulties, it is inappropriate to bring them into counseling or to employ methods that are particularly based in religious or spiritual beliefs or practices. Third, establish a trusting and genuine relationship with the client, and select interventions that are respectful of clients' belief systems (Fukuyama & Sevig, 1999; Richards & Bergin, 1997). Fourth, obtain informed consent to use religious or spiritual practices as counseling interventions (Richards & Bergin, 1997). Fifth, explore the parameters of the work setting to determine appropriateness of implementing religious or spiritual strategies. Some settings such as public schools and government-supported agencies may forbid counselors from discussing religion and spirituality with their clients. Therefore, counselors must know the norms of the work setting regarding these issues. Sixth, work with clients' worldviews and values, taking care not to impose your perspective on clients (Richards & Bergin, 1997). Of course, sometimes it is therapeutically helpful to assist clients in examining their beliefs and to challenge ideas that are contributing to the difficulties presented in counseling. Such confrontation should be done in ways that encourage clients to grow, rather than by means that condemn. Seventh, obtain peer supervision when employing religious or spiritual interventions (Fukuyama & Sevig, 1999). Getting the perspective of others can enhance one's clinical insights and effectiveness. It is especially helpful when venturing into unfamiliar territory such as the use of spiritual or religious strategies. Peers can assist with "person-of-the-therapist" issues and can help counselors be sure they are putting their clients' needs above their own. Eighth, uncover clients' sources of support within the family, the community, and religious or spiritual guides or leaders (Fukuyama & Sevig, 1999). Use these external supports when implementing religious or spiritual strategies in counseling. Finally, know the circumstances under which employing religious and spiritual interventions are contraindicated. (A discussion of these conditions follows later in this chapter).

PRAYER AND MEDITATION

Prayer

Prayer is one of the most universal and personal aspects of almost every world religion and is central to spirituality that is not expressed in religious dogmas, doctrines, or denominations. Prayer is "thoughts, attitudes, and actions designed to express or experience connection to the sacred" (McCullough & Larson, 1999, p. 86). Prayer is a way of accessing a richer, more intense life, and is a means by which people experience transcendent and superempirical reality (McCullough & Larson, 1999).

Research results have indicated that 90% of Americans pray, 97% believe that prayer is heard, and 86% believe that prayer makes them better people (Gallup Organization, 1993). In addition, several researchers have shown that women pray more frequently than men do (Husaini, Moore, & Cain, 1994; Poloma & Gallup, 1991) and that they pray in a more meditative manner with deeper religious experiences than men (Gallup Organization, 1993; Poloma & Gallup, 1991). African Americans have been shown to pray more often than Whites and reported greater satisfaction with their prayer life than did Whites (Gallup Organization, 1993). Older persons have been shown to be more religious than younger ones and to engage in prayers more frequently than younger people do (Chatters & Taylor, 1989; Gallup Organization, 1993; Poloma & Gallup, 1991).

Researchers investigating prayer have discovered that it is often used as a coping mechanism for serious problems (Neighbors, Jackson, Bowman, & Gurin, 1983); that it is positively correlated with life satisfaction, well-being, and religious satisfaction (Markides, 1983; Poloma & Pendleton, 1989, 1991); and that it acts as a buffer for stress (Pargament, 1997). It is impossible to explain what happens during prayer and what makes it efficacious. Dossey (1993) proposed that the effects could be explained by the placebo effect, the mind-body connection, or perhaps transcendent healing.

Some types of prayer include contemplative/meditative, ritual, petitionary, colloquial, and intercessory (McCullough & Larson, 1999). Contemplative/meditative prayer involves a receptivity in which one experiences oneself in God's presence (Poloma & Pendleton, 1989). This involves a transcendence of words and images in which one focuses attention of the experience of the sacred. This type of prayer has been shown to be positively related to recovery from a stressful event (Pargament, Koenig, & Perez, 1998). Ritual prayer involves reciting prayers either from written materials or from memory (Poloma & Pendleton, 1989). Although there is little research conducted in this area, some studies suggest that this type of prayer could be associated with lower well-being (McCullough & Larson, 1999). Petitionary prayer means going to God or one's Higher Power asking for the particular needs of others to be met (Poloma & Pendleton, 1989). This form of prayer is not uniquely associated with measures of well-being and, used exclusively could be an indicator of psychosocial distress resulting from negative life events (Pargament, Smith, Koenig, & Perez, 1998). Colloquial prayer is a conversation with God that might include elements of petition, adoration, and simply sharing feelings with God (Scarlett & Periello, 1991). This type of prayer could be a form of religious coping that is positively related to health and well-being (McCullough & Larson, 1999). Intercessory prayer involves praying for others and has been subjected to many attempts at empirical study. Investigators have raised methodological and interpretive challenges; however, one assumption has been that intercessory prayer may be therapeutic for the agent of prayer as well as for persons for whom prayer has been offered (McCullough & Larson, 1999).

In the therapeutic arena, prayer may be used in three major ways: (a) by clients as an ancillary tool alongside mental health treatment; (b) by practitioners who pray about or for their clients outside of the counseling session; and (c) by practitioners who pray with their clients in the counseling session. Clients who choose to pray for insight, guidance, healing, or change for themselves in the counseling process may find that prayer is a means of collaborating with God [a Higher Power or Supreme Being] and the counselor to bring about change. In a sense, these clients are using their religious or spiritual beliefs to augment the effectiveness of the therapeutic process. Although the efficacy of such a process can be debated on both metaphysical and psychological grounds, it is certainly plausible that the mere act of trusting in the power of prayer could bring about significant cognitive transformation (Propst, Ostrom, Watkins, Dean, & Mashburn, 1992). Because of cognitive shifts, clients might find themselves more open to the influence of counselors. In addition, counselors' who recommend that clients consider meditative/contemplative prayer as an adjunct to therapy might be able to use the data suggesting that this form of prayer is positively associated with well-being (Carlson, Bacaseta, & Simanton, 1988; Finney & Malony, 1985).

Praying for clients outside of the session and without their awareness might bring about positive outcomes, especially if the mental health practitioner believes in the efficacy of intercessory prayer (Richards & Bergin, 1997). Such a practice could open practitioners to insights and wisdom regarding how to work best with their clients. Moreover, Richards and Bergin (1997) argued that prayer for one's clients is apt to change the pray-er as much as the one for whom the prayer is offered. As a result, prayer may be considered a positive strategy, especially when working with difficult clients or those that the counselor does not like (McCullough & Larson, 1999). Regardless of what perspective counselors take in praying for their clients, prayer "should not be viewed as a substitute for counselors' professional competency and psychological health" (Richards & Bergin, 1997, p. 203).

Praying with one's clients in the counseling session is rare (Jones, Watson, & Wolfram, 1992) and controversial at best. In their study of Christian practitioners' use of religious or spiritual strategies in counseling, Ball and Goodyear (1991) found that most counselors either prayed silently within the session or outside of the session rather than with the client. Richards and Bergin (1997) claimed that there are limited situations in which praying out loud with clients is appropriate. These conditions are (a) when the client requests it, (b) when a thorough assessment has been conducted and it has been determined that to pray with a client will not create boundary confusion, (c) when counselors are convinced that competent psychological help is being given, (d) when both the client and the counselor share similar religious and spiritual worldviews, and (e) when the setting supports in-session prayer. Even under these conditions, one runs the risk of ethical violations. First, offering prayer is usually an activity associated with the role of a religious leader or spiritual guide. When counselors participate in verbal prayer with clients within the counseling session, they create the potential for clients to confuse the boundaries around their profession and that of the clergy. Second, offering prayer in a counseling session could set up clients for unhealthy transference (Richards & Bergin, 1997). For example, clients could project onto the counselor negative feelings they have about their priests or clergy. In addition, counselors who pray with their clients in the therapeutic setting are vulnerable to imposing their values on their clients. The words selected and the tone used are powerful vehicles of communicating counselors' values and beliefs. This truth is especially evident when counselors choose to pray with their clients. Before entering this sphere of activity, counselors should consult with supervisors and proceed only when they feel confident they are not violating ethical standards and that their prayer with clients would be in their clients' best interest.

Meditation

Meditation is a form of contemplation "that involves concentrated practice" (Miller, 1994, pp. 2–3) and involves training the attention (Goleman, 1988). Marlatt and Kristeller (1999) noted that there are two basic types of meditation. The first is *concentrative,* in which one focuses on something such as a candle, a mandala, or one's own breathing. The second type of meditation is referred to as *mindfulness,* in which one opens up the self, surrender's control, and awaits insight. In practicing mindfulness, one engages in self-observation or self-monitoring of one's stream of consciousness. Persons who practice mindfulness adopt an accepting and nonjudgmental attitude toward the self (Marlatt & Kristeller, 1999).

Meditation is often associated with Eastern religions, such as Hinduism and Buddhism, and spiritualities that exist outside of religious structures. For this reason, some Christian clients may not be comfortable practicing meditation (McLemore, 1982) despite its similarities with Western practices such as contemplation, imagery, and centering prayer (Carlson et al., 1988; Finney & Malony, 1985).

Meditation has been shown to be effective in managing stress, anxiety, depression, post-traumatic stress disorder (PTSD), health problems (Benson, 1996; Martin & Carlson, 1988), and is useful for the prevention and treatment of addictive behaviors (O'Connell & Alexander, 1994). In addition, the relaxation effects of meditation have also been demonstrated (Cuthbert, Kristeller, Simons, & Lang, 1981).

When attempting to integrate meditation into clinical practice, it might be necessary to teach clients the basics of the meditative process in the session. These steps may include having clients first sitting in a comfortable position and then selecting a word or phrase on which to focus. This word should be grounded in clients' religious or spiritual belief systems. Then, clients should be instructed to close their eyes, relax their muscles, and breathe slowly repeating the focus word as they exhale. Next, counselors should encourage clients to adopt a passive, nonjudgmental attitude, and to quietly dismiss intrusive thoughts if they enter the mind. This meditative practice should continue from 10 to 20 minutes and should be practiced out-side of the session once or twice a day (Marlatt & Kristeller, 1999).

Visualization and Spiritual Imagery

Related to meditation and mindfulness are visualization and spiritual im-agery, which can occur in the context of meditation or in a meditative pos-ture. In these practices, clients are asked to imagine scenes or images that call up issues or concerns. In one approach called guided imagery, leaders (or counselors) take clients on an imaginary journey, reading for them a narra-tive that invites them to reflect on sacred writings and the meaning of these scriptures. For example, Stahl (1977) offered a guided imagery meditation on a piece of scripture from the Bible taken from Matthew 13:45–46: "Here is another picture of the kingdom of Heaven. A merchant looking out for fine pearls found one of very special value: so he went and sold everything he had, and bought it." In beginning the visualization, Stahl suggested having clients close their eyes, pay attention to their breathing, and to imagine themselves in a meadow or grassy area. Part of the guided imagery meditation she devel-oped follows:

> You become aware that you are searching for something of great value . . . Fol-lowing your intuition and god's guidance, choose your path and do whatever is necessary in order to find that for which you are searching . . . Let yourself expe-rience any struggles or barriers along the way . . . also, bring in any help or assis-tance that you want . . . Finally you find this thing of great value for which you have been searching . . . You discover that you must sell or get rid of everything else in your life if you are to obtain this one thing . . . Become aware of your inner experience as you make this discovery . . . (p. 105)

Such a guided imagery or visualization could be adapted to other sacred writ-ings, or could be developed by counselors using other images or archetypes that are relevant to clients' concerns. Tan (1996) cautioned against expecting all clients to be able to be successful at visualization and warned counselors to be on guard against imposing their preferred images, scriptures or agendas onto their clients.

Focusing

Another counseling intervention that draws on the principles of meditation and is based on Gendlin's (1969) work is called the focusing method (Hin-terkopf, 1994). According to Hinterkopf, focusing involves paying attention to something that is unclear and letting new, explicit meanings emerge. There are six steps to this process. Counselors instruct clients to relax, assume com-fortable positions, and quiet their minds. In step one, clients clear a space and take inventory of their problems and issues. In step two, they get a felt sense of the issue. This step involves having clients tune into their sensations in-cluding emotions, images, and body movements. In step three, clients find a handle by thinking of words or images to describe the felt sense. In step four, clients resonate with the felt sense and try to determine if the words or images they chose in step three are the best descriptors of their felt sensations. In step five, the counselor encourages the client to begin asking an open-ended question to the felt sense. In step six, the client takes time to receive the answer that brings a "felt shift" (Hinterkopf, 1994, p. 169).

CASE | LIANN

Liann is a Vietnamese American who was referred to counseling by her co-worker because of almost debilitating grief over the death of her grandmother. As part of his work with her, Liann's counselor, Clayton, used Hinterkopf's (1994) focusing method. He had Liann relax, get into a comfortable position, close her eyes, and attend to her breathing. Then he asked her to "get the felt sense" of her situation. After a few moments, Liann reported that she felt anxious, alone, and cold. She was aware of the street smells in Saigon where she had walked with her grand-mother as a little girl. She heard the sounds of the marketplace as well. Clayton asked Liann to "find a handle" for the emotional qualities—to describe in words or images what was going on for her. Liann indicated she felt isolated, anxious, and lost. Then Clayton asked Liann to linger with the felt sense, to search for other words or images that might better describe her circumstances. Liann said she saw an image of a little girl lost in a Vietnamese marketplace. Clayton asked Liann to ask the "felt sense" an open-ended question. After a few moments, Liann was visibly more calm and less depressed. Liann revealed that she had asked the "felt sense" the question, "What am I supposed to learn from this experience?" She said that the answer she received was this: "You are to learn that you are never alone. Your grandmother's spirit is still with you to guide you. You are also to learn to develop other relationships that can provide you with love, nurture, and support." By listening for an answer, Liann was able to feel both comforted and challenged in her situation.

KEEPING A SPIRITUAL JOURNAL

Having clients keep a diary of their thoughts, feelings, and reactions to what happens to them has long been an effective counseling technique. Keeping a spiritual journal is the same process; however, its focus is on spiritual issues that surface for clients. Counselors may describe a journal to clients as

> A book in which you keep a personal record of events in your life, of your different relationships, of your response to things, of your feelings about things—of your search to find out who you are what the meaning of your life might be. It is a book in which you carry out the greatest of life's adventures—the discovery of yourself. (Cargas & Radley, 1981, p. 8)

By encouraging clients who are wrestling with spiritual or religious concerns to keep a journal, we are providing them with a tool for self-discovery, an aid to concentration, a safety valve for their emotions, and a mirror for the spirit (Klug, 1982). Journaling can be a means through which clients respond to the therapeutic enterprise and by which they integrate their psychological and spiritual growth. In addition, journaling may be viewed as an ancillary tool to meditation. Some clients might find it helpful to keep responses to prayer or meditation in their spiritual journals. Counselors may encourage clients to share relevant excerpts from their journals during counseling sessions, always taking care to safeguard clients' privacy and their freedom not to disclose the content of their journals.

BIBLIOTHERAPY
Spiritual Bibliotherapy

Bibliotherapy is "a family of techniques for structuring interaction between a facilitator and a participant . . . based on their mutual sharing of literature in the broadest sense possible" (Berry, 1978, p. 186). Although bibliotherapy is often considered a technique to be used with children, it is an effective tool for working with adolescents and adults as well. Orton (1997) offered several reasons why bibliotherapy is useful in counseling. First, it enables clients to express problems and concerns that might be outside of their awareness or that clients may be intentionally repressing. Second, it helps clients examine their own thoughts and behaviors and how they compare with that of others. Third, it provides information that could assist in problem-solving or in developing positive thinking. Fourth, bibliotherapy may provide relaxation while promoting emotional release and anxiety reduction. Fifth, bibliotherapy provides a means of trying out new solutions to problems.

In spiritual bibliotherapy, these same possibilities are also possible. The only difference between classic bibliotherapy and spiritual bibliotherapy is in the choice of literature. Spiritual bibliotherapy involves using books, stories, myths, or other literature with spiritual themes.

The process of spiritual bibliotherapy is similar to that of classic bibliotherapy. Gumaer (1984) described the basic technique. Clients select a book or story from a prepared list of literature appropriate to the problem situation. Clients read the story, book, or myth (or if they are too young, counselors read it to them). Counselors then ask clients to retell the story with emphasis on the characters and the action. Then, counselors ask clients to describe their perceptions of the characters' feelings and behaviors. In addition, clients are asked to consider alternate behaviors and consequences that could have occurred in the story. Next, counselors encourage clients to personalize the story and relate it to themes in their own lives. Finally, counselors ask clients to evaluate the effectiveness of various characters' behaviors and to apply their discoveries to their own situations. Bibliotherapy has the potential to provide clients with the opportunity to identify with the protagonist or other story characters and to imagine experiencing similar emotions, ideas, and behaviors (Orton, 1997). As clients identify with the characters, they may undergo a cathartic release of emotions that are tapped by the unfolding story. Optimally, the catharsis results in insight and eventual conflict resolution (Pardeck & Pardeck, 1993).

When gathering materials to be included in a bibliography that are suitable for use in psychotherapy, counselors must read the literature they are considering for inclusion. A recommendation from a colleague or family member is not adequate to ensure that the embedded beliefs, values, worldview, and outcomes are consistent with the principles of good mental health. Moreover, for a book or story or other piece of literature to be an effective means for therapeutic growth and change, it must be a good fit for clients' perspectives and problems. A wealth of literature is available that is being marketed for use in clinical, religious, and spiritual settings. Just because the title or the advertisement touts the material as helpful does not mean that it will be meaningful for a particular client, and some narratives could have significant drawbacks. One problem is the tendency for some stories to offer simplistic or "band-aid" solutions to complex problems, which can discourage clients in their efforts to address their own difficulties (Chatton, 1988). Conversely, other books or narratives present characters who struggle with a myriad of problems such that readers become overwhelmed and come away with a message that some problems cannot be resolved successfully (Chatton, 1988). Thus, it is essential that counselors select materials that support clients' efforts at improving their emotional and spiritual health.

Besides literature that is based in the genre of story, other nonfiction books with religious or spiritual themes could assist counselors. Again, these materials need to be scrutinized for their themes and values. Most often such literature is helpful in clarifying for clients the meaning of certain religious or spiritual concepts, in teaching them about how to practice spiritual disciplines, or how to integrate religious or spiritual values and practices into their daily lives. Seeking out colleagues, clergy, and other professionals for recommendations is a place to begin. After having read the material critically, counselors should write and keep on hand a short annotation about the literature including its premise, purpose, themes relevant to counseling, and any questionable or negative content. This procedure enables counselors to make bibliotherapy suggestions for clients by matching the literature to the person and the problem.

Using Scripture or Authoritative Writings

A particular form of bibliotherapy involves the use of sacred texts or authoritative writings in counseling. In their study of spiritual interventions used by Christian counselors, Ball and Goodyear (1991) found that these counselors used the Bible in several different ways. Some quoted passages to clients, made biblical interpretations, made references to scripture while teaching particular concepts, related biblical stories, encouraged clients to read the Bible outside of the session, and used it to challenge dysfunctional and irrational beliefs. Richards and Potts (1995) found that among 215 Mormon counselors, the use of scriptures and other sacred writings was the most frequently reported spiritual intervention. However, there is no evidence that such strategies have positive psychological effects (Richards & Bergin, 1997). Nevertheless, Richards and Bergin (1997) maintained that some therapeutic benefits have yet to be understood and explained.

Before beginning to employ the Bible, Torah, Qur'an (Koran), or any other sacred writings in counseling, it is important to set some boundaries for this practice. Richards and Bergin (1997) offered the following guidelines: First, be certain to work within clients' belief systems and not to impose your beliefs about these writings onto your clients. Second, avoid setting yourself up as a religious authority or getting into debates or power struggles with clients over the meaning of certain passages or texts. Such an approach rarely meets therapeutic goals and often results in the imposition of counselors' values on clients. Third, if clients' questions are pressing you beyond your competence level, be prepared to refer clients to religious leaders or spiritual guides. These persons may provide clarification of meanings associated with certain traditions.

Although some counselors are comfortable quoting scriptures or sacred texts and using them while teaching clients spiritual concepts (Ball & Goodyear, 1991), many others find these approaches intrusive or inappropriate. One of the most helpful aspects of applying scriptures or sacred texts to counseling is in their narrative power. The stories and passages that are authoritative in clients' religious and spiritual traditions carry within them the potential to shift clients' thinking precisely because they are vehicles of authority. Thus, counselors may make use of both metaphor and narrative to help clients re-author their own stories (Parry & Doan, 1994).

CASE | JONATHAN

Jonathan is a 34-year-old Jewish attorney and local politician. He came to counseling because he was "torn apart by guilt over an affair he had had with a colleague." Although he and his wife, Patti, are currently involved in couples therapy with another counselor, Jonathan sought out Joshua, a Jewish counselor, to help him address his guilt and self-loathing. After hearing Jonathan's story, it became clear to Joshua that Jonathan was being extremely harsh on himself because he saw himself either as almost perfect or as "worthless garbage." Joshua's goal was to help Jonathan become more accepting of his frailties and to be able to integrate his failures with his successes.

Because Jonathan specifically asked for a religious dimension to be included in the counseling, Joshua consulted with his rabbi for a text that might be instructive for Jonathan. Rabbi Rosen suggested using the text from 2 Samuel 5–12:7, which includes the stories of David's kingship, his victories, and his adultery with Bathsheba. First, Joshua asked Jonathan to read the text the rabbi had recommended. Next, he asked Jonathan, "How is your life like that of King David?" Immediately, Jonathan saw the connection. He said, "I am a successful businessman and a leader in my community, but I am also human. Just because I am capable and contributing doesn't mean I am without my faults. And, just because I made a lousy mess of my relationship with Patti by having an affair doesn't mean that I am worthless garbage either." Joshua then asked, "Based on your understanding of the David story, what do you think God would have you do in your life?" Jonathan responded, "There will have to be consequences. I won't be able to weasel out of this one easily. I will have to demonstrate to Patti my remorse, and I'll have to figure out some way to make amends. And, I will need to start trusting God more for guidance, rather than relying solely on myself."

In this case, Joshua was able to consult with his rabbi for help in selecting a text that would speak to his client's situation. By using the text, its narrative power was able to speak to Jonathan about his situation in a way that evoked a shift in Jonathan's thinking about who he was, what he valued, and what changes he needed to make to deal with his guilt. Because Jonathan had allowed this story to function authoritatively in his life, it was able to bring about a transformation that may have been qualitatively different from that of other stories or other voices. In this approach, Joshua did not exacerbate Jonathan's guilt by using the scripture to condemn him for adultery. Instead, it allowed Jonathan to hear and interpret for himself what message God, via the scripture, had for him.

CASE	MONIQUE

Monique, a 29-year-old homemaker and mother of two pre-school children was referred to counseling by her physician because of her stress-related symptoms. Monique reported to her counselor, Vivian, that she had been having difficulty sleeping, had little appetite, and was exhausted. When Vivian asked Monique to describe her day, she indicated that she got up at 5:00 A.M., spent an hour reading the Bible, meditating and prayer, fixed breakfast for her family, and spent most of the day and several evenings a week in volunteer activities. She served lunch in a soup kitchen for the homeless, tutored inner-city children in reading and math, taught Sunday School and directed a children's choir in her church, helped with the actual construction of a home built by Habitat for Humanity, and even traveled to Central America to help with disaster relief. Vivian told Monique she could understand how depleted she was because of her intense caring for others. Vivian asked Monique what motivated her to spend so much energy in serving the needy. Monique revealed that she "had become a Christian" a few years ago and that because she had the privilege of not working outside the home she was determined to express her devotion to God through direct work with God's people. Vivian asked Monique if any biblical texts were especially meaningful for her. Monique said, "Of course. I think all of Jesus' teachings can be summed up in the verse from Mark 12:31: 'You shall love your neighbor as you love yourself.'" Vivian said to Monique, "So all of your service activities are efforts to love your neighbor, correct?" Monique nodded. Then Vivian added, "What are you doing to love yourself?" Monique burst into tears and said she had a hard time loving herself. She confided that she truly believed that she would be more lovable and acceptable if she gave herself to others in their need. Vivian asked Monique, "What would it mean for you to love others as you love yourself?" Monique was asked not to answer the question right away, but to meditate on it, pray about it, write down her thoughts, and to ask her pastor and her friends at church what they thought this verse meant. A discussion of the meaning of this important text carried into the next counseling session with a new interpretation emerging for Monique in the intervening week. Monique said she had come to realize that she was loving others instead of herself and that doing so was damaging her health and her family relationships. She said she needed to learn how to love herself and to have her love for others grow out of her self love and care. Thus, the agenda for Monique's counseling grew both out of her religious understandings and the shift that occurred when her counselor asked her to reconsider an interpretation of a verse of scripture. Because Monique offered a verse that was significant in her spiritual life, Vivian knew that it could be the key to understanding Monique's self-destructive behavior and the catalyst for change.

Counselors who are not conversant with sacred texts need not let lack of familiarity prevent them from using authoritative writings in psychotherapy. As I have stated elsewhere (Frame, 1996), what is required when employing religious or spiritually based sacred writings is openness. When counselors lay aside their interpretations and presuppositions, their biases and beliefs, they could hear fresh meanings and clues to how these texts may support the counseling endeavor. The biblical narrative, or any other sacred text, when linked to personal narrative may reveal clients' values and perspectives and offer potent metaphors for bringing about therapeutic change (Frame, 1996).

FORGIVENESS AND REPENTANCE

An important spiritual issue for many religious clients is that of forgiving those who have wronged them, or asking forgiveness of those whom they have injured. Christian clients, in particular, are likely to view forgiveness as a biblical mandate and as a moral obligation (Kanz, 2000). They are well aware of Jesus' statement in Matthew 18:22 in response to a question concerning how many times one must forgive. Jesus answered 77 times, meaning that the requirement is beyond calculation.

Forgiveness is a word with Indo-European roots meaning "to give up or give away anger and the actions associated with it, *retribution* and *revenge*" (Sanderson & Linehan, 1999, p. 207). Other writers consider forgiveness as "a willingness to abandon one's right to resentment, negative judgment, and indifferent behavior toward one who unjustly injured us (Enright, Freedman, & Risque, 1988, pp. 46–47).

Forgiveness is considered a virtue not only in Christianity, but in other religions as well. The belief in a Supreme Being greatly shapes the way forgiveness is conceived. In Christianity, Judaism, and Islam, there is a God who models forgiveness for humans. Nevertheless, even these religions have some significant differences in how forgiveness is understood. For example, in Judaism only an injured person can grant forgiveness. It is not appropriate to ask God to forgive a wrong committed against another person, nor to offer forgiveness of behalf of others unless requested to do so by the injured party (Sanderson & Linehan, 1999). In Eastern religions, the offenses people commit against each other are considered to be rooted more in ignorance than in evil, and forgiveness grows out of compassion (Sanderson & Linehan, 1999). In Buddhism, for example, everything is connected and all actions can be traced to a web of influences. Forgiveness emerges in this context more as understanding the universal cause of suffering (Sanderson & Linehan, 1999). These religious differences in perceptions regarding forgiveness suggest that counselors who seek to help clients who are wrestling with forgiveness must be familiar with how both the offended and the offender understand the concept.

Forgiveness is one of the spiritual interventions most frequently used by counselors (Ball & Goodyear, 1991; DiBlasio & Benda, 1991; Freedman & Enright, 1996; Richards & Potts, 1995). Some researchers (Bergin, 1988; McCullough & Worthington, 1994) have found that promoting forgiveness among clients results in clients experiencing more positive affect, in improved mental health, a greater sense of personal power, reconciliation between alienated persons, and freedom to grow (Richards & Bergin, 1997).

When clients indicate they are want to be able to forgive an offender and move on with their lives, it is important for counselors to assess clients' readiness for that step. It is not uncommon for forgiveness to become a shortcut to healing such that clients believe they have forgiven an injurious party when they really haven't. This pseudoforgiveness often results in anxiety and depression (Kanz, 2000; Romig & Veenstra, 1998).

Richards and Bergin (1997) outlined a process that leads clients to forgiveness after they have truly addressed the wrongdoing they have experienced. They caution that clients may become frustrated with the process because it is not easy and may take a lot of time. Some stages that clients must negotiate are (a) shock and denial, (b) awareness of the hurt or abuse, (c) acknowledgement of the grief, and anger and the opportunity to express their feelings to others, (d) validation of their feelings, (e) justice and restitution if possible, (f) prevention of further offenses, and (g) forgiveness and moving on (Richards & Bergin, 1997, p. 213). When clients appear ready for forgiveness to occur, some important caveats must be considered. Freedman (1998) underscored the notion that forgiveness does not require reconciliation. She indicated that an apology may be necessary for reconciliation, but not for forgiveness. Freedman stressed that forgiveness can occur "without the offender's involvement or knowledge" (p. 203). Given possibilities, Freedman outlined four possible choices clients may make when faced with a decision about forgiving an offender: (1) forgive and reconcile, (2) forgive and not reconcile, (3) not forgive and interact, (4) not forgive and not reconcile. For clients to be prepared to select one of these four choices, additional steps must be taken. First, clients must be educated about how holding on to anger might hurt them and be given options of dealing with it, including forgiveness (Enright et al., 1998; Kanz, 2000). Clients must then consider the benefits and liabilities to themselves in forgiving or not forgiving the wrongdoer. These outcomes may include the psychological, emotional, and physical implications of either forgiving or not (Sanderson & Linehan, 1999). Second, if clients choose to move toward forgiveness, they must refrain from revenge behaviors (Enright et al., 1998). Third, clients are taught empathy skills and engage in cognitive reframing to understand the offending person's behavior and the feelings he or she is having regarding the fractured relationship (Enright et al., 1998; McCullough, Worthington, & Rachal, 1997). Fourth, clients are to practice conciliatory behavior by not acting angry. Even if reconciliation is not desired, clients may still let go of anger for their own welfare (Sanderson & Linehan, 1999). Ferch (2000) noted that when clients decide to forgive, with or without reconciliation, touch may be a useful vehicle for forgiveness. Of course, this approach must be carefully considered by clients given their relationship with the offender, their comfort with touch, and the meanings attached to such an act.

Whether or not clients are able to forgive their offenders depends on their ability to navigate these steps. Their successes or failures may be explained by how well they have mastered psychosocial developmental challenges (Romig & Veenstra, 1998). Romig and Veenstra (1998) found that persons who resolved trust issues early in life were better able to be empathic about offenders and act in positive ways toward them. Further, persons who have negative attitudes about themselves or are focused on short-term self-gratification might have a more difficult time forgiving than will those who are more other-oriented and have integrated caring (Gilligan, 1982) as a moral model (Romig & Veenstra, 1998). Clients who wish to forgive might not be able to forgive those who have injured them for a variety of reasons: deeper unexplored issues, shame associated with connecting with a perpetrator without justice being served, or that any kind of link to the offender could exacerbate a serious injury or loss. These issues should be explored when counseling clients regarding forgiveness.

In addition, counselors should be especially aware of their own understanding of forgiveness and its salience for their lives. Again, person-of-the-therapist issues could affect the way counselors work with clients regarding this issue. Counselors' own experiences of accepting and offering forgiveness may shape the directions they take with clients. When forgiveness is a sensitive issue for counselors, they are wise to seek consultation and supervision for cases in which forgiveness emerges as a central concern.

CASE | CASSANDRA

Cassandra, a 22-year-old African American woman, was referred to counseling by her pastor because of her angry outbursts and threats to Orlando, her daughter Natasha's father. When Cassandra got pregnant at age 15, Orlando, then 19, had agreed to marry her. However, when Natasha was born, Orlando left town and had no contact with Cassandra or Natasha for five years. Recently, however, Orlando moved back home with his mother and wanted to see his daughter. On the first visit, Cassandra became enraged at Orlando's notion of establishing a relationship with her and Natasha. When he returned a second time, she threatened him with a knife. Cassandra's mother, Emma, called her pastor and asked him to talk with Cassandra. After listening to her rage and sob for over two hours, Pastor Johnson told Cassandra she was going to need to work on forgiving Orlando for the sake of their child. Then he referred Cassandra to counseling with Lola.

Lola spent several sessions with Cassandra helping her to identify her feelings and empathizing with her about the betrayal and rejection she felt as a result of Orlando's leaving her and their child. Eventually, Cassandra said she wanted to be able to forgive Orlando because she "knew God expected her to be forgiving as He [God] had forgiven her." She indicated that she wanted Natasha to have a relationship with her father, and she knew she was standing in the way of such a relationship because of her anger. Lola spent some time teaching Cassandra about the concept of forgiveness, letting her know she had choices, and helping her examine the possible emotional and physical outcomes if she continued to hang on to her anger and rage. In addition, Lola encouraged Cassandra to write a letter to Orlando in which she expressed her feelings and explained why she had behaved the way she had. She told Cassandra that she did not have to mail the letter, but that it was a means of clarifying her own feelings. Later, Lola taught Cassandra about empathy and worked with her to try to imagine Orlando's feelings when he first left and those he had when he returned. Cassandra told Lola she thought Orlando was probably really scared about being a father, that he felt unprepared for a commitment, and that he didn't know what to do, so he left. Cassandra added that she thought Orlando had grown up some, that he felt guilty about abandoning her and Natasha and was trying to make it up to them. Having achieved these insights about her feelings and having made hunches about Orlando's, Cassandra felt more ready to forgive. She told Lola that she thought she could forgive Orlando, but she didn't think she wanted to reconcile with him. She said she had moved on, wanted to go to school and to build a new life for her daughter. Cassandra's major test was to invite Orlando to one of her counseling sessions where, with Lola's support, she would share her feelings with Orlando and demonstrate conciliatory behaviors for Natasha's sake. Although the joint counseling session was painful for Cassandra, she was able to behave civilly and to begin talking to Orlando about child support and visitation.

In this case, Lola was able to work within Cassandra's religious view of forgiveness while giving her permission not to reconcile with Orlando. By being patient and taking Cassandra through the long and painful process, Lola was able to support Cassandra's new ways of thinking about Orlando and to provide opportunities for appropriate behavior in his presence. By avoiding the implication that forgiveness requires reconciliation, Lola was able to assist Cassandra in forgiving Orlando, but to feel free not to reconcile with him.

SURRENDER

One spiritual value related to trust is surrender. Paradoxically, most counselors spend much of their clinical time assisting clients to gain personal control over some of the vicissitudes of their lives, and yet, surrender requires relinquishing control over situations in which there really is none. There are two basic types of control. The first is an attempt to change the world and external circumstances so that it is compatible with persons' needs (Rothbaum, Weisz, & Snyder, 1982). The second is to be willing to change oneself to accept the direction life takes (Cole & Pargament, 1999). Either of these approaches may be adopted during times of severe stress.

Pargament, Smith, Koenig, & Perez (1988) studied the relationship between persons' belief in God and their approach to managing stress and reported five different coping strategies: (1) deferring, (2) pleading, (3) self-direction, (4) collaboration, and (5) spiritual surrender. The strategy of deferring involves clients not being actively involved in dealing with the stressor but, rather, turning it over to God. The pleading strategy involves bargaining with God to intervene and improve the situation or to perform a miracle. Clients employing the self-directing approach take responsibility for making decisions about how to respond to stress without God's help. Those who opt for collaboration manage stressful situations by making themselves partners with God. Those who choose spiritual surrender take control of what they can do and leave the rest to God. Research results revealed that the collaborative approaches tend to be more effective than deferring (Pargament, Kennell, Hathaway, Grevengoed, Newman, & Jones, 1988), pleading (Pargament, 1997), and self-direction strategies (Pargament et al., 1990) especially in situations where personal control is at a minimum (Bickel, Ciarrocchi, Sheers, Estadt, Powell, & Pargament, 1998).

When clients are faced with situations in which there is little personal control, such as chronic or terminal illness, death, or accidents, surrender might be appropriate for clients to consider. This spiritual strategy involves having clients acknowledge that under certain negative circumstances there could be a greater good than personal control (Cole & Pargament, 1999). Moreover, surrender involves not only a cognitive shift, but an experiential one as well in which one is in touch with self-transcendence that leads to serenity (Cole & Pargament, 1999). This strategy seems to have positive associations with psychological and spiritual well-being for persons in crisis (Cole & Pargament, 1999).

Before approaching the notion of surrender with clients, it is important to be clear about clients' situations and their religious or spiritual perspectives and determine if surrender would be a helpful intervention. Cole and Pargament (1999) caution against presenting the concept of surrender as a means of gaining control of a stressful situation. They emphasize the paradoxical reality that a secondary sense of control (accepting life's circumstances as they come) may result from surrender, but that it is certainly not a goal or an expected outcome. In addition, Cole and Pargament suggested that at its best, surrender is an appropriate response to human limitations. However, they warn practitioners that what looks like surrender could really be some form of learned helplessness. Clinicians will want to explore the various dynamics of surrender with clients to understand how it functions for them.

Counselors with clients with spiritual surrender as an option should first explore clients' religious or spiritual beliefs and their compatibility with the concept of spiritual surrender. Second, counselors might want to test clients' receptivity to such an approach by asking a question such as, "What would it be like for you to surrender to God?" (Cole & Pargament, 1999, p. 192). In addition, counselors may ask clients to list aspects of their problem that are within their control and those that are outside of their control. This exercise helps make cognitive errors visible because people both think they can control situations that they cannot and think they cannot control circumstances that are clearly within their control (Cole & Pargament, 1999). When clients have determined that spiritual surrender is an appropriate option in the context of their particular situation, counselors might want to lead these clients through a guided imagery exercise that involves imagery of spiritual surrender (Cole & Pargament, 1999). In this way, clients gain an experiential component of a cognitive decision.

CASE | STAN

Stan, a 44-year-old pediatrician, was referred to counseling by a colleague because of his obsessive attempts to manage the stress associated with his wife, Bonnie's, metastasized breast cancer. When Bonnie was diagnosed with breast cancer, Stan immediately responded with self-direction, attempting to take control of a very scary medical situation. Stan began contacting oncology specialists all over the country arranging for Bonnie to undergo consults and experimental treatments. Furthermore, he spent every free moment in the medical school library reading journal articles about breast cancer treatments. At one point, Bonnie pleaded with him to stay home and spend time with her rather than "trying to play God." Stan's colleague, Norman, noticed Stan's exhaustion and his obsessive preoccupation with cancer research. Norman told Stan he thought he was about to "go over the edge" and that he [Norman] questioned Stan's clinical judgment on two very serious pediatric cases in their practice. Norman referred Stan to Naomi, a well-respected counselor whose office was in their building.

Naomi worked with Stan to enable him to relax and begin to address his fear about Bonnie's illness and her probable death from breast cancer. Naomi asked Stan about his religious or spiritual beliefs. Although Stan reported he "was not religious," he did reveal that he believed there was a "power in the universe that is greater than we are." He said that whenever he was unable to find answers through science, he relied on "the mystery" as he called his notion of the sacred. Once Naomi had been able to connect with Stan on a personal level and to win his trust, she was able to help him think about his situation. Finally, in a fit of despair, Stan confessed that he had met his limit fighting this disease. He told Naomi that he felt guilty that as a physician he could not bring about his wife's healing. He said, "All that training is in vain if I can't cure the person who matters most to me." Naomi helped Stan begin to face the painful realization of his human limitations and supported him in his grief. Then she suggested Stan list all the things about his wife's cancer that he could control and the things that he could not. Stan's list of things he could control included the time he spent with Bonnie, the emotional support he offered her, the amount of help he was willing to accept from others, the energy he put into his practice, and his attitude about her illness. Stan's list of things he could not control included Bonnie's condition and its outcome, the effectiveness of the treatments, her responses to her illness, and other people's responses to her cancer. Ultimately, Stan realized that he was only hurting himself and his relationship with Bonnie by obsessively seeking a cure for her cancer. He confessed that he was ready to surrender control to "the mystery" and concentrate on making the most of each day he was given with Bonnie. Toward the end of his counseling experience, Naomi led Stan through a guided imagery in which he was to surrender control of Bonnie's cancer to "the mystery." Stan reported a physical sense of relief after going through the guided experience. He indicated that he visualized himself putting down a huge bag of boulders he had been carrying on his shoulders. Afterward, Stan hired another physician to assist in his pediatric practice and took a six-month leave of absence to spend time with his wife. After Bonnie's death, Stan contacted Naomi to thank her for helping him lay down his burden in time to truly enjoy some quality time with Bonnie.

12-STEP PROGRAMS

By far, the most popular self-help programs in the United States today are those based on the 12-step model (McCrady & Delaney, 1995). Kurtz (1990) reported the existence of more than 80 12-step related programs and 125,000 individual chapters. It is estimated that more than 3.5 million individuals participate in 12-step programs every year (Room, 1993).

Over the years, there have been several different theories on the nature of addiction. Some clinicians view addiction as an intrapsychic problem rooted in unresolved issues in early childhood (Fenichel, 1945). Others see it as a moral failure (Baron, 1962). Still others characterized it as a disease (Jellinek, 1960). Shaef (1987) claimed addiction is evidence of the failure of cultural values whereas Vaillant (1983) viewed it as a biopsychosocial phenomena. The unique aspect of 12-step programs is their view of alcoholism and other addictions as spiritual problems that can be overcome through the reliance on spiritual principles. In fact, Alcoholics Anonymous (AA) traces its roots to a comment made by Carl Jung to a man identified only as Rowland H. After unsuccessful attempts by Jung to treat Rowland via extensive analytic work, Jung purportedly told his client that he could not help him and declared that only a religious or spiritual experience could rescue him from his condition (Hopson, 1996). Jung's statement became the catalyst for Rowland to join an evangelical religious movement called the Oxford Group through which he eventually became sober. Rowland's networking eventually led him to Edwin T. who was a friend of Bill W., the founder of AA (Hopson, 1996).

Twelve-step programs are voluntary, anonymous, and noninstitutional. Typically, groups meet in rented spaces or religious buildings. The meetings last one hour. They usually begin with the Serenity Prayer: "God grant me the serenity to accept the things I cannot change, the courage to change the things I can, and the wisdom to know the difference."* The basic approach to 12-step programs is for successful sponsors to assist new members in working through the 12 steps (see Table 7.1). Although most groups focus on

---

*In the public domain.

TABLE 7.1 | THE 12 STEPS OF ALCOHOLICS ANONYMOUS

1. We admit we were powerless over alcohol—that our lives had become unmanageable.
2. Came to believe that a Power greater than ourselves could restore us to sanity.
3. Made a decision to turn our will and our lives over to the care of *God as we understood Him.*
4. Made a searching and fearless moral inventory of ourselves.
5. Admitted to God, to ourselves, and to another human being the exact nature of our wrongs.
6. Were entirely ready to have God remove all these defects of character.
7. Humbly asked Him to remove our shortcomings.
8. Made a list of all persons we had harmed, and became willing to make amends to them all.
9. Made direct amends to such people wherever possible, except when to do so would injure them or others.
10. Continued to take personal inventory and when we were wrong promptly admitted it.
11. Sought through prayer and meditation to improve our conscious contact with *God as we understood Him,* praying only for knowledge of His will for us and the power to carry that out.
12. Having had a spiritual awakening as a result of these steps, tried to carry this message to alcoholics, and to practice these principles in all our affairs.

personal sharing by those in attendance, some include speakers, studying the 12-step literature or birthday meetings in which members' sobriety is celebrated (Tonigan, Toscova, & Conners, 1999). Most meetings also include the opportunity for donations to be made for organizational support. Meetings typically close with the Lord's Prayer. Although many AA (and other 12-step programs) are open to anyone, some groups are closed. Some groups cater predominantly to women, people of color, or gay, lesbian, and bisexual constituents (Tonigan et al., 1999). Twelve-step organizations are structured and operated in light of the 12 Traditions (see Table 7.2).

There are several spiritual principles that are fundamental to 12-step programs. The first is the concept of a Higher Power. Acknowledging this spiritual reality is an essential aspect of participating in a 12-step program. The term, "Higher Power" was intentionally ill-defined so that potential members could have the freedom to develop or use their own names that may or may not include the term, "God." Second, participants are expected to develop a personal relationship with their Higher Power through prayer and meditation (Tonigan et al., 1999). Spirituality is considered a means of relapse prevention. Third, participants are expected to acknowledge that transcendent interventions or miracles do occur. Twelve-step members often speak about their

TABLE 7.2 | THE 12 TRADITIONS OF ALCOHOLICS
ANONYMOUS

1. Our common welfare should come first; personal recovery depends upon AA
   unity.
2. For our group purpose there is but one ultimate authority—a loving God as He
   may express Himself in our group conscience. Our leaders are but trusted
   servants; they do not govern.
3. The only requirement for AA membership is a desire to stop drinking.
4. Each group should be autonomous except in matters affecting other groups or AA
   as a whole.
5. Each group has but one primary purpose—to carry its message to the alcoholic
   who still suffers.
6. An AA group ought never endorse, finance, or lend the AA name to any related
   facility or outside enterprise, lest problems of property, money, and prestige divert
   us from our primary purpose.
7. Every AA group ought to be self-supporting, declining outside contributions.
8. Alcoholics Anonymous should remain forever nonprofessional, but our service
   centers may employ special workers.
9. AA, as such, ought never be organized; but we may create service boards or
   committees directly responsible to those they serve.
10. Alcoholics Anonymous has no opinion on outside issues; hence, the AA name
    ought never be drawn into public controversy.
11. Our public relations policy is based on attraction rather than promotion; we need
    always maintain personal anonymity at the level of press, radio, and films.
12. Anonymity is the spiritual foundation of all our traditions, ever reminding us to
    place principles before personalities.

victory over alcoholism or other addictions as "miracles." Although these triumphs might or might not occur all at once, there is a clear assumption that a
Higher Power was involved in achieving sobriety. Indeed, participants claim
that "God does for us what we cannot do for ourselves" (Alcoholics Anonymous, 1976, p. 84). Fourth, the notion of daily spiritual renewal is at the heart
of both obtaining and maintaining freedom from addiction. Finally, discord
and conflict are considered evidence of incongruity with one's Higher Power
and a lack of serenity (Tonigan et al., 1999). Whenever disagreements occur in
interpersonal relationships or if there is conflict in the group, these are considered reminders of one's daily dependence on a spiritual connection.

Working the 12-steps involves four major emphases. First, prayer and
meditation is a fundamental aspect of any 12-step approach. Second, participants are to make amends for the wrongdoings that they have committed because of their addiction and are to develop relationships based on trust,
mutuality, respect, and honesty (Tonigan et al., 1999). Third, participants are
to share their experiences with others regarding their program. This aspect of

the 12-step program has been shown to be significantly and positively related to members' commitment to AA (Kingree, 1997). Fourth, participants are to carefully monitor their behavior and to integrate spiritual principles in their daily lives (Tonigan et al., 1999).

Various writers have analyzed the 12 steps in different ways. Tonigan and colleagues (1999) suggested that steps 1–3 involve acceptance and surrender, that steps 4–10 evoke action, and that steps 11 and 12 refer to maintenance. Faiver and colleagues (2001) characterized the steps like this: Steps 1–3 are the "surrender" steps, 4 and 5 are the inventory and confessional steps, 6 and 7 are the character-change steps, 8 and 9 are the relational steps, 10 and 11 are the maintenance steps, and 12 is the service step. Hopson (1996) analyzed the steps in this way: Steps 1–3 give up, steps 4–7 own up, steps 8–9 make up, and steps 10–12 grow up (p. 543). However conceptualized, the 12-step programs involve surrender to a Higher Power in concert with personal responsibility and lifelong commitment to living according to spiritual principles.

Although there is certainly a wealth of personal testimony supporting the effectiveness of 12-step approaches in treating addiction, these programs are not without criticism. One major objection to 12-step programs is whether or not the notion of surrender is appropriate. Some writers (Bufe, 1998; Ellis & Schoenfeld, 1990) have suggested that this concept reinforces learned helplessness, low self-esteem, and dependency. Others have cited the concept of surrender and the listing of character defects as contraindicated for marginalized persons who constantly struggle with issues of powerlessness and helplessness (Faiver, Ingersoll, O'Brien, & McNally, 2001). Another criticism centers around the belief that 12-step organizations are appropriate for middle-class white men because of the exclusively male language employed in the "Big Book" written in the 1930s (Hopson, 1996). Another criticism focuses on the fact that 12-programs are led by persons who are recovering addicts themselves, thus lending to these organizations an antiscientific and antiprofessional air (Hopson, 1996). In addition, some critics believe that 12-step programs encourage addicts to substitute one form of dependency (on substances) for another (Higher Power) and that by so doing, the intrapsychic pathology that causes addictive behavior is never addressed (Hopson, 1996).

Although there may be some truth in these allegations, AA's oral tradition has a strong message to those who object to aspects of the program: "Take what you want and leave the rest" (Faiver et al., 2001, p. 143). In response to the perceived "white male orientation" of 12-step groups, other self-help organizations have emerged. One such group, Men in Recovery, is aimed at African American males and focuses on their need for empowerment (Zitter, 1987) and community (Williams, 1992). Women for Sobriety's focus is on increasing women's self-esteem, autonomy, and personal responsibility (Hopson, 1996). Two alternative organizations, Secular Organization for Sobriety and Rational Recovery, were initiated in reaction against the spiritual components of 12-step programs (Kasl, 1992).

Regardless of one's opinion about 12-step programs, mental health service providers should be familiar with them for several reasons. First, because clients' beliefs shape their attitudes and their successes in counseling, clinicians need 12-step information for treatment planning (Tonigan et al., 1999). Second, because 12-step programs offer a spiritual approach to addiction recovery, many clients will avail themselves of this opportunity in addition to engaging in personal counseling. Third, correlational studies revealed that 12-step programs reduced target behaviors such as substance abuse and overeating (Emrick, Tonigan, Montgomery, & Little, 1993; Tonigan, Connors, & Miller, 1996). In addition, other research results (Emrick et al., 1993; Tonigan, Connors, & Miller, 1996) demonstrated an improvement in psychosocial functioning. Although much research remains to be conducted on the effectiveness of 12-step programs, their proliferation and perceived effectiveness make them significant spiritual strategies to be considered when undertaking addiction counseling.

| CASE | RALPH |

Ralph is a 60-year-old retired school administrator. He sought counseling because his wife of 35 years, Carole, told him that she would divorce him if he didn't stop drinking. Ralph told his counselor, Rhonda, he had tried to stop drinking several times during the past 20 years, but to no avail. This time, however, he said he knew Carole was serious about her threat. She had even contacted an attorney. In the initial intake session, Ralph revealed that he "believed in God" but always felt so ashamed to attend church because of his alcoholism. He indicated that he was open to tapping the spiritual dimension if it would help him conquer his drinking. Rhonda worked with Ralph using behavioral and cognitive behavioral strategies, and she was supportive when he asked her if she thought he should attend Alcoholics Anonymous. Ralph decided to continue weekly therapy with Rhonda and to explore AA as well.

At his first AA meeting, Ralph introduced himself using the traditional phrase, "My name is Ralph. I am an alcoholic." Ralph told Rhonda that merely uttering those words helped him to begin facing the reality of his addiction. Over the next several months, Ralph attended AA faithfully. He was assigned a sponsor with a similar background and drinking history. He got back in touch with his spiritual side, and even agreed to attend church again with Carole. Although Ralph experienced two severe relapses during his first year in AA, he became zealous about the 12-step program and attended meetings several times a week. Ralph found that attending AA alongside individual therapy was exactly what he needed to turn his life around.

CONTRAINDICATIONS FOR SPIRITUAL INTERVENTIONS

There are circumstances under which using spiritual interventions may be contraindicated. When clients indicate that they are not interested in participating in spiritual approaches to psychotherapy, counselors should refrain from using them. Also, when clients are actively psychotic or delusional such interventions are not appropriate (Bullis, 1996; Richards & Bergin, 1997). Using spiritual interventions when they are not relevant to the presenting problem is highly questionable as is using them when the setting (publicly funded secular school or agency) does not support such an approach (Richards & Bergin, 1997). Counselors should also take care to obtain permission from parents or guardians when considering employing spiritual interventions with children or adolescents (Richards & Bergin, 1997). Moreover, Richards and Bergin (1997) caution that spiritual interventions are not likely to be as effective if there is not a strong therapeutic bond between counselor and client, if the counselor and client have divergent religious or spiritual values, or if the counselor is not sensitive to multicultural, religious, and spiritual diversity. Thus, it is important to consider the entire therapeutic context before employing spiritual strategies in counseling.

SEEKING APPROPRIATE CONSULTATION AND REFERRAL

Sometimes during the course of counseling, religious or spiritual issues arise that signal counselors that they need to seek consultation or possibly referral. Faiver, O'Brien, & McNally (1998) argued that it was important for counselors to identify "friendly clergy" who are qualified to provide assistance. Faiver and colleagues characterized "friendly" clergy as those who, from a variety of religious backgrounds, are known by their congregations and are accessible and humane rather than judgmental. In addition, they should possess some rudimentary communication and counseling skills. Counselors may engage in networking processes to discover the "friendly clergy" in their communities. Such networking can be accomplished by contacting other counselors, lay persons who are active in religious or spiritual organizations, churches, synagogues or mosques, local councils of churches, crisis hotlines, and clients who know of supportive clergy (Faiver et al., 1998). When such a network is in place, it may mean that reciprocal consultation becomes an added benefit to both clergy and counselors.

CASE EXAMPLES
Lillian

Lillian is a 68-year-old retired Caucasian business woman who was referred to counseling by her son, Evan, because of her immobilizing grief following the death of her husband, Lowell, eight months previously. Although Lillian was reluctant to enter counseling because she thought it was a sign of weakness, she agreed to attend at least three sessions to please her son. During the intake session, Lillian revealed she was a religious person and had been active in a United Methodist church all her life except for the past three years because of her husband's illness. Lillian indicated that she had always counted on her faith as a means of coping with difficulties, and she told her counselor, Anna, that she would be most receptive to counseling that incorporated spiritual approaches.

Discussion Questions

1. If you were working with Lillian, what would be your primary goals?
2. What model of faith development seems most useful for working with Lillian? How would you assess what stage she is in?
3. What spiritual interventions would you deem most appropriate for helping Lillian deal with her grief? Why?
4. What spiritual interventions, if any, would you think might be contraindicated? Why?
5. What personal issues does Lillian's case bring up for you? How are your issues connected to this case? What assets or liabilities do you think your personal situation would contribute were you working with Lillian?
6. If you felt overwhelmed by Lillian's circumstances and her request for the use of spiritual interventions, how would you handle the case?
7. What resources within yourself or the community would you seek out to assist you in working effectively with Lillian?

Cindy

Cindy is a 39-year-old African American mother of two daughters, Tiffany, 9, and Taylor, 7. Cindy came to counseling because she was having difficulty dealing with the fact that her father, Jerome, had sexually abused both girls the previous summer on a family camping trip. Cindy reported that her father remained in denial, that she and her husband, Carter, are extremely stressed by their involvement with Social Services and with the legal system. Cindy said that her siblings were all angry at her for "breaking up a happy family" and they were beginning to take sides. When she met with her counselor, Paula, she said, "I just want to be able to forgive him [her father]. Right now, I am so hurt and angry I can't even think about him without getting nauseated. But I know God expects me to forgive him. How will I ever do it?"

Discussion Questions

1. What would be the first steps you would take in working with Cindy?
2. How might you work with her family members and extended family?
3. How would you respond to Cindy's goal of forgiving her father?
4. What questions might you ask Cindy (and possibly her husband or other family members) to clarify her (their) experience?
5. What is your personal understanding of forgiveness? How would your view influence the way you work with Cindy in this case?

Ramon

Ramon is a 27-year-old former truck driver who immigrated from Mexico when he was 10 years old. He was raised in the Catholic Church, but five years ago was "born again" after attending a revival at a fundamentalist Christian church. His former employer, Gerald, referred Ramon to counseling because of his depression about losing his job a month ago. Ramon's driving record was not as good as the company required, given that he had caused two serious accidents in the last year. When Ramon reported for counseling he was a bit hesitant to speak, not knowing fully what to expect, nor how his counselor, Gene, would respond to him. Ramon told Gene about being fired from his trucking job and added, "I feel like God is punishing me for having the accidents. I feel so guilty that I don't know what to do. I want to be a good Christian and bring glory to God in what I do, but I can't even get up enough courage to look for another job."

Discussion Questions
1. If you were Ramon's counselor, how would you approach his presenting problem?
2. What questions would you ask Ramon to get a better understanding of his circumstances and worldview?
3. What spiritual interventions, if any, would you consider using with Ramon? What is your rationale for selecting these interventions?
4. What cultural dimensions of Ramon's situation seem relevant? What steps would you take to demonstrate cultural and spiritual competence?
5. Given your current experience and training, how comfortable would you feel working with Ramon? What aspects of this case make you feel uncomfortable? How would you address your discomfort?

SUGGESTED ACTIVITIES

Experiment with a Spiritual Strategy

In a role-play situation with a partner, select one of the cases just described or develop one of your own that gives you an opportunity to practice implementing one of the specifically spiritual interventions described in this chapter. Ask a third person to observe the role-play and take notes about his or her observations. Debrief the role-play in these groups of three or with an instructor.

Keep a Spiritual Journal

Commit yourself to keeping a spiritual journal for a month or longer. Use the journal to reflect on your own spiritual journey. The journal may be a vehicle for processing your thoughts and feelings about spiritual issues such as prayer, forgiveness, hope, surrender, or others. You could divide your class into small groups and share excerpts from your journal with classmates. Try to discern what implications for counseling emerge in your reflections.

Attend a 12-Step Meeting

Because so many clients with addiction issues get involved in 12-step programs, counselors need to know about them first-hand. Call for information about the various meetings in your community. Be sure to inquire about whether a group is open or closed. When you arrive at the meeting, introduce yourself as a visitor seeking to learn more about AA or whatever the 12-step program is. It is often better not to disclose your profession, so that your presence doesn't make participants uncomfortable. Make notes about your observations and personal reactions to the meeting.

SUPPLEMENTAL READING

Cameron, J. (1992). *The artist's way: A spiritual path to higher creativity.* New York: Putnam. This book is an inviting volume on how to connect with one's creativity through spiritual processes. One approach suggested is daily journaling that the author refers to as "morning pages." This book could be an excellent resource for both clients and counselors who wish to pursue spiritual growth.

Goldstein, J., & Kornfield, J. (1987). *Seeking the heart of wisdom: The path of insight meditation.* Boston: Shambhala. This primer on meditation is useful for those who wish to explore this spiritual discipline in more depth.

Klug, R. (1982). *How to keep a spiritual journal.* Nashville, TN: Thomas Nelson. This book is a practical guide for keeping a spiritual journal. It is easy to read and answers questions about "how to" begin and maintain a spiritual journal.

May, G. G. (1988). *Addiction and grace: Love and spirituality in the healing of addictions.* New York: HarperCollins. May examines attachment issues that lead to addiction and describes the relationship between various addicitions and spiritual awareness.

Progoff, I. (1975). *At a jounal workshop.* New York: Dialouge House Library. This book is a well-known classic on keeping a journal. It is extensive and more comprehensive than some books, but not especially directed at spiritual issues. Serious journal-writers should review this book for hints and support.

Stahl, C. (1977). *Opening to God.* Nashville, TN: Upper Room. This book, written from a Christian perspective, is a handbook for conducted guided imagery and visualization based on biblical texts. It contains actual guided scripts that could be used or adapted for assisting clients in this spiritual discipline. This book could be a model for developing guided imagery scripts from other religious or spiritual traditions.

USING RELIGIOUS AND SPIRITUAL STRATEGIES IN COUPLE AND FAMILY COUNSELING

CHAPTER 8

INTRODUCTION

Chapters 6 and 7 presented specific approaches counselors might use in working with individual clients' religious and spiritual issues. Specifically, Chapter 6 focuses on interventions associated with traditional counseling theories, and Chapter 7 concentrates on strategies considered religious or spiritual in nature. Many of the strategies discussed in the preceding chapters could be tailored to counseling couples and families. Hence, these topics will not be addressed again.

This chapter underscores the systemic perspective of couple and family counseling, present spiritual interventions associated with various family therapy schools, and offer particular strategies designed to build on clients' religious or spiritual worldviews. These approaches, too, may be adapted for working with individuals.

RELIGION, SPIRITUALITY, AND THE FAMILY

The 1990s saw a renewal of interest in religion and spirituality in American culture (Walsh, 1999). In fact, 90% of adults consider religion to be a significant aspect of their lives, and 60% consider it to be very significant (Gallup, 1996). Thus, for most Americans, the interface between family life and religion or spirituality is very important (Burton, 1992; Cornwall & Thomas, 1990).

In addition, Beavers and Hampson (1990) found that religious and spiritual beliefs are critical aspects of healthy family functioning. Indeed, such a values approach to family life seems to buffer the stresses associated with living in intimate family relationships. Indeed, 75% of persons surveyed indicated that religion has been a positive, strengthening force in family life (Gallup, 1996). Because religion and spirituality are prominent features of most families, and because they can serve as positive means of coping and enhancing family life, family counselors must consider ways to build on this dimension in their work.

Religion and spirituality are coping mechanisms that moderate stress in family life, and they surface frequently in life cycle transitions. When couples unite in marriage or other union-forming commitments, one of the first questions raised is whether or not there will be a religious or civil ceremony (Walsh, 1999). This question taps into individuals' personal and family histories with religious institutions, elicits couples' beliefs about the nature and context of their commitment and their relationships, and can be the source of conflict between the partners. Gay and lesbian couples could experience the pain of rejection if their religious traditions forbid participation in celebrations of union, or if their family members' beliefs limit such ceremonies to heterosexual marriage (Laird & Green, 1996). Concerns regarding intermarriage might also arise if the partners come from different religious or spiritual backgrounds. Stress might be increased if one or both families object to the marriage because of religious differences. Couples could have trouble securing clergy who are willing to perform marriage or uniting rituals outside of their particular faith-traditions. Further, couples wishing to remarry after a divorce might find strong opposition to their plans based on the theology of a given religion or denomination. For example, an Orthodox Jewish woman who desires to remarry must obtain permission from her former spouse (Rosen & Weltman, 1996); however, men are not bound by this regulation. In addition, Roman Catholics who have been divorced must first seek an annulment of the previous marriage before obtaining permission to remarry in the Roman Catholic Church. The annulment process is fraught with strain and could engender anger by an individual's children from the previous marriage who might perceive themselves as invalidated by such a move (Walsh, 1999).

The birth of children is also an occasion for religious issues to arise. Parents must decide whether or not to participate in rituals associated with new birth such as baptism, christening, or dedication (Christian) or circumcision (Jewish). Hindu practices involve a birth ceremony, *jatakarman,* that involves ritual washing which is followed by a naming ceremony, the *samskara namakarana* (Crompton, 1998). Immediately after birth, Muslim children are presented to the leader of the local congregation who whispers prayers in Arabic into each ear. These are the first words heard by the child. There may also be a circumcision ceremony, *khitana,* performed either shortly after birth or until the 13th birthday (Crompton, 1998). Again, when intermarriage is a salient concern for the couple, polarization can occur. Loyalty issues to family-of-origin traditions might surface. Or, couples for whom religion and spirituality was unimportant in the initial stages of their relationship might discover that the birth of a child engenders an interest in seeking out religious or spiritual connections. Most adults claim they want their children raised with some kind of religious or spiritual faith (Gallup, 1996).

Adolescence is another period in the life cycle when religious or spiritual concerns could be present. Many religions have rites of passage in which adolescents become full members of their congregations. Bar/Bat Mitzvahs in the Jewish tradition and baptism or confirmation in Christian circles are examples of these rituals. Even if religion has been a marginal aspect of family life during the latency period, many parents feel compelled to involve their young adolescents in religious training out of a sense of duty or loyalty to a tradition. Because the teen years characteristically involve the search for self and the establishment of a personal identity, adolescents are likely to be interested in religious or spiritual issues. They are attaining a level of cognitive development that makes it possible for them to consider the tenets of their family's religious or spiritual beliefs and to come to terms with their own appropriation or rejection of these beliefs.

Young adults typically distance themselves from organized religion (Elkind, 1971), and some even cut themselves off from the religious or spiritual traditions of their families of origin. Others find this life stage to be particularly important for exploring new spiritual directions (Parks, 1986).

Persons at midlife and in their later years find religion and spirituality to be increasingly significant aspects of their lives (Walsh, 1999). During this period, they evaluate life's meaning and grapple with the prospect of death— that of their loved ones and their own. Typically, involvement in religious organizations and attendance at worship increases for persons in midlife and beyond (Walsh, 1999). Thus, issues of religion and spirituality could arise at any point in the client's life cycle, especially during transitional periods. Counselors' knowledge about these moments when spirituality is most salient, and their openness to helping clients explore these issues, could enhance their work with families.

COUPLE AND FAMILY THERAPY: A SYSTEMS APPROACH

The unique aspect of couple and family counseling is its systemic approach. Instead of considering the locus of concern to be *within* the individual client, family therapy approaches consider the locus of concern to be *between* individuals. That is, in family systems theories, problems are viewed as interpersonal rather than intrapersonal. Couples and families constitute systems in which mutual interaction is responsible for both the cause and effect of individual behavior. Indeed, the family forms a system in which the whole is greater than the sum of its parts (Goldenberg & Goldenberg, 1996; Satir, 1964). Within this systemic perspective, there is an emphasis on *what* rather than *why*, a focus on patterns of reciprocal causality, rather than linear views of cause and effect, and an accent on the subjective, rather than the objective (Becvar & Becvar, 1996). Family counselors who work from a systemic position are likely to explore patterns of interaction, contextual aspects of family functioning, and on the here-and-now rather than the past (Sayger, Homrich, & Horne, 2000).

Within the systemic perspective, several schools of family therapy have emerged. Although it is beyond the scope of this chapter to provide a detailed discussion of these theories, brief summaries of several methods will help readers orient themselves to family therapy practices and to grasp how religious and spiritual issues could be integrated into these approaches.

Anderson and Worthen (1997) suggested that family therapies could be organized around three different dimensions of human experience: time (sequential events), space (structures of relationships), and story (language that gives meaning to time and space experiences). Strategic and brief therapies emphasize the time dimension, structural approaches focus on the space dimension, and transgenerational and postmodern constructionist theorists use the story form. According to Anderson and Worthen (1997), therapies emphasizing time and space employ interventionist strategies. Those that draw on stories rely on the conversational mode.

Transgenerational Theory

The quintessential contributor to transgenerational theory was Murray Bowen (1978). His theory is built on the assumption that human beings are part of evolutionary emotional processes that date back to the beginning of time (Friedman, 1991). Thus, families are considered *emotional systems* that have affective connections with each other. These family systems include members' thoughts, feelings, fantasies, physical makeup, genetic heritage, and their individual and collective processes across generations. The emotional system includes all the information that can be included in a genogram, including fusion between members and emotional cut-offs or disengagements (Friedman, 1991).

Another significant tenet of Bowenian theory is that of *differentiation*. This concept refers to the process of keeping oneself in balance while negotiating self-definition and self-regulation. Differentiation involves "knowing where one ends and another begins . . . , being clear about one's own personal values and goals, taking responsibility for one's own emotional being and destiny rather than blaming others or the context" (Friedman, 1991, p. 141). Differentiation is not to be equated with autonomy or independence. Differentiation is much more of an emotional issue than a behavioral one.

The concept of *triangles* refers to the notion that a two-person relationship is unstable. Thus, to manage the anxiety generated by emotional reactivity, one person brings in a third to moderate or reduce the anxiety (Papero, 2000). An extramarital affair is a good example of a triangulation. If the anxiety level is especially high, others will be brought into the system to form interlocking triangles. It is not uncommon, then, for the counselor to be triangulated by one spouse in the process of couple therapy.

When two people, typically a couple, join into a single self, the process is called *fusion* (Papero, 2000). Such fusion creates anxiety produced by intense togetherness. The more undifferentiated each partner is, the greater likelihood there will be emotional reactions designed to minimize anxiety. Some of these mechanisms include (a) withdrawal and seeking emotional distance, (b) couple conflict, (c) the transmission of a problem to a child in the system, or (d) dysfunction emerging in one of the partners (Papero, 2000).

Another major component of Bowenian theory is that of the multigenerational transmission process. This concept suggests that patterns of behaving and interacting, including all the efforts at managing anxiety, are passed along predictably from one generation to another. According to Friedman (1991), this process is not simply the *influence* of the past, but in a real sense it is the past made present. This concept of multigenerational transmission gives rise to the notion of "family-of-origin" work. By analyzing their own family patterns and processes, counselors can attend to their own differentiation issues and reduce the likelihood of being triangulated by their clients.

Counselors working from this theoretical position focus on (a) clarifying couple relationships, (b) resisting triangulation, (c) embodying differentiation, (c) teaching clients about emotional systems, (d) managing client emotional reactivity, and (e) remaining neutral (Papero, 2000). Bowenian counselors help clients intervene in family of origin patterns and work with them toward greater differentiation.

Structural Family Therapy

In structural family therapy, the family is viewed as a living organism that adapts to changing contextual circumstances: "an open sociocultural system in transformation" (Minuchin, 1974, p. 51). Structural counselors view the family as composed of various subgroups, or *subsystems.* Individual members may participate in more than one subsystem. Partners participate together in a couple subsystem, they participate with children in a parental subsystem, and children function together in a sibling subsystem. Rules that dictate who should be in contact with whom are called *boundaries.* Boundaries need to be permeable enough for members to have contact with each other, but strong enough to protect the development of the subsystems (Colapinto, 1991). Patterns of interaction in families move toward *homeostasis,* or maintaining the status quo (Colapinto, 2000). Thus, individual behaviors function in interlocking patterns reminiscent of the pieces of a jigsaw puzzle. This quality is referred to as *complementarity* (Colapinto, 2000).

Ways of managing family conflict surface in one of two ways. Families are either *enmeshed,* in which extreme levels of closeness and loyalty minimize disagreement, or *disengaged,* where the same result occurs via extreme distancing and pseudo-independence.

The notion of *hierarchy* concerns the rules that define different levels of decision-making power for individuals and subsystems (Colapinto, 1991). According to structural theorists, in functional families parents are hierarchically positioned above their children to provide leadership and protection (Colapinto, 1991).

Structural counselors seek to eliminate the presenting problems by transforming the structure of family interactions. Such counselors are active and directive. They might stage *enactments* in which family members are instructed to change places or to engage in alternative transactions with other family members. In addition, they might engage in *boundary-making* to manage over- and under-involved client participation. This strategy involves interrupting detouring patterns and other conflict avoidance mechanisms to allow members to function more effectively. Another technique, known as *unbalancing,* requires that the counselors use their authority to challenge a rigid family hierarchy (Colapinto, 1991). For example, the counselor may ignore an overly involved family member to give voice to a silent one. An even more intense form of unbalance occurs when counselors align themselves with one or more family members against others to highlight other possible interaction patterns. In all these interventions, family counselors and counselors are attempting to change the structure of the family to improve its function.

Strategic Family Therapy

Strategic family therapy is most often associated with the work of Haley (1976), Papp (1980), Madanes (1981), Watzlawick, Weakland, and Fisch (1974), and the Milan group (Selvini-Palazzoli, Boscolo, Cecchin, & Prata, 1978a). In this approach, counselors look for sequences of events and predictable patterns of behavior in a family. A contribution of the Milan Group (Selvini-Palazzoli, Boscolo, Cecchin, & Prata, 1980) was circular questioning. This method involves interviewing family members to generate information for the family regarding changes and differences in their relationships with each other that support symptoms in the family (Smith, Griffin, Thys, & Ryan, 1992). For example, counselors might ask who agrees with whom about a behavioral sequence. Or, perhaps counselors might inquire of a child, "What do you do when your father comes home drunk?" Circular questioning provides new contextual information to the family about the systemic nature of their interactions (Fleuridas, Nelson, & Rosenthal, 1986). Once the patterns are known, counselors then design a strategy for solving client problems. Interventions take the form of directives and involve something the family is assigned to do either within or outside of the counseling session (Madanes, 1991). The focus of counseling is on four constructs: symptoms, metaphors, hierarchy, and power (Smith, 1992). Families use symptoms to signal ways that they are stuck and as means of maintaining homeostasis in the system. Strategic counselors consider symptoms to be metaphors for other problems in the family (Madanes, 1984). For example, a couple engages in violent conflict in the presence of their child. The child begins acting out in school and exhibiting poor academic performance. The child's behavior takes the focus off the embattled couple, and they jointly attend to the needs of their child. Thus, the child's acting out is a metaphor for couple conflict. In addition, the hierarchy in the family is explored and counselors ask about how the family system is maintained, how symptoms, coalitions, and communication processes are connected to the hierarchy (Smith, 1992). Power is evaluated in the family system, and parents are organized to take charge of the family and to establish appropriate rules and consequences.

Therapeutic interventions revolve around four dimensions: (a) domination and control, (b) the desire to be loved, (c) love and protection, and (d) repentance and forgiveness (Keim, 2000). Counselors design interventions that are direct, indirect, or paradoxical to address these themes. Most directives are straightforward, but some may be implied. Through paradoxical interventions, counselors use clients' resistance to promote change. Thus, if the counselor tells the client to continue presenting the symptom, then "in response to the counselor's request not to change, clients resist by changing in a way that solves the presenting problem" (Keim, 2000, p. 190).

Brief Therapy

The brief therapy model grew out of strategic family therapy, especially from work conducted at the Mental Research Institute (MRI) in Palo Alto, California (Homrich & Horne, 2000). Solution-focused therapy, another model of brief therapy, is associated with de Shazer (1985) and O'Hanlon and Weiner-Davis (1989). One major assumption of brief therapy is that the client's complaint is truly the problem, not simply a symptom of the problem (Segal, 1991). Moreover, clients' behavior is shaped and determined by other people's behavior. Thus, in the MRI school of brief therapy, two basic questions are posed: "What makes this behavior persist? What is needed to change it?" (Watzlawick, Weakland, & Fisch, 1974, p. 2). The goal of brief therapy, then, is to reduce or eliminate the client's difficulty (Segal, 1991).

Brief therapy involves defining the problem, asking why the family is coming for help now (Budman & Gurman, 1989), inquiring about what solutions have been tried and their outcome, and ascertaining from the client what would be the smallest indicator that the problem was about to be solved (Segal, 1991).

Some interventions associated with this model include reframing, doing something different or more of the same, mentioning the dangers of improvement, advising clients to "go slowly," or taking a U-turn (Segal, 1991). Reframing involves "changing the conceptual and/or emotional setting or viewpoint in relation to which a situation is experienced and to place it in another frame which fits the 'facts' of the same situation equally or even better, and thereby changes its entire meaning" (Watzlawick et al., 1974, p. 95). For example, a father's incessant inquiry about his son's girlfriend could be cast as the father's opportunity for caring or interacting rather than as intrusiveness. When clients have discovered a strategy that is effective, they are encouraged to continue it. When clients use approaches that are not working, counselors advise them to "do something different," thus interrupting a pattern of unsatisfactory interactions. Mentioning the dangers of improvement involves helping clients imagine what other issues might surface once the presenting problem is solved. Admonishing clients to "go slowly" may either speed up or slow down the therapeutic process. This directive can be tied to predictions of backsliding or relapse, which, in and of itself, could prevent or reduce such action (Segal, 1991). Doing a "U-Turn" means re-evaluating a previous strategy, telling the client the approach was not effective, and offering something completely opposite to it.

Solution-focused brief therapy includes similar principles and interventions to those of the MRI school, but its emphasis is on the exception to the problem rather than the problem itself (Todd, 1992). Some assumptions of solution-focused therapy are that clients have the ability to solve problems, minimal history is needed about the problem, understanding the cause of the problem is unnecessary, and only small changes are necessary because these lead to larger changes (O'Hanlon & Weiner-Davis, 1989).

Some techniques associated with solution-focused therapy are (a) the exception questions, (b) the scaling questions, and (c) the miracle question. With exception questions, counselors ask clients about times when the problem did not occur and what was happening then. Counselors help clients identify what they were doing that contributed to extinguishing the problem. The scaling question takes this form: "On a scale from zero to ten where zero represents things at their worst, and ten presents how things will be when these problems are resolved, where would you place yourself today?" (Cade & O'Hanlon, 1993, p. 105). The answer to this question helps counselors evaluate progress. Similar scaling questions can be used to determine what clients need to do to move up one point on the scale. The miracle question elicits clients' desired outcome of their situation. One version of the question is

> Suppose that one night, while you were sleeping, there was a miracle and the problem was solved. How would you know? What would you be doing the next day that would tell you there had been a miracle? How would other people know without your having told them? (de Shazer, 1990, p. 97)

Social Constructionisim and Narrative Therapy

As described earlier (Chapter 1), social constructionists hold that a totally objective reality, apart from the observer is never fully knowable. They reject the notion that our mental ideas represent some objective truth "out there" as it actually is (Rosen, 1996). In the social constructionist* view, meaning is the product of persons interacting within the context of continuing relationships. Such meaning turns on the use of shared language (Gergen, 1985). As a

---

*There are differences between constructivism and social constructionism. "Constructionism . . . focuses more on an individual's personal construction of reality through the interfacing of senses with the environment. Constructivism accepts the individual psyche as a given, and examines the perceptual mechanisms and properties of the psyche as a reality-constructing instrument. Social constructionism sees the production of reality—not only as an individual phenomenon but as a social one. It focuses more on language use and interaction, and tends to be critical of cognitive science." (Kogan & Gale, 2000, p. 216)

result, multiple perspectives are generated, valued, and become the opportunity for clients and counselors to view presenting problems (and solutions) in alternative ways.

Social constructionist theory is exemplified most often in narrative therapy approaches. In their classic book, *Narrative Means to Therapeutic Ends,* White and Epston (1990) asked clients a variety of circular questions that resulted in clients' altered meanings about problems, each other, and themselves. Narrative therapy is concerned with the construction of reality in both the spaces "between" persons as well as "within" them (Sawicki, 1991). Thus, the very act of therapeutic conversations embodies possibilities for change.

Narrative therapy is based on the assumption that people's experiences compose stories that carry meanings, values, and interpretations about their lives. Stories are influenced by cultural variables such as gender, race, class, sexual orientation, age, disability, and so forth. In this storied context, counseling becomes the process by which clients and counselors collaborate to author alternative stories that will help clients exercise new possibilities and strategies for managing problems (White & Epston, 1990). Unlike other forms of family therapy, the counselors themselves are within the conversations, rather than acting as outside forces attempting to influence family interaction patterns (Kogan & Gale, 2000).

One of the best-known techniques associated with narrative therapy is externalizing the problem. This approach involves reversing the notion of the locus of the problem. Instead of the family having the problem, the problem has (or manages) the family (Kogan & Gale, 2000). In this way, "the problem becomes a separate entity and thus external to the person or relationship that was ascribed as the problem (White & Epston, 1990, p. 38). For example, a counselor might ask,

> When did the tempers begin to push you around? How does your depression get you to think about yourself? When did "conflict" begin to take over your relationship? How does "conflict" enlist you to react to your family? How does anorexia want you to view your body? (Kogan & Gale, 2000, p. 226)

Another intervention in the narrative traditions involves having the counselor write letters to clients sometimes in the place of case notes. Counselors summarize what happened in the session, what changes were noted, and their personal reactions to the process (Kogan & Gale, 2000). Another approach is to help clients look at situations in two different ways: as circumstances that are culturally prescribed and as "family" problems. This method is particularly useful regarding issues of race, gender, ethnicity, class sexual orientation, and disability. Not surprisingly, issues of power and privilege emerge when this strategy is employed. Anderson & Goolishian (1992) suggested having counselors approach clients as ethnographers studying new cultures. They approach each family as an opportunity to experiment with a variety of theories and multiple perspectives for understanding their situation. These efforts and others that facilitate new ways of seeing client situations are typical of social constructionist and narrative approaches to couple and family therapy.

IMPLICIT STRATEGIES FOR COUPLE AND FAMILY THERAPY

Tan (1996) made a distinction between spiritual strategies that were *implicit* in the counseling process and involved the use or adaptation of existing interventions and those that were *explicit* and were particularly spiritual in nature. In both these categories, however, the unique aspect of working with clients' religious and spiritual beliefs is in counselors' acceptance of God as a member of the family (Griffith, 1986). Once it is clear that God is a viable actor in a family system, then many of the traditional techniques in family therapy can be easily adapted to include clients' relationship with God. In this section, I begin with implicit strategies for integrating spirituality into couple and family therapy. These approaches are organized by schools of family therapy.

Transgenerational Theory

One basic tool of Bowenian therapy that addresses multigenerational transmission of family patterns is the genogram (McGoldrick, Gerson, & Schellenberger, 1996). The genogram is a blueprint or a map that depicts family relationships and patterns across three generations. In Chapter 4 of this text, I described in detail how counselors might assist clients in creating a spiritual genogram (Frame, 2000) that illustrates their religious and spiritual traditions across time. Such a genogram reveals the emotionally charged relationships that resulted from events and experiences associated with religion and spirituality in the family of origin and the extended family. Using a genogram helps clients and counselors understand the source of troubling beliefs or practices.

Butler and Harper (1994) used the concepts of *triangles* and *triangulation* in their work with religious couples. Such couples have a real and personal relationship with God and believe that God is "stabilizing interpersonal relationships and engaging in daily family transactions (Griffith, 1986, p. 609). Essentially, to manage the anxiety or tension in the couple relationship, one or both partners (at some time or other) bring in a third party, in this case God, to diffuse conflict and to balance the relationship. When each party in the triangle is fairly differentiated, then each of the partners can use their belief system and their relationship with God to provide support for problem-solving efforts. In this ideal state, couples take responsibility for addressing their issues and enlist God's assistance for reconciliation and problem-resolution (Butler & Harper, 1994).

When individual partners are not well-differentiated, God becomes triangulated in the couple relationship such that God's presence constrains the development of the marriage. Borrowing from structural family therapy concepts, three types of triangles may result: coalition, displacement, and substitutive (Hoffman, 1981; Minuchin, Rosman, & Baker, 1978; Umbarger, 1983). In coalition triangles, each partner "competes intensely for the allegiance of God, but neither is assured that they have it" (Butler & Harper,

1994, p. 282). In this case, each partner attempts to convince the other that God is on his or her side, sometimes engaging in elaborate systems of defense buttressed by quotations from sacred writings or revelatory experiences. Rather than seeking God's help in solving their problems, they co-opt God into participating in their blaming of the other partner.

CASE | BERT AND PEGGY

Bert and Peggy are Christians in their mid-thirties. They came to counseling because of unresolved conflicts regarding equitable division of household labor and child care. When their counselor, Gus, began to address their presenting problem, both Bert and Peggy re-formulated it in terms of the other partner's lack of religiosity. Peggy charged Bert, saying, "If you really loved me as Christ loves the church, then you would do more around the house. Clearly, God wants you to hold up your end of the bargain." Bert retaliated, "I'm definitely walking closer to God than you are. I spend an hour in prayer daily and I am tithing 15% of my hard-earned money to the church. I think God is proud of me and wants me to be the head of this family and make the decisions." The argument escalated as each spouse provided evidence of a more significant relationship with God, justifying God's alliance with him or her. In response to this pattern of triangulation, Gus re-framed God's position and asked the couple how God could "side with either of them against the other without violating the sanctity of their marriage" (Butler & Harper, 1994, p. 282). In this case, the counselor proposed that their interaction suggested that God was having an affair with one or both of them. He then asked how a God who is so supportive of marriage could be so disrespectful of the boundary of their marriage (Butler & Harper, 1994).

In displacement triangles, the couple unites against a common enemy. In this arrangement, God is blamed for the adversity in the marriage and the couple may be connected by their mutual anger at God. According to Butler and Harper (1994), "this triangle yields the tragic situation of painful hostility and emotional cutoff in a relationship with a God whom they can't disavow" (p. 283).

CASE | LINDA AND JUDY

Linda and Judy, lesbians in their forties, sought counseling from Jean because of conflict in their relationship regarding whether or not they would "come out" to their friends and family members. Linda was adamant that they needed to affirm themselves and their relationship so they could live with integrity. Judy was worried about losing significant support from her family of origin and especially her friends in the church. When Jean began to pursue each partner's perspective on coming out, Linda and Judy began to minimize their conflict, to collude with each other, and to direct their anger toward God and the institutional church that denied them the right to live openly as a lesbian couple. In this case, Jean focused on the displacement triangle and commented on how being angry at God and the church kept them from dealing directly with their divergent views and resultant conflict. She asked, "Are you really angry at God or angry at yourselves for your relationship difficulties?"

In substitutive triangles, bringing in a third person, in this case, God, minimizes conflict by diverting attention and intimacy to God rather than to the partner. One form of substitutive triangle occurs when instead of helping the couple work through their difficulties, relating to God becomes a means of enduring rather than solving couple conflict (Butler & Harper, 1994). Another form involves one or both partners working diligently toward God's causes such that they spend their time helping God, rather than dealing with their distress.

| CASE | NED AND ROSEANNE |

Ned and Roseanne, a Jewish couple in their fifties, were referred to counseling by their Rabbi, Steven, because of incidents or arguing and backbiting during public religious events and festivals. Their counselor, Levi, began interviewing each partner to ascertain the root of their conflict. During the initial interview, both Ned and Roseanne shifted the focus from their couple issues to boasting about the time they were spending working on a Holocaust memorial, volunteering in the city's homeless shelter, and tutoring inner-city children. In this case, Levi recognized the substitutive triangle and asked the couple to consider whether in working on God's behalf if God was willing for them to sacrifice their marital satisfaction (Butler & Harper, 1994). In all these strategies, couple counselors used interventions that honored God's place in the relationship, but that also disentangled God from the triangle to increase couple differentiation (Butler & Harper, 1994).

One pitfall of working with couples for whom God is a significant family member is the potential for the counselor to be triangulated by one of the partners. Rotz, Russell, & Wright (1993) suggested that it is not uncommon for the partner who perceives him or herself to be spiritually superior to attempt to recruit the counselor as partner aligned against the spouse. They offered several methods of keeping oneself out of a triangle and maintaining a focus on the process of therapy. First, Rotz and colleagues (1993) advise counselors to ask couples about their expectations of them and of the therapeutic process. One such question is, "If I agree to work with you, you may discover that what I do as a counselor does not fit with your image of me as a spiritual person. How would that affect our ability to work together?" (Rotz, Russell, & Wright, 1993, p. 371). Second, they propose making the issue of spiritual differences explicit. An example of this strategy is to ask, "If one of you believes yourself to be more or less spiritually inclined than the other, will that difference help or hinder the work we need to do here?" (Rotz, Russell, & Wright, 1993, p. 371). Third, Rotz and colleagues (1993) recommend inviting the "spiritually one-down" partner to develop criteria to assess the objectivity of the counselor. The counselor might say to this partner, "I am curious to know whether you think I might team up with your wife (husband) against you? Would you be able to recognize it if it happened? If so, how? Do you think your husband (wife) has you here for another reason than (insert presenting complaint)?" (Rotz, Russell, & Wright, 1993, p. 372). Fourth, disavow conversion efforts. Fifth, predict a sense of betrayal by telling each partner that she or he may experience times of feeling double-crossed or ignored. Rotz and colleagues advocate asking the partner who feels such betrayal to bring up the feeling so it can be discussed. Last, they mention balancing the therapeutic agenda so that if one partner dominates the session with "God talk" the other can have equal time raising issues that are important to him or her. Using these strategies can help counselors minimize the likelihood that they will be drawn into a coalition with one partner who perceives him or herself as spiritually "one-up" compared with the other spouse.

Structural Family Therapy Approaches

Family sculpting (Duhl, Kantor, & Duhl, 1973; Satir, 1983) involves having family members recreate the family system by creating a physical representation of family relationships at a particular time. Family members are asked to design a visual sculpture using themselves as subjects. The sculpture is to depict their view of family interactions (Sayger & Horne, 2000). When working with families where God is a member, it can be especially useful to have family members include God in the sculpture. When this adaptation is made to the technique, it is possible to see how each family member views his or her relationship to God and how he or she represents other family members' God-self relationships.

CASE | **LYDIA AND EDGAR**

Lydia and Edgar, an African American couple in their mid-thirties sought counseling with Jake because their son, Trevor, was acting out in school. The couple reported that they had asked God to help them solve their difficulty, but were frustrated that no answer was forthcoming. Jake asked the couple how important their religious faith was in their family, and all members, including Trevor, reported that it was "very important." Jake asked the family members to sculpt their relationships and to include God in the sculpture. (Jake volunteered to stand in for God.) All three of the family members placed Lydia right up against "God" (Jake) and Edgar and Trevor distant from each other and the Lydia-God pair. When asked what they thought the sculpture revealed about their family, Trevor said,

"Mom is so busy with God she doesn't have time for us." Jake then suggested that perhaps Lydia and God were in charge of the family, functioning as the parental subsystem and that Edgar and Trevor were experiencing themselves as members of the sibling subsystem. Jake reframed Trevor's acting out as a cry for attention and as an attempt to reinstate his father in the parental role. Jake asked the family members how God could be involved in the family without over-stepping the couple boundaries. They all agreed (though Lydia was reluctant) that Edgar and Lydia should spend more time together as a couple and should work as partners in parenting and providing for Trevor. They wanted God to be available to each of them, not just to Lydia. In this case, a popular family therapy technique has been modified to address God's relationship in a religious family.

Strategic Family Therapy

Counselors working from a strategic perspective may discover that God* is an active player in family patterns and interactions. Determining how God functions for individuals in a family system can be explored by using circular questions (Griffith, 1986). For example, counselors using appropriate respect and neutrality might ask each family member, "When Dad stops focusing on his work and attends to his relationship with Mom, what happens to Tyler's relationship to God? Does Tyler move closer to God or farther away? If Tyler moves away from God, who else makes a similar move? Who would be the most upset if the family did not remain close to God?" (Griffith, 1986). Other examples of circular questions (Fleuridas, Nelson, & Rosenthal, 1986) include the following:

> About which relationship in the family do you think God would express the most satisfaction? About which relationship do you think God would express the least satisfaction? If you worked out your sexual relationship with your husband so that you both found it to be satisfying, would you feel closer or further away from God? With whom in the family can you talk about God? With whom would it feel awkward? (Griffith & Griffith, 1992, p. 73)

In these ways, counselors are able to extract information about God as a member of the family and how the God-construct functions in the context of the family's presenting problem.

Relabeling behavior using a religious or spiritual frame may be an effective way to intervene in families that are immobilized by self-defeating patterns. For example, Griffith (1986) related a case regarding a very religious (Christian) young adult son who was overly enmeshed with his mother. He was not able to complete his work without her constant supervision and she was not able to travel because he felt like he needed to protect her. Griffith (1986) reframed the son's obsession with his mother as a sin because he lacked the faith that God would protect her. Griffith (1986) said to the young

*Other names for God may be substituted based on the client's worldview.

man, "For many years you have been more a husband to your mother than her own husband; now, by acting as her protector against every natural disaster, you are trying to be her God" (p. 610). In this case, the counselor was able to use the client's belief system in a way that pitted his loyalty to his mother against his devotion to God. Ultimately, by choosing God, the client was able to begin separating from his mother and establishing an independent identity (Griffith, 1986).

In another case (DiBlasio, 1988), a counselor working with an evangelical Christian family used a strategic directive to put a father in charge of his acting-out child. The counselor based the directive on the biblical injunctions of Ephesians 5:22–23 and I Peter 3:1–7 which call for a father's spiritual leadership and authority in the family.

In all these cases, counselors maintain their focus on the interactional patterns of clients' relationships with God, rather than the theological content of their beliefs (Griffith, 1986). The counselors adopt a neutral stance and take on a perspective of curiosity regarding clients' particular religious or spiritual constructions.

The Milan Group, led by Selvini-Palazzoli and others (1978b), prescribed rituals as interventions in strategic family therapy. Rituals are symbolic acts or interactions that express values, meaning, or the norms of a culture (Bewley, 1995). Rituals are used in family therapy for various purposes. They involve relating (shaping, expressing, and maintaining relationships), changing (marking transitions for ourselves and others), healing (recovering from relationship betrayal, trauma, or loss), believing (voicing beliefs and making meaning), and celebrating (affirming deep joy and honoring life with festivity) (Imber-Black & Roberts, 1992). Rituals are dramatic messages that provide at least three kinds of integration: (a) of the self with itself, as it contemplates change; (b) of the self with culture, by the use of common symbols; and (c) of the self with others, connecting celebrants into an often profound community (Neu, 1995, p. 192).

Because rituals are central to both religion and spirituality, they lend themselves well to being vehicles for incorporating the sacred into secular therapy. When designing rituals that are spiritually informed, counselors and clients co-create them with attention to clients' notions of spirituality (Bewley, 1995). Together, counselor and clients identify an experience embraced by the clients, find significant symbols that represent the experience, and formulate corresponding symbolic acts. Both counselors and clients designate the ritual as a sacred process and set apart a space where Spirit (in whatever form clients describe) can be remembered (Bewley, 1995). Rituals may be used for healing from incest, gay and lesbian persons coming out (Neu, 1995), or dealing with grief and loss (Bewley, 1995). Almost any therapeutic issue can be the impetus for the creation of an appropriate ritual; however, ritual work may be contraindicated for clients with poor ego strength and those who have experienced ritual abuse (Bewley, 1995). Counselors should also avoid rituals that include destruction of others' images, as these symbolic acts may exacerbate feelings of anger and hatred rather than banish them (Bewley, 1995).

| CASE | COLLEEN AND ERIC |

Colleen and Eric are a remarried Caucasian couple in their early forties. They each brought two children from previous marriages into their new family. Since their marriage, Colleen's daughter, Maddy, 8, and her son, Caleb, 10, have been living with Eric's daughter, Lucretia, 9, and his son, Garrett, 12. The family had sought counseling because of constant conflict between the four children in this blended family. All the children were extremely loyal to their parent and insubordinate to their stepparent. Colleen and Eric were overwhelmed with the daily tasks of caring for four children, managing regular fights that erupted among the children, and nurturing their new relationship. After 18 months of intense family therapy as well as individual and sibling group work, significant positive changes had occurred among the children and between the children and their stepparents. Toward the end of therapy, the children were proud to be members of one unified family. Colleen and Eric told their counselor, Eva, they were considering taking a new family name to symbolize their family unity. Eva suggested they work together to develop a naming ritual that would incorporate some of their spiritual beliefs.

The entire family talked together about a new name that would symbolize their experience becoming a family. They came up with the family name, "Lovebridge" because they had "built bridges of love toward one another." As a family, they decided to retain their former names as middle names and to legally change their names to "Lovebridge." Eva worked with the family to develop a family logo and a ritual that incorporated their beliefs about naming as part of creation, revealed in the biblical creation stories in Genesis 1–2. They decided to hold the ritual in their new home and to invite special friends and extended family members.

During the ritual, Eric read from the Bible the story of the naming at creation. Then, each family member shared what the new name meant to him or her and why it was important to have a new family name. Next, each family member lit a candle and said, "I am _____ (first name) Lovebridge." The guests responded affirming the naming saying together, "You are _____ (first name) Lovebridge." At the end of the ritual, Colleen and Eric produced T-shirts that had a family-designed logo on the back including the words, "Lovebridge Family." Eric then led the family in a prayer of thanksgiving and unity. The ritual was followed by a brief reception in the family's home.

In this case, the co-creation of a ritual to mark both a healing and transition was an effective way to celebrate the success of therapy and to launch a blended family.

Brief Therapy

In brief therapy, the focus is on solutions to presenting problems. When those problems include religious or spiritual issues, classic interventions may be adapted to address client issues. Prest and Keller (1993) suggested a strategy that involves identifying solutions that have become part of the problem. In this approach, counselors help clients recognize the solutions that have grown out of their spiritual systems but that have maintained the problem rather than eliminated it. For example, Prest and Keller (1993) described a case in which a couple in their thirties presented with marital problems, including depression, substance abuse, distancing patterns, control issues, and sexual difficulties. The couple's solution was for the wife to become involved in Bible study to learn how to be a better wife and parent. The husband became more controlling as he attempted to apply the control-oriented patriarchal beliefs of his church to his family life. These strategies exacerbated the family difficulties and reinforced the existing problems. According to Prest and Keller (1993), the counselor was able to help the couple see how their spiritual solutions had been ineffective at best and harmful at worst. By examining their attempted solutions, the couple became more open to exploring alternative beliefs that would assist them in dealing with their problems.

Another brief therapy intervention is for counselors to caution clients to "go slowly" when they are attempting to solve problems. This strategy implies that solving the problem might not be simple and that relapse into old patterns might occur. Such an approach could be especially helpful to couples who are attempting to modify their belief systems to manage other difficulties in their relationships.

CASE | ARMEN AND TASHA

Armen and Tasha are Muslims in their mid-forties. They immigrated from Jordan 10 years previously so that Armen could pursue an advanced degree at an American university. They brought their two small children who became very acculturated during their stay in the United States. Armen and Tasha began having marital difficulties as the children moved away from family values and toward American practices. Armen and Tasha first tried to require their children to observe the traditions of family, country, and religion. This approach was unsuccessful and resulted in their now-adolescent children's increased rebellion and disrespectful behavior. When this strategy did not work, Armen withdrew from the family and Tasha was left alone without spousal support, still trying to insist on conformity to religious requirements and cultural traditions.

When Armen and Tasha finally sought counseling, Ross helped them explore their customs and beliefs and to decide what they valued most of all. Ultimately, they decided that being in relationship with each other and their children was their most important value. They indicated that they also wanted to have their children know Allah as the Supreme Being in their lives. Both Armen and Tasha acknowledged that they had been more focused on requirements than relationships (Borg, 1997) and that they could forego some of their rules and rituals if it would bring them into a richer relationship with each other and their children.

Once they had decided to relax their stringent religious and cultural requirements, Armen and Tasha moved so quickly they felt lost in a chaotic world they themselves had created. Ross advised them to "go slowly" as they modified their beliefs and practices. He predicted that a rapid total change in lifestyle would be distressing to both their children and to themselves as a couple. Eventually, Armen and Tasha were able to invite their children to participate in re-thinking their lives together so that family members could integrate their cultural and religious traditions and practices into their current life situation.

From solution-focused interventions, counselors working with couples and families regarding religious or spiritual beliefs may be able to use the "scaling question" to clarify various perspectives. For example, couples assessing their spiritual beliefs might be asked to consider a variety of aspects of their belief systems. Counselors may ask, "On a scale of one to ten (one being not at all; ten being very much), how strongly do you believe in a Higher Power?" Other spiritual content may be introduced and the scaling question applied to these as well. As a result, clients are able to discover for themselves the valence of their particular beliefs. Then, they might explore in more depth the issues about which they were ambivalent or which they rated quite low.

Social Constructionist Approaches

One of the major contributions of social constructionist thinking and therapy has been the centrality of language and the implications for the therapeutic use of language systems. In the religious and spiritual realm, these ideas are particularly salient because language, metaphor, and narrative are some of the important media by which spirituality is experienced and explored.

Language   Language is the primary vehicle for psychotherapy. Anderson and Goolishian (1988) stated, "therapy is being in conversation about a problem, which is a process of developing new meanings and understandings . . . Through therapeutic conversation, fixed meanings and behaviors (the sense people make of things and their actions) are given room, broadened, shifted and changed" (p. 381). Thus, the language that counselors choose reflects their values and assumptions about the therapeutic enterprise, their clients' situation, and the world in general.

When clients are particularly focused on the religious or spiritual aspects of their presenting problems, and when clients' language systems include religious or spiritual beliefs and language, then counselors engage clients appropriately when they use clients' language in the therapeutic conversation (Kudlac, 1991). It is irrelevant whether or not the counselors themselves subscribe to that belief system.

CASE | **LORNA AND CLIFF**

Lorna and Cliff, a Caucasian couple in their mid-fifties, sought counseling with Annette because Lorna had been involved in a brief affair with a co-worker. During an early session, both Cliff and Lorna each expressed pain about the fracture in their relationship as well as confusion about the future of their marriage. Cliff said, "We just want to figure out what God's will is for our lives." Because Annette did not share Cliff and Lorna's religious beliefs, initially she was perplexed about how to respond to Cliff's statement. However, she was able to step inside the couples' language system and ask, "What do you think God wants for each of you and for your marriage?" (Sperry & Giblin, 1996, p. 521). By using their spiritual language, Annette was able to "include God in the conversation" (Kudlac, 1991), honor the couple's religious beliefs, and assist them in difficult decisions within their worldview.

Griffith and Griffith (1992), building on the work of Tomm (1987) and White (1986), designed some questions that "invite fresh dialogue and new linguistic distinctions in the conversations between self and God-construct" (Griffith & Griffith, p. 73). Some of these questions are reflexive (Tomm, 1987, 1988) such as the following:

1. Had you possessed the relationship you now have with God when you first married, how do you suppose your different behavior might have altered the way the relationship evolved?
2. If God were to restructure this interaction, how do you think it would go?
3. If God were to see worth in this relationship that the two of you might not be able to see, what might that be?
4. If you were to discover that God had in fact been present and active in this situation all along, where might that have been? (Griffith & Griffith, 1992, p. 73)

Other questions are outcome and unique account questions (White, 1988). Some of these type questions are

1. Has there ever been even a brief moment when, contrary to your expectations, you did sense approval coming from God?
2. Can you recall a time when your husband might have criticized your relationship with God but didn't?
3. In view of all the betrayals you experienced in your life growing up, are you surprised to discover that you have learned to trust God? (Griffith & Griffith, 1992, pp. 73–74)

Other questions that delve into clients' religious or spiritual perspectives are unique redescription and unique possibilities questions (White, 1986, 1988). Some examples of these types of questions are the following:

1. What difference will your having learned how to trust God make in your learning how to trust your wife?
2. If you see yourself as the person God sees, what new possibilities might you imagine for this relationship?
3. If you were to agree with the outcome you believe God wants for this relationship, what might be the next step in getting there? (Griffith & Griffith, 1992, p. 74)

Metaphor   Haley (1971) stated, "a basic principle of systems approaches is that families express pathologies through metaphors" (p. 225). People also express other aspects of themselves and their relationships through metaphors such that the task of the counselor is to make sense of the metaphors and help the family construct new ones (Kudlac, 1991). Because religious language in particular is metaphorical language (Greeley, 1990), it behooves counselors to inquire of their clients the meanings of these metaphors and to join with them as co-creators of metaphors that could shift client thinking enough to make a difference in their circumstances.

Prest and Keller (1993) suggested the use of metaphors with clients whose spiritual beliefs were nontraditional (e.g., outside the context of Judeo-Christian society). One such metaphor is that human beings are manifestations of God. This notion is supported both by Judeo-Christian religion and by Eastern traditions that view all life as sacred. Prest and Keller claimed that by using this metaphor, anger and abuse are difficult to maintain because clients see all persons as bearers of the holy. Moreover, such a metaphor enhances the belief in the dignity and worth of all persons and may be linked to increased self-esteem. Another metaphor offered by Prest and Keller (1993) is that of God as a stream with all humans in the stream. They indicated that such a metaphor implies that "individuals may try to swim against the stream, deny they are in the stream, or turn and allow the stream to carry them" (p. 145). This metaphor is helpful clinically because it underscores one's personal value compared with others, celebrates the value of human life, and supplies the motivation for caring because all humans are in the stream together. Yet another metaphor offered by Prest and Keller (1993) is that of the divine presence in both "darkness" and "light." The concept here is that the Higher Power is made known in the difficult times as well as in the times of triumph and joy, such that "darkness" is not viewed as abandonment, but a special opportunity to experience the holy.

CASE | MARIBETH AND MONA

Maribeth and Mona came to counseling because of bitterness that neither partner could conquer. Both Maribeth and Mona had each been sexually involved with other women, despite their commitment to monogamy. The anger and resentment had grown so strong that violence had nearly erupted. Moreover, the entire lesbian community in which they were involved was beginning to take sides. Their counselor, Kira, inquired about Maribeth and Mona's spiritual persuasions. Each partner indicated she had been raised in a Protestant [Christian] church, but had left it because of its doctrine that rejected same sex unions. Both Maribeth and Mona reported that they had been intrigued by Eastern religions and New Age practices. They were also drawn to goddess religions and imagined the divine in female form.

After hearing Maribeth and Mona's story, Kira asked them what their goals were for counseling. Both said they wanted to release the anger and hatred that was seething inside them. Kira decided to use the metaphor of the Divine as a stream that carried with it all humanity. In fact, Kira emphasized to Maribeth that Mona's face was a face of the Goddess. And, in turn, she reminded Mona that Maribeth was an incarnation of the Goddess. The metaphor was a powerful statement of faith for this couple that enabled them to begin to address their pain and anger and to make a contract with Kira that they would not engage in violence toward each other.

In addition to the metaphors described in this case, each religion and spiritual tradition embodies a multitude of metaphors. The sacred writings and texts are replete with metaphorical language. Further, the myriad of cultural traditions also contains metaphors that may be used in counseling. For example, in many cultures, the well-known metaphor of the hero (Campbell, 1968) emerges. Counselors who are attentive to the language of metaphor may find they have access to powerful agents for therapeutic change.

Narrative   A popular method of family therapy in the social constructionist milieu is narrative therapy. Well-known writers such as White and Epston (1990) have argued that rather than focusing on absolutes and objective views, the narrative approach is concerned with stories and lifelikeness (Todd, 1992). Working with clients' life narratives includes examining life stories that do not fit with the facts clients are currently experiencing. One major reason why people enter counseling is that their live stories have broken down. Either their lives have lost purpose or the purpose has become derailed because of psychological difficulties (Vitz, 1992).

Lax (1996) argued that narrative models have much in common with Buddhist practice. In Buddhism, the notion of "a permanent self is an illusion that we cling to, a narrative developed in relation to others over time that we come to identify as who we are" (Lax, 1996, p. 200). Narrative therapy is similar in that people's lives are viewed as changing narratives to be freed from one reified version and opened to a host of possibilities. In both Buddhism and narrative therapy, "multiple voices, stories, and views are valued, with the individual's own experience given centrality" (Lax, 1996, p. 201). In addition, both Buddhism and narrative therapy share an emphasis on *reflexivity,* the "process of making oneself an object of one's own observation" (Lax, 1996, p. 206). Thus, we shape and are shaped by our own narratives. As counselors, we inform and are informed by clients' narratives *and* by the changes in their narratives. Buddhist clients who are in the habit of insight meditation and mindfulness (Nhat Hanh, 1976) may respond well to narrative work that asks them to deconstruct their current stories and to disengage from them enough to become observers of their own narratives.

CASE | **MARISSA**

Marissa, 30, sought counseling with Elliot because of ongoing conflicts with her parents and extended family members over her rejection of Lutheranism, the religion of their family for several generations. In college, Marissa had been drawn to the philosophy of the Buddha and had joined a Buddhist group on campus. She had become very disciplined in her meditation and reported that this spiritual practice helped her relax and gain perspective on her life. She was frustrated that her parents, grandparents, and other family members could not see the significance of her religion for her, and that they denigrated it as a departure from "the truth." Marissa reported that family visits consisted largely of heated debates regarding whose religion was superior and why. Although she felt depleted and angry after these exchanges, Marissa was unsure of how to interrupt the patterns of negativity that characterized her family relationships.

Elliot introduced Marissa to the idea of the self as narrative—a story, cast in one's cultural context, fashioned by interactions with others and experiences across time. Marissa was drawn to this fluid concept of self as story because it fit nicely with her Buddhist understanding of impermanence. She was able to grasp the notion that her story was simply another narrative alongside the narratives of her family members—not a story imbued with fixed, immutable meaning. Elliot helped Marissa to see that individual stories could be observed as one views thoughts during meditation—as passing constructions that surface and then fade. Such ideas became the catalyst for Marissa to deconstruct her perceptions of her family's (and her own) religious narratives as eternal bearers of truth. This awareness enabled her to become less defensive and more accepting of family differences. Once Marissa was able to lay aside her need to be right when it came to religion, she was able to consider her religious differences with her family as a metaphor for her leaving home. Over the next several months, Elliot and Marissa worked on ways she could connect with her family of origin and receive a blessing from them to enter into full adulthood.

When working with clients for whom religion and spirituality are central, narrative therapy is a means of addressing these themes. Because most sacred texts and other writings are composed of narrative, these stories may act as metaphors for clients' stories. Indeed, because the sacred writings are authoritative, they might hold clues for clients' re-authoring of their own stories.

CASE | CHERISE

Cherise is a 25-year-old African American woman battling cocaine addiction. Her husband abandoned her and took their only daughter to live with his parents in another state. Cherise's mother and grandmother also told her to find another place to stay until she "kicked the cocaine habit." Cherise was court-ordered to counseling as the result of her last arrest for drug trafficking. Her counselor, Duane, inquired about Cherise's religious and spiritual background. Cherise reported she was raised in an African Methodist Episcopal (AME) church, but that she hadn't attended since high school.

As Cherise told her story of her descent into the hell of alcohol and drug abuse, Duane began externalizing the problem. He asked Cherise, "When did you let the cocaine convince you that you were so weak you had to depend on it to be somebody?" and "how has cocaine affected your relationships with your family?"

Duane also asked Cherise, "What will your life look like in five years if cocaine keeps controlling you?" Duane's approach kept Cherise from feeling guilty and blamed. Instead, she felt anger rising at the abuses cocaine had inflicted on her and her family.

Later in the counseling process, Duane read Cherise the Biblical story of Israel's captivity and bondage in Egypt and their ultimate deliverance by God (Exodus 1–15). The biblical story of Hebrew oppression became a metaphor for Cherise and her addiction to cocaine. Paired with her anger at the drug and her deep, but unclaimed belief in the power of God, Cherise was able to commit herself to drug rehabilitation with new fervor and determination. She was able to write a new script for her future life that included a relationship with her daughter, her mother, and her grandmother.

Narrative approaches that use archetypal stories across cultures and religious and spiritual traditions may also be useful in counseling. Greek and Roman myths, Zen stories, parables, legends, ballads, and other kinds of narratives may connect with clients' stories in ways that provide the catalyst for transformation.

Collaboration and Debriefing

The use of reflecting teams (Andersen, 1987; Hardy, 1993) and debriefing sessions (Kuehl, Newfield, & Joanning, 1990) have contributed greatly to the conduct of postmodern constructionist family therapy. When religious or spiritual concerns are important aspects of family dynamics, these strategies may be especially effective.

Reflecting teams who watch the counseling sessions behind one-way glass share their perspectives with the counselors who then pass along the team's views to the family. Sometimes the entire team actually meets with the family. Information delivered to the family via the reflecting team may open up new possibilities for growth and change that were not previously available.

Debriefing sessions provide the opportunity for family members to share with the counselor their opinions about how the therapy is progressing, what they would like to change, and what other topics they might like to discuss (Joanides, 1996). Often such debriefing sessions are the occasion for families to interject religious or spiritual issues. Debriefing sessions may also be the mechanism for introducing new information into the therapeutic system from the family's perspective (Joanides, 1996).

CASE | LORRAINE

Lorraine, a 51-year-old single mother of two adolescents, Hannah, 14, and Kip, 16, sought counseling with Casey because of difficulty managing her children's acting-out behavior since her divorce from their father. Casey asked Lorraine what she had tried, used narrative approaches with the youth about how they would like to re-write their family story, and externalized the problem so that the "bad-behavior" was construed as interrupting their school and family life. None of these strategies was particularly effective in bringing about change. However, during a debriefing session, Casey asked family members their perceptions of the counseling process. Kip told Casey that nothing was going to change until his mother "gave up her New Age spiritual experiments and became a *normal* person." The debriefing session introduced a hidden, but important aspect of Kip and Hannah's dissatisfaction with their current life. Not only had they lost their father's presence in the family, they had been deprived of their Jewish traditions and practices as a result of their mother's adoption of a new set of spiritual expressions. This information served as a means of re-directing the therapy to bring about change.

EXPLICIT RELIGIOUS AND SPIRITUAL STRATEGIES IN COUPLE AND FAMILY COUNSELING

In the preceding section, I described couple and family interventions for working with religious or spiritual issues *within* the existing theoretical frameworks adapting classic family therapy approaches. In this section, I present four explicitly religious or spiritual counseling methods for working with couples or families: soul healing (Becvar, 1997); prayer (Butler, Gardner, & Bird, 1998); transcendence, relinquishment, and use of self (Anderson, 1994; Anderson & Worthen, 1997); and community-based spiritual linkages (Nakhaima & Dicks, 1995).

Soul-Healing

Becvar (1997) presented a couple and family counseling approach embedded in a spiritual understanding of the world. *Soul-healing* involves the "creation of contexts in which the focus is no longer primarily on problems, but rather emphasizes solutions and the facilitation of wellness in a holistic sense" (Becvar, 1997, p. 4). This approach includes the awareness of a transcendent dimension of existence that is embodied in all relational interactions. Its goal is not only the growth and development of persons but of the "soul of the world" (Becvar, 1997, p. 5).

A soul-healing perspective involves five principles: acknowledging connectedness, suspending judgment, trusting the universe, creating realities, and walking with heart (Becvar, 1997). Acknowledging connectedness means underscoring the interdependence between persons, and persons and the world. Suspending judgment means shifting the focus away from blame toward acceptance and respect for the dignity and worth of persons. It means to "work to bring about a change in context rather than seeing a problem as residing within a particular person" (Becvar, 1997, p. 7). Trusting the universe involves adopting a life-stance of mystery and awe with a basic faith in ourselves and a power beyond ourselves. Creating realities suggests we are participants in forming the realities we experience and that we have the capacity for awareness of ourselves as co-creators of our experiences. "Walking the world with heart" means living and working in such a way that human potential is more fully developed and that the goals of compassion and peace are integrated into our work.

CASE	TRUDI

Trudi, a 25-year-old homeless African American woman with a 4-year-old son, Moses, was referred to the shelter counselor, Toby, because of repeatedly being fired from jobs and getting evicted from various apartments and motels. Trudi was angry and sullen in the initial session and barely made eye contact with Toby. Because Toby had adopted a "soul-healing" approach to his practice, he began by empathizing with Trudi and telling her that he would feel angry, too, if employers, landlords, and family members constantly rejected him. He said he would feel like he didn't have any worth at all. Toby emphasized his belief in the connectedness of all things, and that Trudi and Moses were part of the human family. Toby refrained from focusing on what was wrong with Trudi and how she had failed to negotiate the rules, roles, and relationships of successful living. Instead, he externalized the problem and asked her how long she thought "homelessness" and "unemployment" would tear at her dignity. He aligned himself with Trudi, and by so doing, helped her to acknowledge the ways in which she enabled "homelessness" and "unemployment" to get the best of her. By working out of his own basic faith in the universe and by extending to Trudi and Moses sincere compassion, Toby was able to discover the person who hid behind the anger. He didn't work instant miracles with Trudi, but he was able to set her on a path of growing self-esteem.

Prayer

Using a qualitative method, Butler, Gardner, and Bird (1998) studied the effects of prayer on couple interaction during conflict. Several themes emerged as participant interviews were analyzed. First, when couples perceived God as a personal deity with whom they were in relationship, the act of prayer resulted in a dynamic shift in the constellation of couple behaviors and interactions (Butler, Gardner & Bird, 1998). Second, when couples prayed for each other, they experienced hostility, contempt, and negativity as incompatible with God's care for the spouse and the relationship. Thus, one effect of praying for a spouse during a conflictual period was the reduction in emotional reactivity and a calming of emotions (Butler, Gardner, & Bird, 1998). Third, couples who prayed for each other experienced a "softening" of the relationship, a sense of humility in the face of their individual self-righteous feelings, and an emerging commitment to the partner and to the couple relationship. They seemed to gain "God's metaperspective on their relationship" such that they were able to observe their marital system with neutrality. Fourth, couples who engaged in prayer indicated that they experienced "coaching" in incremental steps toward positive problem resolution, rather than direct answers.

Although the researchers noted a variety of possible explanations of their findings, including the notion of being "fated to see only what we already believe" (Butler, Gardner, & Bird, 1998, p. 470), they offered a "cautious recommendation" to clinicians to consider the use of prayer with conflicted religious couples. In addition, they urged counselors to employ prayer as an intervention in the context of sound clinical judgment.

Transcendence, Relinquishment, and Use of Self

Related to the use of prayer in couple counseling, Anderson (1994) suggested counselors open to a spiritual dimension could alter their approaches with conflicted clients by assuming that "change inducing influence from beyond the partners" (p. 38) may break in to their experience from the transcendent realm.

Anderson (1994) described a couple, Jim and Fran, who presented for counseling after years of struggling with emotional distance. Their attempts to solve the problem centered on each partner's attempts to change the other. After several sessions, the counselor had not seen significant change in the couple and was concerned about their separateness and apparent despair. However, in a subsequent session, Fran reported a spiritual experience during a half-waking period in which she felt her anger and resentment toward Jim melting away and increased warmth toward him encompassing her. Although Jim had not had this experience, he could testify that Fran's behavior toward him had changed and was characterized by warmth and openness. Fran reported she felt compelled to relinquish her need to control Jim and to have him respond in the ways she desired. This spiritual experience was a turning point in the couple's therapy.

Anderson (1994) noted that this spiritual awakening (although more dramatic than most) was similar to many experiences he had had over 25 years of providing couple therapy. Instead of relying solely on their own training, skills, and insight, he suggested counselors allow or even encourage the mysterious and spiritual to be active elements of the therapeutic enterprise.

Another means of employing explicitly spiritual interventions in couple and family counseling has to do with the counselor's use of self and his or her own spiritual practices. Anderson and Worthen (1997) advised counselors with a spiritual bent to consider "listening meditatively or contemplatively" (p. 9) to the couple in the light of the transcendent dimension. Such an approach could result in the counselor's emotional response of compassion and unconditional acceptance (Anderson & Worthen, 1997). In addition, counselors may choose to disclose their own experiences in which they felt changed by "the More" (Anderson & Worthen, 1997, p. 10). Further, counselors may share their spiritual selves nonverbally by visualizing the couple bathed in white or golden light or praying silently for clients. Rosenthal (1992) applied the Buddhist practice of attending to one's thoughts, feelings, sensations, and images during the session such as a means of letting go of one's agenda and leaving room for something new to emerge. In these approaches, the focus is more on the spirituality of the counselor and less on designing interventions that make use of clients' religious or spiritual orientations.

Community-Based Spiritual Linkages

Another strategy proposed by Nakhaima and Dicks (1995) and Weaver, Koenig, and Larson (1997) is that of employing religious consultants in the therapeutic process with religious families. These authors argue that because religious institutions may provide a sense of spiritual orientation, authority, values, community, and practical support, that their representatives may be helpful members of a therapeutic team. Using a religious consultant can be a positive experience for many families because of research suggesting that many people tend to feel comfortable with clergy and use them more than any other resource for counseling and problem-solving (Dayringer, 1989; Veroff, Kulka, & Douvan, 1981; Weaver, 1995).

CASE | **LATISHA**

LaTisha is a 37-year-old African American woman with two children, Roscoe, 12, and Riley, 10. She had been estranged from her family of origin and her extended family because she had married and later divorced a White man. She had also stopped attending church because she felt she was not welcome.

When LaTisha's mother became ill and unable to care for herself, LaTisha felt simultaneously obligated to assist her siblings in helping their mother and guilty for not offering any assistance. She sought counseling with Lavonne, the social worker who had arranged for a short-term home health care worker. Lavonne validated LaTisha's feelings and urged her to reconnect with her family who lived only blocks away. Soon LaTisha was taking her turn helping care for her mother and began initiating conversations with her siblings about being cut off from them and her spiritual roots. Lavonne suggested she invite Pastor Brown to a session so that LaTisha could disclose her fears about involvement in their church. Pastor Brown listened attentively to LaTisha's concerns, invited her to participate fully in their congregation, and gave her his blessing. The power of the religious link enabled LaTisha to move beyond guilt and shame to forge new bonds in her family and community. Moreover, Pastor Brown was able to mobilize additional assistance for LaTisha's mother from within the church community, thus reducing LaTisha and her siblings' burdens of caring for their mother.

When considering using a religious link from the community in family counseling, it is important to ascertain whether or not the selected persons will be an asset or liability to the therapeutic endeavor. Although some clergy and spiritual leaders may, like Pastor Brown in the previous case, be an agent for change, they also reinforce unhealthy practices that are at cross-purposes with the clients' goals. Appropriate networking and interviewing on the counselor's part can reduce or eliminate potential mismatches in a linking process.

CASE EXAMPLES

Calvin and Anita

Calvin and Anita are a Caucasian couple in their mid-twenties. They sought counseling with Kyle because they were contemplating marriage. The difficulty they presented was their differing religions. Calvin is a Roman Catholic and Anita is Jewish. Both partners have been actively involved in their church and synagogue respectively. Their families of origin and extended families are also very religious. Although both sets of parents like their children's partners, neither approves of intermarriage. Calvin and Anita reported to Kyle that they "are very much in love and feel sure they can work things out." However, they are also both close to their families and do not want to hurt or disappoint them.

Discussion Questions
1. If you were their counselor, how would you frame Calvin and Anita's problem?
2. What theoretical perspective would you take in working with them?
3. What questions would you ask each partner?
4. What interventions did you think would be effective? Why?
5. What is your own opinion of intermarriage? What do you think the possibilities and pitfalls might be for Calvin and Anita were they to marry?

Lance and Ashley

Lance and Ashley are a Caucasian couple in their late thirties. They have three children: Dustin, 12, Kelsey, 10, and Lynnea, 6. In the past year, Lance and Ashley joined a nondenominational church that could be described as "evangelical and fundamental." Both Lance and Ashley claimed to have been "born again" and they have spent the last several months re-ordering their lives to put God first in their family. Lance wants the entire family to attend every function at the church, and Ashley believes sports, music, and school activities are also important. Lance and Ashley sought counseling with Eduardo for help dealing with increasing conflict between them. Ashley reported that she was angry with Lance because he had become so domineering and constantly claimed that "God was on his side" whenever an argument occurred.

Discussion Questions
1. How would you conceptualize Lance and Ashley's problem?
2. What couple and family theory seems to fit with your understanding of their dilemma?
3. How would you plan to work with Lance and Ashley and their family?
4. What specific strategies would you use?
5. How do you think you would respond to Lance and Ashley, given their religious perspective?
6. What would be your fears about working with this couple? What would be your strengths?

Bennett

Bennett is a 49-year-old single African American father who has primary custody of his 8-year-old son, Cody. Bennett has been a practicing Buddhist for 10 years, and his adoption of this religion was a major factor in his decision to divorce his wife, Jamie. Bennett sought counseling with Ivan because despite his asking her not to, Jamie was taking Cody to a Southern Baptist church on the weekends when he visits her. Bennett felt that participating in two very different religions would be confusing to Cody, and he told Ivan that he "wanted to bring up his son in peaceful meditative ways." When he asked Jamie to refrain from taking Cody to church and to revivals, Jamie threatened to take him to court to petition a change in custody arrangements.

Discussion Questions
1. How do you see Bennett's problem?
2. What is your opinion about Jamie's right to expose her son to a religion different from his father's?
3. What approach would you take in working with Bennett?
4. If Jamie were available to participate in counseling, would you include her? What about including Cody?
5. What questions would you want to ask the participants?
6. What interventions would you consider?
7. How do you feel personally about the issues in this case?

SUGGESTED ACTIVITIES

Invite a Panel

Work with your peers and instructor in developing a list of intermarried couples in which each spouse or partner has a different religion or spiritual practice. Be intentional about including people of color, and people who represent a wide continuum of religious and spiritual expressions. Invite three or four couples to speak to your group about the religious and spiritual issues in their relationship, how they manage their differences, what they think counselors should know about working with intermarried couples.

Share Your Rituals

In small groups, talk with each other about the rituals in your lives. Indicate which ones are religious and spiritual. Discuss how these practices have changed over time, what is meaningful to you about them, and how you think you could use rituals in counseling couples and families.

Interview a Couple

Select a couple that you know to be particularly religious or spiritual. Talk with them about how their religion or spirituality affects their relationship.

You might use some of the questions posed in various sections of this chapter to assist you in your interview.

SUPPLEMENTAL READING

Family Therapy Theory and Practice

Combs, G., & Freedman, J. (1990). *Symbol, story, and ceremony: Using metaphor in individual and family therapy*. New York: Norton. This book provides a wealth of detailed information about how to employ narrative models in psychotherapy. Its focus is on using metaphors. The authors provide case studies and other examples of integrating this approach into counseling.

Gurman, A. S., & Kniskern, D. P. (Eds.). (1991). *Handbook of family therapy* (Vol. 2). New York: Bruner/Mazel. This comprehensive handbook provides a helpful history of the family therapy movement as well as detailed chapters regarding family therapy theory.

Horne, A. M. (Ed.). (2000). *Family counseling and therapy*. Itasca, IL: F.E. Peacock. This edited book includes chapters on classic family therapy models, including social constructionism. It also includes other approaches such as behavioral, Adlerian, person-centered, object relations and reality therapy as applied to couple and family counseling.

Rituals

Hudson, P. O., & O'Hanlon, W. H. (1991). Unfinished business: Using rituals and symbols to resolve tragedies. In P. O. Hudson & W. H. O'Hanlon, *Rewriting love stories* (pp. 83–101). New York: Norton. In this book, the authors work from a brief marital therapy model. They focus on using rituals as interventions in troubled marriages. Specific examples of prescribed rituals are offered.

Imber-Black, E., & Roberts, J. (1992). *Rituals for our times*. New York: HarperCollins. This book is a groundbreaking contribution to the importance of rituals in family life. It is readable, personal, and offers counselors important strategies for helping clients enrich their ritually impoverished lives.

Spirituality

Becvar, D. S. (Ed.). (1997). *The family, spirituality, and social work*. New York: Haworth Press. This book is a compilation of articles published simultaneously in the *Journal of Family Social Work*, 2(4) 1997. It contains a variety of chapters relevant to the interface between spirituality and mental health practice.

Walsh, F. M. (Ed.). (1999). *Spiritual resources in family therapy*. New York: Guilford Press. This book contains a variety of chapters that address spiritual and religious issues in family therapy. Divergent perspectives are presented. Some chapters are scholarly and others are personal.

RELIGIOUS AND SPIRITUAL APPLICATIONS TO SPECIAL GROUPS

CHAPTER 9

INTRODUCTION

This chapter introduces the religious and spiritual issues that are significant for four special groups: women; lesbian, gay, and bisexual persons; children and adolescents; and the terminally ill and their families. Although entire books could be written on these topics, I underscore the central religious and spiritual themes that counselors should be aware of when working with these populations. In addition, I offer specific strategies counselors might employ with these particular persons.

WOMEN AND SPIRITUALITY

It is nearly impossible to make general statements about women's experience of religion and spirituality—the major feature of women's spirituality is its diversity. Many women feel totally comfortable and secure as members of established religions and spiritual paths and are not especially interested in the issues of gender and feminism that have been raised from within and outside of these religious and spiritual institutions and organizations. Moreover, some women vehemently oppose the feminist movement and its impact on traditional religious and spiritual practices. Counselors who work with these women must consider their religious and spiritual beliefs and experiences and employ strategies that honor their worldviews. Many of these strategies have been presented in the preceding chapters.

In this section, I focus on unique aspects of women's spiritual development, feminist spirituality, including the goddess movement, and strategies for counseling women clients who find themselves outside the boundaries of traditional religions and yet seek an authentic spirituality for their lives.

Women's Spiritual Development

There are few existing models of women's spiritual development. The three described here, those of St. John (2000), Christ, (1995), and Harris (1989) are intimately connected to women's identity development. St. John's (2000) model fits squarely within a Judeo-Christian framework and draws narrative and metaphorical support from stories recorded in the Hebrew scriptures. Christ's (1995) and Harris' (1989) models are more applicable to a broad range of spiritual perspectives, though at points they are very similar to the model offered by St. John (2000).

St. John's Model of Female Identity and Spiritual Development   St. John (2000), influenced by Cross (1991), Downing and Roush (1985), and Russell (1982), presents a four-stage model of women's identity development. She depicts female development as a journey from "Doormat Me" to "Real Me" that involves not only psychological processes, but the spiritual ones as well. She argues that how women see themselves shapes how they view God. St. John claims that the higher stages are not superior to the lower ones—merely different. She also suggests that women might not travel through these stages in linear fashion but, rather, might vacillate between stages depending on their personal histories, their current context, or their perceived inner strength at the time.

Stage I: Doormat Me or Grand Me.   In this stage, women either adopt a subservient role to avoid being controlled by others, or they grasp at power and seek to dominate others. In the *Doormat* pattern, women accept traditional gender stereotypes and placate and serve others to win approval of those whose love they seek. They may feel unworthy of praise, scorn their femaleness, and "consistently project that 'badness' onto their bodies" (St. John, 2000, p. 10). They might excel at nurturing others, but fail to care for themselves.

The Hebrew story of Jephthah's daughter (Judges 11:1ff) exemplifies this aspect of stage one. In the story, Jephthah, an Israelite general, promised God he would sacrifice another's life (his daughter's) if he were victorious in battle. Jephthah's daughter passively accepted her plight and her father's injustice in blaming her for his trouble.

Women in the *Doormat* aspect of stage one might see their human fathers as omnipotent and view God in the same way. They might focus on the angry, punitive, judgmental qualities of God and constantly feel unacceptable in God's eyes.

Women in the *Grand Me* take control when they can. They use whatever means they can to attain power, either directly or through their alliances with others. They might not feel particularly connected to other women, unless such women can assist in the acquisition of power. They tend to emphasize appearances and social acceptability that serve as inadequate substitutes for love.

The Hebrew story of Jezebel (I Kings 21:1) reveals a woman characterized by the notion of herself as the *Grand Me*. Jezebel, wife of King Ahab, saw her husband depressed over not being able to buy a vineyard belonging to Naboth. She arranged to have Naboth unjustly accused and executed so Ahab could have the vineyard. She disregarded the rights of others and used her power to tyrannize others.

Spiritually, women in the *Grand Me* stage might also subscribe to the vengeful God who metes out punishment for sins. However, the unique twist is that they might "see God as a personal ally, a thundering judge who is quite happy to punish others for us" (St. John, 2000, p. 19).

Stage II: Why Me?   The *Why Me?* Stage is characterized by a crisis. A series of episodes or a single event could awaken women to inner emptiness and social oppression. According to St. John (2000), women respond to this crisis point in a variety of ways from facelifts, to affairs, to schooling, to alcohol, to counseling.

In the Hebrew scriptures, Queen Vashti (Esther 1:9) is a model of a woman in stage two. Although she was a pampered wife of King Ahasuerus, she decided not to support his flagrant abuses of power. After a week of gluttonous feasting in a celebration designed to glorify himself, King Ahasuerus decided to have his wife, Queen Vashti dance before the men at the party. When Vashti refused, King Ahasuerus divorced her and banished her from the kingdom. Then he married Esther, an attractive virgin.

At this stage, women's spiritual development might involve the recognition that old beliefs are not adequate, but new alternatives are not forthcoming. As a result of their crisis and resultant awakening, some then abandon God. Others begin serious questioning about God's nature. Many wonder if God is male, as they had always assumed (if not openly, at least unconsciously).

Stage III: Who Am I?   In stage three of identity and spiritual development, women begin an intense process of self-examination and self-discovery. Part of this stage involves acknowledging genuine feelings, including anger, and moving away from passive acceptance of one's circumstances to confrontation of structures and persons who stand in the way of authentic selfhood. Moreover, in this stage, women take responsibility for participating in their oppression and that of other women. They move into new friendships and seek role models in women who have successfully negotiated this tumultuous period. They are open to being part of a sisterhood among women and to forging new notions about who they are.

In the Hebrew scriptures, Rachel and Leah (Genesis 29ff) are sisters who are given to Jacob as wives in exchange for his working for their father, Laban. First, Laban tricked Jacob into marrying Leah instead of Rachel, the

TABLE 9.1 | SUMMARY OF ST. JOHN'S MODEL OF WOMEN'S SPIRITUAL DEVELOPMENT*

	Stage I (Doormat Me)	Stage I (Grand Me)	Stage II (Why Me?)
View of Self	Performer (Acquiescence) Apologizer Unworthy Pleaser Fearful	Performer (Control) Competitive Impressive Superior	Feel Uncomfortable Being Alone with Self Despondent or Depressed Sense of Despair Feel Victimized
Views of Others—Relationships	Power belongs to others Criticisms made by others are "true" Nurture others to be needed/accepted	Control/dominate others Not concerned about welfare of others Oppress others for personal gain	Feel trapped Desire to break free Feel detached from others Feel bitter toward others
Views of Women	Lack sense of kinship with women	Lack sense of kinship with women	Lack sense of kinship with women Continues to stereotype
Views of God	God the Father, you the child God is on my side, not yours God judgmental God rewards and punishes	God the Father, you the child God is on my side, not yours God judgmental God rewards and punishes	Blame God Angry with God Feelings of betrayal Fear God

*Compiled by Sandi Wilson, Ph.D., in St. John, 2000

TABLE 9.1 | *Continued*

	Stage III (Who Am I?)	Stage IV (Real Me)
View of Self	Aware of Feelings— Rage, Anger, Love	In touch with roots
	Growing sense of inner worth	Conscious of self
		Accept self as "human"
	Desire to direct own life	Harmonize inner and outer life
	Reject authority figures	Embrace whole self
	Reject traditional ways of doing things	Balance autonomy and interdependence
	Take responsibility for self	
Views of Others— Relationships	Acknowledge feelings to self	Open to diverse ideas
	Choose to cast off critical friends	Relationships based on mutual trust and caring
	Demand honesty	Risky sharing feelings
	Feel anxiety relating feelings to others	Sense interconnectedness with all things
Views of Women	Notice other strong women	Deep kinship with women
	See sisterhood—ties that link one to all women	
Views of God	Open to seeing God in new ways	Close, personal relationship with God—wisdom within
	God as healer, as the beloved	God is in All

more beautiful sister. Later, after seven years of service to his father-in-law, Jacob was permitted to marry Rachel. When Jacob decided to move to his native country, Rachel stole her father's household gods, symbols of his leadership and his claim to property. Together the sisters refused to cooperate with their father who had sold them for profit.

In stage three, spirituality is characterized by a search for a new and meaningful way of connecting with a deity. This could involve righteous anger at religious institutions and practices that discriminate against women and devalue them.

Stage IV: Real Me   Authenticity is the hallmark of stage four. According to St. John (2000), this stage is a lifelong journey. However, it is characterized by women beginning to take charge of their own nurturance through reciprocally validating relationships, setting their own goals, and being willing to listen to their inner voices. Women in stage four are striving to deal with ambiguity, to accept all parts of themselves, and to confront injustice in whatever forms it appears. In this stage, women are learning to balance their needs for both self-reliance and interdependence. St. John (2000) sums up this stage: "As we acquire greater and greater maturity, we look to share, not acquire; to liberate, not dominate; to seek justice, not safety; to create, not crush; to connect, not detach—to love instead of own" (p. 17).

The Hebrew scriptures reveal the intertwined lives of Ruth and Naomi (Ruth 1–4) who represent the best of stage four development. After being widowed, Naomi advises her daughters-in-law, Orpah and Ruth to return to their people where they will be protected. Orpah does so, but Ruth vows to partner with Naomi in a tale that defies custom and tradition and leads to survival for both. Together they conspire to establish a marriage between Ruth and Boaz, one of Naomi's relatives, thus securing their future.

Spiritually, the *Real Me* stage finds women seeking new definitions of God, rejecting old beliefs and practices, and making their own choices based on their personal experience as their authority. See Table 9.1 for a summary of St. John's model of women's spiritual development.

Christ's Model of Women's Spiritual Quest   Christ (1995) described four aspects of women's spiritual development: nothingness, awakening, insight, and new naming. She indicated that these experiences are not necessarily linear but, rather, a spiral of nonsequential events and moments that result in women's forging a spiritual identity.

Nothingness.   Nothingness refers to the negative self-image many women hold as a result of growing up female in a male-dominated, patriarchal culture. Many women are riddled with anxiety so they search for new ways of conceptualizing and relating to mystery or the Divine. This stage is characterized by letting go of old constructions of reality (Fukuyama & Sevig, 1999) and searching out a set of values that are genuine.

Awakening   Awakening involves women's awareness of the Divine in nature and in themselves. Women in this stage of spiritual development strive to affirm female ways of knowing and experiencing the world, especially through body functions such as menstruation and childbirth and spiritual actions such as care and intuition. Sometimes the *awakening* stage occurs in conjunction with a commitment to a political or social justice initiative. This stage may involve mystical experiences in which women "become aware of something that already exists" in a realm outside of themselves (Fukuyama & Sevig, 1999, p. 40).

Insight   Women gain *insight* on their spiritual journey as a result of mystical, transcendent experiences that connect them with other sources of power. They achieve new awareness of self and new self-confidence that affirm their spiritual experiences as authentic.

Naming   The final dimension of the spiritual journey involves women naming their experiences in language that reflects their own discovered spiritual reality. They might intentionally reject masculine-based language that historically has circumscribed religion and spirituality. By so doing, "not only will they create new life possibilities for women, they will also upset the world order that has been taken for granted for centuries" (Christ, 1995, p. 24). New connections with other women may emerge and spiritual practices may include the "circle" as a symbol for unity and sisterhood.

Harris (1989) also outlined a seven-step process by which women undergo a series of movements, as in a dance, as they choreograph their own brand of spirituality. Harris' steps are similar to Christ's:

1. Awakening, or becoming aware of one's personal identity.
2. Discovering or coming to terms with one's spirituality. During this stage, many women move away from their traditional religious understandings (Hickson & Phelps, 1997).
3. Creating.
4. Dwelling or turning to an inner presence.
5. Nourishing or engaging in spiritual practices such as prayer, meditation, or journaling that feed the soul.
6. Traditioning or becoming a mentor to future generations.
7. Transforming or "becoming a steward of the entire cosmos." (Hickson & Phelps, 1997, p. 53)

CASE | ROXANNE

Roxanne, a 42-year-old salesperson, sought counseling with Gretchen because she had lost a sense of herself, was "at odds with God" and was realizing she needed to "figure some things out about myself." In the process of counseling, Roxanne related her experiences of growing up "like Pollyanna" in a world where she was promised everything as long as she was "nice to everybody" and didn't "rock the boat." She reported she understood her role as that of "taking care of people and things (especially men)" and always looking attractive. Roxanne told Gretchen she had played out her end of the bargain perfectly: she had gotten educated, married a successful businessman, "kept up her looks," and stayed in the background while tending to her husband's every need. Three years ago, she discovered her husband was having an affair with a co-worker in another state. When she tried to convince him to give up the relationship and seek couple counseling, he immediately divorced her and married his lover.

Roxanne said that she was "crushed" by this turn of events, but that it served as a "wake up call" to her to examine her lifestyle, her beliefs, and to "get a life." Roxanne told Gretchen that she was so confused because she was questioning everything: her values, her religious beliefs, and even God.

Gretchen worked with Roxanne for many months, supporting her quest for a new and satisfying identity and spiritual path. She created an accepting environment where Roxanne could explore her feelings, thoughts, and beliefs. Gretchen provided Roxanne with resources about women's consciousness-raising groups and feminist spirituality groups. Over time, Roxanne became both angry and determined. She was enraged at the way she had been controlled in her marriage and was angry at God and her church for "selling me that bill of goods." She was also committed to finding a spiritual path that would free her from her old ways.

Gretchen used bibliotherapy to open up new ideas and possibilities for Roxanne. Roxanne read voraciously, attended spiritual retreats for women, and ultimately rejected her Presbyterian heritage for a new feminist spirituality that incorporated Neo-Paganism, witchcraft, and New Age elements.

In this case, Roxanne moved through St. John's (2000) stages from *Doormat* to *Real Me,* and through Christ's spiral of experiences including nothingness, awakening, insight, and naming. She also exhibited a typical path that many women take from traditional religion to feminist spirituality.

Feminist Dimensions of Christianity and Judaism

Some women go through the spiritual journey described by St. John (2000), Christ (1995), and Harris (1989) within the structures of their religions of Christianity and Judaism. They retain their connections to their churches and synagogues while seeking to reform and reinterpret their religious traditions in light of feminist understandings.

Within the Christian traditions, the 1970s and 1980s produced writers such as Collins (1974), Mollenkott (1977), Ochs (1983), Scanzoni and Hardesty (1986), and others who criticized the patriarchy of the church and the masculine language of the Bible. They suggested that God's true intention was equality and wholeness for both genders. Much careful, scholarly study of biblical texts was conducted (Trible, 1978) and misinterpretations emphasized. Newly discovered feminist interpretations of the Bible emerged. Many Christian women continued to embrace their faith, while growing in their commitment to feminism and expanding their notions about and experiences of women's spirituality (Kidd, 1996; Reilly, 1995). They organized themselves politically within the structures of their churches demanding the ordination of women and full participation of women in aspects of church life.

Many Christian denominations responded (albeit reluctantly) by becoming more inclusive of women in language, ritual, and governance. One notable exception is the Roman Catholic Church, which continues to perpetuate male hierarchy and power and forbid women ordination.

During the past 30 years, many Christian women have opted to stay within the Christian tradition, although some have relocated to more progressive, women-affirming denominations. Others have formed "women-churches" exclusively comprising feminist Christian women who wish to practice their religion without interference from men. Still others have abandoned Christianity altogether, some drifting toward feminist spirituality and others totally rejecting religion and spirituality in any form.

A similar reformation occurred in Judaism beginning in the 1970s. Theological writers such as Trible (1978), Ackelsberg (1986), and Plaskow (1990) criticized Judaism for its male-centeredness and reinterpreted the Torah in light of feminist perspectives. Over time, Reformed congregations responded and eventually women rabbis began to assume leadership positions within Jewish congregations.

Many Jewish women committed themselves to transforming Judaism into a more woman-friendly religion by gathering regularly to create Jewish-feminist ritual, liturgy, and theology (Breitman, 1995; Cantor, 1979; Gross, 1979; Plaskow, 1979). By establishing feminist Jewish communities, many Jewish women have found "a context for the exploration of identities previously suppressed as we have simultaneously been transforming many of the old structures and the language of Judaism that previously shaped our realities" (Breitman, 1995, p. 80). Breitman recalled that Jewish tradition is centered around "a sacred text made up largely of stories of our ancestors' encounters with the Holy" (p. 81) and that in the context of a feminist Jewish community, Jewish women proclaimed their lives to be the text (Alpert, 1991). In this way, they were able to reconstruct for themselves a new vision of Judaism that responded to feminist philosophy.

From the perspective of radical feminism, Judaism has been viewed as a richer source of women's spirituality than has Christianity because some of its rituals relate to menstruation and the moon and because it prescribes particular spiritual duties for women (Eller, 1993). Moreover, because Judaism is not the dominant religion in the United States, and because Jews have experienced oppression and marginalization, many Jews are able to identify with the plight of women. Many Jewish women have stayed connected to their religion despite its patriarchal worldview because "it is an identity not easily cast aside" (Eller, 1993, p. 224).

Feminist Spirituality

For many women, staying within the misogynist walls of Christianity and Judaism was not an acceptable option if they were to continue their spiritual growth and development. Some gravitated toward expressions of feminist spirituality. Feminist spirituality is a phenomenon that emerged in the 1970s alongside and interwoven with the feminist social and political movement (Eller, 1993). It is a diverse movement, paradoxically unified by the notion that feminist spirituality is "whatever works to make a woman stronger" (Eller, 1993, p. 3). Some general themes characterize feminist spirituality. First, empowerment or healing is the goal and the reward of feminist spirituality. Second, the use of ritual, including both traditional religious practices as well as various forms of magic, divination, or psychic skills. Third, feminist spirituality almost always includes a reverence for Nature and sometimes includes the personification of nature as a goddess or Mother Earth (Eller, 1993). Also, women themselves are honored in feminist spiritual systems. Fourth, feminist spirituality tends to include some aspect of gender relationships across history with a goal of dismantling patriarchy and implementing systems that are more female-affirming.

Feminist spirituality is a movement that largely is separatist. Although some women remain connected to traditional religions such as Judaism, Christianity, and Islam and subscribe to the principles of feminist spirituality, they are, by far, in the minority (Eller, 1993). Moreover, a central focus of feminist spirituality is that it is centered on women. Therefore, men are likely to be excluded unless they can defer to the authority of women (Eller, 1993).

In addition, feminist spirituality tends to be located in the English-speaking world, especially in the United States and Canada. It is expressed in a variety of settings: communes, spiritual growth groups, retreats, workshops, training programs, and summer camps (Eller, 1993). There is a loosely structured organization called the Reformed Congregation of the Goddess (RCG) that was created to provide tax-exempt status for feminist spiritual business undertakings and to encourage networking (Eller, 1993).

Demographically, the feminist spirituality movement comprises mostly white, middle-class, educated women in their thirties or forties, raised in either Christian or Jewish backgrounds. A large percentage of participants are openly lesbian (Eller, 1993). One major tension within feminist spirituality is the issue around gender versus race. Many spiritual feminists are dismayed that there are not more women of color involved in the movement. However, some women of color feel caught in the dual oppression of gender and race and do not feel that shared femaleness is enough to overcome their struggles with racism (Eller, 1993). Other women of color find that sharing cultural practices such as African American spirituality and voodoo were a means of mending racism (Eller, 1993).

In her study of feminist spirituality, Eller (1993) reported that many women came to embrace this form of spirituality first by reading a book or other literature espousing feminist ideas. Other women were drawn in through alternative religious movements or therapeutic practices. Yet others were attracted to feminist spirituality because of a life crisis. Still others drifted in slowly as they began to discover that their religious traditions and practices did not fulfill their deepest spiritual longings.

Feminist spirituality is extremely eclectic in that it is connected to the larger New Age movement and it borrows traditions and practices from a variety of religious and spiritual groups. Feminist spirituality has been influenced by Neo-Paganism and Wicca (discussed in Chapter 3), and by various forms of therapy such as 12-step programs and Jungian psychology (Eller, 1993). Moreover, feminist spiritualists have appropriated much from Eastern religions such as Buddhism and Hinduism, including meditation, alternative healing, dietary practices such as macrobiotics, and body work such as acupuncture, massage, yoga, and various forms of dance (Eller, 1993). In addition, some women engaged in feminist spirituality have borrowed from Native American religions and sacred traditions, including sweat lodges, much to the dismay of some Native Americans who consider this appropriation of their culture as continued oppression by whites (Kasee, 1995). African religions, too, are sources of feminist spiritual practices, including voodoo, and the reverence toward black goddesses (Eller, 1993).

Because of its eclectic nature, feminist spirituality includes a diverse number of rituals and practices. It includes meditation and dreamwork, healing practices such as chakras, acupuncture, herbal medicine, chanting, and massage. In addition, divination techniques such as tarot cards, use of the *I Ching,* and astrology are often included in feminist spirituality. Art, music, and theater, as well as pilgrimages to sacred sites such as the Greek temples of Delphi and Eleusis (Downing, 1981). Magic, a major practice of witchcraft or Wicca, is also central to some forms of feminist spirituality (Eller, 1993).

Rediscovering the Goddess

"I found god in myself/ and I loved her/ I loved her fiercely" (Shange, 1976, p. 63), a line from the play *for colored girls who have considered suicide/ when the rainbow is enuf,* embodies many women's search for a deity that encompasses female body and female experience. Thus, the reappropriation of the Goddess from ancient Mediterranean, pre-Christian European, Native American, and African traditions (Christ, 1997) has been one of the most salient features of feminist spirituality. The Goddess is a symbol of life and death as well as the waxing and waning energy in the universe (Christ, 1979). Many women have adopted the Goddess as a religious symbol because it is more in line with their experience of the divine. Moreover, because religion is composed of symbols that create powerful, all-encompassing, and enduring moods and motivations (Geertz, 1972) in the people of a culture, many women find the male deity, God the Father, a symbol of male authority. They also believe that male images of God "create the impression that female power can never be fully legitimate or wholly beneficent" (Christ, 1979, p. 275).

Although there are a variety of explanations about who the Goddess is and how she functions, Christ (1979) suggested three ways of understanding the Goddess:

> (1) The goddess is divine female, a personification who can be invoked in prayer and ritual; (2) the Goddess is symbol of the life, death, and rebirth energy in nature and culture, in personal and communal life; and (3) the Goddess is symbol of the affirmation of the legitimacy and beauty of female power. (p. 278)

The Goddess, according to Christ (1979), is "an affirmation of female power, the female body, the female will and women's bonds and heritage" (p. 276). Goddess worship is typically associated with feminist spirituality and with Wicca, though some women within Christianity and Judaism also incorporate the Goddess in their spiritual experience and expression.

A Model of Psycho-Spiritual Counseling for Women

Hickson and Phelps (1997) offered a counseling approach for women undergoing spiritual transitions. They based the model on Harris' (1989) stages of women's spiritual development. Hickson and Phelps (1997) suggested that counseling "can help women discover essential truths and answer some of life's most basic issues" (p. 53). In their model, they propose several themes that are significant for women delving into spirituality. First, *exploration* involves being invited by the counselor to freely express themselves without censure. Many women clients need counselors who will assist them with the shift from seeking spiritual meaning outside of themselves to listening to their inner voice (Hickson & Phelps, 1997). Second, many women need to be able to affirm the *interdependence* that characterizes their relationships with others and is the context for their spirituality (Hickson & Phelps, 1997). Third, the challenge of obtaining *balance* in one's life is critical for many women in their spiritual growth. They need counselors who will help them respond to the tension between meeting others' needs and caring for their own (Hickson & Phelps, 1997). Fourth, women seek to undergo spiritual *transformation* by letting go of their pain and being open to their counselors' assistance in exploring their vulnerability (Hickson & Phelps, 1997). Finally, a goal of spiritual growth is *wholeness*. Counselors can enable women clients to deal with victimization in whatever forms it might have taken.

CASE | RITA

Rita, a 38-year-old accountant, sought counseling with Beverly because she had been involved in a sexual relationship with her pastor, Kent. Besides causing Rita significant emotional pain and abuse, she told Beverly she had felt "spiritually wounded" because of the way Kent used his position as a minister to take advantage of her vulnerability. Beverly worked with Rita on a variety of issues, but regaining a sense of authentic spirituality was an important goal. Beverly began by creating a safe space where Rita could express a range of emotions, including intense rage. She helped Rita see how she had based her faith in the structures and representatives of her religion, rather than cultivating a personal spirituality. Beverly helped Rita find a support group for women who had been abused by clergy. In that group, Rita discovered mutuality and interdependence. In her individual counseling with Beverly, Rita continued to work on issues of self-care and nurture that had been lacking in her life. She came to see that her overemphasis on caring for others had led her into a vulnerable situation with Kent. In addition, Beverly worked with Rita for many months dealing with her spiritual wounds from her relationship with Kent. Eventually, Rita was able to begin a search for a new spirituality that was an authentic expression of her new, stronger self.

SPIRITUALITY AND GAYS, LESBIANS, AND BISEXUALS

In this section, I focus on counseling clients who already claim or are in the process of claiming a gay, lesbian, or bisexual (GLB) identity and who are interested in integrating that identity with a religious or spiritual worldview. In short, in this chapter, I emphasize counselors' work with clients who want to be "simultaneously gay and spiritual" (Barret & Barzan, 1996, p. 4). The conflict surrounding this dual identity is precisely why many GLB clients come into therapy.

Responses of Religious Institutions to Gays, Lesbians, and Bisexuals

In general, the monotheist religions of Judaism, Christianity, and Islam have been negative at best and often extremely destructive toward homosexual and bisexual people (Lynch, 1996). The denigrating attitudes of the leaders and members of these religions have resulted in many GLB persons experiencing guilt, shame, repression, and self-hatred (Ritter & O'Neill, 1995). Indeed, the prevailing posture of the major religions toward persons with a gay, lesbian, or bisexual identity has been intolerance (Boswell, 1980; Davidson, 2000). As a result, most GLB persons have felt rejected by religious institutions because they believed they were forced to choose between their religion and their personal integrity (Barret & Barzan, 1996).

Judaism   The position taken in traditional Judaism is that sexual acts between same-gendered persons is a sin (Umanksy, 1997) and that the only acceptable sexual relationships are between males and females because heterosexuality is the basis for Jewish family life (Kahn, 1989; Kimelman, 1994). These beliefs are based on a particular interpretation of passages from the Hebrew scriptures (specifically Genesis 1:27 and Leviticus 18:22). Some congregations of Reformed and Reconstructionist Judaism have moved toward more accepting perspectives.

Islam   Sexual acts between two males are considered adultery in Islamic doctrine (Davidson, 2000), and heterosexual marriage is the norm. Sexual relations outside of marriage are considered a sin and ostensibly punishable by death, though extensive if not impossible proof is required to substantiate such allegations (Dynes & Donaldson, 1992). Within the fundamentalist Shiite sect, anal intercourse between males carries with it extremely harsh punishment for the receptive partner (Blumenfeld & Raymond, 1988).

Christianity   Christian churches, too, have taken an overwhelmingly negative position toward homosexuality and bisexuality. The ethic of the Roman

Catholic Church, with its emphasis on procreation, asserts that heterosexual activity within monogamous marriage is the only acceptable form of sexual expression (Nugent & Gramick, 1989). Protestant churches' views range from a punishing and rejecting stance of the fundamentalists to full acceptance by the Quakers (Friends) and the Unitarian Universalists (Davidson, 2000). Certain congregations of other churches welcome gay, lesbian, and bisexual persons as well, despite their denomination's official position toward homosexuality and bisexuality. Other churches bifurcate their position with the notion of "love the sinner (the GLB person) but hate the sin (sexual acts between same-sex partners)" (Davidson, 2000, p. 413). The Church of Jesus Christ of Latter Day Saints (Mormons), one of the fastest growing denominations, holds an especially negative doctrine. For Mormons, sexual activity is affirmed only within heterosexual marriage and premarital and extramarital sex is considered totally unacceptable (Heaton, Goodman, & Holman, 1994). Indeed, same sex attraction is considered perverted and punishable by excommunication (Schow, 1997).

In summary, the major religions in the United States have been unsupportive of GLB persons "professionally, liturgically/pastorally, or doctrinally" (Clark, Brown, & Hochstein, 1990, p. 265). Most of these religious institutions have excluded GLB persons from ordination and from rituals that mark various life commitments and transitions. For example, in most religions, same-sex couples are not permitted to marry or participate in union ceremonies. When a partner dies, there is little support for the surviving one (Boswell, 1980). It is no wonder that many GLB persons have found themselves in a precarious double bind—either they endure the difficulty and pain of living in denial and making futile attempts to change their sexual orientation or they suffer spiritually with the perpetual message that they are sinful and unacceptable to God (Ritter & O'Neill, 1995).

Gay, Lesbian, and Bisexual Persons' Responses to Religion

The often hostile and rejecting environment most GLB persons experience in churches, synagogues, and mosques has required them to make difficult decisions regarding the expression of their spirituality. Some have chosen to stay affiliated with their religious institutions and to hide their sexual orientation so they will feel more accepted. Many of these GLB persons value their faith and the beliefs of their religion more than their sexual orientation. Some, mostly those associated with fundamentalist groups, enroll in conversion or reparative programs designed to cure them of their homosexuality or bisexuality (Clements, 1994).

Other groups of GLB persons choose to stay within their religious institutions with an effort to maintain their identities and self-respect. These persons are as "out" as possible, they affiliate with like-minded people and affirming congregations, including the GLB-oriented Metropolitan Community Church, and they get involved in "Queer Christian based communities" that function as political activist organizations (Goss, 1993). Still others actively fight rejection from their religious institutions by developing new theologies of liberation and by making a "commitment to be a force to be reckoned with in theology" (Clark, 1991, p. 28).

Some GLB persons find organized religion too oppressive and leave it for alternative spiritual paths. Many find themselves attracted to Neo-Paganism, Greek and Eastern mythology, witchcraft, feminist spirituality, New Age spirituality, aspects of Buddhism, Native American rituals, or a combination of these (Davidson, 2000). Others abandon religion and spirituality altogether.

Therapeutic Issues Facing Spiritually Oriented Gay, Lesbian, and Bisexual Clients

Several themes emerge as counselors begin working with GLB clients for whom spirituality is a significant value. First, clients must deal with multiple identities of ethnicity, gender, and sexual orientation (Davidson, 2000). The conflicting claims of these dimensions of self often create difficult internal dilemmas. Some persons feel forced to choose between the religion of their culture (e.g., the Black church) and the GLB community and might feel alienated from both (Folayan, 1992; Gock, 1992).

Especially among Native Americans, gender and sexual orientation are understood to be more fluid than in Western culture. In fact, the concept of the Two-Spirited (Tafoya, 1997), someone who possesses both a male and a female spirit is central in many Native American tribes. According to Tafoya,

> The status of the Two-Spirited person was valued in many Native communities, since an ordinary male sees the world through male eyes and an ordinary female sees the world through female eyes. However, a Two-Spirited person (who possesses both a male and female spirit, regardless of the flesh that is worn) will always see further." (1997, p. 8)

Because of their far-sightedness, many Two-Spirited people have become medicine people, leaders, and mediators in Native communities (Tafoya, 1997). Thus, Native Americans who are gay, lesbian, or bisexual could experience conflict between the messages of their own culture as it interacts with Western culture and religion.

Second, GLB clients must cope with the stress associated with attitudes of their family of origin, often mediated by religious beliefs and values (Davidson, 2000). Some of the pain and rejection by family members directed toward GLB persons can be directly attributed to the assumptions family members make based on religious doctrine and tradition. Sometimes, GLB clients will find themselves forced to choose between family relationships and personal integrity and wholeness.

Third, GLB clients must come to terms with the impact of AIDS (Davidson, 2000). They must deal with the noxious myth that AIDS is punishment for homosexual and bisexual activity and that it is the "scourge of God" (Fortunato, 1987). Clients who contract AIDS themselves or whose partners and associates are infected with HIV/AIDS must confront their religious and spiritual beliefs in search of a means of coping with their circumstances. They might find themselves especially compelled to reconcile with the religion of their families or to forge a new spiritual path that leads to hope and wholeness, rather than to despair.

Counseling Interventions to Facilitate the Spiritual Journey

Counselors have a special opportunity to work with GLB clients in their search for meaning, authenticity, and a spirituality that connects them to the immanent and transcendent experiences of the sacred. Several interventions can help.

Building a Trustworthy Alliance   One major consideration for GLB clients in selecting a counselor is whether or not that person is "safe" and trustworthy. Having experienced the pain from being discounted by significant others, GLB clients need to find counselors who are open and accepting and who do not impose homophobic interpretations on clients' experiences (Bernstein, 2000). Straight counselors working with GLB clients must be especially careful not to respond defensively to clients' rage about the injustices they have experienced, or to focus excessively on sexual orientation if it is not related to the presenting problem (Bernstein, 2000). Employing well-honed cross-cultural counseling skills can be an asset for straight counselors working with GLB clients. Being willing to raise the issue of sexual orientation and what difference it could make in the therapeutic relationship is important. Taking an ethnographic approach (Laird, 2000) of "informed not knowing" (Shapiro, 1996) means being as knowledgeable as possible, but not bringing assumptions into the process that may prevent one from comprehending a person's unique experience.

Conducting a Comprehensive Assessment   One of the first things counselors can do when they receive GLB clients is to assess the importance of religion and spirituality in their lives (see Chapter 5) and to determine how salient it is for the presenting problem (Haldeman, 1996). A spiritual genogram (Frame, 2000) could help determine religious and spiritual influences that are outside the clients' awareness or that continue to affect clients despite their assertion that religion and spirituality have no significance for them. The assessment process can assist clients in shaping their agenda and goals for counseling and can signal counselors about the degree to which religion and spirituality are involved in the clients' concerns.

Reeducation   Many GLB persons come to counseling with misinformation about sexual orientation. Others come indoctrinated with religious, spiritual, or biblical assumptions that contribute to their distress. Supporting clients' reeducation through bibliotherapy can be an important step in self-empowerment (Lynch, 1996) and a crucial tool in rebuilding spirituality for the future.

Reframing Loss   Loss is a pervasive theme for GLB clients because life has handed them so many. They might have lost their relationships with family and friends and their connection to their religious heritage. Some have lost their jobs. They may have lost their loved ones to AIDS, and many feel they have lost respectability in society because of the negative connotations of GLB relationships (Ritter & O'Neill, 1995). Counselors must help GLB clients deal with their multiple losses with the hope that loss "becomes a springboard for spiritual transformation" (Ritter & O'Neill, 1995, p. 135).

Harvey (1992) proposed that counselors help GLB clients examine the wounds that have occurred as the result of their losses, especially their loss of social acceptability. Harvey claimed that a careful scrutiny of the wounds leads clients to confront shame, fear of abandonment, rage, and self-hatred. Clients are encouraged to embrace these feelings—a process that can take them to a transcendent state and bring about their healing.

Search for New Images   Because the images in Western culture of GLB persons are so negative, counselors can support clients' quest for alternative, hope-giving images that could contribute to feelings of positive self-worth. For example, Native traditions can be explored for traces of ancestors who were spiritual leaders and shamans. Such leaders were well-respected and appear in at least 88 Native American tribes (Ritter & O'Neill, 1995). Similar persons existed in other cultures of South America, Polynesia, India, China, Japan, as well as in Greek and Roman cultures (Ritter & O'Neill, 1995).

Support the Creation of a Spiritual Path   Fox (1994) suggested a four-fold path for gays, lesbians, and bisexuals that fosters spiritual development. The first step involves what Fox (1994) calls "creation" or the genuine embracing of the GLB self. The second step is letting go, in which the pain of rejection and loss are recognized and released. The third step is creativity that results in the rebirth of the soul, and the fourth step is transformation in which GLB persons extend compassion and celebration to others. This process is an intense one that could take years to accomplish. It can be facilitated in several ways.

Counselors can assist clients in examining religious and spiritual alternatives or to create a form of spirituality that witnesses their unique experiences. Counselors can also support clients' search for an inner authority to guide them when external authorities (church, clergy, sacred texts, and doctrine) condemn and reject them. Moreover, counselors can provide resources for clients to make connections with GLB communities of support. When these approaches are considered, then counselors may employ other strategies and interventions (see Chapters 7, 8, and 9) to address other religious or spiritual issues.

Person-of-the-Therapist Issues   A persistent theme in this book is the impact that counselors' own issues might have in the therapeutic relationship. Counseling GLB clients is an area that is fraught with possibilities for negative countertransference to occur. Therefore, counselors must examine their own (perhaps unconscious) biases against sexual minorities (Barret & Barzan, 1996). Being immersed in a homophobic society makes the most accepting of counselors vulnerable to internalized homophobia, even GLB counselors! Relatedly, counselors must explore their religions of origin and their current spiritual practices for messages they have received regarding homosexuality. These messages, though intentionally silenced, could surface in unexpected and unpredictable ways. Studying scholarly interpretations of sacred texts that condemn homosexuality might be an important dimension of preparing oneself to counsel GLB clients.

In addition, counselors should examine their feelings about their own sexuality (Barret & Barzan, 1996). Counselors who are aware of "any internal confusion or even curiosity about their own sexual orientation will minimize the possibility of negative countertransference" (Barret & Barzan, 1996, p. 11). Of course, awareness alone does not prevent the projection of homoprejudice onto GLB clients. Being committed to one's own personal growth through counseling and supervision is a critical aspect of being a competent counselor.

For a variety of reasons, some counselors will not feel comfortable working with GLB clients. Some will subscribe to religious or spiritual beliefs that condemn homosexuality and bisexuality as sin or perversion of nature. Their value system will prevent them from taking a supportive therapeutic stance with GLB clients. Such counselors should refrain from working with GLB clients to prevent themselves from doing psychological or spiritual harm. Other counselors will be confused about their perspectives on homosexuality and bisexuality. They might be torn between the beliefs of their family of origin and religious heritage and their general openness and acceptance of diversity. To improve their understanding of GLB issues, these counselors should acquire as much knowledge as they can about the subject, engage in personal therapy if needed, and come to terms with their religious and spiritual beliefs before counseling GLB clients.

CASE | ROY

Roy is a 28-year-old gay journalist who sought counseling with Adrian because of depression related to his "coming out" process. Roy has been in a two-year relationship with Harvey, 10 years his senior. Harvey has been pressuring Roy to "come out" to his family and to co-workers. Although Roy was not totally committed to being "out" in all of the areas of his life, he felt his relationship with Harvey would be in jeopardy if he continued to be closeted. As Roy began to disclose his sexual orientation to his family members, several of them, including his father, shunned him and banished him from their homes. This painful encounter led Roy to seek advice from his pastor. Again, Roy was devastated by the response he received. His pastor, Sean, told Roy that "his lifestyle was sinful" and that he should repent and pray for a healing of his desires. Moreover, Sean suggested that Roy might not feel welcome in a church that could not support his "perverted sexuality." Roy felt utterly alone and abandoned by his family and his church. Harvey suggested he see Adrian, a counselor who had experience working with gay clients.

Adrian immediately put Roy at ease because of his warmth and openness. He empathized with Roy's pain and his losses. He referred Roy to some books to help him gain knowledge about Christian groups that welcomed GLB persons. He also invited Roy to attend a support group of Christian gay men who were struggling with spiritual issues related to being gay. Adrian worked with Roy for more than a year helping him to fully embrace his sexuality and to be able to affirm his innate goodness. Adrian also helped Roy grieve his losses and supported him in his writing of a ritual in which he let go of his anger and broke ties with his former church. Roy continued to participate in the Christian support group for gay men and eventually joined the Metropolitan Community Church in his city.

In this case, Adrian was able to accept Roy unconditionally—something neither Roy's family nor his church could do. Adrian stood by Roy during his painful times, helped him examine his wounds, let go of his rage, and begin to forge a new personal and spiritual identity.

CHILDREN, ADOLESCENTS, AND SPIRITUALITY

One of the most neglected subjects in the literature concerning spirituality and counseling involves issues related to children and adolescents. Perhaps the failure to consider children's and even adolescents' spiritual needs is because of the prevalent myth that children (and some adolescents) are not capable of grasping spiritual and religious concepts (Koepfer, 2000). Although they may not be able to articulate religious ideas or spiritual experiences in philosophical terms or theological categories, children and adolescents are not without awareness and experiences of spirituality (Cloyd, 1997). In fact, many Buddhists hold to the notion that children have greater spiritual understanding than some adults (Koepfer, 1999).

Characteristics of Children's Spirituality

When children are engaged in conversation regarding spiritual ideas, they reveal insatiable curiosity. Children often ask, "Who made God?" "Where does God live?" "What does God look like?" (Cloyd, 1997, p. 17). Furthermore, some children demonstrate insight and sometimes a profound sense of wonder and a deep appreciation of a Creator. When Cloyd (1997) interviewed young children about their understanding of God, a 5-year-old girl responded, "God is good to us and is always by our side" (p. 17). Another 5-year-old offered, "God is very special. He is all around you even though you don't know it. God protects you and heals you too when you are sick" (Cloyd, 1997, p. 17). Brussat and Brussat (1993) related an incident in which a 3-year-old had just experienced the birth of a sibling. The older child pleaded to have a moment alone with her new brother. Her mother hesitated, but eventually agreed. She stood outside the door of the nursery and peeked in. Her daughter leaned over the crib and said to her new brother, "Tell me about God. I think I am beginning to forget" (p. 5). These anecdotes indicate that even young children have some notion of a Higher Power.

Coles (1990) interviewed hundreds of children from diverse ethnic, cultural, and socioeconomic backgrounds regarding their spiritual experiences, their concepts of God, and how they would draw their notions of God. He concluded that children everywhere have a deep awareness of God and the spiritual life. He said his study helped him "to see children as seekers, as young pilgrims well aware that life is a finite journey and as anxious to make sense of it as those of us who are farther along in the time allotted us" (Coles, 1990, p. xvi).

Nye and Hay (1996) studied the spirituality of randomly selected elementary school children in Nottingham and Birmingham, England. The results of their study revealed four core qualities of spirituality in children: *awareness, value, mystery, and meaningfulness or insight.*

Awareness   According to Nye and Hay (1996), childhood spirituality involves attentiveness toward one's attention that might be experienced during periods of quiet or concentration. Awareness also involves *tuning* (Schutz, 1964) that emerges during aesthetic moments such as listening to music or being at home in nature. *Flow* (Csikszentmihalyi & Csikszentmihalyi, 1988), another aspect of awareness, refers to the "experience of concentrated attention, giving way to a liberating sense of one's own activity managing itself, or being managed by some outside influence" (Nye & Hay, 1996, p. 147–148). The ability of children to lose themselves in play or to attend to a butterfly illustrates this notion. Awareness also includes *focusing* (Gendlin, 1963) or "a recovery of respect for the body as a source of spiritual knowledge" (Nye & Hay, 1996, p. 148). The uninhibited sensuality of children enables them to experience pleasure and pain in ways that connect them the sacred. Children's awareness typically occurs in the *here and now* such that it becomes the means through which "entry is gained to the spiritual dimension of adult experiences" (Nye & Hay, 1996, p. 148).

Value   Being able to sense what matters in a given set of experiences is also a dimension of childhood spirituality. Two extreme emotions, delight and despair, seemed to emerge in investigations by Nye and Hay (1996). These feelings are linked to children's perceptions of good and evil in their every day lives.

Mystery   The element of *mystery* is also characteristic of childhood spirituality. It involves both wonder and awe that are connected to the incomprehensible nature of the world and its extreme beauty. Included in the notion of *mystery* is also the role of imagination. Indeed, for children, imagination is a significant key to opening their spiritual perceptions.

> Imagination is central to religious activity through the metaphors, symbols, stories and liturgies which respond to the otherwise unrepresentable experience of the sacred. In children's imagination, seen in their play, stories, art work and perhaps also their fears and hopes, we may at times be encountering a window on this aspect of their spirituality. (Nye & Hay, 1996, p. 149)

Meaningfulness The fourth quality of children's spirituality is sensing *meaningfulness or insight* in which children make connections between their experiences and their reflections on these experiences. *Meaningfulness* emerges as children begin to ask core questions such as, "Where have I come from?," "Where am I going?," and "What am I meant to do?" (Hay, 1995, p. 1271).

These spiritual qualities "embrace children's whole experience including perception and imagination, emotion and intellect, physicality and fantasy, security and discovery" (Crompton, 1998). They enable counselors to identify ways in which childhood spirituality may be present if counselors are attentive and perceptive enough to recognize it.

Concepts of God

Given the ground-breaking work of Fowler (1981) and others who discovered the processes of faith development (see Chapter 2), it is not surprising that children's concepts of God emerge as their cognitive capacity increases. Preschool children can have a natural awareness of God or Spirit (Cavelletti, 1983) and tend to perceive God in human terms as a special man (Tamminen, Vianello, Jaspard, & Ratcliff, 1988). Some children, especially those raised in religious homes, view God as the child Jesus who is to be admired, served, and emulated, just as they would like to be (Mailhiot, 1962). These concepts reflect clearly the egocentric thinking that characterizes this stage of child development.

School-aged children retain anthropomorphic concepts of God. They view God as a human with qualities that are different from other humans. Some see God as a giant, a magician, or possibly an invisible man (Cloyd, 1997; Tamminen & Ratcliff, 1992). In another study, Johnson (1955) found that most young school-aged children thought God was "in the sky" or "in heaven" and saw God's role as creator, protector, and judge, attributes also associated with their parents.

Heller (1986) discovered sex differences in children's God concepts. All children reported God to be a great father, but rationality and participation in events marked boys' notions about God. Boys had no doubt God was male, someone who could function as a role model. Indeed, the idea of a feminine God created anxiety for boys (Heller, 1986). Girls also saw God as male; however, they hinted at more androgynous characteristics of God. Their God was more passive than the boys' God and was often described as an observer rather than a participant (Heller, 1986).

By adolescence, ideas about God are more abstract. Adolescents tend to see God as a Spirit (Cloyd, 1997). In late adolescence, youth begin to question the doctrines of their churches and synagogues and some become agnostic or atheist (Hyde, 1990). Others become increasingly religious or spiritual as a function of their developing sense of personal identity (Strommen, 1974).

Religious and Spiritual Issues for Children and Adolescents

Several issues emerge as counselors begin to work with children and adolescents. Some of these concerns are raised in the context of life cycle transitions (Crompton, 1998; Pellebon & Anderson, 1999). The birth of children carries with it religious and spiritual beliefs, practices, and expectations depending on the background of the particular family. Sometimes specific roles are assigned to the child based on gender or birth order. In some spiritual circles (Hinduism, New Age), there are issues of how the birth is related to a past life (Pellebon & Anderson, 1999). Family conflict around these issues can bring couples into counseling.

Another issue regarding children, religion, and spirituality relates to family expectations about social interactions. Some families hold worldviews that children are not to interact with "nonbelievers," whereas other families are more open about their children's exposure to diverse populations. For example, Jehovah's Witness children are not permitted to participate in Christmas parties or celebrations because it is inconsistent with their belief system (Rosten, 1975). Thus, peers could exclude such a child, resulting in anger or sadness. These issues may be exacerbated if particular religious attire is required. A tefillin (head cover for Jewish boys) (Eckstein, 1984) is an illustration of a religious custom that could contribute to children's social isolation if they are the exceptions in their peer group.

Family socialization and discipline are rooted in religious and spiritual understandings concerning the spiritual state of their children (Pellebon & Anderson, 1999). For example, parents who believe their children are born innately good may be permissive. Those who believe their children are spiritually neutral could think that producing a "good" child depends on spiritually guided parenting (Pellebon & Anderson, 1999). Other parents believe that their children are born into a spiritually negative state and that they as parents must discipline them in ways to extricate evil (Pellebon & Anderson, 1999). In the latter case, counselors may observe the potential for child abuse and/or neglect.

Relatedly, many parents believe they have the divine right to exercise parental authority over their children. As a result, counselors working with children must understand this parenting perspective and take care not to undermine parental authority when a child is the identified client (Pellebon & Anderson, 1999). Of course, religious or spiritually based parenting practices are not exempt from legal standards, and counselors are obligated to report evidence of child abuse or neglect.

A unique issue that can arise is precocious spirituality exhibited by gifted children. Lovecky (1997) described such children as individuals who

> understand the universality of spiritual concepts such as forgiveness of others, develop spiritual self-awareness through asking questions and finding spiritual problems to solve, develop a systematic philosophy of life and death, or are seekers of the transcendent in the universe, other people and themselves. (p. 178)

Other gifted children might report mystical or transcendental experiences and could begin to ask spiritual and religious questions earlier than their peers do

(Lovecky, 1997). Because of these experiences, some gifted children might become anxious and stressed because they are not taken seriously by adults or peers. Therefore, counselors working with such children must provide support and be open to receiving such disclosures from children.

Adolescence presents some challenges for families in which there is strong religious or spiritual affiliation. During this period, adolescents typically explore their world and question their beliefs. They are exposed to ideas and values that may be diametrically opposed to their parents' worldview. Conflicts can arise when youth stray from the family value system, especially in peer contacts and sexual experimentation. Moreover, teens may experience heightened guilt and anxiety if they violate parental codes of behavior that are religiously or spiritually based (Pellebon & Anderson, 1999). For example, a Hindu teen might be frustrated that her family has rigid rules about dating (Frost, 1972) and act out or become depressed. Counselors working within such cultural and religious contexts must be sensitive to the worldviews expressed without undermining important principles. Such an approach helps parents understand that if their adolescent chooses to reject a religious or spiritual practice, then the decision is based on client judgment and not counselor influence (Pellebon & Anderson, 1999).

Counseling Strategies

In working with children's and adolescents' religious and spiritual issues, counselors who exhibit nonjudgmental attitudes, who are receptive to a variety of beliefs and practices, and who approach children and youth with warm, supportive inquisitiveness are likely to be effective. The social constructionist principle involving taking the position of "not knowing" (Andersen, 1991; Anderson & Goolishian, 1988, 1991) can be useful for counselors who are surprised by children's disclosures. Giving up the need to be an expert enables counselors to encourage spiritual and religious expression and to assist their young clients to explore these concerns.

Classic play therapy techniques including the use of dolls, puppets, sand play, and games (Orton, 1997) to facilitate children's expression of feelings and themes that characterize their distress. Astute counselors may be able to detect clues about childhood spirituality through their clients' play.

CASE | **BLAKE**

Blake, a 5-year-old, selected a figure of the Devil for his sand tray. When he was finished with his tray his counselor, Clay, asked Blake about his creation. Blake pointed to the devil figure and said, "That's me." Clay was alarmed by this response and worried that Blake might be experiencing excessive fear related to his exposure to religion. Clay asked Blake to tell him more about the devil. Blake said, "Oh, that's what my Mommy calls me—'her little devil.'" In a meeting with Blake's mother following the session, Clay asked about "her little devil." Blake's mother realized that her affectionate term for her son was confusing and frightening to him. Blake had often heard the pastor at his church talk about "the Devil and hell" and, in his child-like way Blake had thought of himself as evil. A family conversation, facilitated by Clay, enabled Blake's mother to assure her son "that he was not a bad boy."

Creative activities such as art, music, and dance may also be useful ways of tapping into children's religious and spiritual issues. Because experiences of the transcendent or the sacred often defy verbalization, and because children are often incapable of articulating faith verbally, drawing is an exceptionally useful vehicle for spiritual expression.

Koepfer (1999) related the case of Julio, an 11-year-old boy who was hospitalized for an acute asthmatic attack. During his work with Julio, Koepfer asked the boy to create an image of his illness and subsequently asked him how he would change the image to make it healthy. In his first image, Julio drew turtles in his lungs "painfully burning and cutting him" (Koepfer, 1999, p. 193) representing how the asthma attacks felt. When asked to change that image to a healthy one, Julio drew a picture of doves whose job it was "to fly around my lungs and turn the turtles into new doves" (Koepfer, 1999, p. 193). Without prompting, Julio stated, "The dove is like Jesus flying around healing people" (Koepfer, 1999, p. 193). Later, when asked to explain what he meant, Julio explained that Jesus had the power to heal people and that is what the doves were doing. In this case, drawing helped Julio access his religious beliefs and use them positively toward his healing.

Stories, myths, and legends are the heart and soul of religion and spirituality. Children learn the stories of their faith and are unconsciously influenced by the images that embody religious and spiritual values and beliefs (Crompton, 1998). In fact, Coles (1992) found that religious stories had considerable impact on children from various traditions. Coles wrote:

> The stories are not mere symbolism, giving expression to what people go through emotionally. Rather, I hear children embracing religious stories because they are quite literally inspiring—exciting their minds to further thought and fantasy and helping them become more grown, more contemplative and sure of themselves. (1992, p. 121)

Counselors may find they can use stories from various religious and spiritual traditions to help children cope with their problems. In addition, counselors can use bibliotherapy using books and stories that address religious or spiritual themes. Counselors should preview the materials before using them to ensure that the values therein do not conflict with those of the child's family, religion, or culture.

Another powerful strategy for working with children involves having children create their own stories. This process often reveals children's anxieties and fears that could interrupt their emotional or spiritual growth (Crompton, 1998).

Techniques associated with child therapy can also be adapted for work with adolescents. In addition, using guided imagery activities can be especially helpful for older children and adolescents. This intervention involves counselors developing their own scripts or adapting others in response to religious or spiritual concerns raised by their clients. For example, Stahl (1977) developed several guided imagery exercises based on biblical themes that could be useful.

CASE | MONICA

Monica, a 15-year-old Christian client, was referred to counseling by her homeroom teacher because of poor school performance and increasing irritability. In the intake session, her counselor, Audrey, learned that Monica's parents had recently separated and were planning to divorce. Monica, an only child, was devoted to both of her parents and felt caught in the crossfire between them. She told Audrey she felt like she was being whirled around in a tornado and couldn't get free. Knowing that Monica was active in her church and a zealous Christian, Audrey decided to engage Monica in a guided imagery exercise. She had Monica read the biblical text from Matthew 8:23–27 that tells of Jesus calming the storm at sea. Then she proceeded to have Monica relax, take some deep breaths, and imagine herself in a similar storm:

> Visualize yourself in a boat . . . Notice the size and type of boat . . . discover who is with you . . . Become aware of how you feel being there . . . Now you notice the water is very troubled, a storm is surrounding you . . . Stay in touch with your feelings in this storm . . . When you are ready, become aware of the calming presence in your midst . . . Before you disembark, look around on the boat for a symbol or image that represents this deep calm for you . . . (Stahl, 1977, p. 67–68)

After completing the guided imagery, Audrey asked Monica to write a short response to her experience and to share what she felt comfortable sharing. Monica said she was aware of a paralyzing fear when she was in the boat, but was comforted because her grandparents were in the boat with her. She also said she felt God's Spirit surrounding her "like a cozy blanket" and she felt much more calm and relaxed. Monica also revealed that the symbol she had chosen was an anchor because she needed to feel anchored in the storm she was experiencing in her family. Audrey suggested that when Monica felt afraid and caught in the storm that she take a few moments to relax, breathe deeply, and remember the calming experience she had had during the exercise. In the next session, Monica reported she had used her birthday money to purchase a silver anchor on a necklace that she decided to wear as a reminder that she could rely on God as her anchor in the storm.

DEATH, DYING, AND SPIRITUALITY

Even though persons may speak glibly of death "being a part of life," in modern American culture, death is treated as something taboo and alien to our experience. This "denial of death" (Becker, 1973) has contributed to the removal of death from our immediate experience and placed it at a distance in hospitals or nursing homes. Because of this shift, death is "viewed not as an inevitable part of life but as a failure of medical technology" (Baker, 1999, p. 22). Because many people have not come in direct contact with death, they may be afraid or unsure of how to respond to the sudden or impending death of a loved one, or to their own eventual death. Counselors are not immune from these feelings of fear and confusion. However, through education and work on their personal issues, counselors can be useful resources to assist others in the grief process.

A wealth of literature deals with various aspects of death and dying, but the focus of this section is on religious/spiritual beliefs, tasks, and strategies that may be useful for counselors working with dying or grieving clients.

Religious and Spiritual Beliefs About Death and the Afterlife

One of the most important pieces of information counselors can have as they prepare to counsel a terminally ill person or a grieving client is knowledge about that person's religious or spiritual beliefs concerning death and the afterlife. These beliefs are the vehicles through which people make meaning of death and are able to cope with the losses that surround it. Unsurprisingly, there is much diversity of belief regarding death and the afterlife. Some of this diversity is based on religion, culture, ethnicity, or the interaction between all those variables. Moreover, individuals, though associated with a particular religion or cultural group, might not subscribe to the traditional beliefs held by that group. Counselors will want to be informed of the classic beliefs about death and the afterlife, but should refrain from making assumptions about their clients' belief systems.

Western Concepts of Death and the Afterlife   The ancient Greeks conjectured about what happens to people after they die, and they contributed an enduring belief to western thought about death and the afterlife: the immortality of the soul (Corr, Nabe, & Corr, 1997). This notion can be traced to the writings of Plato who viewed the human being as composed of two parts, a body (earthly, mortal) and a soul (immortal) (Corr, Nabe, & Corr, 1997). At death, the body is separated from the soul, but the soul continues eternally.

Judaism, on the other hand, holds that the body is an integrated whole. It is not a soul in a body, but rather, a living body. For Jews, any life after death must be an embodied life. Thus, in some strands of Judaism there is a belief in resurrection, the act of God raising a human being (living body) from the dead. However, many Jews do not believe in an afterlife except for ongoing life in the community of descendents and the continuation of the family line (Bowker, 1991). Because of their belief in the sacredness of the body, many Jews do not believe in cremation or in embalming the body for viewing (Baker, 1999). Funerals and burial take place soon after death and relatives observed a weeklong *Shiva*, or period of mourning.

Christianity, based in Judaism, has retained its concept of resurrection, claiming that Jesus inaugurated access to eternal life through his own bodily resurrection. Many Christians, however, hold beliefs that are far closer to the idea of the immortality of the soul than that of resurrection. Other Christians, especially those of a fundamentalist bent, believe (a) that death itself is the result of humanity's sin; (b) that God is the ruler over death; (c) death has been conquered in Jesus Christ; (d) that believers are assured eternal life with God; (e) that they will be judged and rewarded based on their faithfulness; and (f) that unbelievers will go to hell (Anderson, 1995).

Islam's belief is that humans originated in Heaven where Adam and Eve were living. They were the first persons on earth and are the ancestors of all living people (Sakr, 1995). The human life cycle, according to Islam, involves eight phases. Phase 1 is life in the womb where the fetus develops. Phase 2 is life on earth. Phase 3 is life in the grave where the flesh is separated from the soul (Knappert, 1989). The only thing that remains is the seed for new life (Sakr, 1995). It stays in the grave until the Day of Judgment. The soul, on the other hand, stays in Isthmus and visits the grave for rewards or punishments. Life in the grave is either in Paradise or in Hell. Phase 4 involves a process of rebirth in which the original seeds of life are re-germinated and re-joined to the souls. They will "come out of their graves in a state of shock and will be unclothed and shoeless" (Sakr, 1995, p. 52). Phase 5 is the Assembly Day when everyone awaits judgment and reflects on his or her destiny. Phase 6 is Judgment Day in which Allah judges everyone personally. Those with whom Allah is pleased will receive Books in their right hands that include their "activities, appearance, and intention" (Sakr, 1995, p. 53). Those who did not win Allah's approval will receive Books in their left hands. Phase 7 involves life in hell "where everybody is to go and to be visited" (Sakr, 1995, p. 53). However, while some people will be exempt from eternal Hell, others, who don't deserve to enter Paradise or Hell will be sent to *Al-A'raf*. One group will go to Hell either to be purified or to stay forever. Phase 8 is life in paradise that is eternal bliss without the existence of any vices. There is also the belief that if a dying person recites the *Kahlimah* ("There is nothing worthy of worship except Allah") he or she will be spared from Hell. Muslims believe it is important for family members to be with a dying person, and there are elaborate rituals associated with death, burial, and funeral rites (Knappert, 1989; Sakr, 1995).

Eastern Concepts of Death and the Afterlife   In Hinduism, humans are considered an unborn and undying soul *(atman)* that is incarnated in bodies based on what the person has done in previous lives (Corr, Nabe, & Corr, 1997). This concept is commonly known as reincarnation. Because each rebirth brings with it suffering, the goal is to end this continual transmigration of souls. A passage from the Bhagavad Gita explains the Hindu understanding of death:

> Wise men do not grieve for the dead or for the living . . . never was there a time
> when I was not, nor thou . . . nor will there ever be a time hereafter when we

shall cease to be . . . Just as a person casts off worn-out garments and puts on others that are new, even so does the embodied soul cast off worn-out bodies and take on others that are new. (Radhakrishnan, 1948, pp. 102–108)

Living rightly ends the repeated rebirths and joins the soul with a transcendent reality (Corr, Nabe, & Corr, 1997). Like Islam, if Hindus die with the name of God (Brahman) on their lips, they are promised a favorable future. Hindus believe that after death the *atman* is either reborn immediately, is in one of the heavens awaiting rebirth, or is joined eternally with Brahman (transcendent reality) (Corr, Nabe, & Corr, 1997).

In Buddhism, a derivative of Hinduism, reincarnation is a major tenet, however, Buddha taught that there is no soul (Corr, Nabe, & Corr, 1997). Thus, upon death, some aspect of the person undergoes rebirth or achieves *nirvana,* a state of serenity and peace (Becker, 1989; Radhakrishnan & Moore, 1957) or absolute calm (Chan, 1963). One's destiny is based on karma, the result of one's actions in this life. Upon death, Buddhists believe that there is an "intermediate body" the person takes on before the next birth (Yeung, 1995). Tibetan Buddhists refer to this intermediary body as *Bardo* or the gap. Because of this transitional period between death and rebirth, Buddhists must guide the being to the right path. Such guidance takes place with chanting the name of the Buddha (Yeung, 1995).

African Concepts of Death and the Afterlife   The size of Africa with its diverse cultures means that there are a variety of beliefs and practices surrounding death depending on which tribe and location is being studied. In general, however, Africans view human beings as part of the world, rather than separate from it (Corr, Nabe, & Corr, 1997). Life is considered a process and that those who are the "living dead" (not alive as we are) are only at a different stage. The living dead are not in another world, they are in another part of this world (Corr, Nabe, & Corr, 1997). Thus, as ancestors, they are respected and venerated. Most African religions are devoid of concepts such as Heaven and Hell.

Native American Concepts of Death and the Afterlife   Similar statements can be made about Native American beliefs as have been made about African ones. Native American beliefs are characterized by diversity. In most cases, however, Native Americans hold that life and death are not linear events, but occur in a circular or interwoven way (Brown, 1987). Death, then, is viewed as a part of life. Within this general perspective, however, are a variety of beliefs. Some Native American groups accept death and experience little anxiety about it. Others exhibit high levels of fear in the face of death (Corr, Nabe, & Corr, 1997). Many Native Americans believe that death means a transition from one form of life to another and that the dead are involved in this life. Ancestors are believed to influence the living.

Spiritual Tasks for the Dying

Clients who are dying face many challenges: physical, emotional, and spiritual. When there is time, terminally ill clients may need to address the spiritual aspects of their lives so they have a sense of completion and well-being when they come to the end of their lives. Doka (1993) suggested three spiritual tasks for clients who are dying. First, terminally ill clients need to find meaning in life, whether it be in a personal god and religious faith, a connection with nature, a set of significant relationships, a secular philosophy, or something else that provides ultimate value. Second, such clients need to be able to die with integrity and in a way that is congruent with their self-identities. They need to make sense of death and to interpret it in a meaningful way. Third, dying clients need to find hope (in whatever form they construe it) that extends beyond death. Another spiritual need some terminally ill clients might have is that of reconciliation (Callanan & Kelley, 1992). Sometimes as people approach death, they become aware of unfinished business they have with another person, a supreme being, or with themselves. Some terminally ill clients prolong dying to bring about a reconciliatory meeting (Callanan & Kelley, 1992).

Counseling Strategies to Address Dying Clients' Spiritual Needs

In helping clients identify and claim what gives life meaning, Dudley, Smith, and Millison (1995) suggested asking several questions of dying clients. After having established rapport with the client and ascertained the client's willingness to explore questions of meaning, the following may be asked:

1. Do you have a philosophy about illness (or your illness)?
2. How do you understand hope? For what do you hope?
3. What is especially meaningful or frightening to you now?
4. How has being sick made any difference in how or what you believe?
5. What does death mean to you? Do you have a belief in an afterlife?
6. Has spiritual support been helpful to you in the past?
7. What is your source of strength during your current illness?

If it does not seem appropriate to ask these questions directly of the client, they could be used as springboards for a spiritual journal that clients may keep. Such journals often focus on helping terminally ill clients focus on what gives their lives meaning and purpose.

Another method for assisting dying clients to capture the meaning and purpose of their lives is to help them engage in a life review. In this process, clients look back on their lives, relationships, and experiences and get a sense of what aspects of life have been significant for them. A useful tool for beginning a life review or life narrative is *A Guide for Recalling and Telling Your Life Story* (Pelaez & Rothman, 1994). This resource includes a videotape, workbooks, and a place to store mementos.

In helping clients deal with their concepts of death, Smith (1993) recommended asking clients to write a "healthy death story." In this story, clients are to include as much detail as possible, describing where they will be, what they will look like, who will be with them, and what they will be doing, thinking, and feeling. Clients are also advised that they may draw a picture that represents their view of a healthy death. Through this strategy, clients are able to think about what death means to them, to gain awareness and possibly some control over the circumstances and surroundings of their death. Counselors can assist their clients and the clients' families in creating a "healthy death" situation that will be in keeping with the client's wishes.

To assist clients in clarifying what constitutes hope for them, Smith (1993) suggested having them build a shrine that reveals their notion of the divine. This strategy may be adapted to have clients focus on a shrine or an altar or even a collage of materials that represent hope. Clients are encouraged to gather a variety of mementos including pictures, special objects, books, artwork, music, and other items that signify hope. In subsequent sessions, clients may explain their shrines and may be encouraged to keep these objects assembled in a special place so they may serve as constant reminders of the hope that is in them.

For clients who are open to meditation and who feel ready to contemplate the experience of death, Levine (1991) offered meditation scripts that facilitate this experience. In "A Guided Meditation on Dying," Levine (1991) suggests that dying persons read the meditation silently to themselves or aloud to a friend. One passage is representative of the meditation:

> Gently, gently, let it all go. Let it all float free. Let yourself die. Leave the body behind and follow the light into luminous space. Go into it. Let yourself die into space. Each breath vanishes. Each thought dissolving into space. Don't hold now. Just let go once and for all. Let go of fear. Let go of longing. Open to the wonder . . . (p. 313)

Counselors may be instrumental in helping dying clients accomplish the task of reconciliation. Counselors may ask if there is unfinished business between the terminally ill client and another person, if the client feels at peace with God, a supreme being or Higher Power, and if the client has any internal issues that are standing in the way of a peaceful death. Counselors may assist by helping clients do what they need to do to effect reconciliation with others. That task could involve locating and actually bringing the other person into the counseling setting or the client's home. It could involve empty chair exercises or perhaps letter-writing. Clients need to specify the means by which they feel reconciliation could best take place. To bring about reconciliation with God or the sacred in a client's life, counselors can help arrange for clients to speak with a priest or other clergyperson, participate in some rite or ritual or blessing sanctioned by their religion, have a special person say a prayer, or engage in another type of spiritual practice that would accomplish the goal of reconciliation. In addressing the need for resolving personal issues that could interfere with clients' obtaining inner peace, counselors may ask, "What, if anything, stands in the way of your being able to die in peace?"

Callanan and Kelley (1992) described the struggle of a woman named Janine who was dying of cancer. She had separated from her husband several years previously, but he refused to grant her a divorce. For many years, she had lived with Jeff, but secretly felt guilty for living with him without being married. The hospice worker arranged for a chaplain to come to Janine's bedside, to bless her relationship with Jeff, and to celebrate her life with a few friends and family members. This blessing enabled Janine to die that night in peace, having resolved the final issue that kept her from being able to let go of this life.

Spiritual Issues for Grieving Families

When a family member dies, the entire family system is disoriented and experiences various levels of upheaval. When death is sudden and unexpected, the tumult and chaos engendered might last longer and healing might be slower in coming. When a family member has a terminal illness, others have time to prepare for death, to say goodbye, and to let go. Through the process of watching their loved one die, they might experience anticipatory grief (Rando, 1986). Nevertheless, the full impact of the loss is often not felt until after the actual death.

Rosen (1990) indicated that grieving families must negotiate a set of tasks or psychological experiences and behavioral changes that enable them to survive their loss. First, families must corporately acknowledge the reality of death. Although forms of denial are expected in the early stages of grief and can actually be effective coping mechanisms, prolonged denial is detrimental to healing. Second, family members must share the pain of grief by accepting in each other a wide range of emotions without judgment or criticism. Failure to express grief-related emotions could result in other symptoms. Third, the family system must undergo reorganization through the realignment of relationships and the reallocation of roles (Rosen, 1990). Families must then redirect their relationships and their goals. This process usually takes at least a year and sometimes longer. However, to be successful with moving on with their lives, family members must resist idealizing the deceased member such that his or her memory interferes with creating a new future.

Related to these family tasks, grieving family members face similar spiritual challenges to those dying persons face: finding meaning in life, making sense of death, and finding hope that buoys them up enough to negotiate the previously described tasks. For some family members, the deceased *was* the meaning in their lives and they feel they can no longer go on living without their loved one. In this case, the grieving person must reassess his or her values and belief system to transfer meaning to another life arena or focus. Some people are able to make this shift by carrying on a project that was important to the deceased such as volunteer work. Others pour themselves into caring for the dying; others get sustenance from their religious or spiritual beliefs and community and refocus their lives in a spiritual direction.

Making sense of death from a spiritual perspective is often very difficult. Some of the challenge has to do with clients' beliefs about death and the afterlife and their interpretation of their loved one's death. For example, some people believe that death is the result of not having enough faith or praying hard enough. They feel guilty because "if I'd only believed in a miracle she wouldn't have died." Others find themselves angry at God because they have interpreted death as "God's will" and believe God has taken their loved one from them. Counselors may encourage clients to explore more deeply these thoughts and beliefs. Bibliotherapy is often a helpful approach because clients are exposed to a wider range of explanations and interpretations of death. Leslie Weatherhead's (1944) *The Will of God* and Harold Kushner's (1981) *When Bad Things Happen to Good People* are useful resources in this regard.

In addition to addressing particular spiritual beliefs about death, Rosen (1990) suggested creating genograms with surviving family members to trace the patterns of loss and to become aware of the transgenerational messages and meanings attached to death throughout the family system. Such a strategy helps externalize the problem of grief so that clients can learn about their family patterns and better understand their own grieving process.

Asking families to view particular movies whose themes deal with death, dying, and family relationships might be especially helpful. Rosen (1990) recommended *I Never Sang for my Father* written by Robert Anderson; *The Great Santini* by Pat Conroy, and a docudrama, *Time Flies When You're Alive*. These films can be the springboard for conversations that link the issues in the movies to those surviving family members are experiencing.

Clients who need to acquire a sense of hope in the wake of a loved one's death might discover it through ritual (Imber-Black & Roberts, 1992; Rosen, 1990; Roberts, 1999). Certainly traditional religious or cultural ritual surrounding death such as funerals and wakes are means to building hope in survivors. Other rituals, developed by the family, assisted by counselors, can be especially meaningful.

CASE | KINGSTON FAMILY

The Kingston family had celebrated Thanksgiving at the family ranch for as long as anyone could remember. The entire extended family, including aunts, uncles, cousins, and friends attended the annual pig roast and turkey shoot. The thought of orchestrating such an event in the recent aftermath of John's death was overwhelming to the family. John had always overseen the food preparation and so to continue the celebration seemed both impossible and meaningless without John.

Leo, the family's counselor, suggested the family elect a successor to John, and create a ritual to remember John and to "pass the torch" to the one selected to carry on the tradition of the pig roast and turkey shoot. The family sent a letter to their relatives explaining the situation, indicating that they wanted to continue the family thanksgiving, and they asked if anyone were interested in being the bearer of the tradition. A nephew, Greg, volunteered and wrote a touching letter to the family saying how honored he would be to carry on the legacy of Uncle John.

John's immediate family asked everyone to bring pictures and other mementos of John's life when the family gathered at Thanksgiving. The night before Thanksgiving, they shared the memories and then participated in a ceremony to pass the torch to Greg. This ritual enabled the family to acknowledge John's life and the impact his death had on them, and to move the family into the future without losing a valuable tradition. This process created hope across the extended family.

Using narrative approaches in counseling grieving survivors has been offered as a means of reviving hope (Rosenblatt & Elde, 1990; Weinbach, 1989; Wrye & Churilla, 1977). Counselors help clients construct a future-directed narrative that includes the past and those who have died. Counselors encourage clients to reframe the loss as a challenge (Bogolub, 1991). By approaching the narrative of their lives in this way, the story of loss becomes part of an ongoing life-story that can be a turning point for regaining hope.

Children, Death, and Spirituality

Children often experience the death of a grandparent, sometimes a parent or sibling, and sometimes they become terminally ill themselves. Their ability to grasp the meaning and implications of death vary with age and developmental stage (see Table 9.2).

One of the major considerations for counselors is in helping parents approach the topic of death with their children in an honest and straightforward manner (Crompton, 1998). As Erikson (1963) rightly said, "Healthy children will not fear life if their elders have integrity enough not to fear death" (p. 269). Counselors can help parents and other caregivers think carefully about the language they use with children to talk about death and dying. For example, referring to death as "going to sleep" could create sleep phobias in young children. In addition, despite a strong belief in the afterlife, telling children that "God needed a loved one more than we needed him" may result in the child's harboring anger at God. A spirituality that is intended to be comforting to children can cause fear if the ideas are not explained in a positive, concrete fashion.

Children can be helped to cope with death through bibliotherapy (see Table 9.2) provided that counselors select age-appropriate materials, evaluate them thoroughly, prepare themselves to deal with the books' limitations, and work alongside the children so that they can respond to "teachable moments" (Corr, Nabe, & Corr, 1997).

Play, art, music, and other creative activities can help children express their understandings and feelings about death (Crompton, 1998). One such activity includes having older children make collages from tidbits of the belongings of each family member, including the person who has died. This strategy elicits conversation about the family members and helps to bring about healing.

Involving children in support groups for the bereaved is also a helpful strategy. Churches, synagogues, and other religious organizations often

Age	Concepts of Death	Feelings
Birth to 2 years	Separation; absence Reacts to change in routine and emotional climate	Miss and ache for sound, smell, sight or feel of someone Fears of being abandoned General anxiety
3–5 years	Death is temporary and reversible Finality of death is not evident To be dead is to be sleeping or on a trip May wonder what deceased is doing Magical thinking and fantasies, often worse than realities Understanding is limited	Sad Anxious Insecure Withdrawn Confused Angry Scared Cranky Agitated
6–9 years	Thinks about the finality of death Thinks about the biological process of death Death is associated with bodily harm, mutilation and disintegration Personify death—a spirit, monster, death man, ghost gets you when you die Who will care for me if my caregiver dies? My actions or words caused the illness or death. Death is punishment	Sad Anxious Withdrawn Confused Angry Scared Cranky

TABLE 9.2 | *Continued*

Age	Behaviors	How to Help
Birth to 2 years	Thrashing, rocking, throwing Crying Sucking, biting Sleeplessness Indigestion	Physical contact and reassurance Attend to immediate physical needs Maintain routines Include child in mourning Be patient
3–5 years	Crying Fighting Interested in dead things Acts as if death never happened Regressive behaviors Regressive questions Expressing strong feelings in his/her sleep and dreams Expressing feeling through play	Answer repetitive questions Give simple and truthful answers to questions Include child in family rituals and mourning process Provide safe ways to express feeling Maintain structure and routines Encourage children to play and to have fun Tolerate the child's need to regress for a while (being held, sleeping with others, thumb sucking, etc.) Physical contact Let the child cry Talk
6–9 years	Aggressive acting out Withdrawal Nightmares/sleep disturbances Acting as if the death never happened Lack of concentration Declining or greatly improving grades Regressive behaviors Specific questioning, looking for details	Answer questions truthfully Look for confused thinking Encourage expression of feelings Offer physical outlets Encourage drawing, reading, playing, art, music, dance, acting, sports Physical contact Have intentional times to grieve together Let child choose how to be involved in the death and mourning process Find peer support for the child Work with school to tailor workload Talk

continued

TABLE 9.2 | *Continued*

Age	Concepts of Death	Feelings
12 years	Understanding of the finality of and universality of death Death may happen again What will happen if my caregiver dies My actions and words caused the illness or death	Vulnerable Anxious Scared Lonely Confused Angry Sad Abandoned Guilty Fearful Worried Isolated Shock Denial Emotional turmoil heightened by physical changes
Adolescents	Understanding of the finality of death If I show my feelings I will be weak I need to be in control of my feelings Can sense own impending death Self-centered and thus have an exaggerated sense of their own role in regards to death	Vulnerable Anxious Scared Lonely Confused Angry Sad Abandoned Guilty Fearful Worried Isolated Shock Denial Depression Highly self-conscious about being different because of grief

TABLE 9.2 | *Continued*

Age	Behaviors	How to Help
12 years	Aggressive acting out Withdrawal Talks about physical aspects of illness or death Acts like illness or death never happened Does not show feelings Nightmares/sleep disturbances Lack of concentration Declining or greatly improved grades Regressive behavior Changing behavior Acting out Role confusion	Answer questions Expect and accept mood swings Give choices about how to be involved in death and mourning rituals Find peer support groups Encourage expression of feelings Encourage reading, writing, art, music, sports Talk
Adolescents	Impulsive behavior Fighting, screaming, and arguing High risk behavior Grieving for what might have been Acts like the illness or death never happened Lack of concentration Changes in grades Sleep disturbances Changes in eating patterns Changes in peer groups Acting out; role confusion Conflict within teen about moving to independence and remaining dependent	Expect the thoughts and feelings of the teen to be contradictory and inconsistent Allow their coping behavior in covering up their grief if it is basically harmless to themselves and others Encourage expression of feelings Look for high risk behavior Encourage relationships with other supportive adults Listen Display honest grief, share in discussions Answer questions truthfully Give choices about involvement in death and mourning rituals Encourage peer support groups Talk

sponsor such groups. Through interaction with peers who have experienced loss, children are able to share their feelings and gain information, comfort, and hope for the future.

Counselors might also want to develop rituals that are appropriate for children who have experienced the death of a loved one. Although it is often helpful for children to be included in traditional religious services or funerals, alternate rituals can assist children in understanding the finality of death and in celebrating the life of someone special. One such ritual involves having children select balloons in the deceased's favorite color, fill them with helium, and attach written notes or pictures to them with ribbons. Poems are read or prayers said and the balloons released. This ritual enables children to say good-bye and move on with the process of healing.

CASE EXAMPLES

Cecelia

Cecelia is a 41-year-old Caucasian interior decorator. She was raised in the Methodist church, and was an active laywoman until about 10 years ago when she went through a painful divorce. Cecelia stopped attending church about the time of her divorce because her husband had a major leadership role. According to Cecelia, "I got the house. He got the church."

As part of her recovery, Cecelia joined a group of other women who were dealing with divorce. During that process, Cecelia read voraciously and became passionate about women's issues. She sought counseling with Marla because she was unable to reconcile her Methodist upbringing with her new interest in feminist spirituality.

Discussion Questions
1. What dilemma do you perceive is the central focus for Cecelia?
2. If you were her counselor, what questions would you ask Cecelia to help her explore the relationship between her religious background and her feminist ideas?
3. What information do you think you need but do not currently have in order to work effectively with Cecelia? What resources do you have to obtain such information?
4. What is your personal reaction to the ideas associated with feminist spirituality? How do you think you would respond to Cecelia's desire to explore this spiritual avenue?

Marco

Marco is a 32-year-old Latino musician who immigrated to the United States from Puerto Rico when he was 14. After a stormy adolescence in which Marco attempted suicide twice, he finally acknowledged that he was gay.

During his early twenties, Marco engaged in multiple sexual encounters, and, as a result contracted AIDS. His partner of three years, Jeremy, a Caucasian, is currently not infected. Marco's health is deteriorating, and both he and Jeremy are seeking spiritual support for dealing with Marco's impending death. Marco's family members live in Florida, and his father, Pedro, has not spoken to him since Marco shared with him his sexual orientation. However, Pedro has made it clear that Jeremy is not welcome in their home. Both Marco and Jeremy were raised as Roman Catholics, but neither has attended church since childhood.

Discussion Questions

1. What are the issues you believe to be central for Marco and Jeremy?
2. What tasks seem necessary for Marco and Jeremy to complete so they can come to terms with Marco's condition and his eventual death?
3. What sources of spiritual support might be available for Marco and Jeremy? How would you go about connecting them with this type of support?
4. After Marco's death, what barriers might exist for Jeremy to successfully complete his grieving process? How could you facilitate this process in the present?
5. What is your personal reaction to this case? How equipped do you feel to work with Marco and Jeremy? How do your views on homosexuality influence your response to these clients?

Elise

Elise is a 9-year-old Caucasian who is intellectually gifted. She excels academically and is especially talented in music and the arts. According to her mother, Anne, Elise "has always has a deep sense of the spiritual." She is mesmerized by natural beauty and is brought to tears by a violin concerto. Recently, Elise began asking questions in school related to spiritual concerns. During a science lesson about the origin of the world, she asked her teacher, "If God created the universe, who created God?" Elise has been experiencing difficulty with peers at school because of her precocious questions. Other children bully her, call her names, and exclude her from their play. Anne wants to encourage Elise's spiritual inquisitiveness, but not at the expense of her social and emotional development.

Discussion Questions

1. How would you conceptualize Elise's situation?
2. If you were Elise's counselor, what strategies would you employ to support her spiritual quest and to assist her in her social relationships?
3. How would you work with Elise's mother to reach her goals?
4. What specific challenges would this case present for you?

SUGGESTED ACTIVITIES

Join a Chat

Search the Internet for Web sites related to feminist spirituality. Locate a chatroom related to feminist interests and participate in an online dialogue with others about your reading and responses to it.

Invite a Speaker

Contact your local chapter of PFLAG (Parents and Friends of Lesbians and Gays) and ask someone from their speaker's bureau to visit your class. Or, attend one of the workshops or seminars sponsored by this organization.

Go to Church

If there is a congregation of the Metropolitan Community Church nearby, visit one of the Sunday morning worship services, or attend another church function. Try to ascertain the mood and the type of spiritual experience that is offered.

Interview Children and Adolescents

Select three children (ages 4–6; 7–9; 10–12) and one adolescent to interview about their understanding of God, religion, and spirituality. Be sure to get informed consent from the parents. Write a summary of your findings.

Invite a Chaplain

Contact a chaplain from your local Hospice program and invite him or her to speak to your class about spiritual and religious issues associated with death and dying.

Write Your Own Epitaph

Get in touch with your feelings and responses to death by writing your own epitaph or designing your own funeral service. Be as specific as possible. Share your writings and experiences with your peers if you wish.

SUPPLEMENTAL READING

Feminist Spirituality
Christ, C. P. (1997). *Rebirth of the goddess: Finding meaning in feminist spirituality*. New York: Addison-Wesley. In this book, the author traces her academic and personal experience with goddess thea-ology. She provides a rich history of the goddess, discusses resistance to goddess history, and suggests meanings attached to goddess worship.

Eller, C. (1993). *Living in the lap of the goddess: The feminist spirituality movement in America.* New York: Crossroad. This book is a comprehensive treatise on feminist spirituality based on interviews and research conducted by the author. Descriptions of beliefs and practices and their sources are included.

Reilly, P. L. (1995). *A God who looks like me: Discovering a woman-affirming spirituality.* New York: Ballentine Books. In this book, the author describes the experience of women who find themselves out of sync with traditional religious frameworks and are seeking a spirituality that embraces their experiences as females.

Spirituality and Gay, Lesbian, and Bisexuals

Davidson, M. G. (2000). Religion and spirituality. In R. M. Perez, K. A. DeBord, & K. J. Bieschke, (Eds.), *Handbook of counseling and psychotherapy with lesbian, gay and bisexual clients* (pp. 409–433).Washington, DC: American Psychological Association. This book chapter provides an overview of religious and spiritual issues faced by GLB clients and ways that counselors can be helpful in addressing them.

Children and Spirituality

Coles, R. (1990). *The spiritual life of children.* Boston: Houghton Mifflin. In this book, the author describes his interviews with racially and ethnically diverse children about their understanding and experience of spirituality and religion.

Crompton, M. (1998). *Children, spirituality, religion, and social work.* Aldershot, England: Ashgate. In this book, the author addresses a variety of topics related to children and spirituality, including children's concepts of God, religious and spiritual rites of passage, fasts and festivals, worship, symbols, and sacred objects. She discusses strategies for working with children's spiritual issues in the context of mental health practice.

Hyde, K. E. (1990). *Religion in childhood and adolescence.* Birmingham, AL: Religious Education Press. This book is a comprehensive review of the research literature regarding children and adolescents and religion. Topics include children and adolescents' concepts of God, gender differences, beliefs, and the relationship between spirituality and other mental health concerns.

Death, Dying, and Spirituality

Callanan, M., & Kelley, P. (1992). *Final gifts: Understanding the special awareness, needs, and communications of the dying.* New York: Bantam Books. Written by two hospice nurses, this book describes the process of dying and how survivors can help the terminally ill die peacefully.

Levine, S. (1998). *A year to live.* New York: Bell Tower. This book is full of exercises to help terminally ill persons accept and prepare for death. It is also a helpful resource for family members of dying patients.

Menten, T. (1991). *Gentle closings: How to say goodbye to someone you love.* Philadelphia: Running Press. This book is about people who said goodbye to loved ones and how they did it. Examples of effective leave-taking are found in this compassionate, warm, and even humorous book.

ETHICAL
CONSIDERATIONS

CHAPTER 10

INTRODUCTION

Ethical behavior is at the core of sound mental health practice. Such behavior grows out of knowing the ethical codes that govern one's profession and understanding the philosophical principles that underlie them (Bersoff, 1996). The term *ethics* refers to our beliefs about what constitutes right conduct (Corey, Corey, & Callanan, 1998). Ethics is concerned with counselors' behaviors related to client welfare. Moreover, ethics involves the "intended and unintended consequences of counselor's behavior to clients, their social networks, to the public and to the profession" (Haug, 1998, p. 183). According to Welfel (1998), ethics covers four dimensions:

1. Having sufficient knowledge, skill, and judgment of use efficacious interventions
2. Respecting human dignity and freedom of the client
3. Using the power inherent in the counselor's role responsibly
4. Acting in ways that promote public confidence in the profession of counseling (pp. 3–4)

Virtually all the codes of ethics of the mental health professions (AAMFT, 1991; ACA, 1995; APA, 1992; NASW, 1996; NOHSE, 1995) contain these themes and present specific standards for clinician's behavior in concert with them. What is missing, however, are guidelines for practitioners who intend to integrate religion and spirituality into psychotherapy.

In this chapter, I present the major points of ethical concern related to religious and spiritual interventions in counseling. These areas include the welfare of the client, informed consent, competence and training, person-of-the-therapist issues, imposition of values, dual relationships, work-setting boundaries, and consultation and referral. Most of these topics are addressed in the professional codes of ethics, but the introduction of religion and spirituality raises unique challenges in some arenas. Included in this chapter are case vignettes that illustrate ethical dilemmas as well as guidelines for practice.

WELFARE OF THE CLIENT

Perhaps the overarching goal of ethical mental health practice is to protect client welfare. To do so means safeguarding clients from harm (nonmaleficence), whether it is overt or covert. In a sense, the other dimensions of ethical practice are a means of making sure clients' well-being is promoted and defended.

One way we secure client welfare is to address religious and spiritual issues when they arise. As we have seen throughout this book, clients' issues are often complex and involve their thoughts, feelings, behaviors, and context, *including* a possible religious or spiritual context. When we as counselors neglect any aspect of our clients' experiences and perceived reality, we run the risk of doing them harm. It is incumbent on us, then, to prepare ourselves as best we can to take seriously clients' worldviews, which could include religious or spiritual perspectives.

One way to support client well-being is to become familiar with the religious or spiritual language clients use to talk about their transcendent experiences, their doctrines, and their beliefs (Haug, 1998). For example, in some Christian circles the terms *sin, grace,* and *salvation* have particular meanings or interpretations. When counselors are able to use these terms appropriately in communicating with their clients about significant religious or spiritual concepts, they honor their clients' worldviews and demonstrate that they are conversant with their clients' tradition. Clients are more apt to trust counselors' insights, interventions, and challenges when counselors are multilingual when it comes to religion and spirituality.

Another way to safeguard client welfare is to work within clients' belief systems (Bergin & Payne, 1991; Nelson & Wilson, 1984; Tan, 1994). To counsel in this way means to step inside clients' constructed reality and learn about their beliefs and practices and how these are connected to both their distress and their well-being. Once counselors understand clients' religious and spiritual perspectives, counselors can assist clients in exploring the degree to which these perspectives are contributing to distress or serving as a buffer against it. In addition, counselors who work within their clients' belief systems are able to facilitate congruence between clients' beliefs and behaviors so that clients' welfare may be enhanced.

INFORMED CONSENT

The notion of informed consent is one of the best ways counselors have of protecting client welfare. This concept involves the rights of clients to know what will transpire during treatment and to make autonomous decisions about their participation in it (Corey, Corey & Callanan, 1998). Informed consent involves disclosing enough information about the risks and benefits of particular interventions so clients can voluntarily agree to engage in the process. Legally, the three aspects that pertain specifically to informed consent are capacity (the ability to make rational decisions), comprehension of information, and voluntariness (Anderson, 1996; Crawford, 1994; Stromberg & Dellinger, 1993).

Informed consent procedures should be part of every counselor's intake process, however, it is especially critical when clients might not be expecting to have religious or spiritual concerns addressed in counseling. Counselors who intend to work with clients' religious or spiritual issues are obligated to inform clients of their approach at the outset of therapy (Richards & Potts, 1995). Furthermore, counselors who are associated with religious institutions have a duty to inform clients in both their advertising efforts and face to face about their affiliations and the religious doctrines therein. Taking care to obtain informed consent is especially important when clients are minors because legally they do not have the capacity to make choices for themselves about treatment interventions (Haug, 1998). In addition, it is a counselor's duty to protect clients' rights to decline the use of spiritual interventions or to delve into their religious or spiritual beliefs in any way and provide referrals to other persons for spiritual guidance and support (Haug, 1998).

| CASE | ALFONSO |

Alfonso was employed in a Catholic counseling center where he provided outpatient therapy to members of the community. One of his clients, Jessica, a 17-year-old high school drop out, disclosed that she was pregnant after being raped during a drug deal. Jessica said to Alfonso, "I have enough problems as it is without bringing a baby into the world. I'd like to consider having an abortion." Alfonso carefully summarized Jessica's situation, and then began to share with her the doctrine of the Catholic Church regarding abortion. He said, "While I understand you are in a lot of pain and distress about being pregnant, surely you know that abortion is not God's will for your baby." Jessica was visibly upset by Alfonso's remark and left the counseling session immediately in tears. Alfonso ran after her, but she refused to talk with him and screamed expletives at him as she ran across the parking lot. In a session with his supervisor, Jim, later that afternoon, Alfonso related the incident with his client, Jessica. Jim asked Alfonso if he had talked with Jessica on intake about the center's philosophy and treatment approaches. Alfonso indicated that he had mentioned the Catholic connection casually to Jessica, but had not dwelt upon it. Instead, he noted that he had tried to form a strong therapeutic alliance with her "without going into a lot of detail about the Catholic stuff."

In this case, Alfonso made several ethical errors. First, he should have explained his agency's philosophy to Jessica from the beginning, providing her with detailed information concerning sensitive issues such as birth control, abortion, divorce, and other activities that are viewed as incompatible with Catholic doctrine. Next, Alfonso should have talked with Jessica about his counseling approach and should have disclosed to her the fact that he would be working with her on several fronts, including the religious or spiritual ones. Then, Alfonso should have obtained written informed consent from Jessica herself and from her parent(s) or guardian because she is not of legal majority. In addition, Alfonso should have inquired about Jessica's religious or spiritual background and beliefs and worked within her worldview to help her come to a decision regarding her pregnancy that was congruent with her belief system. Instead, Jessica likely perceived his referring to the Catholic position on abortion as insensitive. Alfonso's failure to reluctance to discuss his approach with Jessica and his failure to obtain informed consent cost him his counseling relationship with his client.

COMPETENCE AND TRAINING

Another hallmark of general counseling ethics is that clinicians do not practice beyond the level of their competence and training. Until recently, little training was available for mental health practitioners in the area of integrating religion and spirituality into psychotherapy (Collins, Hurst, & Jacobson, 1987; Genia, 1994; Jensen & Bergin, 1988; Shafranske & Malony, 1990). In the last several years, however, more and more courses are being offered that are specifically oriented toward training students to work with clients' religious and spiritual concerns (Fukuyama & Sevig, 1997; Ingersoll, 1997). A growing body of professional literature also addresses this topic (Kelly, 1995; Fukuyama & Sevig, 1999; Miller, 1999; Richards & Bergin, 1997). Moreover, the program offerings at professional conferences, conventions, and workshops currently list many training opportunities for counseling professionals. Currently, counselors have numerous resources to obtain additional training in working with clients' religious and spiritual issues.

In addition to availing themselves of training opportunities, counselors should become familiar with the world's major religious traditions and spiritual movements, regardless of their own personal persuasions. Indeed, it has been shown (Propst, 1980, 1992) that it is not necessary for counselors to share clients' religious or spiritual perspectives to use clients' belief systems in therapy. On the contrary, what is needed is understanding and receptivity that may be the key to determining how frequently clients share their religious and spiritual beliefs in the first place (Sheridan & Bullis, 1991).

To practice ethically, counselors should seek supervision and consultation (or both) when they begin working with clients from a particular religious or spiritual background or when clients' issues are new and challenging for the counselor (Richards & Bergin, 1997). In addition, counselors should solicit consultation and supervision when they initiate novel religious or spiritual interventions.

CASE	COURTNEY

Courtney is a counselor in private practice. Her client, Maggie, a 22-year-old graduate student, sought counseling because she was "not finding fulfillment or spiritual depth" in her religion as a Mormon. Maggie told Courtney that there was a tremendous amount of pressure on her from her parents and extended family to participate in worship, study, and missionary service in their Latter Day Saints congregation. Maggie indicated that she found her religion too confining, and that she wanted an opportunity to explore other religions, including Buddhism, so she could satisfy her curiosity and her longing "for meaning and spiritual connectedness."

Although Courtney had no knowledge about the Mormon faith, nor was she particularly familiar with other religions, she thought that she could help Maggie find a meaningful spiritual experience. In addition, Courtney believed she could help Maggie deal with the negativity she would experience from her family members should she abandon Mormonism for some other spiritual path.

As she began her work with Maggie, Courtney felt overwhelmed by the tenets of the Mormon religion and had difficulty understanding the basic concepts Maggie herself took for granted. Further, Courtney began to feel angry that Maggie's extended family would expect her to ascribe to such a belief system. Courtney's strategy was to support Maggie in what Courtney perceived as Maggie's attempt to separate from a family that was entirely too enmeshed. Rather than creating an open space where Maggie could explore her emerging beliefs and evaluate her religion, Courtney created a loyalty conflict for Maggie between her family and the counseling process. Eventually, Maggie terminated counseling because she could not tolerate feeling so torn between Courtney and her family.

In this case, had Courtney been familiar with Mormon doctrine and practice, she could have avoided the double bind she created for Maggie. In addition, she could have been more helpful to Maggie by asking her questions that would reveal how her religion was failing her. Had Courtney been better trained in dealing with religious and spiritual concerns, and had she consulted a competent supervisor, Courtney could have helped Maggie unravel the aspects of her religion that were not effective for her. Relatedly, Courtney could have enabled Maggie to explore whether it was the religion per se that was troubling Maggie, or whether Maggie was choosing to discard her religion as a means of gaining independence from her family.

PERSON-OF-THE-THERAPIST ISSUES

One major theme I have developed in this book is the need for counselors to continue to work on their personal issues, especially with regard to religion and spirituality, to avoid harming their clients. Because counselors' effectiveness is only partly the result of knowledge and skill and mostly the result of personal characteristics and relational quality (Haug, 1998), counselors must attend to their own religious and spiritual issues so that their unfinished business is not projected onto their clients. In addition, to minimize countertransference, counselors need to confront their own belief systems and seek personal therapy or spiritual guidance to resolve dilemmas that might create difficulties for them in the therapeutic milieu.

One area in which counselors are most vulnerable is in placing their own needs above those of their clients. This liability comes into play in unique ways when counselors work with clients religious and spiritual concerns. For example, counselors who are highly invested in their own beliefs could attempt to satisfy their needs to share their faith by proselytizing clients who are struggling to find a meaningful spiritual direction. Conversely, counselors who are hostile toward religion in general or toward a particular expression of religion might inadvertently discourage clients from exploring certain belief systems for fear of receiving disapproval from their counselors. For example, a counselor who was raised in a fundamentalist Christian church might have rejected this form of Christianity. As a result, he gives subtle, nonverbal cues to his clients that their views of the Bible, the role of women in the church, and their conservative social mores are unacceptable to him. Thus, fearing rejection by their counselor, clients maintaining a fundamentalist Christian perspective might terminate counseling prematurely.

Continual self-examination and personal counseling can enable counselors to increase their awareness of how they are vulnerable to placing their own needs ahead of those of their clients. Because introducing religious and spiritual material into counseling is a value-laden enterprise (Haug, 1998), counselors' increased clarity regarding their own values reduces the likelihood that they will seek to have clients conform to their values.

CASE	WARREN

Warren is a 42-year-old counselor who works in a residential facility for adolescent males who have committed juvenile offenses. Warren likes his work because he can identify with his clients with whom he shares a similar history. Warren turned his life around after attending a Transcendental Meditation retreat with his older brother. Being introduced to meditation helped Warren to get in touch with himself and to set some personal goals. Meditation also helped him gain control over stress and the powerlessness he had felt growing up in a substance-abusing family.

One of Warren's clients is Adam, a 15-year-old boy who was arrested for stealing a car. Adam is angry at the world, especially his father who abandoned him when Adam was 7. Warren believes that finding a spiritual path is what Adam needs to assuage his anger and pain and to gain peace in his life. Rather than dealing with Adam's presenting issues regarding the car theft and his anger at being placed in the facility, Warren suggests that Adam learn to meditate. Adam is not interested in meditation or "any crazy religion stuff like that." Instead of responding to Warren's approach, Adam violates facility regulations and, because of violent behavior, is placed in a more confining situation.

In this case, Warren's need to rescue Adam in the same way he was rescued (through discovering a spiritual path and practice) backfired and resulted in Adam's placement outside the facility. Rather than focusing on Adam's needs and problems, Warren's personal convictions led him to place his needs above those of his client. Warren offered his personal solution to Adam when such an approach was neither invited nor desired. Warren's failure to recognize that he was re-living his experience through Adam led him to approach Adam in a way that had been effective for him, but that, at that time and under those circumstances was not appropriate. Warren's unresolved personal issues interfered with his effectiveness in counseling Adam.

IMPOSITION OF VALUES

All the mental health professions have ethical codes or standards that expect their members to respect clients' diverse opinions and values (AAMFT, 1991; ACA, 1995; APA, 1992; NASW, 1996; NOHSE, 1995). Because counseling is not a value-free enterprise (Bergin, 1980; Corey, 2001; Tjeltveit, 1986) working with clients' religious and spiritual values makes clinicians particularly vulnerable to violating this standard of practice.

Imposing one's values suggests that counselors could be coercive in attempting to influence clients' beliefs and value-based choices. Such an imposition of values can occur overtly or covertly. *Exposing* one's values means that counselors disclose their perspectives to clients regarding religious or spiritual beliefs or values. There is a controversy in the mental health field about whether or not *exposing* one's values is a subtle form of *imposing* such values. For example, Aponte (1996) proposed that counselors make their beliefs explicit. Such an approach respects clients' right to informed consent and honors counselors' right to their convictions (Haug, 1998). When a conflict of conscience arises because of divergent views and values, counselors may then refer clients to other providers. On the other hand, it might not be wise under all circumstances to share one's beliefs and values with clients. For example, children, adolescents, persons with fragile egos or low self-esteem could be especially vulnerable to adopting their counselor's values because of the counselor's authority and power in the relationship. These same persons could be influenced by counselor self-disclosure precisely because they have not yet formulated their own beliefs, or because they are searching for something to value and to trust and thus they attach themselves to counselors' belief systems. In such cases, *exposing* one's values could inadvertently result in *imposing* them on clients. Practitioners must evaluate each situation and make a decision about sharing beliefs and values based on their clinical judgment regarding which course of action appears to be in the client's best interest.

Employing spiritual interventions such as prayer often raise questions about whether or not such a strategy involves imposing one's values on a client. For example, there is disagreement among practitioners about whether or not praying for one's client out loud in the counseling session constitutes an imposition of values. Certainly if such an activity were to be used, it would be important for the counselor to consider the following safeguards: (a) to obtain informed consent from the client before engaging in prayer, (b) to be sure that praying audibly in a session would not violate work-setting standards, (c) to discuss the purpose of using prayer with the client in advance, and (d) to have a clear rationale regarding how this strategy connects to the presenting problem and therapeutic goals. Another approach proposed by Fukuyama and Sevig (1999) is to invite the client to lead such a prayer because doing so reveals the client's concern and effectively avoids the potential for values imposition by the counselor.

Another example of possible imposition of values would be for counselors to teach religious doctrine, distribute religious or spiritual literature, or engage in any form of proselytizing during counseling sessions or other contexts with clients (Richards & Bergin, 1997). These activities are clearly unethical.

Another form of value imposition involves telling clients that their beliefs are wrong or that they themselves are spiritually deluded or ineffective. Examples of such behavior could include counselors implying clients' choices to have abortions, to engage in same-sex unions, or to participate in extramarital relationships are morally unacceptable. As Richards and Bergin (1997) pointed out, such behavior is inappropriate for mental health practitioners, although it may be well within the purview of ecclesiastical leaders.

These prohibitions do not preclude counselors' making judgments about the outcomes of client behaviors and sharing those perspectives with them (Richards & Bergin, 1997). For example, counselors might wish to confront clients who reveal they are abusing drugs and stealing money to support their addiction by pointing out the consequences of such a lifestyle. However, counselors must remember that clients are free to choose their way of life, unless it is clearly illegal (e.g., child or elder abuse).

In addition, it is appropriate for counselors to help clients identify their beliefs and examine them with the goal of assisting clients to determine which beliefs make a positive difference in their lives and which ones are destructive (Nelson & Wilson, 1984). Working with clients to enable them to restructure their belief systems so that they are able to live more functional and meaningful lives is a worthy goal for counselors to pursue. However, telling clients what to believe or indoctrinating them toward a certain set of values or lifestyle would constitute imposition of values.

CASE | DOROTHY

Marvin and Sybil are in their fifties. They have been married for 7 years, each having been divorced previously. They sought couples' counseling with Dorothy because they were having a disagreement about how to handle certain household responsibilities. Marvin said he believed "it was the woman's duty to prepare the meals and clean the house." He indicated that "it was the man's responsibility to do yard work, manage the finances, and take care of the cars." Dorothy was offended by such rigid gender roles and told the couple that she believed such an arrangement was oppressive to women. She said she could work with Marvin and Sybil to come to a more equitable division of labor based on their interests, skills, and freedom to choose. Marvin got angry at Dorothy's implication that he was being oppressive to Sybil, and he told Dorothy that "the Bible says the man is the head of the house." Dorothy countered saying, "that statement is just a reflection of cultural values. It has nothing to do with how couples arrange their lives today."

In this case, Dorothy is clearly violating ethical standards by imposing her beliefs (about women's roles and about biblical interpretation) on her clients. Although Dorothy is certainly entitled to her personal beliefs, the way she chose to disclose them resulted in offending her clients and thwarting the therapeutic process.

DUAL RELATIONSHIPS

The ethical codes of the mental health professions (AAMFT, 1991; ACA, 1995; APA, 1992; NASW, 1996; NOHSE, 1995) caution against and sometimes prohibit dual relationships because engaging in them makes clients vulnerable to being exploited by their counselors. A dual relationship exists when counselors have other connections with clients besides that of counselor (Welfel, 1998). When counselors have overlapping relationships with their clients, there is a potential for counselors to be caught in a conflict of interest that could impair their clinical judgment, reduce their objectivity, and possibly result in harm to the client.

Two types of dual relationships are of particular interest for those counselors integrating religious and spiritual issues into counseling: relationships that have the potential to blur social and professional boundaries, create role confusion, and thus, boundary violations (Haug & Alexander, 1992). First, there are dual relationships in which the counselor is also a religious or spiritual leader such as a minister, rabbi, or priest. In this case, counselors are functioning in two different roles relative to their clients who are also parishioners. Clergy have ecclesiastical authority over their members and if they serve as counselors, the dual role has the potential to create boundary violations. For example, Richards and Bergin (1997) noted that clients might not feel free to discuss all aspects of their lives (e.g., sexual and financial problems) with their counselors who are also their religious or spiritual leaders. Moreover, conflicts of interest could arise because clergypersons are privy to information that would influence their judgment when working with clients in the ecclesiastical setting. For example, if a priest who is counseling a parishioner knows that his client has suffered with bouts of depression, he might not recommend that client for a position as a church official. Had he not had the counseling relationship and possessed intimate knowledge of the client, the client might well have been elected to a church office.

Another dilemma that might arise from dual relationships involving religious or spiritual leaders and their constituents is the possibility that clients in a worshipping congregation may personalize statements from the pulpit. For example, if a clergy-counselor is preaching a sermon about forgiveness and her client is present, the client could interpret the sermon to mean that he must forgive his father for the physical abuse he suffered as a child. The dual role has the potential to confuse clients regarding the intended meaning of the sermon, lecture, or presentation when the content is relevant to issues in the counseling setting.

Certainly, these potential hazards do not mean that clergy and other religious or spiritual leaders should not ever engage in counseling their parishioners. Indeed, counseling is considered one responsibility of spiritual leaders in many religions. However, Richards and Bergin (1997) offer several guidelines that help protect boundaries and minimize role confusion. First, ecclesiastical leaders should provide counseling free of charge and in the religious setting. Second, they should make it clear that they are providing counseling as part of their pastoral or spiritual role. Third, they should refer clients who have significant emotional issues that may be better treated by a mental health professional in another setting.

Another form of dual relationship that can pose potential difficulties is that of counselors who provide mental health services to members of their congregations, meditation groups, or other religious or spiritual organizations. In this situation, it is likely that counselors and clients will have frequent social contacts in the religious or spiritual setting. As a result, some clients might avoid attending religious or spiritual functions for fear of encountering their counselor and feeling embarrassed because the counselor is privy to the details of their lives (Richards & Bergin, 1997). Further, there is also a greater risk that counselors could violate confidentiality by accidentally disclosing information obtained in a counseling session. In addition, clients might reveal some issues that are pertinent to counseling in the religious or spiritual context, thus creating an awkward situation for both the client and the counselor (Richards & Bergin, 1997). Although many religious people prefer to receive counseling by those who share their values and religious beliefs (Worthington, 1986), such relationships are best avoided if possible.

Avoiding these dual relationships is difficult if not impossible in some situations. Geyer (1994) compared counseling within religious or spiritual contexts with the challenges that arise by counseling in rural settings. In addition to the dilemma described earlier, Geyer noted that both rural and religious/spiritual settings pose the following special problems. First, there are increased power differentials in which counselors are viewed as possessing "special information" (p. 190) that increases their power over their clients and might provide them some immunity from criticism by their clients. Second, client anonymity can be difficult in that people in small towns and in religious or spiritual communities are known by others. It is difficult to provide individual and especially group counseling in this context because of the likelihood that clients will run into each other, and therapeutic content may travel outside of the counseling setting. Third, professional isolation can be a potential problem in religious or spiritual contexts because "there are few situations in which they feel free to relax or talk about pressures they themselves are experiencing" (Geyer, 1994, p. 190).

In response to these challenges, Geyer (1994) proposed guidelines for managing the hazards of dual relationships that occur when counselors and clients are members of the same religious or spiritual organization or community. First, clients should be informed in advance of consultation services being used as well as any leadership roles the counselor has that might compromise client confidentiality or counselor objectivity. In this way, clients have the right to seek counseling elsewhere if they believe a conflict of interest could arise. In addition, counselors assert from the outset their need for consultation and supervision, and clients may give informed consent for those persons or agencies to be involved. Second, churches, synagogues, mosques, and other religious and spiritual organizations can consider collaborating among themselves to provide mental health services for each other's staffs, families, and members. Thus, persons for whom a particular religious or spiritual perspective is important could obtain counseling from providers with similar backgrounds but who are not participants in their congregations. Third, counselors who are involved in leadership roles in religious or spiritual contexts could reserve the right not to comment on situations in which they have inside information related to a client's right to confidentiality. According to Geyer (1994), counselors would not disclose whether the refusal was "related to a client or indirect information shared about another person by a client" (p. 193). Such a policy would help protect the integrity of roles and "would involve generally recognized limitations on performance in one setting based on commitments made in another" (p. 193). Fourth, dual relationships should be avoided where the role responsibilities and activities are incompatible. For example, clients and counselors would not participate together in study groups, meditation groups, or other situations where personal disclosure is expected.

Fifth, clear personal boundaries should be established with clients where there is a particular risk of dual relationships. For example, policies should be established regarding clients' calling counselors at home, how emergencies are to be handled, and how counselors will manage casual contacts that are unavoidable. Sixth, financial and other obligations and procedures should be defined clearly. Doing so creates a contractual agreement between counselor and client and underscores the professional nature of their relationship. Large gifts or expensive services should be avoided because they could create an inappropriate sense of entitlement for the client or they might foster a level of intimacy between client and counselor that could be detrimental to the therapeutic enterprise. In addition to these suggestions made by Geyer (1994), counselors who find themselves in situations where dual relationships could abound should maintain regular supervision to help them maintain their integrity and to minimize the risk of compromising the ethical standards of the profession.

CASE | MOHAMMED

Mohammed is the only Muslim counselor within a 100-mile radius in his southwestern United States community. He has obtained professional credentials and is often called upon by other Muslims to provide counseling for them and their families. In addition, Mohammed is a leader in his religious community, serving on the personnel committee. Mohammed's client, Ali, also a Muslim who worshipped in the same mosque, was struggling with alcohol abuse and allegations of battering made by his wife. Unbeknownst to Mohammed, Ali applied for a position to work with children and youth in the religious community. When he read the list of applications, Mohammed found himself in a double bind. As a member of the personnel committee of his mosque, he did not feel comfortable hiring Ali to work with youth and children because of his addiction and his violent temper. However, to disclose this information to the personnel committee would be a violation of Ali's confidentiality. Instead of revealing his reasons for not supporting Ali's employment, Mohammed emphasized the positive qualities of other applicants. Nevertheless, Ali was hired and Mohammed felt guilty that he had betrayed his religious leaders by remaining silent.

In this case, Mohammed should have known that dual relationship dilemmas would characterize his professional life since he had focused his practice on working with other Muslims. Mohammed should have had clear guidelines established both with his mosque and his clients about the nature of their relationship, about the ways in which he would manage potential conflicts of interest, and should have obtained informed consent from his clients about consultation and supervision. In this situation, had Mohammed done the preliminary groundwork, from the outset he could have refused to take on a leadership role in the mosque that might give him authority over potential clients. In addition, if he had learned from Ali about his application to work with children and youth, he could have talked with his client about whether or not that particular job was appropriate given Ali's presenting problems.

WORK-SETTING BOUNDARIES

One major ethical challenge facing counselors who work with clients' religious and spiritual issues is practicing within legal and policy limits of their settings. Counselors who work in government-funded agencies and public schools could find themselves in precarious positions relative to the law or their institutional regulations if they use explicit spiritual interventions with their clients. Given the legal precedent of separation of church and state, employing religious or spiritual strategies in civic settings could be construed as a violation of the First Amendment to the United States Constitution (Fischer & Sorenson, 1985). This amendment prohibits governments from promoting, endorsing, or establishing a religion.

Certainly, counselors have the right to explore clients' values and beliefs as they are related to clients' mental health issues. In addition, counselors have the right to disclose their own religious or spiritual beliefs if clients request this information and if counselors believe that revealing it would not constitute imposing their values on their clients. However, any activities in civic settings that could be interpreted as proselytizing or attempting to convert clients to one's spiritual or religious perspective would be unethical and quite probably illegal (Richards & Bergin, 1997). Counselors who want to use spiritual interventions of any kind should obtain informed consent from their clients and permission from their supervisors and other agency authorities before implementing them. Also, counselors might consult an attorney to clarify legal restraints related to their therapeutic approach.

Another work-setting boundary issue has to do with displacing or usurping the authority of religious or spiritual leaders (Richards & Bergin, 1997). One form of this situation occurs when counselors engage in activities that are not typically associated with the role of a mental health provider and more typically belong to that of a religious or spiritual leader. For example, leading religious rituals, pardoning sins, or giving blessings are ecclesiastical functions not associated with counselors' roles. To engage in them as a counselor is to create role and boundary confusion for clients.

Another way in which counselors might displace religious or spiritual authority is by failing to consult with religious or spiritual leaders when working with clients for whom religion or spirituality is significant. Often, clergy and other spiritual directors can be exceptional resources for client support. A more obvious form of displacing religious or spiritual authority occurs when counselors criticize or denigrate religious leaders and make negative comments about belief systems or spiritual practices (Richards & Bergin, 1997). Not only are these behaviors unethical, they might offend clients who hold their religious and spiritual leaders in high esteem. Certainly clients may express their contempt for or disagreement with their ecclesiastic authorities, and counselors may wisely empathize with them. However, overtly and intentionally lashing out at persons or beliefs with which one disagrees is inappropriate professional conduct.

CASE | **MEREDITH**

Meredith is a counselor who has been in private practice for 10 years. She describes herself as a Christian, but says she is not currently involved in a local church congregation. When her client, Wayne, learned that Meredith was a Christian he began to disclose a complex story of childhood trauma and ritual abuse by his parents and their friends who were members of a satanic cult. Wayne indicated that he had always been frightened by life and asked Meredith, "If there is a God, why didn't he protect me from such horrible experiences?" Although Meredith had not studied Satanic practices, she thought that Christian beliefs could be an antidote to the abuse Wayne had experienced at the hands of his parents.

Meredith then asked Wayne if he would like for her to perform an exorcism to rid him of the satanic demons that remained from his childhood. Wayne agreed, and during the next session, Meredith performed an elaborate and emotionally wrenching exorcism ritual in which she commanded the abusive, Satanic demons to leave Wayne. After the exorcism, Wayne was disappointed that he was not miraculously healed of his lifelong trauma and he became angry with Meredith for "playing charades with my spirit."

In this case, Meredith took on the role of an ecclesiastical leader and performed a religious ritual that was both outside her role and beyond her level of training. She engaged in a religious activity that both confused and angered her client and interfered with his therapeutic goals. Moreover, Meredith did not consult with religious leaders, nor did she seek consultation or supervision with peers or superiors. In short, Meredith failed to be clear about her professional role as that of a counselor, rather than as a spiritual guide whose responsibility it is to assist in the ongoing development of the spiritual self (Ganje-Fling & McCarthy, 1991).

CONSULTATION AND REFERRAL

In many cases, it can be extremely helpful for counselors to consult with respected clergy and other spiritual leaders regarding questions of doctrine, belief, or practice. Doing so assists counselors in understanding their clients' presenting problems and in detecting when clients may have misunderstood or misinterpreted a significant tenet in a religious or spiritual system. In addition, sometimes clients present problems related to a loss of purpose and direction as a result of losing or letting go of their faith (Lukoff, Lu, & Turner, 1992). These circumstances, too, warrant consultation with or referral to clergy. There are also times when exploring clients' religious delusions can be beneficial and therapeutic, however, a referral to a psychiatrist for a medication evaluation and possible ongoing care is desirable (Haug, 1998).

Although referring clients to religious or spiritual leaders might be appropriate in some situations when counselors are aware of having reached their limits, there could also be occasions when to do so would be counterproductive. For example, clients who are struggling with revising their belief systems, or are in the midst of dealing with inner conflict over particular religious doctrines or spiritual practices, might not be helped by religious or spiritual leaders who are rigid and authoritarian. Religious or spiritual leaders who are intent on having their constituents maintain orthodoxy with regard to beliefs and practices could frustrate the therapeutic process. Further, there might be religious or spiritual leaders who are popular in a given community, but who espouse beliefs and values that are contrary to basic axioms of mental health. These persons, though well meaning, might reinforce beliefs and behaviors that are contributing to client distress.

It is prudent for counselors to develop a network of "friendly clergy" (Faiver, Ingersoll, O'Brien, & McNally, 2001) and other spiritual leaders who represent a variety of religions and perspectives. These professionals are persons who can be trusted to support clients' psychological and spiritual growth, and to be positive adjuncts to the therapeutic endeavor.

CASE EXAMPLES

Gordon

Gordon is a Caucasian Episcopal priest who is also a Licensed Professional Counselor (LPC). He is the rector of a large parish in an upper-middle-class suburb of a large city. During the last five years, Gordon has established a private counseling practice that he operates out of his church-owned home. He was given approval by church authorities to use church property for his practice, with the understanding that he would contribute 10% of his profits to the church. Gordon has a caseload of 10 clients whom he sees two evenings a week and on Saturday mornings. Most of these clients are members of Gordon's church. Gordon believes that his practice is an extension of his ministry and contends that he is able to provide both psychological help and spiritual guidance to his clients. Moreover, Gordon boasts that he is free to pray with his clients, bless them, and offer the Sacrament of Holy Communion if circumstances warrant doing these things. He maintains that he is able to assist clients with their doctrinal questions and to enable "the healing of the whole person."

Discussion Questions
1. What ethical issues, if any, do you think Gordon's case raises?
2. What do you think are the positive aspects of Gordon's practice? What are the negative ones?
3. What advice would you give Gordon to help him ensure that he is practicing ethically?
4. If you were a member of Gordon's church and one of his clients, how would you feel about Gordon being both your priest and your counselor?

Dong Chen

Dong Chen is a Chinese American school counselor in a public high school in a large West Coast city. She has the opportunity to work with teens in a variety of capacities, including personal counseling. During several sessions, students reported that Dong Chen had taught them basic meditation techniques and had suggested they use them to manage test anxiety and other forms of stress. In addition, Dong Chen shared with one student the fundamental tenets of Buddhism, including the Four Noble Truths and the paths to enlightenment. When asked by one parent about her religious beliefs, Dong Chen disclosed that she was a Buddhist, but that she didn't force her views on others. She simply shared her religion with students who were interested because she thought it was a way for them to grow in their appreciation of cultural diversity.

Discussion Questions
1. Do you think Dong Chen was practicing ethically? Why or why not?
2. What changes, if any, would you recommend Dong Chen implement in her practice of public school counseling?
3. If you were a parent of one of the students exposed to Dong Chen's counseling approach, how would you feel about her employing spiritual strategies?
4. What alternative ways would you suggest for Dong Chen to increase cultural appreciation in her high school?

Lori

Lori, a Caucasian licensed marriage and family counselor in private practice is a Wicca practitioner. She is a member of a small coven that meets regularly in various homes. Recently, she has been counseling other members of her coven and their partners. During her counseling sessions, Lori often uses themes and symbols that are part of her Wiccan spiritual beliefs. Lori believes that her willingness to counsel others who practice Wicca is a service to them. She is especially aware of the stigma attached to witchcraft in some religions and among many people, especially evangelical and fundamentalist Christians. Therefore, she maintains that she is able to help her Wiccan clients integrate their beliefs into their daily struggles and triumphs because she understands their perspectives. Moreover, Lori claims that most Wicca practitioners do not feel free to reveal their spiritual beliefs to mainstream counselors because of fear of rejection or reprisal.

Discussion Questions
1. What ethical issues does Lori's practice raise for you?
2. What questions would you ask Lori about her desire to counsel members of her own coven?
3. What benefits and liabilities do you see for Lori's approach to spiritual counseling?
4. What recommendations would you make to Lori if she continues to counsel Wiccan clients?
5. If you were one of Lori's clients, how would you feel about having her as your counselor?
6. If you were a member of Lori's coven, how would you feel about other members' being in therapy with Lori?

SUGGESTED ACTIVITIES

Invite a Bureaucrat

If it is geographically and logistically feasible, invite a member of your state's licensure board or grievance committee to attend your class. Prepare a set of questions for him or her about your board's position on counselors' integrating religious and spiritual issues into their practices. Use the cases in this chapter or develop your own to which your guest may respond. If it is not possible for a licensure board member to visit your class, arrange a telephone interview that could be audiotaped and shared with other class members.

Call a Colleague

Contact a colleague in one of the mental health disciplines in your community. Ask him or her what ethical issues come to mind for counselors who want to use religious or spiritual strategies in their practice. Share the case vignettes in this chapter, or develop your own and ask your colleague how he or she would handle these dilemmas.

Interview a Religious or Spiritual Leader

Arrange interviews with at least two religious or spiritual leaders in your community. Ask them whether or not they counsel their constituents and what kinds of ethical concerns they have if they do provide such counseling. Ask them about the nature of their counseling training and how they handle cases that they believe are too time-consuming or are beyond their level of expertise. Share with them some of the issues raised in this chapter, especially regarding dual relationships, imposition of values, and work-setting boundaries and get their reactions to these ideas.

SUPPLEMENTAL READING

Haug, I. E. (1998). Including a spiritual dimension in family therapy: Ethical considerations. *Contemporary Family Therapy, 20,* 181–194. In this article, the author addresses many important ethical issues that arise in the context of counselors providing mental health services with a spiritual dimension. Haug organizes her article around the moral principles of autonomy, beneficence, nonmaleficence, justice, and fidelity advocated by Kitchener (1984).

Rave, E. J., & Larsen, C. C. (Eds.). (1995). *Ethical decision-making in therapy: Feminist perspectives.* New York: Guilford Press. In this book, the authors present a feminist viewpoint as they address the major ethical themes in the mental health profession's code of ethics. Although this book is not focused specifically on religious and spiritual issues, chapters dealing with overlapping relationships provide challenging ideas. Included is a feminist code of ethics that expands the existing professional ethical codes.

Richards, P. S., & Bergin, A. E. (1997). Ethical issues and guidelines. In P. S. Richards and A. E. Bergin, *A spiritual strategy for counseling and psychotherapy* (pp. 143–169). Washington, DC: American Psychological Association. This chapter provides an in-depth treatment of the ethical issues that surface when counselors work with clients' religious and spiritual issues in therapy. Although the authors focus much of their material on theistic religions, applications to other types of spirituality are readily made.

REFERENCES

Ackelsberg, M. (1986). Spirituality, community, politics: B'not Esh and the feminist reconstruction of Judaism. *Journal of Feminist Studies of Religion, 2*, 107–120.

Adler, M. (1986). *Drawing down the moon.* New York: Beacon Press.

Alcoholics Anonymous. (1976). *Alcoholics Anonymous* (3rd ed.). New York: Alcoholics Anonymous World Services.

Allen, J. (1989). *We the people: An atlas of America's ethnic diversity.* New York: Macmillan.

Alpert, R. (1991). Our lives *are* the text: Exploring Jewish women's rituals. *Bridges, 2*, 66–80.

Allport, G. W. (1950.) *The individual and his religion.* New York: Macmillan.

Allport, G., & Ross, J. M. (1967). Personal religious orientation and prejudice. *Journal of Personality and Social Psychology, 5*, 432–443.

American Association for Marriage and Family Therapy (AAMFT). (1991). *AAMFT code of ethics.* Washington, DC: Author.

American Counseling Association (ACA). (1995). *Code of ethics and standards of practice.* Alexandria, VA: Author.

American Psychiatric Association. (1994). *Diagnostic and statistical manual of mental disorders* (4th ed.). Washington, DC: Author.

American Psychological Association (APA). (1992). *Ethical principles of psychologists and code of conduct.* Washington, DC: Author.

Andersen, T. (1987). The reflecting team: Dialogue and meta-dialogue in clinical work. *Family Process, 26*, 415–428.

Andersen, T. (1991). *The reflecting team: Dialogue and dialogues about the dialogues.* New York: Norton.

Anderson, B. S. (1996). *The counselor and the law* (4th ed.). Alexandria, VA: American Counseling Association.

Anderson, G. (1995). Walking through the valley of the shadow of death: Grief and fundamentalism. In J. K. Parry & A. S. Ryan (Eds.), *A cross-cultural look at death, dying, and religion.* Chicago: Nelson-Hall.

Anderson, D. A. (1994). Transcendence and relinquishment in couple therapy. *Journal of Systemic Therapies, 13,* 36–41.

Anderson, D. A., & Worthen, D. (1997). Exploring a fourth dimension: Spirituality as a resource for the couple counselor. *Journal of Marital and Family Therapy, 23,* 3–12.

Anderson, H., & Goolishian, H. (1988). Human systems as linguistic systems: Preliminary and evolving ideas about the implications for clinical theory. *Family Process, 27,* 371–393.

Anderson, H., & Goolishian, H. (1991, October). *"Not Knowing": A critical element of a collaborative language systems therapy approach.* Plenary address presented at the 1991 Annual American Association for Marriage and Family Therapy Conference, Dallas, TX.

Anderson, H., & Goolishian, H. (1992). The client is the expert: A not-knowing approach to therapy. In S. McNamee & K. J. Gergen (Eds.), *Therapy as social construction* (pp. 25–39). London: Sage.

Anderson, W. T. (1990). *Reality isn't what it used to be.* San Francisco: Harper & Row.

Aponte, H. J. (1994). *Bread and spirit: therapy with the new poor.* New York: Morton Press.

Aponte, H. J. (1996). Political bias, moral values, and spirituality in the training of psychotherapists. *Bulletin of the Menninger Clinic, 60,* 488–502.

Aponte, H. J., & Winter, J. E. (1987). The person and practice of the therapist: Treatment and training. *Journal of Psychotherapy and the Family, 3,* 85–111.

Applewhite, S. L. (1995). *Curanderismo:* Demystifying the health beliefs and practices of elderly Mexican Americans. *Health and Social Work, 20,* 247–253.

Argyle, M., & Beit-Hallahmi, B. (1975). *The social psychology of religion.* London: Routledge & Kegal Paul.

Armstrong, K. (1993). *A history of God.* New York: Knopf.

Assagioli, R. (1965). *Psychosynthesis: A manual of principles and techniques.* New York: Viking Penguin.

Assagioli, R. (1989). Self-realization and psychological disturbances. In S. Grof & C. Grof (Eds.), *Spiritual emergency: When personal transformation becomes a crisis* (pp. 27–48). Los Angeles: Tarcher.

Assagioli, R. (1993). *Transpersonal development: The development beyond psychosynthesis.* San Francisco: Harper.

Attneave, C. (1982). American Indians and Alaska Native families: Emigrants in their own homeland. In M. McGolddrick, J. K. Pearce, & J. Giordano (Eds.), *Ethnicity and family therapy* (1st ed., pp. 55–83). New York: Guilford Press.

Baker, B. (1999). Mourning in America. *Common Boundary, 17,* 20–26.

Ball, R. A., & Goodyear, R. K. (1991). Self-reported professional practices of Christian psychologists. *Journal of Psychology and Christianity, 10,* 144–153.

Bandura, A. (1986). *Social foundations of thought and action: A social-cognitive theory.* Englewood Cliffs, NJ: Prentice-Hall.

Banks, J. (1991). *Teaching strategies for ethnic studies* (5th ed.). Boston: Allyn & Bacon.

Baron, S. (1962). *Brewed in America: A history of beer and ale in the United States.* Boston: Little, Brown.

Barret, D. G. (1996). Religion: World religious statistics. In *Encyclopedia Britannica Book of the Year* (p. 298). Chicago: Encyclopedia Britannica.

Barret, R., & Barzan, R. (1996). Spiritual experiences of gay men and lesbians. *Counseling and Values, 41,* 4–15.

Batson, C. D., Schoenrode, P., & Ventis, W. C. (1993). *Religion and the individual: A social-psychological perspective.* New York: Oxford University Press.

Batson, C. D., & Ventis, W. L. (1982). *The religious experience.* New York: Oxford University Press.

Bean, R. A., Perry, B. J., and Bedell, T. M. (2001). Developing culturally competent marriage and family therapists: Guidelines for working with Hispanic families. *Journal of Marital and Family Therapy, 27,* 43–54.

Beavers, W. R., & Hampson, R. B. (1990). *Successful families: Assessment and intervention.* New York: Norton.

Beck, V., & Walters, A. L. (1977). *The sacred ways of knowledge: sources of life.* Tsaile (Navajo Nation), AZ: Navajo Community College Press.

Becker, C. B. (1989). Rebirth and afterlife in Buddhism. In A. Berger, P. Badham, A. H. Kutscher, J. Berger, M. Perry, & J. Beloff (Eds.), *Perspectives on death and dying: Cross-cultural and multi-disciplinary views* (pp. 108–125). Philadelphia: Charles Press.

Becker, E. (1973). *The denial of death.* New York: Free Press.

Becvar, D. S. (1997). Soul healing and the family. *Journal of Family Social Work, 2,* 1–11.

Becvar, D. S., & Becvar, R. J. (1996). *Family therapy: A systematic integration.* Boston: Allyn & Bacon.

Beit-Hallahmi, B. (1989). *Prolegomena to the psychology of religion.* Lewisburg, PA: Bucknell University Press.

Benningfield, M. F. (1998). Addressing spiritual/religious issues in therapy: Potential problems and complications. In D. S. Becvar (Ed.), *The family, spirituality and social work* (pp. 25–42). New York: Haworth Press.

Benson, H. (1996). *Timeless healing: The power and biology of belief.* New York: Scribner.

Benson, P. L., & Spilka, B. (1973). God image as a function of self-esteem and locus of control. *Journal for the Scientific Study of Religion, 12,* 297–310.

Bergin, A. E. (1980). Psychotherapy and religious values. *Journal of Consulting and Clinical Psychology, 48,* 75–105.

Bergin, A. E. (1983). Religiosity and mental health: A critical reevaluation and meta-analysis. *Professional Psychology: Research and Practice, 14,* 170–184.

Bergin, A. E. (1988). Three contributions of a spiritual perspective to counseling, psychotherapy, and behavior change. *Counseling and Values, 32,* 21–31.

Bergin, A. E. (1991). Values and religious issues in psychotherapy and mental health. *American Psychologist, 46,* 394–403.

Bergin, A. E. (1993). *Adaptive/healthy versus maladaptive/unhealthy religious lifestyles.* Unpublished manuscript, Brigham Young University, Provo, UT.

Bergin, A. E., & Jensen, J. P. (1990). Religiosity of psychotherapists: A national survey. *Psychotherapy, 27,* 3–7.

Bergin, A. E., Masters, K. S., & Richards, P. S. (1987). Religiousness and mental health reconsidered: A study of an intrinsically religious sample. *Journal of Counseling Psychology, 34,* 197–204.

Bergin, A. E., & Payne, I. R. (1991). Proposed agenda for a spiritual strategy in personality and psychotherapy. *Journal of Psychology and Christianity, 10,* 197–210.

Bernal, G. (1982). Cuban families. In M. McGoldrick, J. K. Pearce, & J. Giordano (Eds.), *Ethnicity and family therapy,* (1st ed., pp. 187–207). New York: Guilford Press.

Bernal, G., & Gutierrez, M. (1988). Cubans. In L. Comas-Diaz & E. H. Griffith (Eds.), *Clinical guidelines in cross-cultural mental health.* New York: Wiley.

Bernstein, A. (2000). Straight therapists working with lesbians and gays in family therapy. *Journal of Marital and Family Therapy, 46,* 443–454.

Berry, F. (1978). Contemporary bibliotherapy: Systematizing the field. In R. Rubin (Ed.), *Bibliotherapy sourcebook* (pp. 185–190). Phoenix, AZ: Oryz Press.

Bersoff, D. N. (1996). The virtue of principle ethics. *Counseling Psychologist, 24*(1), 86–91.

Bewley, A. R. (1995). Re-membering spirituality: Use of sacred ritual in psychotherapy. In J. Ochshorn & E. Cole (Eds.), *Women's spirituality, women's lives* (pp. 201–214). New York: Haworth Press.

Bianchi, E. C. (1989). Psychotherapy as religion: Pros and cons. *Pastoral psychology, 38,* 67–81.

Bickel, C. O., Ciarrocchi, J., Sheers, N. J., Estadt, B. K., Powell, D. A., & Pargament, K. (1998). Perceived stress, religious coping styles, and depressive affect. *Journal of Psychology and Christianity, 17,* 33–42.

Billingsley, A. (1968). *Black families in White America*. Englewood Cliffs, NJ: Prentice-Hall.

Billingsley, A. (1992). *Climbing Jacob's ladder: The enduring legacy of African-American families*. New York: Simon & Schuster.

Bilu, Y., Witztum, E., & Van der Hart, O. (1990). Paradise regained: "Miraculous Healing" in an Israeli psychiatric clinic. *Culture, Medicine, and Psychiatry, 14*, 105–127.

Bloch, J. P. (1998). *New spirituality, self, and belonging: How new agers and neo-pagans talk about themselves*. Westport, CT: Praeger.

Blumenfeld, W. J., & Raymond, K. (1988). *Looking at gay and lesbian life*. New York: Philosophical Library.

Bobin, C. (1999). *The secret of St. Francis of Assisi: A meditation*. Boston: Shambhala.

Bogolub, E. (1991). Women and mid-life divorce: Some practice issues. *Social Work, 36*, 428–433.

Booth, L. (1992). The stages of religious addiction. *Creation Spirituality, 8*(4), 22–25.

Borg, M. J. (1997). *The God we never knew*. New York: HarperCollins.

Boswell, J. (1980). *Christianity, social tolerance, and homosexuality*. Chicago: University of Chicago Press.

Boswell, T. D., & Curtis, J. R. (1984). *The Cuban-American experience: Culture, images, and perspectives*. Totowa, NJ: Rowman & Allanheld.

Bowen, M. (1972). Toward differentiation of self in one's own family. In J. L. Framo (Ed.), *Family interaction* (pp. 111–173). New York: Springer.

Bowen, M. (1978). *Family therapy in clinical practice*. New York: Jason Aronson.

Bowker, J. (1991). *The meaning of death*. Cambridge: Cambridge University Press.

Boyd-Franklin, N. (1989). *Black families in therapy: A multisystems approach*. New York: Guilford Press.

Boyd-Franklin, N., & Lockwood, T. W. (1999). Spirituality and religion: Implications for psychotherapy with African American clients and families. In F. Walsh (Ed.), *Spiritual Resources in Family Therapy* (pp. 90–103). New York: Guilford Press.

Breitman, B. E. (1995). Social and spiritual reconstruction of self within a feminist Jewish community. *Women & Therapy, 16*, 73–82.

Brice-Baker, J. (1996). Jamaican families. In M. McGoldrick, J. Giordano, & J. K. Pearce (Eds.), *Ethnicity and family therapy* (2nd ed., pp. 85–96). New York: Guilford Press.

Brown, J. E. (1987). *The spiritual legacy of the American Indian*. New York: Crossroad.

Brown, M. H. (2001). A psychosynthesis twelve step program for transforming consciousness: Creative explorations of inner space. *Counseling and Values, 45*, 103–117.

Brown, T., Stein, K., Huang, K., & Harris, D. (1973). Mental illness and the role of mental health facilities in Chinatown. In S. Sue & N. Wagner (Eds.), *Asian Americans: Psychological perspectives* (pp. 213–231). Palo Alto, CA: Science & Behavior Books.

Brussat, F., & Brussat, M. (1993). Children's spirituality: A resource companion. *Value and Visions, 24*, 5.

Bucko, R. A. (1999). *The Lakota ritual of the sweat lodge: History and contemporary practice*. Lincoln: University of Nebraska Press.

Budman, S. H., & Gurman, A. S. (1989). *Theory and practice of brief therapy*. New York: Guilford Press.

Bufe, C. (1998). *Alcoholics Anonymous: Cult or cure* (2nd ed.). San Francisco: Sharp Press.

Bullis, R. K. (1996). *Spirituality in social work practice*. Washington, DC: Taylor & Francis.

Burke, M. T. (1998, Winter). From the chair. *The CACREP Connection, 2*.

Burrows, R. J. L. (1986, May 16). Americans get religion in the new age: Anything is permissible if everything is God. *Christianity Today, 30*, 17–23.

Burton, L. A. (1992). *Religion and the family: When God helps*. New York: Haworth Press.

Burtt, E. (1955). *The teachings of the compassionate Buddha*. New York: New American Library.

Busto, R. V. (1996). The gospel according to the model minority?: Hazarding an interpretation of Asian American Evangelical college students. *Amerasia Journal, 22,* 133–147.

Butler, K. (1990, September/October). Spirituality reconsidered. *Family Therapy Networker,* 26–37.

Butler, M. H., Gardner, B. C., & Bird, M. H. (1998). Not just a time-out: Change dynamics of prayer for religious couples in conflict situations. *Family Process, 37,* 451–478.

Butler, M. H., & Harper, J. M. (1994). The divine triangle: God in the marital system of religious couples. *Family Process, 33,* 277–286.

Cade, B., & O'Hanlon W. H. (1993). *A brief guide to brief therapy.* New York: Norton.

Callanan, M., & Kelley, P. (1992). *Final gifts: Understanding the special awareness, needs, and communications of the dying.* New York: Bantam Books.

Cameron, J. (1992). The artist's way: A spiritual path to higher creativity. New York: Putnam.

Campbell, D. (1992). *Campbell Interest and Skill Survey.* Minneapolis: NCS Assessments.

Campbell, J. (1968). *The hero with a thousand faces.* Princeton, NJ: Princeton University Press.

Campbell, J. (1971). *The portable Jung.* New York: Viking Press.

Campbell, J. (1986). *The inner reaches of space: Metaphor as myth as religion.* New York: Alfred Van Der Marck.

Campbell, J. (1988). *The power of myth.* New York: Doubleday.

Campbell, V. L. (1990). A model for using tests in counseling. In C. E. Watkins, Jr., & V. L. Campbell, *Testing in counseling practice* (pp. 1–7). Hillsdale, NJ: Lawrence Erlbaum.

Cantor, A. (1979). A Jewish woman's Haggadah. In C. Christ & J. Plaskow (Eds.), *WomanSpirit Rising* (pp. 185–194). San Francisco: Harper & Row.

Cargas, H. J., & Radley, R. J. (1981). *Keeping a spiritual journal.* Garden City, NY: Doubleday.

Carlson, C. R., Bacaseta, P. E., & Simanton, D. A. (1988). A controlled evaluation of devotional meditation and progressive relaxation. *Journal of Psychology and Theology, 16,* 362–368.

Cavelletti, S. (1983). *The religious potential of the child.* New York: Paulist Press.

Cervantes, J. M., & Ramirez, O. (1992). Spirituality and family dynamics in psychotherapy with Latino children. In L. A. Vargas & J. D. Koss-Chioino (Eds.), *Working with culture: Psychotherapeutic interventions with ethnic minority children and adolescents* (pp. 103–128). San Francisco: Jossey-Bass.

Chan, W-T. (1963). *A sourcebook in Chinese philosophy.* Princeton, NJ: Princeton University Press.

Chandler, C. K., Holden, J. M., & Kolander, C. A. (1992). Counseling for spiritual wellness: Theory and practice. *Journal of Counseling and Development, 71,* 168–175.

Chandler, R. (1988). *Understanding the new age.* Dallas, TX: Word Publishing.

Chatters, L. M., & Taylor, R. J. (1989). Age differences in religious participation among black adults. *Journal of Gerontology, 44,* S183–S189.

Chatton, B. (1988, Spring). Apply with caution: Bibliotherapy in the library. *Journal of Youth Services in Libraries, 1,* 334–338.

Chien, C. P., & Yamamoto, J. (1982). Asian-American and Pacific-Islander patients. In F. X. Acosta, J. Yamamoto, & L. A. Evans (Eds.), *Effective psychotherapy for lower income and minority patients* (p. 117–145). New York: Plenum Press.

Christ, C. P. (1979). Why women need the Goddess: Phenomenological, psychological, and political reflections. In C. Christ & J. Plaskow (Eds.), *WomanSpirit Rising* (pp. 273–287). San Francisco: Harper & Row.

Christ, C. P. (1995). *Diving deep and surfacing: Women writers on a spiritual quest* (3rd ed.). Boston: Beacon Press.

Christ, C. P. (1997). *Rebirth of the goddess: Finding meaning in feminist spirituality.* New York: Addison-Wesley.

Christensen, C. P. (1989). Cross-cultural awareness development: A conceptual model. *Counselor Education and Supervision, 28,* 270–289.

Clark, J. M. (1991). Prophesy, subjectivity, and theodicy in gay theology: Developing a constructive methodology. In M. L. Stemmeler & J. M. Clark (Eds.), *Constructing gay theology* (pp. 27–44). Las Colinas, TX: Monument Press.

Clark, J. M., Brown, J. C., & Hochstein, L. M. (1990). Institutional religion and gay/lesbian oppression. In F. W. Bozett & M. B. Sussman (Eds.), *Homosexuality and family relations* (pp. 265–284). New York: Haworth Press.

Clements, P. (1994, April 22). From gay to ex-gay, part I: The ex-gays. *Stonewall News* (Tampa, FL), 5–8.

Clinebell, H. (1984). *Basic types of pastoral care and counseling.* Nashville, TN: Parthenon Press.

Cloyd, B. S. (1997). *Children and prayer: A shared pilgrimage.* Nashville, TN: Upper Room Books.

Colapinto, J. (1991). Structural family therapy. In A. S. Gurman & D. P. Kniskern (Eds.), *Handbook of family therapy,* (Vol. 2, pp. 417–443). New York: Bruner/Mazel.

Colapinto, J. (2000). Structural family therapy. In A. M. Horne (Ed.), *Family counseling and therapy* (3rd ed. pp. 140–169), Itasca, IL: Peacock.

Cole, B. S., & Pargament, K. I. (1999). Spiritual surrender: A paradoxical path to control. In W. R. Miller (Ed.), *Integrating spirituality into treatment* (pp. 179–198). Washington, DC: American Psychological Association.

Coles, R. (1990). *The spiritual life of children.* Boston: Houghton Mifflin.

Coles, R. (1992). *The spiritual life of children.* London: HarperCollins.

Collins, J. J. (1991). *The cult experience: An overview of cults, their traditions, and why people join them.* Springfield, IL: Charles C. Thomas.

Collins, J. R., Hurst, J. C., & Jacobson, J. K. (1987). The blind spot extended: Spirituality. *Journal of College Student Personnel, 28,* 274–276.

Collins, P. H. (1990). *Black feminist thought: Knowledge, consciousness, and the politics of empowerment.* New York: Routledge.

Collins, S. D. (1974). *A different heaven and earth: A feminist perspective on religion.* Valley Forge, PA: Judson Press.

Comas-Diaz, L. (1989). Culturally relevant issues and treatment implications for Hispanics. In D. R. Koslow & E. Salett (Eds.), *Crossing cultures in mental health.* Washington, DC: Society for International Education Training and Research (SIETAR).

Comas-Diaz, L. (1993). Hispanic/Latino communities: Psychological implications. In D. R. Atkinson, G. Morten, & D. W. Sue (Eds.), *Counseling American minorities: A cross-cultural perspective,* (4th ed., pp. 245–263). Madison, WI: Brown & Benchmark.

Comas-Diaz, L., & Griffith, E. (1988). *Clinical guidelines in cross cultural mental health.* New York: Wiley.

Combs, G., & Freedman, J. (1990). *Symbol, story, and ceremony: Using metaphor in individual and family therapy.* New York: Norton.

Constantine, M. G., Lewis, E. L., Conner, L. C., & Sanchez, D. (2000). Addressing spiritual and religious issues in counseling African Americans: Implications for counselor training and practice. *Counseling and Values, 45,* 28–38.

Cook, D. A. (1993). Research in African American churches: A mental health counseling imperative. *Journal of Mental Health Counseling, 15,* 320–333.

Cook, D. A., & Wiley, C. Y. (2000). Psychotherapy with members of African American churches and spiritual traditions. In P. S. Richards & A. E. Bergin (Eds.), *Handbook of Psychotherapy and Religious Diversity* (pp. 369–396). Washington, DC: American Psychological Association.

Corey, G. (2001). *Theory and practice of counseling and psychotherapy* (6th ed.). Pacific Grove, CA: Brooks/Cole.

Corey, G., Corey, M. S., & Callanan, P. (1998). *Issues and ethics in the helping professions* (5th ed.). Pacific Grove, CA: Brooks/Cole.

Cornwall, M., & Thomas, D. L. (1990). Family, religion, and personal communities: Examples from Mormonism. *Marriage and Family Review, 15,* 229–252.

Corr, C. A., Nabe, C. M., & Corr, D. M. (1997). *Death and dying, life and living* (2nd ed.). Pacific Grove, CA: Brooks/Cole.

A Course in Miracles. (1992). Glen Ellen, CA: Foundation for Inner Peace.

Crawford, R. L. (1994). *Avoiding counselor malpractice.* Alexandria, VA: American Counseling Association.

Crompton, M. (1998). *Children, spirituality, religion, and social work.* Aldershot, England: Ashgate.

Cromwell, R. E., & Peterson, G. W. (1983). Multisystem-multimethod family assessment in clinical contexts. *Family Process, 22,* 147–163.

Cross, W. (1991). *Shades of black: Diversity in African-American Identity.* Philadelphia: Temple University Press.

Csikszentmihalyi, M., & Csikszentmihalyi, I. (1988). *Psychological studies of flow in consciousness.* New York: Cambridge University Press.

Curtis, R. C., & Davis, K. M. (1999). Spirituality and multimodal therapy: A practical approach to incorporating spirituality in counseling. *Counseling and Values, 43,* 199–210.

Cuthbert, B., Kristeller, J. L., Simons, R., & Lang, P. J. (1981). Strategies of arousal control: Biofeedback, meditation, and motivation. *Journal of Experimental Psychology: General, 110,* 518–546.

Davidson, M. G. (2000). Religion and spirituality. In R. M. Perez, K. A. DeBord, & K. J. Bieschke (Eds.), *Handbook of counseling and psychotherapy with lesbian, gay and bisexual clients* (pp. 409–433).Washington, DC: American Psychological Association.

Davis, J. B. (1914). *Moral and vocational guidance.* Boston: Ginn.

Dayringer, R. (1989). *The heart of pastoral counseling: Healing through relationships.* Grand Rapids, MI: Zondervan.

Delbane, R., & Montgomery, H. (1981). *The breath of life: Discovering your breath prayer.* San Francisco: Harper & Row.

Delgado, M. (1978). Folk medicine in Puerto Rican culture. *International Social Work, 21,* 46–54.

Denny, F. M. (1993). Islam and the Muslim community. In H. B. Earhart (Ed.), *Religions and traditions of the world* (pp. 605–712). San Francisco: HarperSanFrancisco.

de Shazer, S. (1985). *Keys to solution in brief therapy.* New York: Norton.

de Shazer, S. (1990). What is it about brief therapy that works? In J. K. Zeig & S. L. Gilligan (Eds.), *Brief therapy: Myths, methods, and metaphors* (pp. 90–99). New York: Bruner/Mazel.

DeStefano, T. J., & Richardson, P. (1992). The relationship between paper and pencil wellness measures to objective physiological indexes. *Journal of Counseling and Development, 71,* 226–230.

Deutsch, A. (1975). Observations on a sidewalk ashram. *Archives of General Psychiatry, 32,* 166–175.

DiBlasio, F. A. (1988). Integrative strategies for family therapy with evangelical Christians. *Journal of Psychology and Theology, 16,* 127–134.

DiBlasio, F. A., & Benda, B. B. (1991). Practitioners, religion and the use of forgiveness in the clinical setting. *Journal of Psychology and Christianity, 11,* 181–187.

Dilthey, W. (1978). *Dilthey's philosophy of existence: Introduction to Weltanschauungslehre* (W. Kluback & M. Weinbaum, Trans.). Westport, CT: Greenwood Press.

Dinges, N. G., Trimble, J. E., Manson, S. M., & Pasquale, F. L. (1981). Counseling and psychotherapy with American Indians and Alaska Natives. In A. J. Marsella & P. B. Pedersen (Eds.), *Cross-cultural counseling and psychotherapy* (pp. 243–276). New York: Pergamon.

Doka, K. J. (1993). The spiritual needs of the dying. In K. J. Doka & J. D. Morgan (Eds.), *Death and spirituality* (pp. 143–150). Amityville, NY: Baywood.

Domino, G. (1990). Clergy's knowledge of psychopathology. *Journal of Psychology and Theology, 18,* 32–39.

Dossey, L. (1993). *Healing words.* New York: HarperCollins.

Downing, C. (1981). *The goddess: Mythological images of the feminine.* New York: Crossroad.

Downing, N., & Roush, K. (1985). From passive acceptance to active commitment: A model of feminist identity development for women. *Counseling Psychologist, 13,* 695–709.

Dudley, J. R., Smith, C., & Millison, M. B. (1995, March/April). Unfinished business: Assessing the spiritual needs of hospice clients. *American Journal of Hospice and Palliative Care,* 30–37.

Dugan, K. M. (1985). *The vision quest of the plains Indians: Its spiritual significance.* Lewiston, NY: Mellen Press.

Duhl, F. S., Kantor, D., & Duhl, B. S. (1973). Learning space and action in family therapy: A primer of sculpting (pp. 47–63). In D. Block (Ed.), *Techniques in family psychotherapy: A primer.* New York: Grune & Stratton.

Dukepoo, P. C. (1980). *The elder American Indian.* San Diego, CA: Campanile.

Duncan, H. D., Eddy, J. P., & Haney, C. W. (1981). Using religious resources in crisis intervention. *Counseling and Values, 25,* 178–191.

Dynes, W. R., & Donaldson, S. (1992). *Studies in homosexuality: Vol. XII. Homosexuality and religion and philosophy.* New York: Garland.

Earhart, H. B. (1993). Religions of Japan: Many traditions, one sacred way (pp. 1077–1187). In H. B. Earhart (Ed.), *Religions and traditions of the world.* San Francisco: HarperSanFrancisco.

Eckstein, Y. (1984). *What you should know about Jews and Judaism.* Waco, TX: Word.

Efran, J., Lukens, R., & Lukens, M. (1988). Constructivism: What's in it for you? *Family Therapy Networker, 12,* 26–35.

Elkind, D. (1971). The development of religious understanding in children and adolescents. In M. P. Strommen (Ed.), *Research of religious development* (pp. 655–685). New York: Hawthorne Books.

Elkins, D. N., Hedstrom, L. J., Hughes, L. L., Leaf, J. A., & Saunders, C. (1988). Toward a humanistic-phenomenological spirituality. *Journal of Humanistic Psychology, 28,* 5–18.

Eller, C. (1993). *Living in the lap of the goddess: The feminist spirituality movement in America.* New York: Crossroad.

Ellis, A. (1980). Psychotherapy and atheistic values: A response to A. E. Bergin's "Psychotherapy and religious values." *Journal of Consulting and Clinical Psychology, 48,* 635–639.

Ellis, A. (1989). History of cognition in psychotherapy. In A. Freeman, K. M. Simon, L. E. Beutler, & H. Arkowitz (Eds.), *Comprehensive handbook of cognitive therapy* (pp. 5–19). New York: Plenum.

Ellis, A., & Schoenfeld, E. (1990). Divine intervention and the treatment of chemical dependency. *Journal of Substance Abuse, 2,* 459–468.

Ellison, C. W. (1983). Spiritual well-being: Conceptualization and measusrement. *Journal of Psychology and Theology, 11,* 330–340.

Ellwood, R. S. (1993). Witchcraft. *Encarta Encyclopedia.* Redmond, WA: Microsoft Corp.

Emrick, C. D., Tonigan, J. S., Montgomery, H., & Little, L. (1993). Alcoholics Anonymous: What is currently known? In B. S. McCrady & W. R. Miller (Eds.), *Research on Alcoholics Anonymous: Opportunities and alternatives* (pp. 41–76). New Brunswick, NJ: Rutgers Center of Alcohol Studies.

Enright, R. D., Freedman, S., & Risque, J. (1998). The psychology of interpersonal forgiveness. In R. D. Enright & J. North (Eds.), *Exploring forgiveness* (pp. 46–47). Madison: University of Wisconsin Press.

Erikson, E. H. (1963). *Childhood and society* (2nd ed.) New York: Norton.

Erikson, E. H. (1966). Ontogeny of ritualization in man. In J. Huxley (Organizer), A discussion of ritualization of behaviour in animals and man. *Philosophical Transactions of the Royal Society of London: Series B, Biological Sciences, 251* (772), 337–349.

Estes, C. P. (1997). *Women who run with the wolves: Myths and stories of the wild woman archetype.* New York: Ballentine Books.

Etemad, B. (1978). Extrication from cultism. *Current Psychiatric Therapy, 18,* 217–223.

Eugene, T. M. (1995). There is a balm in Gilead: Black women and the Black church as agents of a therapeutic community. *Women and Therapy, 16,* 55–71.

Fabrega, H., & Manning, P. K. (1973). An integrated theory of disease: Latino-Mestizo views of disease in the Chiapas Highlands. *Psychosomatic Medicine, 35,* 223–239.

Faiver, C., & O'Brien, E. M. (1993). Assessment of Religious Beliefs Form. *Counseling and Values, 37,* 176–178.

Faiver, C., O'Brien, E. M., & McNally, C. (1998). The "friendly clergy": Characteristics and referral. *Counseling and Values, 42,* 217–221.

Faiver, C., Ingersoll, R. E., O'Brien, E., McNally, C. (2001). *Explorations in counseling and spirituality.* Pacific Grove, CA: Brooks/Cole.

Falicov, C. J. (1996). Mexican families. In M. McGoldrick, J. Giordano, & J. K. Pearce (Eds.), *Ethnicity and family therapy* (2nd ed., pp. 169–182). New York: Guilford Press.

Falicov, C. J. (1999). Religion and spiritual folk traditions in immigrant families: Therapeutic resources with Latinos. In F. Walsh (Ed.), *Spiritual resources in family therapy* (pp. 104–120). New York: Guilford Press.

Fanon, F. (1967). *Black skin. White masks.* New York: Grove Press.

Fenichel, O. (1945). *The psychoanalytic theory of neurosis.* New York: Norton.

Ferch, S. R. (2000). Meanings of touch and forgiveness: A hermeneutic phenomenological inquiry. *Counseling and Values, 44,* 155–173.

Ferguson, M. (1980). *The aquarian conspiracy: Personal and social transformation in the 1980s.* Los Angeles: Tarcher.

Finn, M., & Rubin, J. B. (2000). Psychotherapy with Buddhists. In P. S. Richards & A. E. Bergin (Eds.), *Handbook of psychotherapy and religious diversity* (pp. 317–340). Washington, DC: American Psychological Association.

Finney, J. R., & Malony, H. N. (1985). An empirical study of contemplative prayer as an adjunct to psychotherapy. *Journal of Psychology and Theology, 13,* 284–290.

Fischer, L., & Sorenson, G. P. (1985). *School law for counselors, psychologists, and social workers.* New York: Longman.

Fishbane, M. (1993). Judaism: Revelation and traditions. In H. B. Earhart (Ed.), *Religious traditions of the world.* San Francisco: HarperSanFrancisco.

Fleuridas, C., Nelson, T. S., & Rosenthal, D. M. (1986). The evolution of circular questions: Training family therapists. *Journal of Marital and Family Therapy, 12,* 113–127.

Folayan, A. (1992). African-American issues: The soul of it. In B. Berzon (Ed.), *Positively gay: new approaches to gay and lesbian life* (pp. 235–239). Berkeley, CA: Celestial Arts.

Fong, M. L., & Cox, B. G. (1983). Trust as an underlying dynamic in the counseling process: How clients test trust. *Personnel and Guidance Journal, 62,* 163–166.

Fortunato, J. E. (1987). *AIDS: The spiritual dilemma.* San Francisco: Harper & Row.

Fortune, M. (1989). *Is nothing sacred? When sex invades the pastoral relationship.* San Francisco: Harper & Row.

Foster, G. M. (1960). *Culture and conquest.* Chicago: Quadrangle Books.

Fowler, J. W. (1981). *Stages of faith.* New York: Harper & Row.

Fowler, J. W. (1987). *Faith development and pastoral care.* Philadelphia: Fortress Press.

Fowler, J. W. (1991). Stages in faith consciousness. *New Directions for Child Development, 52,* 27–45.

Fowler, J. W. (1996). *Faithful change: The personal and public challenges of postmodern life.* Nashville, TN: Abingdon Press.

Fowler, J. W., & Keen, S. (1978). *Life maps: Conversations on the journey of faith.* Waco, TX: Word Books.

Fox, M. (1994). The spiritual journey of the homosexual . . . and just about everyone else. In R. Nugent (Ed.), *A challenge to love: Gay and lesbian Catholics in the church.* New York: Crossword.

Frame, M. W. (1996). A social constructionist approach to counseling religious couples. *Family Journal, 4,* 299–307.

Frame, M. W. (2000). The spiritual genogram in family therapy. *Journal of Marital and Family Therapy, 26*, 211–216.

Frame, M. W., & Williams, C. B. (1996). Counseling African Americans: Integrating spirituality in therapy. *Counseling and Values, 41*, 16–28.

Framo, J. (1976). Family of origin as a therapeutic resource for adults in marital therapy: You can and should go home again. *Family Process, 15*, 193–210.

Frankiel, S. S. (1993). Christianity: A way of salvation. In H. B. Earhart (Ed.), *Religious Traditions of the World*. San Francisco: HarperSanFrancsico.

Frankl, V. E. (1963). *Man's search for meaning*. Boston: Beacon Press.

Freedman, S. (1998). Forgiveness and reconciliation: The importance of understanding how they differ. *Counseling and Values, 42*, 200–216.

Freedman, S., & Enright, R. D. (1996). Forgiveness as an intervention goal with incest survivors. *Journal of Consulting and Clinical Psychology, 63*, 983–992.

Freud, S. (1953). Totem and taboo: Some points of agreement between the mental lives of savages and neurotics. In J. Strachey (Ed. and Trans.), *The standard edition of the complete psychological works of Sigmund Freud* (Vol. 13, pp. 1–161). London: Hogarth Press and the Institute of Psycho-analysis. (Original work published 1913.)

Freud, S. (1961). The future of an illusion. In J. Strachey (Ed. and Trans.), *The standard edition of the complete psychological works of Sigmund Freud* (Vol. 21, pp. 1–56). London: Hogarth Press and the Institute of Psycho-analysis. (Original work published 1927.)

Friedman, E. H. (1991). Bowen theory and therapy. In A. S. Gurman & D. P. Kniskern (Eds.), *Handbook of family therapy* (Vol. 2, pp. 134–170). New York: Bruner/Mazel.

Friedman, H., Rohrbaugh, M., & Krakauer, S. (1988). The timeline genogram: Highlighting temporal aspects of family relationships. *Family Process, 27*, 293–304.

Frohlich, M. (1994). *The intersubjectivity of the mystic: A study of Teresa of Avila's interior castle*. Atlanta, GA: Scholars Press.

Frost, S. E., Jr. (1972). *The sacred writings of the world's great religions*. New York: McGraw-Hill.

Frost, W. P. (1992). *What is the new age? Defining the third millennium consciousness*. Lewiston, NY: Mellen Press.

Fukuyama, M. A. & Sevig, T. D. (1997). Spiritual issues in counseling: A new course. *Counseling and Values, 36*, 333–344.

Fukuyama, M. A., & Sevig, T. D. (1999). *Integrating spirituality into multicultural counseling*. Thousand Oaks, CA: Sage.

Gafner, G., & Duckett, S. (1992). Treating the sequelae of a curse in elderly Mexican Americans. *Clinical Gerontologist, 11*, 145–153.

Galanter, M. (1996). Cults and charismatic groups. In E. Shafranske (Ed.), *Religion and the clinical practice of psychology* (pp. 269–296). Washington, DC: American Psychological Association.

Galanter, M., & Buckley, P. (1978). Evangelical religion and meditation: Psychotherapeutic effects. *Journal of Nervous Mental Disorders, 166*, 685–691.

Galanter, M., Rabkin, J., Rabkin, R., & Deutsch, A. (1979). The "Moonies": A psychological study. *American Journal of Psychiatry, 136*, 165–170.

Gallup, G. H., Jr. (1993). *Religion in America*. Princeton, NJ: Princeton Religious Research Center.

Gallup, G. H., Jr. (1996). *Religion in America: 1996 Report*. Princeton, NJ: Princeton Religious Research Center.

Gallup Organization. (1993). GO LIFE survey on Prayer. Princeton, NJ: Author.

Ganje-Fling, M. A., & McCarthy, P. R. (1991). A comparative analysis of spiritual direction and psychotherapy. *Journal of Psychology and Theology, 29*, 103–117.

Garcia-Preto, N. (1996a). Latino families: An overview. In M. McGoldrick, J. Giordano, & J. K. Pearce (Eds.), *Ethnicity and family therapy* (2nd ed., pp. 141–154). New York: Guilford Press.

Garcia-Preto, N. (1996b). Puerto Rican families. In M. McGoldrick, J. Giodano, & J. K. Pearce (Eds.), *Ethnicity and family therapy* (2nd ed., pp. 183–199). New York: Guilford Press.

Gardner, G. (1995). *Witchcraft today*. New York: Citadel.

Gardner, G. (1999). *Witchcraft today*. Ghame, England: Mandrake Press.

Garnett, L. M. (2000). *Mysticism and magic in Turkey: An account of the religious doctrines, monastic organisations and ecstatic powers of the Dervish orders*. New York: AMS Press.

Gartner, J. (1996). Religious commitment, mental health, and prosocial behavior: A review of the empirical literature. In E. P. Shafranske (Ed.), *Religion and the clinical practice of psychology* (pp. 187–214). Washington, DC: American Psychological Association.

Gartner, J., Larson, D. B., & Allen, G. D. (1991). Religious commitment and mental health: A review of empirical literature. *Journal of Psychology and Theology, 19*, 6–25.

Gathman, A. C., & Nessan, C. L. (1997). Fowler's stages of faith development in an honors science and religion seminar. *Zygon, 32*, 407–414.

Geertz, C. (1972). Religion as a cultural system. In W. L. Lessa & Evon V. Vogt (Eds.), *Reader in comparative religion* (3rd ed., pp. 167–178). New York: Harper & Row.

Gendlin, E. T. (1963). *Focusing*. Toronto: Bantam Books.

Gendlin, E. T. (1969). Focusing. *Psychotherapy: Theory, Research and Practice, 6*, 4–15.

Genia, V. (1994). Secular psychotherapists and religious clients: Professional considerations and recommendations. *Journal of Counseling and Development, 72*, 395–398.

Genia, V. (1995). *Counseling and psychotherapy of religious clients: A developmental approach*. Westport, CT: Praeger.

Genia, V. (2000). Religious issues in secularly based psychotherapy. *Counseling and Values, 44*, 213–220.

Gergen, K. (1985). The social constructionist movement in modern psychology. *American Psychologist, 40*, 266–275.

Gergen, K. (1991). *The saturated self*. New York: Basic Books.

Geyer, M. (1994). Dual role relationships and Christian counseling. *Journal of Psychology and Theology, 22*, 187–195.

Gilligan, C. (1982). *In a different voice: Psychological theory and women's development*. Cambridge, MA: Harvard University Press.

Giordano, J., & McGoldrick, M. (1996). European families: An overview. In M. McGoldrick, J. Giordano, & J. K. Pearce (Eds.), *Ethnicity and family therapy* (2nd ed., pp. 427–441). New York: Guilford Press.

Glen, N. D., & Weaver, C. N. (1978). A multivariate, multi-survey study of marital happiness. *Journal of Marriage and the Family, 40*, 269–282.

Gock, T. (1992). Asian-Pacific Islander issues: Identity integration and pride. In B. Berzon (Ed.), *Positively gay: New approaches to gay and lesbian life* (pp. 247–252). Berkeley, CA: Celestial Arts.

Goldenberg, I., & Goldenberg, H. (1996). *Family therapy: An overview* (4th ed.). Pacific Grove, CA: Brooks/Cole.

Goldman, L. (1990). Qualitative assessment. *Counseling Psychologist, 18*, 205–213.

Goldstein, J., & Kornfield, J. (1987). *Seeking the heart of wisdom: The path of insight meditation*. Boston: Shambhala.

Goleman, D. (1988). *The meditative mind*. Los Angeles: Tarcher.

Gonzalez, D. (1992). What is the problem with Hispanic? Just ask a Latino. *New York Times*, November 15.

Gonzalez-Wippler, M. (1992). *The Santeria experience*. St. Paul, MN: Llewellyn.

Gordon, M. (1964). *Assimilation into American life*. New York: Oxford University Press.

Gorsuch, R. L. (1995). Religious aspects of substance abuse and recovery. *Journal of Social Issues, 5*, 65–83.

Gorsuch, R. L., & Miller, W. R. (1999). Assessing spirituality. In W. R. Miller (Ed.), *Integrating spirituality into treatment* (pp. 47–64). Washington, DC: American Psychological Association.

Goss, R. (1993). *Jesus acted up: A gay and lesbian manifesto*. San Francisco: Harper & Row.

Goud, N. (1990). Spiritual and ethical beliefs of humanists in the counseling profession. *Journal of Counseling and Development, 68*, 571–574.

Greeley, A. (1969). *Why can't they be like us?* New York: American Jewish Committee.

Greeley, A. (1974). *Ethnicity in the United States: A preliminary reconnaisance.* New York: Wiley.

Greeley, A. W. (1989). *Religious change in America.* Cambridge, MA: Harvard University Press.

Greeley, A. (1990). *The Catholic myth: The behaviors and beliefs of American Catholics.* New York: Scribner.

Griffith, J. L. (1986). Employing the god-family relationship in therapy with religious families. *Family Process, 25*, 609–618.

Griffith, J. L., & Griffith, M. E. (1992). Therapeutic change in religious families: Working with the God-construct. In L. A. Burton (Ed.), *Religion and the family: When God helps.* New York: Haworth Press.

Grist, T., & Grist, A. (2000). *The illustrated guide to Wicca.* New York: Godsfield Press.

Grof, S. (1975). *Realms of the human unconscious.* New York: Viking Press.

Grof, S., & Grof, C. (Eds.). (1989). *Spiritual emergency: When personal transformation becomes a crisis.* Los Angeles: Tarcher.

Gross, R. (1979). Female God language in a Jewish context. In C. Christ & J. Plaskow (Eds.), *WomanSpirit Rising* (pp. 167–173). San Francisco: Harper & Row.

Guba, E. G., & Lincoln, Y. S. (1989). *Fourth generation evaluation.* Newbury Park, CA: Sage.

Guerin, P. J., & Hubbard, I. M. (1987). Impact of therapists' personal family system on clinical work. *Journal of Psychotherapy and the Family, 3*, 47–60.

Guiley, R. E. (1991). *Harper's encyclopedia of mystical and paranormal experience.* San Francisco: HarperSanFrancisco.

Gumaer, J. (1984). *Counseling and therapy for children.* New York: Free Press.

Gunn, P. A. (1989). *Spider Woman's granddaughters: Traditional tales and contemporary writing by Native American women.* New York: Fawcett Columbine.

Gurman, A. S., & Kniskern, D. P. (Eds.). (1991). *Handbook of family therapy* (Vol. 2). New York: Bruner/Mazel.

Haddad, Y., & Lummis, A. (1987). *Islamic values in the United States: A comparative study.* London: Oxford University Press.

Haldeman, D. C. (1996). Spirituality and religion in the lives of lesbians and gay men. In R. P. Cabaj & T. S. Stein (Eds.), *Textbook of homosexuality and mental health* (pp. 881–896). Washington, DC: American Psychiatric Press.

Haley, J. (1971). Communication and therapy: Blocking metaphors. *American Journal of Psychotherapy, 25*, 214–227.

Haley, J. (1976). *Problem-solving therapy.* New York: Harper/Colophon Books.

Halifax, J. (1982). *Shaman: The wounded healer.* London: Thames & Hudson.

Hall, T. W., & Edwards, K. J. (1996). The initial development and factor analysis of the Spiritual Assessment Inventory. *Journal of Psychology and Theology, 24*, 233–246.

Hammerschlag, C. (1988). *The dancing healers: A doctor's journey of healing with Native Americans.* New York: HarperCollins.

Hardy, K. V. (1993). Live supervision in the postmodern era of family therapy: Issues, reflections, and questions. *Contemporary Family Therapy, 15*, 20.

Harris, M. (1989). *The dance of the spirit: The seven steps of women's spirituality.* New York: Bantam Books.

Hartz, P. R. (1993). *Taoism.* New York: Facts on File.

Hartz, P. R. (1997). *Shinto.* New York: Facts on File.

Harvey, A. (1992). *Hidden journey: A spiritual awakening.* New York: Arkana/Penguin Books.

Harwood, A. (1981). *Ethnicity and medical care.* Cambridge, MA: Harvard University Press.

Haug, I. E. (1998). Including a spiritual dimension in family therapy: Ethical considerations. *Contemporary Family Therapy, 20*(4), 181–194.

Haug, I. E., & Alexander, C. (1992). Dual relationships among clergy therapists. In G. Brock (Ed.), *Ethics Casebook* (pp. 125–139). Washington, DC: American Association for Marriage and Family Therapy.

Hay, D. (1995, October). Children and God. *The Tablet: Educational supplement, 7,* 1270–1271.

Heaton, T., Goodman, K., & Holman, T. (1994). In search of a peculiar people: Are Mormon families really different? In M. Corwall, T. Heaton, & L. Young (Eds.), *Contemporary Mormonism: Social science perspectives* (pp. 87–117). Urbana: University of Illinois Press.

Hedayat-Diba, Z. (2000). Psychotherapy with Muslims. In P. S. Richards & A. E. Bergin (Eds.), *Handbook of psychotherapy and religious diversity* (pp. 289–314). Washington, DC: American Psychological Association.

Heller, D. I. (1986). *The children's God.* Chicago: University of Chicago Press.

Helminiak, D. (1987). *Spiritual development: An interdisciplinary study.* Chicago: Loyola University Press.

Helms, J. E., & Cook, D. A. (1999). *Using race and culture in counseling and psychotherapy: Theory and process.* Boston: Allyn & Bacon.

Henderson, L. (1994). African Americans in the urban milieu: Conditions, trends, and development needs. In B. Tidwell (Ed.), *The state of Black America* (pp. 11–26). New York: National Urban League.

Hendlin, S. J. (1989). Evolving spiritual consciousness: Is "religious maturity" all there is? *Counseling Psychologist, 17,* 617–620.

Hickson, J., & Phelps, A. (1997). Women's spirituality: A proposed practice model. *Journal of Family Social Work, 2,* 43–57.

Hill, R. (1972). *The strength of African American families.* New York: Emerson-Hall.

Hines, P. M., & Boyd-Franklin, N. (1996). African American families. In M. McGoldrick, J. Giordano, & J. K. Pearce, (Eds.), *Ethnicity and family therapy* (2nd ed., pp. 66–84). New York: Guilford Press.

Hinterkopf, E. (1994). Integrating spiritual experiences in counseling. *Counseling and Values, 38,* 165–175.

Ho, D. Y. F. (1985). Cultural values and professional issues in clinical psychology: Implications from the Hong Kong experience. *American Psychologist, 40,* 1212–1218.

Hof, L. & Berman, E. (1986). The sexual genogram. *Journal of Marital and Family Therapy, 12,* 39–47.

Hoffman, L. (1981). *Foundations of family therapy: a conceptual framework for systems change.* New York: Basic Books.

Holifield, E. B. (1983). *A history of pastoral care in America.* Nashville, TN: Abingdon.

Hoge, D. R. (1996). Religion in America: The demographics of belief and affiliation. In E. P. Shafranske (Ed.), *Religion and the clinical practice of psychology* (pp. 21–41). Washington, DC: American Psychological Association.

Homrich, A. M., & Horne, A. M. (2000). Brief family therapy. In A. M. Horne (Ed.), *Family counseling and therapy* (3rd ed., pp. 243–271). Itasca, IL: Peacock.

Honer, S. M., & Hunt, T. C. (1987). *Invitation to philosophy: Issues and options* (5th ed.). Belmont, CA: Wadsworth.

Hopfe, L. M. (1983). *Religions of the world.* New York: Macmillan.

Hopson, R. E. (1996). The 12-Step program. In E. P. Shafranske (Ed.), *Religion and the clinical practice of psychology* (pp. 533–558). Washington, DC: American Psychological Association.

Horne, A. M. (Ed.). (2000). *Family counseling and therapy.* Itasca, IL: Peacock.

Howden, J. W. (1992). Development and psychometric characteristics of the Spirituality Assessment Scale. *Dissertation Abstracts International, 54*(01), 166B. (University Microfilms No. AAG 9312917).

Hudson, P. O., & O'Hanlon, W. H. (1991). Unfinished business: Using rituals and symbols to resolve tragedies. In P. O. Hudson & W. H. O'Hanlon, *Rewriting love stories* (pp. 83–101). New York: Norton.

Hultkrantz, A. (1993). Native religions of North America: The power of visions and fertility. In H. B. Earhart (Ed.), *Religious traditions of the world: A journey through Africa, Meso-America, North America, Judaism, Christianity, Islam, Hinduism, Buddhism, China, and Japan.* San Francisco: HarperSanFrancisco.

Husaini, B. A., Moore, S. T., & Cain, V. A. (1994). Psychiatric symptoms and help-seeking behavior among the elderly: An analysis of racial and gender differences. *Journal of Gerontological Social Work, 21,* 177–195.

Hyde, K. E. (1990). *Religion in childhood and adolescence.* Birmingham, AL: Religious Education Press.

Ibrahim, F. A. (1985). Effective cross-cultural counseling and psychotherapy: A framework. *Counseling Psychologist, 13,* 625–638.

Ibrahim, F. A. (1991). Contribution of cultural worldview to generic counseling and development. *Journal of Counseling and Development, 70,* 13–19.

Ibrahim, F. A. (1996). A multicultural perspective on principle and virtue ethics. *Counseling Psychologist, 24,* 78–85.

Imber-Black, E., & Roberts, J. (1992). *Rituals for our times.* New York: HarperCollins.

Imbrie, G. S. (1985). Untwisting the illusion. *Journal of Orthomolecular Psychiatry, 14,* 143–145.

Indowu, A. I. (1992). The Oshun Festival: An African traditional religious healing process. *Counseling and Values, 36,* 192–200.

Ingersoll, R. E. (1997). Teaching a course on counseling and spirituality. *Counseling and Values, 36,* 224–232.

Ivey, A. E., & Authier, J. *Microcounseling: Innovations in interviewing, counseling, psychotherapy and psychoeducation.* Springfield, IL: Thomas.

Jack, A. (1990). *The new age dictionary.* New York: Japan Publications.

Jagers, R. J., & Smith, P. (1996). Further examination of the Spirituality Scale. *Journal of Black Psychology, 23,* 429–442.

Jellinek, E. M. (1960). *The disease concept of alcoholism.* Harlan Park, NY: Hillhouse Press.

Jensen, J. P., & Bergin, A. E. (1988). Mental health values of professional therapists: A national interdisciplinary survey. *Professional Psychology: Research and Practice, 19,* 290–297.

Joanides, C. J. (1996). Collaborative family therapy with religious family systems. *Journal of Family Psychology, 7,* 19–35.

John of the Cross. (1991). *The dark night.* In K. Kavanaugh & O. Rodriguez (Trans.), *The collected works of St. John of the Cross* (Rev. ed., pp. 353–457). Washington, DC: Institute for Carmelite Studies.

Jones, A. C. (1993). *Wade in the water: The wisdom of the spirituals.* Maryknoll, NY: Orbis.

Jones, S. L. (1996). A constructive relationship for religion with the science and profession of psychology: Perhaps the boldest model yet. In E. P. Shafranske (Ed.), *Religion and the clinical practice of psychology* (pp. 113–147). Washington, DC: American Psychological Association.

Jones, S. L., Watson, E. J., & Wolfram, T. J. (1992). Results of the Rech conference survey on religious faith and professional psychology. *Journal of Psychology and Theology, 20,* 147–158.

Jung, C. G. (1969). Psychotherapists or the clergy. In H. Read, M. Fordham, & G. Adler (Eds.), *The collected works of C. G. Jung* (Vol. 11, 2nd ed., pp. 327–347). Princeton, NJ: Princeton University Press. (Original work published 1932.)

Kahn, Y. H. (1989). Judaism and homosexuality: The traditionalist/progressive debate. In R. Hasbany (Ed.), *Homosexuality and religion* (pp. 47–82). New York: Haworth Press.

Kanz, J. E. (2000). How do people conceptualize and use forgiveness? The forgiveness attitudes questionnaire. *Counseling and Values, 44,* 174–188.

Kasee, C. R. (1995). Identity, recovery, and religious imperialism: Native American women and the new age. *Women and Therapy, 16,* 83–93.

Kasl, C. D. (1992). *Many roads, one journey: Moving beyond the twelve steps.* New York: HarperPerennial.

Kass, J. D., Friedman, R., Leserman, J., Zuttermeister, P. C., & Benson, H. (1991). Health outcomes and a new index of spiritual experience. *Journal for the Scientific Study of Religion, 30,* 203–211.

Keim, J. (2000). Strategic family therapy. In A. M. Horne (Ed.), *Family counseling and therapy* (3rd ed., pp. 170–207). Itasca, IL: Peacock.

Kelly, E. W., Jr. (1994). The role of religion and spirituality in counselor education: A national survey. *Counselor Education and Supervision, 33,* 227–237.

Kelly, E. W., Jr. (1995). *Spirituality and religion in counseling and psychotherapy.* Alexandria, VA: American Counseling Association.

Kelly, E. W., Jr. (1997). Religion and spirituality in variously accredited counselor training programs: A comment on Pate and High. *Counseling and Values, 42,* 7–11.

Kidd, S. M. (1996). *The dance of the dissident daughter: A woman's journey from Christian tradition to the sacred feminine.* New York: HarperCollins.

Kimelman, R. (1994). Homosexuality and family-centered Judaism. *Tikkun, 9,* 53–57.

Kingree, J. B. (1997). Measuring affiliation with 12-step groups. *Substance Use and Misuse, 32,* 181–194.

Kitchener, K. S. (1984). Intuition, critical evaluation and ethical principles: The foundation for ethical decisions in counseling psychology. *Counseling Psychologist, 12,* 43–55.

Kleinman, A. M. (1982). Neurasthenia and depression: A study of somatization and culture in China. *Culture, Medicine, and Psychiatry, 6,* 117–189.

Kluback, W., & Weinbaum, M. (1957). *Dilthey's philosophy of existence: Introduction to Weltanschauungslehre.* Westport, CT: Greenwood Press.

Klug, R. (1982). *How to keep a spiritual journal.* Nashville, TN: Thomas Nelson.

Knappert, J. (1989). The concept of death and the afterlife in Islam. In A. Berger, P. Badham, A. H. Kutscher, J. Berger, M. Perry, & J. Beloff (Eds.), *Perspectives on death and dying: Cross-cultural and multi-disciplinary views.* Philadelphia: Charles Press.

Knipe, D. M. (1993). Hinduism: Experiments in the sacred. In H. B. Earhart (Ed.), *Religions and traditions of the world* (pp. 715–846). San Francisco: HarperSanFrancisco.

Knox, D. H. (1985). Spirituality: A tool in the assessment and treatment of Black alcoholics and their families. *Alcoholism Treatment Quarterly, 76,* 477–483.

Koch, G. R. (1998). Spiritual empowerment: A metaphor for counseling. *Counseling and Values, 43,* 19–27.

Kochems, T. (1993). Countertransference and transference aspects of religious material in psychotherapy. In M. L. Randour (Ed.), *Exploring sacred landscapes: Religious and spiritual experiences in psychotherapy* (pp. 34–54). New York: Columbia University Press.

Koepfer, S. R. (2000). Drawing on the Spirit: Embracing spirituality in pediatrics and pediatric art therapy. *Art Therapy: Journal of the American Art Therapy Association, 17,* 188–194.

Kogan, S. M., & Gale, J. E. (2000). Taking a narrative turn: Social constructionism and family therapy. In A. M. Horne (Ed.), *Family counseling and therapy* (3rd ed., pp. 208–242). Itasca, IL: Peacock.

Koltko, M. E. (1990). How religious beliefs affect psychotherapy: The example of Mormonism. *Psychotherapy, 27,* 132–141.

Kramer, J. R. (1985). *Family interfaces: Transgenerational patterns.* New York: Bruner/Mazel.

Kropf, R. W. (1990). *Faith, security, and risk.* Mahwah, NJ: Paulist Press.

Kudlac, K. E. (1991). Including God in the conversation: The influence of religious beliefs on the problem-organized system. *Family Therapy, 18,* 277–285.

Kuehl, B. P. (1995). The solution-oriented genogram: A collaborative approach. *Journal of Marital and Family Therapy, 21,* 239–250.

Kuehl, B. P., Newfield, N. A., & Joanning, H. (1990). A client-based description of family therapy. *Journal of Family Psychology, 3,* 310–321.

Kuhn, T. (1970). *The structure of scientific revolutions* (2nd ed.). Chicago: University of Chicago Press.

Kung, H. (1979). *Freud and the problem of God* (Rev. ed.). New Haven, CT: Yale University Press.

Kurtz, E. (1999). The historical perspective. In W. R. Miller (Ed.), *Integrating spirituality into treatment* (pp. 19–46). Washington, DC: American Psychological Association.

Kurtz, L. P. (1990). 12-step programs. In T. J. Powell (Ed.), *Working with self-helps* (pp. 93–119). Washington, DC: National Association of Social Work Press.

Kushner, H. S. (1981). *When bad things happen to good people.* New York: Schocken.

LaDue, R. A. (1994). The coyote returns: Twenty sweats does not an Indian expert make. *Women and Therapy, 15,* 93–111.

Laird, J. (2000). Gender in lesbian relationships: Cultural, feminist, and constructionist reflections. *Journal of Marital and Family Therapy, 26,* 455–468.

Laird, J., & Green, R.-H. (Eds.). (1996). *Lesbians and gays in families and family therapy.* San Francisco: Jossey-Bass.

Larson, D. B., Pattison, E. M., Blazer, D. G., Omran, A. R., & Kaplan, B. H. (1986). Systematic analysis of research on religious variables in four major psychiatric journals, 1978–1982. *American Journal of Psychiatry, 143,* 329–334.

Larson, D. B., Sherrill, K. A., Lyons, J. S., Craigie, F. C., Jr., Thielman, S. B., Greenwold, M. A., & Larson, S. S. (1992). Associations between dimensions of religious commitment and mental health reported in the *American Journal of Psychiatry* and *Archives of General Psychiatry: 1978–1989. American Journal of Psychiatry, 149,* 557–559.

Lax, W. D. (1996). Narrative, social constructionism, and Buddhism. In H. Rosen & K. T. Kuehlwein (Eds.), *Constructing realities: Meaning-making perspectives for psychotherapists* (pp. 195–220). San Francisco: Jossey-Bass.

Lazarus, A. A. (1984). Multimodal therapy. In R. J. Corsini & D. Wedding (Eds.), *Current psychotherapies* (pp. 491–530). Itasca, IL: Peacock.

Lechner, N. (1992). Some people die of fear: Fear as a political problem. In J. E. Corradi, P. W. Fagen, & M. Garreton (Eds.), *Fear at the edge: State terror and resistance in Latin America.* Berkeley: University of California Press.

Ledbetter, M. G., Smith, L. A., Vosler-Hunter, W. L., & Fischer, J. D. (1991). An evaluation of the research and clinical usefulness of the Spirtual Well-Being Scale. *Journal of Psychology and Theology, 19,* 49–55.

Lee, C. C., & Armstrong, K. L. (1995). Indigenous models of mental health intervention: Lesson from traditional healers. In J. G. Ponterotto, J. M. Casa, L. A. Suzuki, & C. M. Alexander. *Handbook of Multicultural Counseling* (pp. 441–456). Thousand Oaks, CA: Sage.

Lee, E. (1996a). Asian American families: An overview. In M. McGoldrick, J. Giordano, & J. Pearce (Eds.), *Ethnicity and family therapy* (2nd ed., pp. 227–248). New York: Guilford Press.

Lee, E. (1996b). Chinese families. In M. McGoldrick, J. Giordano, & J. Pearce (Eds.), *Ethnicity and family therapy* (2nd ed., pp. 249–267). New York: Guilford Press.

Lesser, E. (1999). *The seeker's guide: Making your life a spiritual adventure.* New York: Villard.

Lester, R. C. (1993). Buddhism: The path to Nirvana. In H. B. Earhart (Ed.), *Religions and traditions of the world* (pp. 849–971). San Francisco: HarperSanFrancisco.

Levin, J. S. (1994). Religion and health: Is there an association, is it valid, and is it causal? *Social Science and Medicine, 38,* 1475–1482.

Levin, J., & Vanderpool, H. (1987). Is frequent religious attendance really conducive to better health?: Toward an epidemiology of religion. *Social Science Medicine, 24,* 589–600.

Levine, S. (1991). *Guided meditations, explorations and healings.* New York: Anchor Books.

Levine, S. (1998). *A year to live.* New York: Bell Tower.

Levine, S., & Salter, N. E. (1976). Youth and contemporary religious movements: Psychological finds. *Canadian Psychiatric Association, 21,* 411–420.

Lewis, K. G. (1989). The use of color-coded genograms in family therapy. *Journal of Marital and Family Therapy, 15,* 169–176.

Liddle, H. A. (1982). Family therapy training: Current issues, future trends. *International Journal of Family Therapy, 4,* 81–97.

Lifton, R. J. (1961). *Thought reform and the psychology of totalism.* New York: Norton.

Lin, T., & Lin, M. (1981). Love, denial and rejection: Responses of Chinese families to mental illness. In A. Kleinman & T. Lin (Eds.), *Normal and abnormal behavior in Chinese culture* (pp. 387–401). Dordrecht, The Netherlands: D. Reidel.

Lindenthal, J. J., Myers, J. K., Pepper, M. P., & Stern, M. S. (1970). Mental status and religious behavior. *Journal for the Scientific Study of Religion, 9,* 143–149.

Liu, W-C. (1993). Confucianism. *Encarta Encyclopedia.* Redmond, WA: Microsoft Corp.

London, P. (1986). *The modes and morals of psychotherapy* (2nd ed.). Washington, DC: Hemisphere.

Lovecky, D. V. (1997). Spiritual sensitivity in gifted children. *Roeper Review, 20,* 178–183.

Lovinger, R. J. (1984). *Working with religious issues in therapy.* Northwale, NJ: Jason Aronson.

Lovinger, R. J. (1990). *Religion and counseling.* New York: Continuum.

Lovinger, R. J. (1996). Considering the religious dimension in assessment and treatment. In E. Shafranske (Ed.), *Religion and the clinical practice of psychology* (pp. 327–364). Washington, DC: American Psychological Association.

Lownsdale, S. (1997). Faith development across the life span: Fowler's integrative work. *Journal of Psychology and Theology, 25,* 49–63.

Lukoff, D., Lu, F., & Turner, R. (1992). Toward a more culturally sensitive DSM-IV; Psychoreligious and psychospiritual problems. *Journal of Nervous and Mental Disease, 180,* 673–681.

Lynch, B. (1996). Religious and spirituality conflicts. In D. Davies & C. Neal (Eds.), *Pink therapy: A guide for counsellors and therapists working with lesbian, gay, and bisexual clients* (pp. 199–207). Buckingham, England: Open University Press.

Mack, M. L. (1994). Understanding spirituality in counseling psychology: considerations for research, training, and practice. *Counseling and Values, 39,* 15–31.

Madanes, C. (1981). *Strategic family therapy.* San Francisco: Jossey-Bass.

Madanes, C. (1984). *Behind the one-way mirror.* San Francisco: Jossey-Bass.

Madanes, C. (1991). Strategic family therapy. In A. S. Gurman & D. P. Kniskern (Eds.), *Handbook of family therapy* (Vol. 2, pp. 396–416). New York: Bruner/Mazel.

Mahoney, M. (1976). *Scientist as subject.* Cambridge, MA: Ballinger.

Mahrer, A. R. (1996). Existential-Humanistic psychotherapy and the religious person. . In E. P. Shafranske (Ed.), *Religion and the clinical practice of psychology* (pp. 433–460). Washington, DC: American Psychological Association.

Mailhiot, B. (1962). And God became a child: The reactions of children and child-groups under school age. *Lumen Vitae, 16,* 277–288.

Malony, H. N. (1985). Assessing religious maturity. In E. M. Stern (Ed.), *Psychotherapy and the religiously committed patient* (pp. 25–33). New York: Haworth Press.

Malony, H. N. (1993). The relevance of "Religious Diagnosis" for counseling. In E. L. Worthington (Ed.), *Psychotherapy and religious values* (pp. 105–120). Grand Rapids, MI: Baker Book House.

Manson, S. M., & Trimble, J. E. (1982). American Indian and Alaska Native communities: Past efforts, future inquiries. In L. R. Snowden (Ed.), *Researching the underserved: Mental health needs of neglected populations* (pp. 143–163). Beverly Hills, CA: Sage.

Marin, G. (1992). Issues in the measurement of acculturation among Hispanics. In K. F. Geisinger (Ed.), *Psychological testing of Hispanics* (pp. 235–251). Washington, DC: American Psychological Association.

Markides, K. S. (1983). Aging, religiosity, and adjustment: A longitudinal analysis. *Journal of Gerontology, 38,* 621–625.

Marlatt, G. A., & Kristeller, J. L. (1999). Mindfulness and meditation. In W. R. Miller (Ed.), *Integrating spirituality into treatment* (pp. 67–84). Washington, DC: American Psychological Association.

Marsden, G. M. (1987). *Reforming fundamentalism: Fuller Seminary and the new Evangelism.* Grand Rapids, MI: William B. Eerdmans.

Marsella, A., Kinzie, D., & Gordon, P. (1973). Ethnic variations in the expression of depression. *Journal of Cross-Cultural Psychology, 4,* 435–458.

Martin, J. E., & Booth, J. (1999). Behavioral approaches to enhance spirituality. In W. R. Miller (Ed.), *Integrating spirituality into treatment* (pp. 161–175). Washington, D.C.: American Psychological Association.

Martin, J. E., & Carlson, C. R. (1988). Spiritual dimensions of health psychology. In W. R. Miller & J. E. Martin (Eds.), *Behavior therapy and religion* (pp. 57–110). Newbury Park, CA: Sage.

Marty, M. E. (1991). *Modern American religion: Vol.2. The noise of conflict, 1919–1941.* Chicago: University of Chicago Press.

Marty, M. E. (1993). Where the energies go. *Annals of the American Academy of Political and Social Science, Issue on Religion in the Nineties, 527,* 97–112.

Maslow, A. (1968). *Toward a psychology of being.* New York: Van Nostrand.

Maslow, A. (1970). *Motivation and personality* (2nd ed.). New York: Harper & Row.

Matheson, L. (1996). Valuing spirituality among native American populations. *Counseling and Values, 41,* 51–58.

Matsui, W. T. (1996). Japanese families. In M. McGoldrick, J. Giordano, & J. Pearce (Eds.), *Ethnicity and family therapy* (2nd ed., pp. 268–280). New York: Guilford Press.

May, G. G. (1988). *Addiction and grace: Love and spirituality in the healing of addictions.* New York: HarperCollins.

Mbiti, J. S. (1969). *African religions and philosophy.* London: Heinemann Educational.

Mbiti, J. S. (1970). *African religions and philosophies.* Garden City, NY: Anchor Books (Doubleday).

Mbiti, J. S. (1991). *Introduction to African religion* (2nd ed.). Oxford, England: Heinemann Educational.

McCrady, B. S., & Delaney, S. I. (1995). Self-help groups. In R. K. Hester & W. R. Miller (Eds.), *Handbook of alcoholism treatment approaches* (2nd ed., pp. 160–175). Boston: Allyn & Bacon.

McCubbin, H. I., & Thompson, A. I. (Eds.). (1991). *Family assessment inventories for research and practice* (2nd ed.). Madison: University of Wisconsin–Madison.

McCullough, M. E., & Larson, D. B. (1999). Prayer. In W. R. Miller (Ed.), *Integrating spirituality into treatment* (pp. 85–110). Washington, DC: American Psychological Association.

McCullough, M. E., Weaver, A. J., Larson, D. B., & Aay, K. R. (2000). Psychotherapy with mainline protestants: Lutheran, Presbyterian, Episcpal/Anglican, and Methodist (pp. 105–129). In P. S. Richards & A. E. Bergin (Eds.), *Handbook of psychotherapy and religious diversity.* Washington, DC: American Psychological Association.

McCullough, M. E., & Worthington, E. L., Jr. (1994). Encouraging clients to forgive people who have hurt them: Review, critique, and research prospectus. *Journal of Psychology and Theology, 22,* 15–29.

McCullough, M. E., Worthington, E. L., Jr., & Rachal, K. C. (1997). Interpersonal forgiving in close relationships. *Journal of Personality and Social Psychology, 73,* 321–336.

McDermott, J. P. (1993). Buddhism. *Encarta Encyclopedia.* Redmond, WA: Microsoft Corp.

McGill, D. W., & Pearce, J. K. (1996). American families with English ancestors from the colonial era: Anglo Americans. In M. McGoldrick, J. Giordano, & J. K. Pearce, (Eds.), *Ethnicity and family therapy* (2nd ed., pp. 451–466). New York: Guilford Press.

McGoldrick, M., Gerson, R., & Shellenberger, S. (1996). *Genograms in family assessment.* (2nd ed.), New York: Norton.

McGoldrick, M., & Giordano, J. (1996). Overview: Ethnicity and family therapy. In M. McGoldrick, J. Giordano, & J. K. Pearce (Eds.), *Ethnicity and family therapy* (2nd ed., pp. 1–27). New York: Guilford Press.

McGoldrick, M., Giordano, J., & Pearce, J. K. (Eds.). (1996). *Ethnicity and family therapy.* (2nd ed.). New York: Guilford Press.

McGoldrick, M., & Rohrbaugh, M. (1987). Researching ethnic family stereotypes. *Family Process, 26,* 89–98.

McLemore, C. (1982). *The scandal of psychotherapy.* Wheaton, IL: Tyndale House.

Meadow, M. J., & Kahoe, R. D. (1984). *Psychology of religion: Religion in individual lives.* New York: Harper & Row.

Meissner, W. W. (1991). The phenomenology of religious psychopathology. *Bulletin of the Menniger Clinic, 55,* 281–298.

Meissner, W. W. (1996). The pathology of beliefs and the beliefs of pathology. In E. P. Shafranske (Ed.), *Religion and the clinical practice of psychology* (pp. 241–267). Washington, DC: American Psychological Association.

Menten, T. (1991). *Gentle closings: How to say goodbye to someone you love.* Philadelphia: Running Press.

Miller, J. P. (1994). *The contemplative practitioner: Meditation in education and the professions.* Westport, CT: Bergin & Garvey.

Miller, W. R. (Ed.). (1999). *Integration of spirituality into treatment: Resources for practitioners.* Washington, DC: American Psychological Association.

Miller, W. R., & Thoresen, C. (1999). Spirituality and health. In W. R. Miller (Ed.), *Integrating spirituality into treatment* (pp. 3–18). Washington, DC: American Psychological Association.

Minuchin, S. (1974). *Families and family therapy.* Cambridge, MA: Harvard University Press.

Minuchin, S., Montalvo, B., & Guerney, B. J. R. (1967). *Families of the slums.* New York: Basic Books.

Minuchin, S., Rosman, B. L., & Baker, L. (1978). *Psychosomatic families: Anorexia nervosa in context.* Cambridge, MA: Harvard University Press.

Mitchell, E. P., & Mitchell, H. H. (1989). Black spirituality: The values in that ol' time religion. *Journal of the Interdenominational Theological Center, 17*(1/2), 98–109.

Mitchell, H., & Lewter, N. (1986). *Soul theology: The heart of American Black culture.* San Francisco: Harper & Row.

Mollenkott, V. R. (1977). *Women, men, and the Bible.* Nashville, TN: Abingdon Press.

Moody, R. (1975). *Life after life.* New York: Bantam Books.

Mooney, R. L. (1950). *Mooney Problem Check List.* San Antonio, TX: Psychological Corporation.

Moore, T. (1991). The African American church: A source of empowerment, mutual help, and social change. *Prevention in Human Services, 10,* 147–167.

Moos, R. H., & Moos, B. S. (1981). *Manual for the Family Environmental Scale.* Palo Alto, CA: Consulting Psychologist Press.

Morrison, M., & Brown, S. F. (1991). *Judaism.* New York: Facts on File.

Moss, D. (Ed.). (1999). *Humanistic and transpersonal psychology: A historical and biographical sourcebook.* Westport, CT: Greenwood Press.

Moy, S. (1992). A culturally sensitive, psychoeducational model for understanding and treating Asian American clients. *Journal of Psychology and Christianity, 11,* 358–367.

Mull, J. D., & Mull, D. S. (1983, November). Cross-cultural medicine: A visit with a *curandero. Western Journal of Medicine, 139,* 728–736.

Murgatroyd, W. (2001). The Buddhist spiritual path: A counselor's reflection on meditation, spirituality and the nature of life. *Counseling and Values, 45,* 94–102.

Nakhaima, J. M., & Dicks, B. H. (1995). Social work practice with religious families. *Families in Society, 76,* 360–368.

National Association of Social Workers (NASW). (1996). *Code of ethics.* Washington, DC: Author.

National Organization for Human Service Education (NOHSE). (1995). *Ethical standards of the National Organization for Human Service Education.* Author.

National Wellness Institute. (1983). *Lifestyle Assessment Questionnaire* (2nd ed.). Stevens Point: University of Wisconsin Stevens Point Institute for Lifestyle Improvement.

Needleman, J. (1970). *The new religions.* Garden City, NY: Doubleday.

Neighbors, H. W., Jackson, J. S., Bowman, P. J., & Gurin, G. (1983). Stress, coping, and Black mental health: Preliminary finds from a national survey. *Prevention in Human Services, 2,* 5–29.

Neimeyer, R. A. (1995). An appraisal of constructivist psychotherapies. In M. J. Mahoney (Ed.), *Cognitive and constructive psychotherapies* (pp. 163–194). New York: Springer.

Nelson, A. A., & Wilson, W. P. (1984). The ethics of sharing religious faith in psychotherapy. *Journal of Psychology and Theology, 12,* 15–23.

Neu, D. L. (1995). Women's empowerment through feminist rituals. In J. Ochshorn & E. Cole (Eds.), *Women's spirituality, women's lives* (pp. 185–200). New York: Haworth Press.

Nhat Hanh, T. (1976). *The miracle of mindfulness!* Boston: Beacon Press.

Nicholi, A. M. I. (1974). A new dimension of the youth culture. *American Journal of Psychiatry, 131,* 369–401.

Nobles, W. (1980). African philosophy: Foundations for black psychology. In R. Jones (Ed.), *Black psychology* (2nd ed., pp. 18–32). New York: Harper & Row.

Nugent, R., & Gramick, J. (1989). Homosexuality: Protestant, Catholic and Jewish issues: A fishbone tale. In R. Hasbany (Ed.), *Homosexuality and religion* (pp. 7–46). New York: Haworth Press.

Nye, R., & Hay, D. (1996, Summer). Identifying children's spirituality: How do you start without a starting point? *British Journal of religious Education, 9,* 144–154.

Nye, W. (1993). Amazing grace: Religion and identity among elderly Black individuals. *International Journal of Aging and Human Development, 36,* 103–114.

Ochs, C. (1983). *Women and spirituality.* Totowa, NJ: Rowman & Allanheld.

O'Connell, D. F., & Alexander, C. N. (1994). *Self-recovery: Treating addictions using transcendental meditation and Maharishi Ayur-Veda.* New York: Haworth Press.

O'Donohue, W. (1989). The (even) bolder model: The clinical psychologist as metaphysician-scientist-practitioner. *American Psychologist, 44,* 1460–1468.

O'Flaherty, W. D. (1993–1996). Hinduism. *Encarta Encyclopedia.* Redmond, WA: Microsoft Corp.

O'Hanlon, W. H., & Weiner-Davis, M. (1989). *In search of solutions: A new direction in psychotherapy.* New York: Norton.

O'Hare-Lavin, M. E. (2000). Finding a "lower, deeper power" for women in recovery. *Counseling and Values, 44,* 198–212.

O'Malley, J. W. (1993–1996). Roman Catholicism. *Encarta 97 Encyclopedia.* Redmond, WA: Microsoft Corp.

Orton, G. L. (1997). *Strategies for counseling with children and their parents.* Pacific Grove, CA: Brooks/Cole.

Oser, F. K. (1991). The development of religious judgment (pp. 5–25). In F. K. Oser & W. G. Scarlett (Eds.), *Religious development in childhood and adolescence* (pp. 5–25). San Francisco: Jossey-Bass Inc.

Overmyer, D. L. (1993). Religions of China: The world as a living system (pp. 975–1073). In H. B. Earhart (Ed.), *Religions and traditions of the world.* San Francisco: HarperSanFrancisco.

Otto, R. (1958). *The idea of the holy.* New York: Oxford University Press.

Pagels, E. H. (1981). *The gnostic gospels.* New York: Vintage Books.

Palombi, B. J. (1992). Psychometric properties of wellness instruments. *Journal of Counseling and Development, 71,* 221–225.

Paniagua, F. A. (1994). *Assessing and treating culturally diverse clients: A practical guide.* Thousand Oaks, CA: Sage.

Papero, D. V. (2000). The Bowen theory. In A. M. Horne (Ed.), *Family counseling and therapy* (3rd ed., pp. 272–299). Itasca, IL: Peacock.

Papp, P. (1980). The Greek chorus and other techniques of family therapy. *Family Process, 19,* 45–57.

Pardeck, J. T., & Pardeck, J. A. (1993). *Bibliotherapy: A clinical approach for helping children.* Landhorne, PA: Gordon & Breach.

Pargament, K. I. (1996). Religious methods of coping: Resources for the conservation and transformation of significance. In E. Shafranske (Ed.), *Religion and the clinical practice of psychology* (pp. 215–249). Washington, DC: American Psychological Association.

Pargament, K. I. (1997). *The psychology of religion and coping.* New York: Guilford Press.

Pargament, K. I., Echemendia, R. J., Johnson, S., Cook, P., McGath, C., Myers, J. G., & Brannick, M. (1987). The conservative church: Psychosocial advantages and disadvantages. *American Journal of Community Psychology, 15,* 269–286.

Pargament, K. I., Ensing, D., Falgout, K., Olsen, H., Reilly, G., Van Haitsma, K., & Warren, R. (1990). God help me: 1. Religious coping efforts as predictors of the outcomes to significant negative life events. *American Journal of Community Psychology, 18,* 793–825.

Pargament, K. I., Kennell, J., Hathaway, W., Grevengoed, N., Newman, J., & Jones, W. (1988). Religion and the problem-solving process: Three styles of coping. *Journal for the Scientific Study of Religion, 27,* 90–104.

Pargament, K. I., Koenig, H. G., & Perez, L. M. (1998, August). *The many methods of religious coping: Development and initial validation of the RCOPE.* Paper presented at the 106th Annual Convention of the American Psychological Association, San Francisco.

Pargament, K. I., & Park, C. L. (1995). Merely a defense? The variety of religious means and ends. *Journal of Social Issues, 51,* 13–32.

Pargament, K. I., Silverman, W., Johnson, S., Echemendia, R., & Snyder, S. (1983). The psychological climate of religious congregations. *American Journal of Community Psychology, 11,* 351–381.

Pargament, K. I., Smith, B. W., Koenig, H. G., & Perez, L. (1998). Patterns of positive and negative religious coping with major life stressors. *Journal for the Scientific Study of Religion, 37,* 711–725.

Parks, S. (1986). *The critical years: Young adults and the search for meaning, faith, and commitment.* San Francisco: HarperCollins.

Parry, A., & Doan, R. E. (1994). *Story re-visions: Narrative therapy in the postmodern world.* New York: Guilford Press.

Parsons, F. (1909). *Choosing a vocation.* Boston: Houghton Mifflin.

Pate, R. H., & Bondi, A. M. (1992). Religious beliefs and practice: An integral aspect of multicultural awareness. *Counselor Education and Supervision, 32,* 109–115.

Pate, R. H., & High, H. J. (1995). The importance of client religious beliefs and practices in the education of counselors in CACREP-accredited programs. *Counseling and Values, 40,* 2–5.

Payne, I. R., Bergin, A. E., Bielema, K. A., & Jenkins, P. H. (1991). Review of religion and mental health: Prevention and the enhancement of psycho-social functioning. *Prevention in Human Services, 9,* 11–40.

Pearce, J. K., & Friedman, L. (Eds.). (1980). *Family therapy: combining psychodynamic and family systems approaches.* New York: Grune & Stratton.

Peck, M. S. (1978). *The road less traveled: The unending journey toward spiritual growth.* New York: Simon & Schuster.

Pedersen, P. (1990). The multicultural perspective as a fourth force in counseling. *Journal of Mental Health Counseling, 12,* 93–95.

Pelaez, M., & Rothman, P. (1994). *A guide to recalling and telling your life story.* Miami Beach, FL: Hospice Foundation of America.

Pelikan, J. (1968). *Spirit versus structure.* New York: Harper & Row.

Pelikan, J. (1993–1996). Christianity. *Encarta 97 Encyclopedia.* Redmond, WA: Microsoft Corp.

Pellebon, D. A., & Anderson, S. C. (1999). Understanding the life issues of spiritually-based clients. *Families in Society: The Journal of Contemporary Human Services, 80,* 229.

Perlmutter, P. (1992). *Divided we fall.* Ames, IA: Iowa State University Press.

Perls, F. (1969). *Gestalt therapy verbatim.* Moab, UT: Real People Press.

Percesepe, G. (1991). *Philosophy: An introduction to the labor of reason.* New York: Macmillan.

Piercy, F., Soekandar, A., & Limansubroto, C. D. M. (1996). Indonesian families. In M. McGoldrick, J. Giordano, & J. Pearce (Eds.), *Ethnicity and family therapy* (2nd ed., pp. 316–323). New York: Guilford Press.

Plaskow, J. (1979). Bringing a daughter into the covenant. In C. Christ & J. Plaskow (Eds.), *WomanSpirit Rising* (pp. 179–184). San Francisco: Harper & Row.

Plaskow, J. (1990). *Standing again at Sinai: Judaism from a feminist perspective*. New York: HarperCollins.

Poloma, M. M., & Gallup, G. H., Jr. (1991). *Varieties of prayer*. Philadelphia: Trinity Press International.

Poloma, M. M., & Pendleton, B. F. (1989). Exploring types of prayer and quality of life: A research note. *Review of Religious Research, 31,* 46–53.

Poloma, M. M., & Pendleton, B. F. (1991). The effects of prayer and prayer experiences of measures of general well-being. *Journal of Psychology and Theology, 19,* 71–83.

Polster, M. (1987). Gestalt therapy: Evolution and application. In J. K. Zeig (Ed.), *The evolution of psychotherapy* (pp. 312–325). New York: Bruner/Mazel.

Power, C. (1998, March 16). The new Islam. *Newsweek Magazine,* 35–37.

Presley, D. (1992). Three approaches to religious issues in counseling. *Journal of Psychology and Theology, 20,* 39–46.

Prest, L. A., & Keller, J. F. (1993). Spirituality and family therapy: spiritual beliefs, myths, and metaphors. *Journal of Marital and Family Therapy, 19,* 137–148.

Progoff, I. (1975). *At a jounal workshop*. New York: Dialouge House Library.

Propst, L. R. (1980). The comparative efficacy of religious and nonreligious imagery for the treatment of mild depression in religious individuals. *Cognitive Therapy and Research, 4,* 167–178.

Propst, L. R. (1992). Spirituality and the avoidant personality. *Theology Today, 49,* 165–172.

Propst, L. R. (1996). Cognitive-behavioral therapy and the religious person. In E. P. Shafranske (Ed.), *Religion and the clinical practice of psychology* (pp. 391–407). Washington, DC: American Psychological Association.

Propst, L. R., Ostrom, R., Watkins, P., Dean, T., & Mashburn, D. (1992). Comparative efficacy of religious and nonreligious cognitive-behavioral therapy for the treatment of depression in religious individuals. *Journal of Consulting and Clinical Psychology, 60,* 94–103.

Pruyser, P. (1971). Assessment of the patient's religious attitudes in the psychiatric case study. *Bulletin of the Menniger Clinic, 35,* 272–291.

Queralt, M. (1984, March-April). Understanding Cuban immigrants: A cultural perspective. *Social Work,* 115–121.

Radhakrishnan, S. (1948). *The Bhagavadgita: With an introductory essay, Sanskrit text, English translation and notes*. New York: Harper & Brothers.

Radhakrishnan, S., & Moore, C. (1957). *A sourcebook in Indian philosophy*. Princeton, NJ: Princeton University Press.

Rahman, F. (1993). Islam. *Encarta Encyclopedia*. Redmond, WA: Microsoft Corp.

Rando, T. A. (1986). *Loss and anticipatory grief*. Lexington, MA: Lexington Books.

Rave, E. J., & Larsen, C. C. (Eds.). (1995). *Ethical decision-making in therapy: Feminist perspectives*. New York: Guilford Press.

RavenWolf, S. (2000). *To ride a silver broomstick: New generation witchcraft*. St. Paul, MN: Llewellyn.

Rayburn, C. A. (1985). The religious patient's initial encounter with psychotherapy. In E. M. Stern (Ed.), *Psychotherapy of the religiously committed patient* (pp. 35–46). New York: Haworth Press.

Reilly, P. L. (1995). *A God who looks like me: Discovering a woman-affirming spirituality*. New York: Ballentine Books.

Richards, P. S. (1991). Religious devoutness in college students: Relations with emotional adjustment and psychological separation from parents. *Journal of Counseling Psychology, 38,* 189–196.

Richards, P. S., & Bergin, A. E. (1997). *A spiritual strategy for counseling and psychotherapy*. Washington, DC: American Psychological Association.

Richards, P. S., & Bergin, A. E. (Eds.). (2000). *Handbook of psychotherapy and religious diversity*. Washington, DC: American Psychological Association.

Richards, P. S., & Potts, R. (1995). Using spiritual interventions in psychotherapy: Practices, successes, failures, and ethical concerns of Mormon psychotherapists. *Professional Psychology: Research and Practice, 26,* 163–170.

Ricoeur, P. (1967). *The symbolism of evil* (E. Buchanan, trans.). Boston: Beacon Press.

Ritter, K. Y., & O'Neill, G. W. (1995). Moving through loss: The spiritual journey of gay men and lesbian women. In M. T. Burke & J. G. Miranti (Eds.), *Counseling: The spiritual dimension* (pp. 126–141). Alexandria, VA: American Counseling Association.

Rizzuto, A.-M. (1981). *The birth of the living God: A psychoanalytic study.* Chicago: University of Chicago Press.

Rizzuto, A-M. (1993). Exploring sacred landscapes. In M. L. Randour (Ed.), *Exploring religious landscape: Religious and spiritual experiences in psychotherapy* (pp. 409–431). Washington, DC: American Psychological Association.

Rizzuto, A-M. (1996). Psychoanalytic treatment and the religious person. In E. P. Shafranske (Ed.), *Religion and the clinical practice of psychology* (pp. 409–431). Washington, DC: American Psychological Association.

Roberts, J. (1999). Heart and soul: Spirituality, religion, and rituals in family therapy training. In F. Walsh (Ed.), *Spiritual resources in family therapy* (pp. 256–271). New York: Guilford Press.

Roberts, S. (1995). *Who we are: A portrait of America based on the latest U.S. Census.* New York: Times Books.

Robertson, B. (1990). Storytelling in pastoral counseling: A narrative pastoral theology. *Pastoral Psychology, 39,* 33–45.

Rogers, C. (1961). *On becoming a person.* Boston: Houghton Mifflin.

Rogers, C. (1967). The conditions of change from a client-centered viewpoint. In B. Berenson & R. Carkhuff (Eds.), *Sources of gain in counseling and psychotherapy.* New York: Holt, Rinehart, Winston.

Rogers, C. (1986). Carl Rogers on the development of the person-centered approach. *Person-Centered Review, 1,* 257–259.

Romano, E. L. (Ed.). (1996). *In the silence of solitude: contemporary witnesses of the desert.* Staten Island, NY: Alba House.

Romig, C. A., & Veenstra, G. (1998). Forgiveness and psychosocial development: Implications for clinical practice. *Counseling and Values, 42, 185–199.*

Room, R. (1993). Alcoholics Anonymous as a social movement. In B. S. McCrady & W. R. Miller (Eds.), *Research on Alcoholics Anonymous: Opportunities and alternatives* (pp. 167–188). New Brunswick, NJ: Rutgers Center of Alcohol Studies.

Rose, T. (1994). *Black noise: Rap music and Black culture in contemporary America.* Hanover, NH: University Press of New England.

Rosen, E. J. (1990). *Families facing death: Family dynamics of terminal illness.* Lexington, MA: D. C. Heath.

Rosen, E. J., & Weltman, S. F. (1996). Jewish families: An overview. In M. McGoldrick, J. Giordano, & J. K. Pearce (Eds.), *Ethnicity and family therapy* (2nd ed., pp. 611–630). New York: Guilford Press.

Rosen, H. (1996). Meaning-making narratives: Foundations for constructivist and social constructionist psychotherapies. In H. Rosen & K. T. Kuehlwein (Eds.), *Constructing realities: Meaning making perspectives for psychotherapists* (pp. 3–51). San Francisco: Jossey-Bass.

Rosenblatt, P., & Elde, G. (1990). Shared reminiscence about a deceased parent: Implications for grief education and grief counseling. *Family Relations, 39,* 206–210.

Rosenthal, J. (1992). The Bodhi-therapist. In B. J. Brothers (Ed.), *Spirituality and couples: Heart and soul in the therapy process* (pp. 27–52). New York: Haworth Press.

Rosten, L. (Ed.). (1975). *Religions of America: Ferment and faith in an age of crisis.* New York: Simon & Schuster.

Roth, N. (1990). *The breath of God: An approach to prayer.* Cambridge, MA: Cowley.

Rothbaum, R., Weisz, J., & Snyder, S. (1982). Changing the world and changing the self: A two process model of perceived control. *Journal of Personality and Social Psychology, 42,* 5–37.

Rotz, E., Russell, C. S., & Wright, D. W. (1993). The therapist who is perceived as "spiritually correct": Strategies for avoiding collusion with the "spiritually one-up" spouse. *Journal of Marital and Family Therapy, 19,* 369–375.

Rubin, L. (1976). *Worlds of pain: Life in the working class family.* New York: Basic Books.

Russell, L. (1982). *Becoming human.* Philadelphia: Westminster Press.

Sabogal, R., Marin, G., Otero-Sabogal, R., Marin, B.V., & Perez-Stable, E. J. (1987). Hispanic familialism and acculturation: What changes and what doesn't? *Hispanic Journal of Behavioral Sciences, 9,* 397–412.

Sakr, A. H. (1995). Death and dying: An Islamic perspective. In J. K. Parry & A. S. Ryan (Eds.), *A cross-cultural look at death, dying ,and religion* (pp. 47–73). Chicago: Nelson-Hall.

Sanderson, C. & Linehan, M. M. (1999). Acceptance and forgiveness. In W. R. Miller (Ed.), *Integrating spirituality into treatment* (pp. 199–216). Washington, DC: American Psychological Association.

Sarason, R. S. (1993–1996). Judaism. *Encarta 97 Encyclopedia.* Redmond, WA: Microsoft Corp.

Sarason, S. B. (1981). *Psychology misdirected.* New York: Free Press.

Satir, V. M. (1964). *Conjoint family therapy,* 1st ed. Palo Alto, CA: Science and Behavior Books.

Satir, V. M. (1983). *Conjoint family therapy,* 3rd ed. Palo Alto, CA: Science and Behavior Books.

Sawicki, J. (1991). *Disciplining Foucault: Feminism, power, and the body.* New York: Routledge.

Sayger, T. V., Homrich, A. M., & Horne, A. M. (2000). Working from a family focus: The historical context of family development and family systems. In A. M. Horne (Ed.), *Family counseling and therapy* (3rd ed. pp. 12–40). Itasca, IL: Peacock.

Sayger, T. V., & Horne, A. M. (2000). Common elements in family therapy theory and strategies. In A. M. Horne (Ed.), *Family counseling and therapy* (3rd ed., pp. 41–61). Itasca, IL: Peacock.

Scanzoni, L. D., & Hardesty, N. A. (1986). *All we're meant to be: Biblical feminism for today* (2nd ed.). Nashville, TN: Abingdon Press.

Scarlett, W. G., & Periello, L. (1991). The development of prayer in adolescence. *New Directions for Child Development, 52,* 63–76.

Schow, W. (1997). Homosexuality, Mormon doctrine, and Christianity: A father's perspective. In G. D. Comstock & S. E. Henking (Eds.), *Que(e)rying religion: A critical anthology* (pp. 255–264). New York: Continuum.

Schultz, D., & Schultz, S. E. (1998). *Theories of personality* (6th ed.). Pacific Grove, CA: Brooks/Cole.

Schumacher, J. E. (1992). *Religion and mental health.* New York: Oxford University Press.

Schutz, A. (1964). Making music together: A study in social relationship. In A. Brodersen (Ed.), *Collected Papers II: Studies in Social Theory* (pp. 135–158). The Hague: Martinus Nijhoff.

Segal, L. (1991). Brief therapy: The MRI approach. In A. S. Gurman & D. P. Kniskern (Eds.), *Handbook of family therapy* (Vol. 2, pp. 171–199). New York: Bruner/Mazel.

Selvini-Palazzoli, M., Boscolo, L., Cecchin, G., & Prata, G. (1978a). *Paradox and counterparadox.* New York: Jason Aronson.

Selvini-Palazzoli, M., Boscolo, L., Cecchin, G., & Prata, G. (1978b). A ritualized prescription in family therapy: Odd days and even days. *Journal of Family Counseling, 4,* 3–9.

Selvini-Palazzoli, M., Boscolo, L., Cecchin, G., & Prata, G. (1980). Hypothesizing—circularity—neutrality: three guidelines for the conductor of the session. *Family Process, 19,* 3–12.

Shaef, A. W. (1987). *When society becomes an addict.* New York: Harper & Row.

Shafranske, E. P. (1996). Religious beliefs, affiliations, and practices of clinical psychologists. In E. P. Shafranske (Ed.), *Religion and the clinical practice of psychology* (pp. 149–162). Washington, DC: American Psychological Association.

Shafranske, E. P., & Maloney, H. N. (1990). Clinical psychologists' religious and spiritual orientations and their practice of psychotherapy. *Psychotherapy, 27,* 72–78.

Shange, N. (1976). *For colored girls who have considered suicide when the rainbow is enuf.* New York: Macmillan.

Shapiro, V. (1996). Subjugated knowledge and the working alliance: The narratives of Russian Jewish immigrants. *In Session: Psychotherapy in Practice, 1,* 9–22.

Sharma, A. R. (2000). Psychotherapy with Hindus. In P. S. Richards & A. E. Bergin, (Eds.). *Handbook of psychotherapy and religious diversity* (pp. 341–365). Washington, DC: American Psychological Association.

Sheldrake, P. (1992). *Spirituality and history: Questions of interpretation and method.* New York: Crossroad.

Sheler, J. (1994, April 4). Spiritual America. *U.S. News and World Report,* 48–59.

Sheridan, M. J., & Bullis, R. K. (1991). Practitioners' views on religion and spirituality: A qualitative study. *Spirituality and Social Work Journal, 2,* 2–10.

Shon, S., & Ja, D. (1982). Asian families. In M. McGoldrick, J. Giordano & J. K. Pearce (Eds.), *Ethnicity and family therapy* (1st ed., pp. 208–228). New York: Guilford Press.

Siegel, B. (1990). *Love, medicine, and miracles: Lessons learned about self-healing from a surgeon's experience with exceptional patients.* New York: HarperPerennial.

Singer, M. T., & Lalich, J. (1995). *Cults in our midst.* San Francisco: Jossey-Bass.

Skinner, B. F. (1953). *Science and human behavior.* New York: Macmillan.

Slife, B. D., & Williams, R. N. (1995). *What's behind research: Discovering hidden assumptions in the behavioral sciences.* Thousand Oaks, CA: Sage.

Smith, H. (1958). *The religions of man.* New York: Harper & Row.

Smith, R. L. (1992). Marital and family therapy: Direction, theory, and practice. In R. L. Smith & P. Stevens-Smith (Eds.), *Family counseling and therapy* (pp. 55–79). Ann Arbor, MI: ERIC Counseling and Personnel Services Clearinghouse.

Smith, R. L., Griffin, J., Thys, K., & Ryan, E. (1992). The use of circular questioning in marriage and family counseling/therapy. In R. L. Smith & P. Stevens-Smith (Eds.), *Family counseling and therapy* (pp. 222–227). Ann Arbor, MI: ERIC Counseling and Personnel Services Clearinghouse.

Snipp, C. M. (1989). *American Indians: The first of this land.* New York: Russell Sage.

Sodowsky, G. R., Kwan, K.-L. K., & Pannu, R. (1995). Ethnic identity of Asians in the United States. In J. G. Ponterotto, J. M. Casa, L. A. Suzuki, & C. M. Alexander. *Handbook of multicultural counseling* (pp. 123–154). Thousand Oaks, CA: Sage.

Spero, M. H. (Ed.). (1985). *Psychotherapy of the religious patient.* Springfield, IL: Charles C. Thomas.

Spero, M. H. (1990). Parallel dimensions of experience in psychoanalytic psychotherapy of the religious patient. *Psychotherapy, 27,* 53–71.

Sperry, L., & Giblin, P. (1996). Marital and family therapy with religious persons (pp. 511–532). In E. P. Shafranske (Ed.), *Religion and the clinical practice of psychology.* Washington, DC: American Psychological Association.

Spiegler, M. D., & Guevremont, D. C. (1998). *Contemporary behavior therapy* (3rd ed.). Pacific Grove, CA: Brooks/Cole.

St. John, I. (2000). *Creative spirituality for women.* Springfield, IL: Charles C. Thomas.

Stahl, C. (1977). *Opening to God.* Nashville, TN: Upper Room.

Stanard, R. P., Sandhu, D. S., & Painter, L. C. (2000). Assessment of Spirituality in Counseling. *Journal of Counseling and Development, 78,* 204–210.

Stander, V., Piercy, F. P., MacKinnon, D., & Helmeke, K. (1994). Spirituality, religion, and family therapy: Competing or complementary worlds? *American Journal of Family Therapy, 22,* 27–41.

Staples, R. (1994). *Black family: Essays and studies* (5th ed.). New York: Van Nostrand Reinhold.

Stark, R. (1971). Psychopathology and religious commitment. *Review of Religious Research, 12,* 165–176.

Statler, O. (1971). Sacred writings of the past. In M. Severy (Ed.), *Great religions of the world* (pp. 132–169). Washington, DC: National Geographic Society.

Stoll, R. I. (1979). Guidelines for spiritual assessment. *American Journal of Nursing, 79*, 1574–1577.

Stoudenmire, J., Batman, D., Pavlov, M., & Temple, A. (1985). Validation of a Holistic Living Inventory. *Psychological Reports, 57*, 301–311.

Stoudenmire, J., Batman, D., Pavlov, M., & Temple, A. (1986). The Holistic Living Inventory: Correlations with MMPI. *Psychological Reports, 58*, 577–578.

Stromberg, C., & Dellinger, A. (1993, December). Malpractice and other professional liability. *The Psychologist's Legal Update*. Washington, DC: National Register of Health Service Providers in Psychology.

Strommen, M. (1974). *Five cries of youth*. New York: Harper & Row.

Sue, D. W., & Sue, D. (1990). *Counseling the culturally different: Theory and practice* (2nd ed.). New York: Wiley.

Sue, S., Allen, D. B., & Conaway, L. (1981). The responsiveness and equality of mental health care to Chicanos and Native Americans. *American Journal of Community Psychology, 6*, 137–146.

Sue, S., & Morishima, J. (1985). *The mental health of Asian Americans*. San Francisco: Jossey-Bass.

Sue, S., Nakamura, C. Y., Chung, R. C., & Yee-Bradbury, C. (1994). Mental health research on Asian Americans. *Journal of Community Psychology, 32*, 570–579.

Sue, S., & Sue, D. (1974). MMPI comparisons between Asian-American and non-Asian American students utilizing a student health psychiatric clinic. *Journal of Counseling Psychology, 21*, 423–427.

Summit results in information of spirituality competencies. (1995, December). *Counseling Today*, p. 30.

Sutton, C. T., & Broken Nose, M. A. (1996). American Indian families: An overview. In M. Mc-Goldrick, J. Giordano, & J. Pearce (Eds.), *Ethnicity and family therapy* (2nd ed., pp. 31–44). New York: Guilford Press.

Szasz, C. M. (1988). *Indian education in the American colonies, 1607–1783*. Albuquerque: University of New Mexico Press.

Tafoya, N., & Del Vecchio, A. (1996). Back to the future: An examination of the Native American holocaust experience. In M. McGoldrick, J. Giordano, & J. Pearce (Eds.), *Ethnicity and family therapy* (2nd ed., pp. 45–54). New York: Guilford Press.

Tafoya, T. (1997). Native gay and lesbian issues: The two spirited. In B. Greene (Ed.), *Ethnic and cultural diversity among lesbians and gay men* (pp. 1–10). Thousand Oaks, CA: Sage.

Tamminen, K., & Ratcliff, D. (1992). Assessment, placement, and evaluation. In D. Ratcliff, (Ed.), *Handbook of children's religious education* (pp. 239–262). Birmingham, AL: Religious Education Press.

Tamminen, K., Vianello, R., Jaspard, J-M, & Ratcliff, D. (1988). The religious concepts of preschoolers. In D. Ratcliff (Ed.), *Handbook of pre-school religious education* (pp. 59–81). Birmingham, AL: Religious Education Press.

Tan, S.-Y. (1991). Counseling Asians. *Urban Mission, 9*, 42–50.

Tan, S.-Y. (1994). Ethical considerations in religious psychotherapy: Potential pitfalls and unique resources. *Journal of Psychology and Theology, 22*, 389–394.

Tan, S.-Y. (1996). Religion in clinical practice: Implicit and explicit integrations. In E. P. Shafranske (Ed.), *Religion and the clinical practice of psychology* (pp. 365–387). Washington, DC: American Psychological Association.

Tan, S.-Y., & Dong, N. J. (2000). Psychotherapy with members of Asian American churches and spiritual traditions In P. S. Richards & A. E. Bergin (Eds.), *Handbook of psychotherapy and religious diversity* (pp. 421–444). Washington, DC: American Psychological Association.

Tataki, R. (1993). *A different mirror: A history of multicultural America*. Boston: Little, Brown.

Teish, L. (1985). *Jambalaya: The natural woman's book of personal charms and practical rituals*. New York: HarperCollins.

Thernstrom, S., Orlov, A., & Handlin (Eds.). (1980). Anglo Americans. In S. Thernstrom, A. Orlov, & O. Handlin (Eds.), *Harvard encyclopedia of American ethnic groups* (p. 125). Cambridge, MA: Harvard University Press.

Thurston, N. S. (2000). Psychotherapy with evangelical and fundamentalist Protestants. In P. S. Richards & A. E. Bergin (Eds.), *Handbook of psychotherapy and religious diversity* (pp. 131–153). Washington, DC: American Psychological Association.

Tillich, P. (1959). *Theology of culture.* New York: Oxford University Press.

Tjeltveit, A. C. (1986). The ethics of value conversion in psychotherapy: appropriate and inappropriate therapist influence on client values. *Clinical Psychology Review, 6,* 515–537.

Todd, T. (1992). Brief family therapy. In R. L. Smith & P. Stevens-Smith (Eds.), *Family counseling and therapy* (pp. 162–175). Ann Arbor, MI: ERIC Counseling and Personnel Services Clearinghouse.

Toelken, B. (1976). How many sheep will it hold? In W. H. Capps (Ed.), *Seeing with a native eye* (p. 23). New York: Harper & Row.

Tomine, S. I. (1991). Counseling Japanese Americans: From internment to reparation. In C. Lee & B. Richardson (Eds.), *Multicultural issues in counseling: New approaches to diversity* (pp. 91–105). Alexandria, VA: American Association for Counseling and Development.

Tomm, K. (1987). Interventive interviewing: part II. Reflexive questioning as a means to enable self-healing. *Family Process, 26,* 167–183.

Tomm, K. (1988). Interventive interviewing part III. Intending to ask linear, circular, strategic, or reflexive questions? *Family Process, 27,* 1–15.

Tonigan, J. S., Conners, G. J., & Miller, W. R. (1996). The Alcoholics Anonymous Involvement Scale (AAI): Reliability and norms. *Psychology of Addictive Behaviors, 10,* 75–80.

Tonigan, J. S., Toscova, R. T., & Conners, G. J. (1999). Spirituality and the 12-step programs: A guide for clinicians. In W. R. Miller (Ed.), *Integrating spirituality into treatment* (pp. 111–131). Washington, DC: American Psychological Association.

Travis, J. W. (1981). *The Wellness Inventory.* Mill Valley, CA: Wellness Associates.

Trible, P. (1978). *God and the rhetoric of sexuality.* Philadelphia: Fortress Press.

Trotter, R. T., & Chavira, J. A. (1981). *Curanderismo: Mexican American folk healing.* Athens, GA: University of Georgia Press.

Trujillo, A. (2000). Psychotherapy with native Americans: A view into the role of religion and spirituality (pp. 445–466). In P. S. Richards & A. E. Bergin (Eds.), *Handbook of psychotherapy and religious diversity.* Washington, DC: American Psychological Association.

Tseng, W. S. (1975). The nature of somatic complaints among psychiatric patients: The Chinese case. *Comparative Psychiatry, 16,* 237–245.

Turner, R. P., Lukoff, D., Barnhouse, R. T., & Lu, F. G. (1995). Religious or spiritual problem: A culturally sensitive diagnostic category in the DSM-IV. *Journal of Nervous and Mental Disease, 183*(7), 435–444.

Uba, L. (1994). *Asian Americans: Personality patterns, identity, and mental health.* New York: Guilford Press.

Umansky, E. M. (1997). Jewish attitudes toward homosexuality: A review of contemporary sources. In G. D. Comstock & S. E. Henking (Eds.), *Que(e)rying religion: A critical anthology* (pp. 181–187). New York: Continuum.

Umbarger, C. C. (1983). *Structural family therapy.* New York: Grune & Stratton.

U. S. Census Bureau (1998). *Statistical Abstract of the United States: 1998* (118th ed.). Washington, DC: Author.

Vaillant, G. E. (1983). *The natural history of alcoholism.* Cambridge, MA: Harvard University Press.

Vande Kemp, H. (1982). The tension between psychology and theology: I. The etymological roots. *Journal of Psychology and Theology, 10,* 105–112.

Vande Kemp, H. (1996). Historical perspective: Religion and clinical psychology in America. In E. P. Shafranske (Ed.), *Religion and the clinical practice of psychology* (pp. 71–112). Washington, DC: American Psychological Association.

Van Eenwyk, J. R. (1996). Switching tracks: Parallel paradigms in psychology and religion. In E. P. Shafranske (Ed.), *Religion and the clinical practice of psychology* (pp. 461–482). Washington, DC: American Psychological Association.

Vaughan, F., Wittine, B., & Walsh, R. (1996). Transpersonal psychology and the religious person. In E. P. Shafranske (Ed.), *Religion and the clinical practice of psychology*. Washington, DC: American Psychological Association.

Veatch, T. L., & Chappel, J. N. (1992). Measuring spiritual health: A preliminary study. *Substance Abuse, 13,* 139–147.

Veroff, J., Kulka, R. A., & Douvan, E. (1981). *Mental health in America: Patterns of seeking help from 1957–1976.* New York: Basic Books.

Vitz, P. C. (1992). Narratives and counseling, Part 1: From analysis of the past to stories about it. *Journal of Psychology and Theology, 20,* 11–19.

Walker, J. R. (2000). *The Sun Dance and other ceremonies of the Oglala division of the Teton Dakota.* New York: AMS Press.

Walsh, F. (1999). Religion and spirituality: Wellsprings for healing and resilience. In F. Walsh (Ed.), *Spiritual resources in family therapy.* New York: Guilford Press.

Walsh, R., & Vaughan, F. (Eds.). (1993). *Paths beyond ego.* New York: Putnam.

Wangu, M. B. (1991). *Hinduism.* New York: Facts on File.

Wangu , M. B. (1993). *Buddhism.* New York: Facts on File.

Washburn, M. (1988). *The ego and the dynamic ground.* Albany: State University of New York Press.

Watts, A. W. (1993). Shinto. *Encarta Encyclopedia.* Redmond, WA: Microsoft Corp.

Watzlawick, P. (1993). *The language of change: Elements of therapeutic communication.* New York: Norton.

Watzlawick, P., Weakland, J., & Fisch, R. (1974). *Change: Principles of problem formation and problem resolution.* New York: Norton.

Weatherhead, L. D. (1944). *The will of God.* Nashville, TN: Abingdon-Cokesbury Press.

Weaver, A. J. (1995). Has there been a failure to prepare and support parish-based clergy in their role as front-line community mental health workers?: A review. *Journal of Pastoral Care, 49,* 129–149.

Weaver, A. J., Koenig, H. G., & Larson, D. B. (1997). Marriage and family therapists and the clergy: A need for clinical collaboration, training, and research. *Journal of Marital and Family Therapy, 23,* 13–25.

Webster's Ninth New Collegiate Dictionary (1987). Springfield, MA: Merriam-Webster.

Weinbach, R. (1989). Sudden death and secret survivors: Helping those who grieve alone. *Social Work, 34,* 57–60.

Welfel, E. R. (1998). *Ethics in counseling and psychotherapy: Standards, research, and emerging issues.* Pacific Grove, CA: Brooks/Cole.

Wenhao, J., Salomon, H. B., & Chay, D. M. (1993). Transcultural counseling and people of Asian origin: A developmental and therapeutic perspective. In J. McFadden (Ed.), *Transcultural counseling: Bilateral and international perspectives* (pp. 239–250). Alexandria, VA: American Association for Counseling and Development.

Wheat, L. W. (1991). Development of a scale for the measurement of human spirituality. *Dissertation Abstracts International,* 9205143.

Whitaker, C. A., & Keith, D. V. (1981). Symbolic-experiential family therapy. In A. S. Gurman & D. P. Kniskern (Eds.), *Handbook of family therapy* (pp. 187–225). New York: Bruner/Mazel.

White, J. L. (1984). *The psychology of Blacks.* Englewood Cliffs, NJ: Prentice-Hall.

White, M. (1986). Negative explanation, restraint, and double description: a template for family therapy. *Family Process, 25,* 169–184.

White, M. (1988, Winter). The process of questioning: A therapy of literary merit? *Dulwich Centre Newsletter,* 8–14.

White, M., & Epston, D. (1990). *Narrative means to therapeutic ends.* New York: Norton.

Wilber, K. (1977). *The spectrum of consciousness.* Wheaton, IL: Quest.

Wilber, K. (1980a). *The Atman project.* Wheaton, IL: Quest.

Wilber, K. (1980b). *No boundary.* Boston: Shambhala.

Wilber, K. (1983). *A sociable god.* New York: McGraw-Hill.

Wilber, K. (1993). The pre-trans fallacy. In R. Walsh & F. Vaughan (Eds.), *Paths beyond ego: The transpersonal vision* (pp. 256–266). Los Angeles: Tarcher.

Wilber, K. (1995). *Sex, ecology, spirituality.* Boston: Shambhala.

Williams, C. (1992). *No hiding place.* San Francisco: HarperCollins.

Williams, C. B., Frame, M. W., & Green, E. (1999). Counseling groups for African American women: A focus on spirituality. *Journal for Specialists in Group Work, 24,* 260–273.

Williamson, D. S. (1981). Personal authority via termination of the intergenerational hierarchical boundary: A "new " stage in the family life cycle. *Journal of Marital and Family Therapy, 7,* 441–452.

Wimberly, E. P. (1991). *African American pastoral care.* Nashville, TN: Abingdon Press.

Winarsky, M. (1991). *AIDS-related psychotherapy.* New York: Pergamon.

Witmer, J. M., Sweeney, T. J., & Myers, J. E. (1994). *Wellness Evaluation of Lifestyle: The WEL Inventory.* Palo Alto, CA: Mind Garden.

Wormser, R. (1994). *American Islam: Group up Muslim in America.* New York: Walker.

Worthington, E. L. (1986). Religious counseling: A review of published empirical research. *Journal of Counseling and Development, 64,* 421–431.

Worthington, E. L. (1988). Understanding the values of religious clients: A model and its application to counseling. *Journal of Counseling and Development, 64,* 421–431.

Worthington, E. L. (1989). Religious faith across the life span: Implications for counseling and research. *Counseling Psychologist, 17,* 555–612.

Worthington, E. L., & Scott, G. G. (1983). Goal selection for counseling with potentially religious clients by professional and student counselors in explicitly Christian or secular settings. *Journal of Psychology and Theology, 11,* 318–328.

Wrye, H., & Churilla, J. (1977). Looking inward, looking backward: Reminiscence and the life review. *Frontiers, 2,* 98–105.

Wulff, D. M. (1996). *The psychology of religion: An overview.* In E. P. Shafranske (Ed.), *Religion and the clinical practice of psychology.* Washington, DC: American Psychological Association.

Yalom, I. D. (1980). *Existential psychotherapy.* New York: Basic Books.

Yalom, I. D. (1995). *The theory and practice of group psychotherapy (*4th ed.*).* New York: Basic Books.

Yeung, W. (1995). Buddhism, death & dying. In J. K. Parry & A. S. Ryan (Eds.), *A cross-cultural look at death, dying, and religion* (pp. 74–83). Chicago: Nelson-Hall.

Yost, J. L. (1986). For god, country, and family: A personal tribute to Christian Fredrik Midelfort, M.D. *Family Process, 25,* 149–151.

Young, T. R. (2000). Psychotherapy with Eastern Orthodox Christians. In P. S. Richards & A. E. Bergin (Eds.), *Handbook of psychotherapy and religious diversity* (pp. 89–104). Washington, DC:American Psychological Association.

Zea, M. C., Mason, M. A., & Murguia, A. (2000). Psychotherpay with members of Latino/Latina religions and spiritual traditions. In P. S. Richards & A. E. Bergin (Eds.), *Handbook of psychotherapy and religious diversity* (pp. 39–7-419). Washington, DC: American Psychological Association.

Zea, M. C., Quezada, T., & Belgrave, F. Z. (1997). Limitations of an accultural health psychology for Latinos: Reconstructing the African influence on Latino culture and health-related behaviors. In J. G. Garcia & M. C. Zea (Eds.), *Psychological interventions and research with Latino populations* (pp. 255–266). Boston: Allyn & Bacon.

Zinnbauer, B. J., & Pargament, K. I. (2000). Working with the sacred: Four approaches to religious and spiritual issues in counseling. *Journal of Counseling and Development, 78,* 162–171.

Zitter, M. L. (1987, March–April). Culturally sensitive treatment of black alcoholic families. *Social Work,* 130–135.

Zukav, G. (1989). *The seat of the soul.* New York: Simon & Schuster.

INDEX

TO THE OWNER OF THIS BOOK:

We hope that you have found *Integrating Religion and Spirituality into Counseling: A Comprehensive Approach* useful. So that this book can be improved in a future edition, would you take the time to complete this sheet and return it? Thank you.

School and address:_____

Department:_____

Instructor's name:_____

1. What I like most about this book is:_____

_____

_____

2. What I like least about this book is:_____

_____

_____

3. My general reaction to this book is:_____

_____

4. The name of the course in which I used this book is:_____

_____

5. Were all of the chapters of the book assigned for you to read?_____

   If not, which ones weren't?_____

6. In the space below, or on a separate sheet of paper, please write specific suggestions for improving this book and anything else you'd care to share about your experience in using the book.

_____

_____

_____

_____

_____

Optional:

Your name: _____ Date: _____

May Brooks/Cole quote you, either in promotion for *Integrating Religion and Spirituality into Counseling: A Comprehensive Approach* or in future publishing ventures?

Yes: _____ No: _____

Sincerely,

Marsha Wiggins Frame

IN-BOOK SURVEY

At Brooks/Cole, we are excited about creating new types of learning materials that are interactive, three-dimensional, and fun to use. To guide us in our publishing/development process, we hope that you'll take just a few moments to fill out the survey below. Your answers can help us make decisions that will allow us to produce a wide variety of videos, CD-ROMs, and Internet-based learning systems to com-plement standard textbooks. If you're interested in working with us as a student Beta-tester, be sure to fill in your name, telephone number, and address. We look forward to hearing from you!

In addition to books, which of the following learning tools do you currently use in your counseling/human services/social work courses?

_____ **Video** _____ in class _____ school library _____ own VCR

_____ **CD-ROM** _____ in class _____ in lab _____ own computer

_____ **Macintosh disks** _____ in class _____ in lab _____ own computer

_____ **Windows disks** _____ in class _____ in lab _____ own computer

_____ **Internet** _____ in class _____ in lab _____ own computer

How often do you access the Internet? _____

My own home computer is a:

_____

The computer I use in class for counseling/human services/social work courses is a:

_____

If you are NOT currently using multimedia materials in your counseling/human services/social work courses, but can see ways that video, CD-ROM, Internet, or other technologies could enhance your learning, please comment below:

_____
_____
_____

Other comments (optional): _____
_____

Name _____Telephone _____

Address _____

School _____

Professor/Course_____

You can fax this form to us at (650) 592-9081; or detach, fold, secure, and mail.

Attention Professors:

Brooks/Cole is dedicated to publishing quality publications for education in the social work, counseling, and human services fields. If you are interested in learning more about our publications, please fill in your name and address and request our latest catalogue, using this prepaid mailer. Please choose one of the following:

☐ social work   ☐ counseling   ☐ human services

Name: _____

Street Address: _____

City, State, and Zip: _____